Spoken from the Heart

My parents and me at the Texas State Fair.

Spoken from the Heart

Laura Bush

SIMON &
SCHUSTER

London · New York · Sydney · Toronto

A CBS COMPANY

First published in Great Britain by Simon & Schuster UK Ltd, 2010
A CBS COMPANY

1 3 5 7 9 10 8 6 4 2

Simon & Schuster UK Ltd
1st Floor
222 Gray's Inn Road
London
WC1X 8HB

www.simonandschuster.co.uk

Simon & Schuster Australia
Sydney

A CIP catalogue copy for this book is available
from the British Library.

ISBN: 978-1-84737-898-9

Printed in the UK by CPI Mackays, Chatham ME5 8TD

For the joys of my heart,
my husband, George;
my daughters,
Barbara and Jenna;
my mother;
and the memory of my dad.

CONTENTS

Through
the Nursery Glass

My first birthday.

What I remember is the glass. It was a big, solid pane, much bigger than our little rectangles at home, which sat perched one on top of the other. I can still picture that window and the way it seemed to float on the wall without any curtains or wood. Beyond the glass was the nursery, where they kept the babies. I don't remember looking at a baby. In my mind, there is only the window, although my brother, John Edward Welch, is lying on the other side of the glass. It is June of 1949 in Midland, Texas, and I am two and a half years old.

I do not remember if I stood on my tiptoes or if my father held me, smelling as he often did of strong coffee and unfiltered cigarettes. He would have dressed me himself that morning in a pretty cotton dress that my grandmother had made. She made almost all of my clothes, choosing her own cute patterns and fabrics, sewing them on her old treadle Singer sewing machine, the needle clacking up and down as she pumped the pedal with her foot. Whatever scraps her scissors had left behind she would take and carefully turn into matching doll dresses. Then she would bundle them up, a few at a time, and mail them from El Paso to Midland. Later, when the ranchers' daughters and the oilmen's girls were riding with their mothers on the train into Dallas to buy their first school dresses, pink or ruffled, with white lace or pert satin bows, at Neiman Marcus or Young Ages, my grandmother was still posting her cotton creations for me on the mail train from El Paso.

Although the Western Clinic was less than ten blocks from our little house on Estes Avenue, with its hint of a front porch and postage stamp yard, where the grass was continually battling drought and dust, we would have driven there, in my father's Ford.

I was born on November 4, 1946, at the same little Western Clinic, a one-story building, concrete and cinder block, with rows of decorative thick block glass and thin windows. It was built over a decade earlier, in the lean years of the 1930s, when Midland was a town of some 9,000 people. But by 1949, Midland was closing in on 22,000 people, and Western Clinic was still all there was. It had a scant thirty-six beds. Patients were simply patched up and moved on. There was a long waiting list for surgeries. The clinic could not afford to let anyone dawdle; as soon as they were able, perhaps even before, patients went home. Dr. Britt, who ran the clinic, had been brought in to practice in Midland by the oil companies. He birthed babies, treated sick toddlers, set broken bones, and watched hearts fail. Western Clinic didn't have a blood bank until 1949. Its X-rays were packed up and sent by commercial bus to a radiologist in Fort Worth. The drive alone was more than six hours. And once that bus had left, Dr. Britt could only wait until the next one was ready to depart from the depot. The city also kept a small Cessna-style plane parked alongside the grassy landing strip at the airport to fly patients in and out and to ferry pathology samples over to a doctor in San Angelo. When the brand-new, $1.4 million Midland Memorial Hospital opened, in 1950, the X-rays were still bussed and the surgery samples still flown.

But this was 1949. There was barely an obstetrical or surgical unit inside Western Clinic by the end of that year. My parents would have known this. My father's brother, Mark, was a doctor in Dallas. But we lived in Midland, and there was no way to move a fragile baby, born unexpectedly two months too soon.

My father had always wanted a son. In February of 1944, when he and my mother had been married for a few weeks, he wrote her a letter from a training base in North Carolina. A thirty-one-year-old GI, he was waiting there to be shipped to England. On thin airmail paper, in his tall, narrow, and meticulous script, Harold Welch wrote to his new bride, Jenna, who was not yet twenty-five, "Honey, what do you want, a little boy or a little girl? What you want, I want, it makes no difference to me, but I'd kind of like to have a little boy, would you?"

I see them now in an old photograph, my grandfather Hal Hawkins, looking hot, uncomfortable, and a bit dour in his jacket and tie, his belly straining against the buttons of his white shirt, his hair refusing to stay slicked back and instead slipping down over his forehead. On the other side of the picture is my father, a head taller, hair neatly cropped, in his dress uniform, grinning and handsome, "so handsome," as my mother says, "with the most beautiful blue eyes." And between them is my mother, her arms through the arms of the men beside her, her head flung back in laughter, her whole face alive with a look of pure joy. Harold and Jenna waited two years for each other. My father shipped home in January of 1946. Two years beyond their vows, they were still newlyweds.

My mother was an only child, and when I was growing up, she would say with a wink in her quick, witty West Texas way that she would have been "insulted" if her parents had had more children. But that is only part of the story, the way when you dig down through the dry West Texas flatlands you discover the fossilized remnants of shells and underwater life, what remains of the ancient, vanished Permian sea.

Only when I was much older did I learn that my grandmother had lost her own babies, two babies, my mother thinks, both of whom were born too soon and died. But she never truly knew because no one spoke of it. You might talk about the wind and the weather, but troubles you swallowed deep down inside. My mother's own pregnancy with me had been hard. She did as the doctors told her and spent most of it in bed. This time she had gone to bed too, but the baby still came early, gasping, with no high-tech incubator to warm him, no pediatric IV line to put in his tiny arm, nothing but swaddling blankets and a few sips of formula from a glass bottle or given with an eyedropper, the way one feeds an injured baby bird.

He would never know the sting of a baseball hitting a leather mitt, or ride his bike up to the edge of Big Spring Street, where the road turned abruptly from pavement to flattened dust, or get his first tooth or report card or walk into church in shiny, stiff shoes.

He would never come home from the Western Clinic. He would never have his intended name. My parents had planned on naming him Hal, after both my father and my grandfather. But no one wanted to bury Hal Welch, three days old. So his official name was John Edward. Hal or Harold was a name they would save for another boy.

John Edward lived only for those few days and then he died. He had a birth certificate, but I never heard him spoken of as a live birth. A "late miscarriage" was how it was euphemistically put. Newnie Ellis, the city undertaker, tended to his lifeless body. He was buried in a tiny box coffin

5

in an unmarked grave alongside other Midland babies who had, over the years and decades, come ever so briefly into the world and then passed on.

There were two more lost babies, a girl, Sarah Elizabeth, when I was eight and another boy when I was thirteen. The doctors called them late miscarriages too. I remember when I was eight that my mother had a blue and white polka dot maternity dress and I had a little navy blue and white polka dot dress. They weren't really matching, but they were the same polka dot, and I loved that we almost matched when we wore them. But by mid-summer, her dress and the baby, who would have been my sister, were gone.

I don't know if my mother cried for these babies when I was out playing in the yard, or rapping on the door of our back-door neighbors over the fence, or darting with the other kids between the gangly, dark limbs and feathery, green leaves of the mesquite bushes that grew over the vacant lot down the street. I don't know if the tears came when she smoothed sheets in the linen closet or hung wash on the clothesline to grow stiff and dry in the hot Midland wind. Or if she trained her eyes to look away whenever she caught sight of a baby carriage or glimpsed a big, boisterous family being herded into a wood-paneled station wagon. In those times, in West Texas, in the 1950s, we did not talk about those things.

The mother I knew laughed and loved. But there remained a corner of her heart that longed for those vanished babies, a corner that dreamed of a big family of her own. Now, at ninety, when she cannot recall someone she met the day before, she remembers those babies. She sits in her green chair in her plain Midland living room and says, "We would have had two boys and two girls if they had all lived. It would have been quite a family, wouldn't it? I sure wish one of those little boys could have lived at least, because my husband wanted a boy so bad."

But even back when nothing was said, I knew how much both my parents wanted those other children. I wanted them too. I remember as a small girl looking up at the darkening night sky, waiting for the stars to pop out one by one. I would watch for that first star, for its faint glow, because then I could make my wish. And my wish on a star any time that I wished on a star was that I would have brothers and sisters.

But year after year, the sound of feet darting down the sidewalk, and up over the front porch, and through the screen door was always mine and mine alone.

Dreams and Dust

On the porch in Canutillo with our dog Bully.
Grammee laid the orange brick by hand.

When my dad was fighting in Europe in the war, he made a bargain with God. He promised God that if he got home alive, he'd never own another gun. And he never did. There was never any kind of a gun in our house, although most boys in Midland by the time they were fourteen could knock off a row of cans with a .22. My father did not go hunting for dove or quail or geese or shoot for sport, like a lot of other Texans do. He drank and he gambled, he bet on football games. He played cards and rolled dice. But he never had a gun. Ever.

He and his friends were passionate gamblers, especially on football. They used to meet on Sunday afternoons at Johnny's Bar-B-Q on Big Spring Street, right at the edge of downtown Midland, when the tables were empty and the restaurant was closed to huddle over pro games. They bet on pro games, on college games, even on the high school games that packed the stadium in Midland every Friday night. They played cards, especially gin rummy, rolled dice, and a few of them, including Daddy, occasionally packed up and flew to Vegas. Once, I came home from college with a boy I wanted my parents to meet, and my dad was squatting down on the kitchen floor, shooting craps with his buddies, the dice skidding across the flat tile and bouncing against the cabinets. The lot of them barely looked up. I was mortified, but I think my college boy loved it.

The gambling part was a West Texas thing. People who live in this place where the desert meets the tip of the plains, where the soil fractures and cracks and blows up against you with the wind, are risk takers, and my dad had grown up in the heart of West Texas, in Lubbock, which is about 120 miles or two hours north of Midland. My mother told me that he had learned to shoot craps in the basement of Lubbock High when he was sixteen or seventeen. He shot a lot of craps in the Army in World War II.

But unlike some of the men in Midland, and a few women too, there was never, ever an occasion when he gambled what he didn't have, or if he did, I certainly never knew of it. We never wanted because of his gambling.

My dad always considered himself lucky, and he was. He carried himself with a confidence that made it impossible to believe he could lose. Even his meeting my mother was luck. Or so the story went. She spotted him on the street in El Paso when she was looking out a second-floor window of the Popular Dry Goods Company, where she worked in the advertising department. Of course, it helped that one of her friends in the department was married to a man who knew Harold Welch. She remembers her friend saying, "Look, there's Hal," which was what they called him then. But the fact is that my mom went over and looked out the window at that exact moment, and there he was.

They had their first date at the Tivoli nightclub in Ciudad Juárez, directly across the border from El Paso. My mother remembers how everyone parked in El Paso and then, all dressed up, paid six cents to walk across the footbridge into Mexico. Juárez was a glamorous place. When I was little and we went to visit my grandparents, I remember Mother and Daddy getting ready to go over into Juárez for the evening, Mother in a big circle dress, Daddy fussing with the knot on his tie to get it just so. I begged to go with them.

The first club, right at the base of the bridge, was the Tivoli, and then a little farther down was another place, called Lobby Number Two, and other clubs fanned out from that. The "braver people" ventured farther out into the city, where at one time there was a jockey club and bullfights staged for the Americans, but my mother says that she and Harold never did any of that. The clubs had exotic—exotic at least for West Texas—floor shows and orchestras for dancing, and that first night over in Juárez, my mother and father ordered Boquilla black bass for dinner. The next morning, a little item ran in the gossip column of the El Paso paper noting that "Jenna Hawkins had been seen dancing with a handsome stranger at the Tivoli."

More than sixty-five years later, my mother still claims that she didn't want to be written up in the newspaper. But the Popular Dry Goods Company was the biggest advertiser in the local paper, and Jenna Hawkins worked in the advertising department. And making the news didn't seem to deter Harold Welch.

My parents started dating, and they were smitten fast. It was wartime. The Japanese had bombed Pearl Harbor, and the United States was also at war with the Germans. My father was nearly thirty years old, but he enlisted. His assignment was an antiaircraft brigade attached to the 104th Infantry Division, known as the Timberwolves. His unit trained in Florida, Louisiana, and outside of El Paso at Fort Bliss, the Army's massive military installation in the West. When he was on leave, he courted my mother. Once she invited him on a picnic up in the El Paso foothills. She carefully packed a basket and a blanket, but Daddy, who was spending his days mired in the dirt of basic training, declined to eat on the ground. They balanced their plates on their laps and ate sitting inside the car with the windows rolled down.

My father was seven years older than my mother, but both of them had left school after two years of college to make their own way. In Daddy's case, it was because his own father had died and he needed to support his mother. My father's parents, Mark and Lula Lane Welch, were truly Victorians, born in 1870, five years after the Civil War had ended and while Queen Victoria was still on the throne. My grandmother even had a biography of Queen Victoria with a big oval picture on the cover and heavy embossing. My paternal grandparents were both from Arkansas, but they met in Ada, Oklahoma, and married when they were forty years old. My uncle Mark was born when they were forty-one and Daddy when they were forty-two. They moved to Fort Worth for a while and then ended up in Lubbock, where my grandfather built homes. He was, I think, a jack-of-all-trades, a carpenter who could put up a frame, lay pipe, shingle a roof, and run some rudimentary wires as well. I never knew him. My mother never met him either. By the time my parents met, only my grandmother was left. I remember her as a big, sturdy, but very elderly woman with heavy, black lace-up shoes. For years she had belonged to the Methodist Church and the Temperance Society, which apparently did nothing to stop her son from driving over to the county line to buy his liquor at Pinkie's package store. Midland was a dry county back then, so people simply drove out along the highway to the next county to buy their alcohol. When Grandma Welch came to visit, Daddy would still drink, but out of deference to his mother, he poured his bourbon into a Coca-Cola bottle.

When I was little, we drove to Lubbock every other weekend to visit my grandmother so that Daddy could check on her, make sure her house was tended to and her bills were paid. She came to our house for Thanksgiving and Christmas. My parents would go up and get her, and she would bring a bag of her pickled peaches that she put up each summer in heavy glass jars. Each Christmas she would make her famous coconut cake. Santa would leave a big, fresh coconut in my stocking, and then Daddy, with great ceremony, would crack the coconut with a hammer. My grandmother carefully drained the clear, sweet milk and grated the coconut meat with a hard box grater, which if you weren't careful, would cut your fingers raw. Then she sprinkled the tender curls over the frosting like a fine, white snow. She would spend Christmas Day making the cake for Christmas dinner. I'm not sure if she had a recipe or if she merely mixed the proportions in her mind, but every bite was delicious.

The Christmas after I turned eight, she carefully wrapped two pieces of jewelry, a pretty gold bracelet and a gold pin that my grandfather had given her, and put them under the Christmas tree for me. She sent my little cousin Mary Mark two other pieces of jewelry, including her opal ring. Those were the only four pieces of jewelry she owned. She must have known that this was going to be her last Christmas. She died right after that. My mother was with her. When Grandma Welch was sick and needed tending, it was my mother who drove to Lubbock to look after her. I was asleep in my parents' bed when the phone rang deep in the night. Daddy woke me and said simply, "Your grandmother died." That was all. My grandmother, his mother, was eighty-four.

Afterward, Mother discovered that Grandma Welch had taken her few nice things—a couple of cut glass vases, platters, a sugar bowl—and had carefully marked each possession with a strip of masking tape on the bottom, writing "Jenna" or "Catherine," and dividing what little she had between her two daughters-in-law.

My parents were married in a chapel at Fort Bliss in January of 1944, right before Daddy was to be shipped off to Europe. He wore his Army dress uniform. Mother followed him briefly to his next base, in Alexandria, Louisiana, but within a week my father was sent east. A hasty good-bye and he was gone. Whirlwind romances with GIs were common back then, but this wedding was no whim for my mother and certainly not for my father. One of his first letters to his new bride before he boarded the ship for England was a detailed accounting of their finances—he began by telling her that he didn't want her to be worried about money and proceeded to explain how much they had if Jenna ever needed to turn in their war bonds for cash.

With nothing to do except wait, Mother went back to El Paso and the Popular Dry Goods advertising department, got a roommate, and hung on every letter. One weekend, Mother and another of her married friends took turns snapping photos of each other immersed in fluffy bubble baths inside an old-fashioned claw-foot tub, flashing Kewpie doll smiles, and mailed the pictures over to their husbands. Daddy carried Mother's photo across northern Europe. He wrote to her from France, from Belgium, from Aachen, the ancient medieval town on the German border where Emperor Charlemagne once lived. It was the first German city to be captured by the Americans. His battalion, the 555th, was an antiaircraft battalion. My dad was a master gunner. His primary mission was to keep the unit's gun batteries in working order and to train new gunners, who arrived wide-eyed and green. He drew maps for the soldiers, and when U.S. forces entered Germany's fourth largest city, Cologne, under a hail of bullets, it would have been the guns under Daddy's command firing. After Germany surrendered, Daddy stayed on in Europe because the plan was that the troops would then be shipped over to Japan. By the time he was released to go home, it was nearly December of 1945, and the seas were too stormy to cross. He wrote to Mother from Paris and Dieppe on thin sheets of USO airmail paper. In one letter, he told her that he didn't like to go to a club and have too many beers with his friends, "because then I get to missing you so much that I can't stand it."

He finally arrived home in January of 1946. Along with his meager gear, he carried with him eight tiny two-by-three-inch photos from Nordhausen, Germany, the site of the Mittelbau-Dora concentration camp. Mother kept them along with some letters in an old latch-top cigar box. As a child, I used to take them out one by one and examine them, holding them up to the light to study the tiny images frozen in time by the camera's lens, trying to decipher them. They were pictures of row upon row of bodies of the dead, some bloated, some so skeletal that they were little more than bones with the last remnants of skin stretched over them, stark white, sunken torsos in which you could count every rib. There were three separate rows of bodies, some naked, some still wearing the rough striped pants and shirts that the Nazis had forced upon them. A few were covered, looking like hastily wrapped mummies in half decay. The rows of human beings stretched out beyond the buildings. My dad had written on the back of one of the photos how the lines of corpses continued well beyond "the second white building." On another photo, showing the grotesque contorted final death grips of naked men, he wrote, after a long explanation, "Tear it up if you wish." But no one ever could, ever did, ever wanted to. He had photos too of a baby and a small child alongside, the child's arm reaching out in one last, futile effort to cover and to comfort the baby. Beside them are the bare legs of a horribly shrunken young man. Starvation had consumed his legs to the point of nothingness. In one last photo, the bodies seem to stretch as far as the eye or camera could see. There were, I now know, about five thousand of them.

Daddy's overall unit, the 104th, the Timberwolves, had liberated Nordhausen. His battalion had fought its way into the heavily fortified German town. He was among the early wave of troops to enter the camp, sent to render aid and to witness what had happened at Mittelbau-Dora. In the photos, you can see clusters of GIs, their feet in the same dirty, scarred combat boots that most of them had worn since Normandy, standing at silent attention beside the field of corpses. Barely one thousand prisoners were alive when they arrived. A plea had gone out for every Army medic in the region to come to the camp to treat anyone who might have survived. Many of the living were hiding among the dead or were too weak even to roll away from those who had died next to them. They lay amid disease and human waste, sometimes covered with dust from a bombing. Three or four living men had spent almost a week trapped under decaying bodies in a bomb crater. Some of the newly freed tried with their last remaining strength to salute their liberators. The American GIs dropped their heads into their hands and wept.

My father carried these photos home, most of them taken by one of his unit buddies. He wrote on the back of one small rectangle that he thought the photo would look different, but the camera lens had been too small to capture the enormity of the scene. Yet Daddy did not talk about Nordhausen. Once every year or two, when the three of us would open the box of photos, he could not bring himself to say a single word. Not long after he returned, Daddy told my mother that while inside the camp he had come upon an American Army nurse wielding a shovel in her hand. Before her stood a group of captured German Army officers. She thrust the shovel toward one man and said, "Dig." He pulled himself up straight and said, "No, I am an officer," and she lifted the shovel, whacked him across the bottom, and again said, "Dig." The officer took the shovel and started to dig. Each scoop of earth widened the space to bury the dead.

I was born in November, just over nine months after Daddy returned home, and to me, growing up, the war was like ancient history, but to him, it must have been very fresh and raw.

My dad came home to El Paso, but my parents didn't stay there long. Before the war, my father had worked for Universal CIT Credit Corporation, a loan company that, among other things, sold auto financing to people who bought cars. Today banks and car manufacturers handle auto financing, but in those postwar years people primarily applied to Universal CIT or another company like it. My father had started out in the Amarillo office and then moved to El Paso to be the district manager, but during the war one of his good friends had been promoted to run the El Paso office. Daddy had no wish to take away his job. The company offered Daddy several other posts, and he picked district manager for Midland. To sweeten the deal, CIT threw in a company car for him to drive.

Across the United States in 1946, there were thousands of towns like Midland and hundreds of thousands of men like my father. Midland became a boomtown because of the oil, but there are towns all over the country—auto towns in Michigan, steel towns in Pennsylvania or Ohio, textile towns in the Carolinas, other industry towns in other states—where veterans came back and settled to live their lives and make their homes. They put the war behind them, went to work, and built the economy. As kids, we knew small parts of their stories. We heard the adults talk in hushed sentences about neighborhood women whose first husbands had died in the war and who were now married to someone else. I had a couple of friends whose dads had been killed overseas, so they no longer had their dad, they had whomever their mother married next. That was the man who raised them, and most kids called him "Dad." Their dads from the war were gone. Many of my parents' best friends had war stories. Johnny Hackney, who owned Johnny's Bar-B-Q, had fought in the Pacific. Charlie White, who started out renting the house behind Mother and Daddy's, had contracted tuberculosis in a training camp during the war. Instead of going overseas, he was shipped to a sanitarium and his first wife left him. He met his second wife, Mary, when he came to Midland to work as an accountant for the Shell Oil Company.

There were families like the Hackneys or the Whites on almost every block, yet most people rarely mentioned the war. Midland had American Legion posts and Veterans of Foreign Wars posts, but they blended in with the Kiwanis clubs and the Elks. The adults I knew did not sit around trading stories of the war, of buddies who had been shot, friends who never came home, of men blown to bits by the side of the road, of the nights they were afraid to go to sleep because they might freeze to death in the bitter snows and cold, or of the emaciated Jews in the camps, many hiding among corpses in their rough, striped clothes, and the overwhelming stench of human dead. Only later would I learn that those were the things so many of them had seen.

Instead, they put the war years behind them and looked forward. I think too that my father seldom spoke of those years because he wanted to shield me. He didn't want me to know, and didn't want to admit to himself, how horrible man could be. He could manage the horrors if he did not examine them, did not dwell on them, if he did not lift the lid of that cigar box too many times to recall what lay within. In Midland, where the sky arced over us in one enormous dome of blistering blue and where people doggedly imported acres of elm seedlings and chinaberry trees to plant the green ribbons of shade that lined their streets at the edge of the desert, we were quite literally an ocean and almost a continent removed. All those years, though, Daddy kept those photos tucked away. He might not wish to remember, but neither would he ever allow himself to forget.

In November of 2002, I went to a luncheon in Prague during one of the NATO summits, and I was seated next to a Czech Holocaust survivor. Over the china plates and clinking crystal, with jacketed waiters hovering near our half-eaten meals, we started talking, and I told him that my father had helped to liberate one of the camps but that he had never actually talked about it. And this man, Arno Lustig, paused and looked at me and said, "Well, I was in one of the camps, and I never talked about it to my kids either. I never told them about it." Like my father, he added, he had wanted to shelter his own children from what he had seen and from all that he knew.

The El Paso that my parents left was a city of over one hundred thousand people. It had tall brick, quarried stone skyscrapers and crowded downtown blocks. The National Bank of El Paso building covered a full city corner and climbed seven stories into the sky. Chubby streetcars clanged up and down the avenues. By comparison, Midland was a sleepy backwater, a cattle drive and railway town bent on growing beyond itself. My father saw something in it and bet on Midland. I don't know if he had heard about the oil strikes when he picked Midland or if he simply wanted to be closer to his mother, in Lubbock. Once my father chose Midland, there was no turning back. However, Harold and Jenna Welch didn't stay put. They had lived in three homes before the first one that I remember, on Estes Avenue. Like all Midland houses, it was a low one-story. Land was abundant, and the swirling desert winds and the tornadoes that periodically threatened to rip past made going up impractical. If you were wealthier, you just had a longer house.

Their first home was a room at the Crawford Hotel. Almost everyone who moved to Midland moved into the Crawford or the slightly fancier Scharbauer Hotel, which had been built by one of the area's early ranching families. The Scharbauer's lobby was where cowboys and roughnecks and geologists tramped in and out looking for jobs and where oil landmen tried to corral ranchers into leasing them the mineral rights to their grazing acres in the hope of striking black gold. My mother was already pregnant when they arrived, and Daddy quickly found a little house on North Loraine, right at the edge of downtown, and put down a deposit. The owner had left behind some furniture and a puppy from a new litter. They named the dog Bully because he was the bully of the lot, and Bully lasted longer than the house. By the time I was two, we had moved over to a house on Estes Avenue. We would live in almost every house on that block before I turned seven.

My father's office was only a few blocks away, and he drove his company car to work each morning. Mother walked to the grocery or into town, although, in 1946, Midland didn't have much of a downtown. The city's first real skyscraper, finished in 1929 by the former Montana senator T. S. Hogan, had been promptly dubbed Hogan's Folly. It was a towering creation of glass windows and intricately carved sandstone, with a top that looked like the points in a king's crown. When the building opened, the town celebrated for a week with barbecues, rodeos, concerts, fireworks, speeches, aerial acts, and a formal dance with an orchestra in the Crystal Ballroom at the Scharbauer Hotel. Within five years, barely 10 percent of the offices had been leased, and the building was used mostly to store grain and hay, one of the most expensive and ornate silos ever built.

My father had the same job that he'd had before the war, but now his territory ran east and south and west, spanning more than one hundred miles in each direction. From Midland, it stretched east to Abilene, south to San Angelo and Fort Stockton, and west to Pecos and Monahans. And it covered a swath of small towns in between, towns with names like Notrees, Texon, and Iraan. Daddy regularly got behind the wheel and made the three-, four-, and five-hour drives to call on car dealers or customers in the region. He knew every dealer in every small town. Occasionally, he took me with him, my legs growing hot and prickly from the heat that rose in glistening waves from the road. Mostly, though, he went alone, and I would cry when his car pulled away from the curb. Today, West Texas salesmen still ply the same routes, this time selling medical devices and high-tech equipment across that vast triangle of land.

My mother stayed home and waged her own constant battle with the land right outside our door. Midland sits at the bottom of the High Plains, nearly three thousand feet above sea level. When the first settlers drove their wagons across it, they found a rich plateau of shimmering grass-lands; "higher than a horse" is how some of them described the grass. Buffalo grazed along its wide stretches and wallowed in its dips, where the hard, fast rains would collect and swell into muddy bottoms. On the grasslands, the Comanche Indians chased the buffalo and then battled the settlers. But the settlers kept coming. Train tracks were laid. The new arrivals drove in cattle from the east and set up ranching. And then they plowed the ground. The land was plowed all the way from Minnesota to Texas. And then the drought came. Without rain, nothing would grow in the soil, and when the winds raced out of Canada and down through the plains, the soil blew, acres and acres of topsoil, more soil in one single storm back in the 1930s than was dug out of the entire Panama Canal, until there was nothing left except the hard, dry land underneath.

Once the soil was gone and the ground was thoroughly razed, the wind would blow clouds of sand and dust. We thought Midland had to be the worst place for sand in all of Texas because it sat at the bottom of this wind range. The land to the north, running up to Lubbock, had been turned into miles and miles of dry-land cotton farming. But for seven years, even what was called the "dry land" got no rain. In the 1950s, Texas suffered its worst drought in history, worse than the Dust Bowl. Not even a trace of rain fell in Lubbock for the entire twelve months of 1952. All those years, acres of rough, reddish sand would blow straight down into Midland, riding in thick swirls on the wind.

People latched their windows tight, not to keep out the heat or the desert cold in the winter, but to hold back the billowing sand. The sand covered our clothes drying on the line; sometimes they were hardly clean by the time Mother brought them in. My mother spent her days with a broom and a wet rag, wiping up the reddish grit that snuck in under the sills or attached itself to your feet or clothes and lodged deep in your hair or skin whenever the wind blew. And it seemed as if the wind was constantly blowing. There were sandstorms too, where the sand raced in so thick you couldn't see down the block or over to the next car. I remember the sand stinging my legs like a layer of acrid skin and its gritty taste in my mouth, peppering my teeth and tongue. When it blew, you scrunched up your eyes and stayed indoors. Only giant tumbleweeds roamed the streets with the wind. They traveled on the gusts until they butted up against something hard that the wind couldn't topple over. We'd find tumbleweeds wedged under cars or landing smack against front doors; one of the most popular pictures of Midland from the early 1950s is of a woman standing in front of a nice ranch house blocked up to the roof with tumbleweeds.

At Christmas, people gathered up the tumbleweeds, tied them together in threes, and sprayed them with white flocking to make desert snowmen for their lawns. Some even added jaunty hats or scarves, their versions of Frosty of the Wild West.

In West Texas, the wind and the sand were things you lived with. If you were born there, you never knew anything else. But if you moved there, it must have seemed sometimes to be a land forsaken. Cowboys who came out to work the Midland range in the late 1800s recalled that many days in the winter they did not hear a sound except for their own footsteps and the moan of the wind. I remember finding a Texas book from the 1920s called *The Wind* by a writer named Dorothy Scarborough. In it, a woman who has moved to West Texas ranchland eventually goes mad from listening to the wind's constant howl and drone.

But it wasn't just the wind. There was an underlying sense of hardship, a sense that the land could quickly turn unforgiving. One of the earliest stagecoach riders, in the 1850s, recalled passing through the grasslands and seeing a vast expanse of the remains of animals and men. "For miles and miles," he wrote, "these bones strew the plain." They were the bones of would-be prospectors who had attempted to cut through Texas to reach the burgeoning California goldfields. Later, in the 1870s, when the Indians battled the buffalo hunters, who had come to shoot the herds for money and sport, they would not simply kill them. The far crueler punishment was to take all the hunters' supplies and leave them to wander the plains, until they collapsed and died of thirst or starvation.

The first family to live in what would become Midland resided in a dugout: they dug a hole in the ground big enough for a room and strung a tent across for a roof. They burned mesquite roots for heat. Their daughter had no dolls; she tied strings to sticks to build a corral, collected rocks to serve as sheep, and played at ranching. One of Midland's oldest ranching families, the Cowdens, had a cow fall through the roof into their dugout room and land on a bed. They had to dig up their home to get the cow out.

By the time I was born in Midland, in the mid-1940s, not all of the local ranchers lived on their ranchlands. Many whose properties encircled the town like a giant, grassy ring, starting at the very edge where streets dead-ended into dust, had already moved their families into houses inside Midland, mostly for the schools. Each morning, the dads would hop in their cars and head out to their ranches just like other fathers heading into the office. Only the cowboys stayed out on the range full-time to work the cattle and keep up the land. But Midland itself was barely two generations removed from the raw, hard days of the frontier. My grandmother Welch had been eleven when Midland (it was called Midway back then, because it stood exactly midway between Fort Worth and El Paso on the railroad line) got its first official building, an old railroad mail car that was shunted onto a siding to make a post office. Our own street, Estes Avenue, was named for a cattleman who had boldly driven his herd out onto the drought-scorched plains in 1886.

And living in town did not silence the wind.

It helped to be fearless if you lived in Midland. It wasn't so much an insular world as an isolated one. Aside from neighboring Odessa, any town of consequence was at least a two-hour drive away. The city fathers like to call Midland "the Capital City of the Great Permian Basin Empire," and they put out a huge write-up on the town, detailing everything down to the neon lights at Agnes's Drive-In. Still, whatever human empire there was, was sparse. What Midland had by the early 1950s were oil storage tanks and junctions of vast pipelines that carried petroleum and natural gas miles away to more populous areas. Sometimes there would be fires at the storage tanks, explosions followed by big, rushing plumes of flame that turned the sky a smoky red. The incinerating heat would pour into the already scorched air and sky.

Midland called itself a city although it remained very much a small town. There was still a blacksmith shop right at the edge of Main Street, its weathered wood siding emblazoned with the cattle brands of all the local ranches. Whenever the smithy designed a new brand, its mark was burned into a fresh section of dry wood.

Midland was so small that Mother and Daddy allowed Bully, our rather daring dog, who had come with the house on North Loraine, to trot down the sidewalks alone every afternoon. At three o'clock, Bully would walk to Daddy's office, and one of the men who worked for Daddy would buy Bully an ice cream cone, which he would hold as Bully proceeded to lick with his bright pink tongue until all the ice cream was gone. Bully also had a habit of following my mother to Anthony's on Main Street. Bully would set off behind her, and she would ignore him. Once they reached the store, Mother would walk inside while Bully sat by the front door waiting until another customer came along to let him in.

There were a lot of things about Anthony's that Bully liked, but he was particularly fond of the pneumatic tubes, which the checkers used to deposit cash and checks and then sent them flying with the push of a button to the cashier who sat high up on the mezzanine. Bully would hear those tubes take off, and he would take off too, chasing the tubes through the store. And Mother would pretend that she didn't know him. He was, she maintained, my father's dog, and everyone agreed that my father was a man who never met a dog that he didn't like.

Bully was a wire-haired terrier mix, and he was quite simply incorrigible. He once bit a passerby on the seat of his pants. The man had kicked Bully's best friend, Happy, a yappy little dog who lived next door. Bully raced up behind the man and bit him. Incensed, the man banged on our door and promptly turned around to show Mother his backside, hollering, "Look what your dog did."

Bully often ended up in the pound, which in Midland was a bleak fenced-in pen by a little shack, and each time Daddy would go to pick him up. Once when Daddy arrived, the gate was already open and all the dogs had bolted out except for one bitch, who was in heat and was locked up in her own little pen, and Bully, who sat waiting for her outside. The dogcatcher blamed Bully for opening the gate.

Eventually, Bully was sent to live with my grandparents in the upper valley of the Rio Grande above El Paso, where he could have more space to roam. They drove him to Midland whenever they came to visit, and we saw him anytime we went to El Paso. The moment he caught sight of my father, Bully would cry and jump on Daddy, because he never forgot him. But Bully was only the first of our many colorful pets—dogs, cats, a box turtle, a parakeet who lived on the back porch, and horny toads out in the garden, which Mother would gently coax into the palm of her hand. We laughed over the antics of our animals, and they were our beloved companions. We were warmed by their unconditional love. I played with the dogs and dressed my cat in doll clothes. Time and again, our animals found us, arriving as if by canine or feline navigation at our front door.

After Bully came Rusty, a cocker spaniel who was particularly close to my mother and was tragically run over on Big Spring Street. Then came sweet Roman, named because he roamed up to the house one day. Roman stayed with us for a few years and then roamed off again. In his lifetime, my father bought only one dog, Duke, a full-blooded boxer with papers, but Duke didn't last. He was a hyper barker who grew too big for our small backyard. Daddy finally sold him to another family in Midland. But for several years, he drove up and down the alley next to Duke's new home to make sure Duke was being treated well. After Duke came Freckles and then Bo, a beagle mix, who was remarkably dumb and was also dispatched to live out the remainder of his days in El Paso. Our last dog, Marty, came to us when I was in high school. He was a mutt, found in a litter of abandoned pups alongside a highway near Waco. One of my friends' sisters spotted them as she was driving home. He lived with Mother and Daddy until shortly before I married. When we left Estes Avenue, my mother adopted the first of several cats. The last cat actually belonged to the Robbins family, who lived across the street from Mother and Daddy on Humble Avenue, but when Daddy charmed him with cat chow, Henry moved in with my parents. After Daddy died, Henry stayed with Mother until she left for her retirement home. Only then did Henry pick up and return to his true owners across the street.

<hr />

Long before the war, Daddy was ambitious. He had done his two years at Texas Tech, the new college in Lubbock, before he dropped out to help support his mother. His brother, Mark, was in medical school, so taking care of her fell to Dad. He had started at the bottom and worked his way up at CIT. But in Midland, Daddy hoped for more.

He had grown up in the Depression, in the Dust Bowl. His family and others had survived on backyard gardens and the fact that most people kept a cow tethered behind their homes. Otherwise, they had lost everything, so Daddy refused to waste anything. He did not buy fancy clothes, wouldn't spend the money to join a country club. He was generous, but he didn't give my mother Christmas presents. In his world, Christmas was for children. Adults had no need for frivolous gifts. If Mother gave something to Daddy, it was likely socks or pajamas. A couple times before Christmas, Daddy gave me a dollar to spend on gifts at Woolworth's. I counted out my change to buy dish towels and other sensible things. Daddy sold credit, yet he didn't like to have too much owed to the bank, and he always walked around with a wad of cash. Some of it was for the gambling, mostly gin rummy games played around the desks in other people's offices, but some was for the security of knowing that he had several hundred dollars, enough for at least a month, right there in his pocket, should everything dry up and blow away again. Much later, when his brain began to betray him and he was no longer able to go to the bank and withdraw a stack of crisp, green bills, he would reach into his pocket and then forlornly look over to my mother and say, "We're busted, honey, we're busted." And she would smile and flash her eyes, and say, "Harold, you may be, but I'm not."

In addition to working at CIT, Daddy soon began building houses on the side. After the big oil strike in the fall of 1946, landmen, engineers, geologists, roughnecks, and roustabouts began crowding into Midland and nearby Odessa, and there weren't enough new homes for all of them. Car financing was a good business. Home building might prove to be even better. And building a house was something that Daddy could make his own.

When we went to Lubbock on the weekends, he loved to drive around and point out houses that his father had built. Daddy taught himself how to draw a floor plan and the basics of construction. By the late 1940s, about the time my baby brother was born and died, Daddy had begun buying small plots of land and putting up houses, starting with our own new block on Estes Avenue.

Sometimes we lived in a house after Daddy built it. Once he sold it, we simply packed up and moved down the street into another house. It was like a game of leapfrog along the block. Daddy also built houses to rent. The house behind us was rented, and my second-grade teacher and her husband briefly rented a duplex that he built. Except for the paint, the houses were largely indistinguishable. Each had a little front door with a covered overhang and windows on either side, and they were all packed in tight, one right next to another. You could practically hand your neighbors a cup of sugar through the window. Or hear most everything that was being said.

From the time of the first settlers, West Texas was a land of magnificent distances and empty range, and the promise and the risk that come with both. Even in the mid–twentieth century, many of the cities and towns that sprang up across its flatlands and ridgelines were unconsciously made to resemble the old stockade forts that were built to hold off Indian war parties or offset fears of a second Mexican invasion. People pulled together and looked inward, rather than out to the unknown. Shared experience was a powerful bond, and transplants and new arrivals created second families out of friends.

That was how it was for Harold and Jenna Welch and Charlie and Mary White, who rented the tiny white house behind us on Estes Avenue. When I was three, I loved running over to Charlie and Mary's; I was forever rapping at their door. My mother told them they could just ignore me. But I was persistent. I'd knock on the front door, and if they didn't answer, I'd go around to the kitchen door in the back and catch them sitting at their table. And I'd say, "Oh, there you are." I never got the hint that they didn't answer the door on purpose.

When I was five, Mary got pregnant, and the day Linda, their daughter, was born, Charlie came to tell me first. He walked in the front door early in the morning. No one ever thought about locking up in Midland. When I came out of my room, Mother was already heading for the kitchen to whip up a celebratory batch of pancakes. Charlie and Mary were so much like family that we had Christmas with them every year. At first, when I was little and they didn't have children, they would come and have Christmas with us. After Linda and then Larry were born, we alternated, one house hosted Christmas Eve, the other Christmas Day. Mary, Charlie, and my mother would cook Christmas Eve dinner, a huge production of intricately stuffed Hungarian cabbage rolls. Daddy provided the recipe, courtesy of one of his CIT employees who was Hungarian. Over time, the cabbage rolls gave way to bubbling platters of enchiladas or tamales. For Christmas Day, either Mary or my mother roasted a turkey. Long after we had moved from Estes Avenue, long after I was grown, we still celebrated Christmas with the Whites. For Mother and Daddy, those shared Christmases with a house full of eager children and paper and presents were the holidays that they had dreamed of but that had remained just beyond their grasp.

When my own daughters, Barbara and Jenna, were born, Linda made them elaborate felt stockings to recall our Christmases together. The girls still hang them in front of the fireplace every December 24.

All told, Estes Avenue had five houses crammed on one little block, with their bits of patchy front lawn and matching concrete front walks. Because it was right after the war and supplies were costly and scarce, the houses were built with the most basic materials—plain board siding, no shutters on the windows. Their walls couldn't go up fast enough. The oil companies were bringing people into Midland, and nearly everyone who arrived needed a house. At one point, during an earlier boom, the Humble Oil and Refining Company, which would later become Exxon, picked up over seventy houses, packed them onto trucks, and moved them from a temporary oil camp into Midland. They were deposited all over the city, where families added rooms and stuck brick veneers on the fronts. They became many of Midland's earliest homes.

Indeed, for about a century, you can chart Midland's progress like the rings of a tree, the fat years of the oil or cattle booms, the thin years of the busts. From Hogan's Folly, the downtown expanded out into the steel office towers of the fifties, then the smoky glass high-rises of the late seventies and early eighties. The houses were the same, the early, wide-porch wooden ranch houses with lattice and gables and their own windmills to pump precious water, then the tiny 1930s and '40s ramblers, then the comfortable brick ranch houses of the 1950s, with their big picture windows and wood trim, then the slant-roofed, brown-brick town homes of the late 1970s and early '80s. Midland would build and then stop, wait years, and then begin the frenzy of building all over again.

On Estes Avenue, parents could turn their children loose and let them roam. Mothers sent their kids outside every afternoon. We'd play kick the can, tag, Red Rover, and other games that were mostly excuses to run through the vacant lots nearby. The lots were scrubby little squares of land where no one had built anything yet, and they were covered with mesquite trees, which are considered trash trees in large parts of Texas. A few people darkly swear that horse thieves brought them up from Mexico and planted them to hide their stolen animals in. More likely, their seeds rode north on the flanks of longhorns during endless cattle drives. Some of the cattle also ate mesquite beans and dropped the pods back down to the ground in their manure. Whatever its origin, mesquite seemed to be the only tree that actually thrived in the arid Midland ground. "Thrived" may be too strong a word. Our mesquite trees were stunted little things, parched and dry like most everything around them, with fluttery leaves that looked like ferns. But when I was young, it seemed very exotic to race through the mesquite, following the narrow paths that other kids' feet had already worn. Because Midland was so new, there were kids all over the neighborhood, growing hot and restless in their tiny postwar homes.

When the streets and lots were quiet, my mother would still turn me out, bundling me off on adventures of her own creation. One of her particular favorites was the solo picnic, where I ate lunch among the soft flurry of birds and leaves. I remember her carefully packing a sack, handing me a jug of milk, and sending me scampering off to the park over on the next street. It was hardly a park; it was little more than an oddly shaped triangle of leftover land where two streets intersected. Someone had planted a cluster of elms at each end. But there was a shiny metal swing, and to a small child, it was a big expanse, far larger than the few square feet of our own yard. I would sit under the rustling trees, unwrap my sandwich, open my milk jug, and eat my solo picnic.

The last house that Daddy built on Estes Avenue sat on the corner of Estes and Big Spring. It was the only brick home on the whole block. We lived there until I was eight. When television came to Midland, Daddy had the garage bricked over and enclosed to make a den.

By then, Daddy was building houses almost full-time. He had gone in with a partner, Lloyd Waynick. Lloyd didn't have children and he liked to sleep late, so Daddy would head to the house sites early and Lloyd would take the afternoon shift while Daddy slipped home for a quick nap. They were always looking for new sites. They bought land from ranchers or cotton farmers who wanted to get out of farming as well as empty tracts along the ever-expanding edges of Midland. Daddy's face was perpetually sunburned, his left arm twice as dark as his right from resting it on the open car window as he drove from job site to job site, from strip of land to strip of land.

Daddy built houses for people moving in with the oil business, and in the boom years, the buyers just kept coming. He built only spec houses.

No matter how many times someone asked, he refused to build a custom home. "Too expensive with people changing their minds," he maintained. Daddy had no interest in ripping out cabinets or carpeting or moving a den simply because someone had seen a picture in a furniture catalog or a magazine. Nearly all of Daddy's houses had the identical floor plan. The few times that he experimented and built a different plan, the house took months to sell. Buyers wanted their houses to have a living room at the front, a den behind it, and a hallway with three bedrooms, one hall bath, and one bath in the master bedroom, plus a kitchen and a utility room. They were sturdy, ranch-style houses, not very different from thousands of other homes all over the United States. By the time he had finished building, Daddy had put up dozens of homes in and around Midland.

Yet if anything ever needed fixing in our house, that was purely my mother's domain. Daddy wasn't handy at all. He didn't even change light-bulbs. My mother did those things and repaired what she could or had a serviceman or one of Daddy's men do it. He could oversee construction and draw floor plans, but he wasn't much good with an actual hammer or wrench in his hands.

Now on the weekends, instead of going to Lubbock, we would drive around Midland. We'd ride slowly up and down the streets, and Daddy would point and say, "I built that house. I built that house. That's one of my houses."

But mostly we drove just to drive. It was how we got out of the house. People in Midland didn't walk, they drove everywhere. Kids rode their bikes until they turned fourteen and could get behind the wheel of a car on their own. On restless days, we merely drove longer and farther. Daddy could drive from Midland to Dallas in six hours and from Midland to El Paso in another six. And those were the drives we did. After he got home from work on a Friday night, we'd head for the car and drive six hours to my grandparents in El Paso or my uncle Mark in Dallas. Occasionally, when I was little, we would drive into Arkansas to visit my mother's grandmother, who lived on a small slip of a dairy farm right near my grandfather's two old-maid sisters and bachelor brother. Each time we crossed the border, my father would joke about all the trees in Arkansas, making it sound as if we were people who had never seen a tree.

The Texas roads of my memory, seen from the backs of our roomy Fords, were wide, flat, and smooth, in part because it was an energy-producing state but also because Texas was so very big and everything was so far away. You could drive for an entire day and still be inside Texas. A hundred years before, men had set out in wagons and on horseback to follow trampled grass trails; today it was gas-powered engines from Detroit humming over million-dollar roads. Modern-day Texas was designed around driving, and vast sums were spent on the state's highways. I remember the minute we drove across the state line into New Mexico, the roads became pitted and rutted and I would rattle and bump around on the long bench seat, pressing my legs down and digging in with my knees. No one ever thought of using seat belts; there weren't any in the car. Sometimes in the heat my skin stuck to the upholstery until I would have to peel it off like a thick roll of sticky tape.

In New Mexico, my parents liked to drive to a horse track with the fancy name of Ruidoso Downs. Although it officially opened in 1947, the owners must have had dreams of becoming the Churchill Downs of the West. Ruidoso was up in the mountains, about four or five hours away. Mother and Daddy would watch the quarter horse races, which had big purses, and gamble. They liked to splurge and buy a day pass to the Jockey Club, where the seats were shaded and the food was rich but not fancy. There were steaming bowls of hot New Mexican chili, and alcohol, of course, cold beers and mixed drinks. I might have had a Coke or a Shirley Temple with a fat, bright red cherry. We would sit in the club, and Mother and Daddy would lean in to see the races, their eyes riveted to the thundering hooves of the horses, the dirt track smarting as they barreled along in a full run.

I loved going to Ruidoso because it was cool up in the mountains and there was a hint of dampness to the air. It was the closest cool place to Midland. Occasionally, you could see snowcaps and, in summer, tall, heavy pines that pierced the sky. It was so very different from the long, flat land around Midland, where the roads stretched unchanged toward the oblivion of the horizon.

We made long drives every summer. We drove all the way to California, to Newport Beach and Balboa and Catalina Island, where the water was a deep turquoise blue, almost as mesmerizing as the Midland sky, and blubbery brown sea lions screeched and sunned themselves on the jagged rocks. We kayaked over the tops of silent kelp forests, and my mother stared in wonder at pelicans scanning for fish in the sea. We slept in a no-frills motel outside the newly opened Disneyland, with its horse-drawn streetcars and King Arthur Carrousel. A few years, we headed east to the swampy bayou port cities of New Orleans and Houston. We drove to San Antonio almost every summer, and each time we'd visit the Alamo. We'd stay at the old Menger Hotel, which kept alligators in a couple of planters on either side of the cavernous lobby fireplace. It had a swimming pool too, which to me was one of the best things about vacations.

Yet it was on those trips, when there were only the three of us, that I felt the overwhelming absence of a brother or sister. Mother and Daddy sat chatting in the front of the car, while I rode in the back alone. If we stopped at a motel with a pool, Daddy might swim a few laps with me, but there were no games of Marco Polo, no splashing races or dives to touch the bottom. Other times, Mother came down and sat by the pool to watch me while I went in by myself. I'm not sure what she would have done if I had suddenly started struggling in the chlorinated water. She had never learned to swim.

And there was the particular loneliness of being an only child among the throngs at a crowded amusement park. Once, in New Orleans, when we had stopped at the park next to Lake Pontchartrain, it was my mother who was drafted to ride behind me in the two-seater Wild Mouse roller-coaster car. She screamed the entire time.

As I grew older, when we went to Ruidoso, my parents would let me invite a friend. A few times, other families traveled with us on our summer jaunts, two cars setting off in a caravan to whatever destination the fathers had picked. When we drove to Newport Beach, at the edge of the Pacific Ocean, it was with our next-door neighbors Ann and Joe Morse and their daughter, Laurie. After a few days in California, Mother and Daddy and Ann and Joe left Laurie and me with her grandparents while they got in the car and headed off across the desert to Vegas to gamble, and then drove all the way back to get us and head home.

By the time I was six, my parents decided that I was ready to travel on my own and sent me on the train to El Paso to visit my grandparents. They handed my ticket to the porter at the Midland station and waved me off. Mother had packed a lunch for me because she didn't think I was old enough to go into the dining car and write down what I wanted on the little pad of paper. It was a nearly six-hour train ride, through Pecos, Van Horn, and Sierra Blanca, across sparse, open land and long-vanished buffalo trails. My grandparents, Grammee and Papa, would meet me at the station in their old pickup truck and drive me out to Canutillo, in the upper Rio Grande Valley outside El Paso, where they had their home.

I loved my Grammee with a particular devotion. Jessie Laura Hawkins, my mother's mother, had been only twenty-one when Mother was born. She was nearly three decades younger than Grandma Welch and still quite young. And she loved to play. Not only did she make my clothes and doll clothes but she also built my doll furniture by hand, little couches covered in lush brown velvet with tiny navy velvet pillows edged in rich gold braid. I thought they were the most elegant things I had ever seen. Grammee, whose own childhood had been cut perilously short, lovingly created so much of my own.

Jessie and Hal had moved to El Paso in 1927; like the Welches, both had been born in Arkansas. But Grammee's mother's family had come from France. Grammee always thought that her mother, Eva Louise LaMaire, had been born in Paris, which no doubt sounded infinitely more glamorous, but in fact she was born in New York City not long after her own parents arrived on an immigrant ship and passed through the gates of Ellis Island. From the teeming crowds and clanking noise of New York, the LaMaires headed west to landlocked Arkansas. However it was spelled, they always pronounced their name "la mer," French for the sea. My great-grandmother was eighteen when she married Joseph Sherrard, who had been born in Mississippi in the middle of the Civil War. On the actual day of his birth, April 7, 1862, the Battle of Shiloh was raging 150 miles away. They settled on a small dairy farm beyond Little Rock, in a place so tucked away and destitute that no one bothered to paint the houses, they simply left the wood to gray, swell, and shrink under the cycle of rain and sun. My great-grandmother bore eight children, seven girls who lived, and one boy, Joseph Jr., who died. Then one morning when my great-grandmother was about forty-two, and newly pregnant with her last daughter, her husband headed out into the field where his cows grazed.

He had his shotgun with him, loaded, and he held it up to his head and pulled the trigger. The family whispered that he did it because of all those girls. I sometimes wonder if any of those same girls were tasked that day with helping their mother carry in their father's corpse. Eva Louise buried her husband and kept on milking the cows, whose udders were full each morning whether someone had died or not. She ran the farm and raised her brood of girls for the rest of her days. I remember stopping to visit her a few times on those trips to Arkansas, when she was a shrunken old woman still living a hard, rural life.

My grandmother never told my mother about the suicide. Instead, Mother heard the story from Papa's side of the family, his two old-maid sisters, who lived with his bachelor brother in Little Rock. Jessie Sherrard was barely nine when her father marched out into that field. After he died, she drove the milk truck for the dairy farm. When she met my grandfather, he worked as a postman, driving a postal truck. He had barely any memories of his own father, who died when Papa was three.

Papa's health was what drove the Hawkinses to move west. He had asthma, and everyone believed that the dry desert air in the Southwest contained some kind of magical cure. Thousands of World War I veterans who had been gassed in the trenches across France had moved to New Mexico, Arizona, and the far reaches of West Texas, seeking a balm for their ravaged lungs. My grandparents settled in the upper valley, one block from the Rio Grande, which rolled and lapped in its riverbed before it turned narrow and sluggish alongside the city of El Paso itself. They chose a place right off Highway 80, the main road to California before the government put through the interstate. As late as the 1950s, it hummed with cars making their way west. Jessie and Hal built a small tourist court, a cluster of tiny one-room cottages with a single communal bathroom in the middle. During the Depression, carloads of people fleeing the devastation of the Dust Bowl and the complete collapse of life back east would stop at a tourist court to shower and sleep in the primitive cottages or doze in their cars or outside on the warm ground before moving on to California's promised land. To supplement what little they made from the tourist court, my grandparents opened a grocery, where they sold bologna, pickles, loaves of bread, and a few other staples that people might buy before they crossed the New Mexico line to traverse the desert beyond.

They also ran a lumberyard, and at one point Hal Hawkins had enough money to buy a small block off of Highway 80 and put up a few houses, just as my father later did in Midland. Grammee and Papa built their own house on that street. It was an orange house, covered in smooth, orange-glazed brick, surplus from the Army's rush to slap up vast new kitchens and dining halls for the freshly minted troops converging on Fort Bliss. My grandfather may have gotten it for free or talked his way into buying it at a cut rate. However he got it, every brick was a bright, shocking orange. One day in 1943, when Mother brought Daddy home to meet her parents, the first thing he saw was Jessie Hawkins down on her knees with a bucket of mortar that she had mixed herself and a trowel in her hand, laying brick. That was how Harold Welch met his future mother-in-law. My father always enjoyed telling that story, invariably adding his own punch line: that when he first saw Jessie, he thought, Great, I'm marrying into a family whose women can do anything.

I loved going to visit Grammee and Papa for those two or three weeks in the summer, to be enveloped by the desert heat and lulled by the simple repetition of Grammee's daily routine. It was, I suppose now, not so far removed from daily chores in Midland—cooking, watering the yard, doing the wash and the cleaning, and the endless sweeping out of the house. But the location was infinitely more interesting, with the Rio Grande on one side and the Franklin Mountains bumping up against us on the other. And Grammee was fascinating. Unlike most mothers I knew, who wore dresses and aprons, she wore pants, hats, gloves, and big, long-sleeved shirts to cover her skin because out in the valley the sun is especially bright and searing. The Texas poet Marian Haddad wrote once about El Paso, "The sun is different here." "Drastic and dense," she called it, and it truly is. There is something thick and liquid about the light, more than can be accounted for by the fact that El Paso sits up closer to the sun than Midland.

Grammee was a collector too, her house and garden an artful arrangement of what man and nature had left behind. She saved old Mexican coins, many of them gold, and smooth Indian grindstones that wandering or fleeing tribes had abandoned along the rough paths in the Franklin foothills. Tucked away in a wooden drawer was a little box of shells and the tiny, perfect skeleton of a sea horse, what remained of an all but forgotten, long-ago visit to the sea. She collected rocks, each with its own lengthy geological tale, and empty glass bottles that others casually tossed aside. Her bottles grew so numerous that she built a ring of shelves for them above the windows on her modest, window-covered porch. The less interesting and more ubiquitous beer bottles she dispatched to her garden, where she marked off her flower beds by planting their stubby necks deep in the ground until only the glinting round bottoms peeked up from the earth.

Most of Grammee's garden, aside from where she grew a patch of asparagus that reliably sprouted year after year, was a wonderful, vast rock garden. There was no trash collection out where she and Papa lived, hence the bottles, so whatever they couldn't reuse was recycled into that garden. She planted flowers inside the well of an enormous rubber tire that must have rolled off a truck plodding along the highway or gone flat and been left behind. In another corner, a faded wagon wheel stuck up from the sand. She took broken bits of pottery and cemented them onto urns that she placed along a wall constructed of her own homemade cinder block, which she made from a rectangular mold that she filled with concrete mix. She grew yuccas, ocotillos, magueys, and pomegranate trees, and a big, bright swath of daffodils. The bulbs had come from her mother's house in Arkansas. When my mother moved to Midland, Grammee divided up the bulbs and gave some to Mother, who planted them in her yard and lovingly dug them up and replanted them each time she moved to another house. When I married George and came back to Midland, Mother did the same for me, appearing on my doorstep with one hundred bulbs, the offspring of that long-fallow Arkansas yard, four generations removed.

Sometimes I would follow Grammee around, but mostly I played, staking out a corner of the garden. I built sprawling sand ranches that stretched across the ground and meticulously arranged the plump mesquite beans that I had chosen to be my cattle. But I was rarely alone. Nuway Drive, Grammee and Papa's block, was teeming with other children, and they became my friends all those summers. Mornings were spent outside in the baking heat. Then, once the blazing sun settled atop the sky, we retreated inside to eat our main meal and lie down for a siesta. Only in the late afternoon did we get up and bathe. My grandmother would put on a dress, and my grandfather would change his shirt and pants, and we'd all go for a ride in his pickup truck. If it was just the three of us, I sat wedged between them in the cab, but most of the time, I piled in the flatbed with an assortment of neighborhood kids and

Bully, our old Midland dog. Then we'd be off, bumping along the levee road that edged right up against the Rio Grande.

Papa would stop, lift Bully out of the truck, and send him running toward the river. Bully would plunge in and paddle about the placid Rio Grande. Then he'd get out, shake, and run after the truck until he had dried off, and Papa would hoist Bully back in. To a six- or seven-year-old, those late-afternoon rides seemed like the greatest adventures in the world.

There was a wildness too in the upper valley that did not exist among the imported trees and rectangular subdivision grids of Midland. Once, behind the orange house, I came upon Bully shaking a rattlesnake to death in his terrier teeth. I watched as the rattler's body broke into pieces, one portion of his scales flying through the open window of the truck cab. It was terrible and mesmerizing at the same time.

In the evenings, we'd sit in our clean, "dressed-up" clothes in Grammee and Papa's living room and talk. Then Grammee would fix supper, usually a bowl of cereal or a dish of ice cream, which we ate at the kitchen table. The kitchen of my childhood memory is a large and spacious room; only much later did I step inside and discover that it was quite small.

The whole house was small. It was a four-square house, only four rooms—two bedrooms, the living room, and the kitchen—with a little center hall. There was an evaporative air conditioner set up on the roof over the center hall to mitigate the heat, a "swamp cooler," we called it. Papa would finally turn it on around four in the afternoon, when the heat had become almost unbearable. But at night, because of the desert, the house was cool. We slept with the windows open. I spent the night on a double bed in the little guest room, but I was not alone. When the lights went out, Grammee would slip in wearing her plain cotton nightie to sleep with me. I can still remember how great it felt to lie there in the quiet dark, with only a sheet resting on top, as the cool desert breeze wafted in.

And I remember too the unspoken comfort of those nights as we drifted off and Grammee held my hand, not letting go until long after we were both asleep.

Grammee and Papa had a pattern to their life that I liked, and I could imagine living like that, in the quiet of the valley, with the sand and the river and the sun. Sometimes, particularly when Mother and Daddy came, we went for longer drives, following the valley out into neighboring New Mexico, heading past the acres of pecan trees at the Stahlman Farm and past San Miguel, with its tiny church built entirely of black volcanic rock, all the way up past the rich farmland to Las Cruces. I would sit in the back of the car, the bright light radiating through the window, and daydream about living on a ranch in the upper valley, raising hot green chilies, onions, and pecans.

For years, every visit to El Paso included a McGinney and a trip to Juárez. The McGinney was Papa's own creation. He liked to drink a beer before lunch, and when I visited, he would fix me what he called a McGinney, a little shot glass filled with a swallow of cold, foamy beer. I drank Papa's McGinneys until I turned seven. That year, I signed the temperance pledge card that sat in the back of every seat in the pews at the First Methodist Church in Midland. Worshipers were expected to sign the pledge and drop it in the collection plate. Once I signed, I gave up McGinneys, at least for a little while.

But I did not give up Juárez. When they visited, Mother and Daddy would go over at night for dinner or to sit in a club with their El Paso friends. In the daylight, it was my turn to cross into Mexico, with Grammee and Papa and sometimes with Mother and Daddy as well. We'd drive to El Paso, park the car, and walk across the barbed-wire-laced bridge with the river draining below. On the other side, Grammee and Papa would stop for a Mexican beer; then we headed for the open-air market, which beckoned with baskets, embroidered cotton tops, hand-hewn guitars, and wooden puppets. The pottery was my favorite. I ambled from stall to stall, comparing brightly painted birds and red and green leaves on miniature tea sets, carefully selecting my purchase. Today, at home in Crawford and Dallas, I have cabinets and shelves lined with vibrant Mexican jugs and bowls.

Afterward, we'd make our way back across the bridge, bundles tied and clutched in our hands. But before we could reenter El Paso, each of us had to speak to a U.S. Customs officer. Grammee and Papa made me thoroughly rehearse "I am a citizen of the United States," so I would not suddenly go mute or say the wrong thing. As much as I relished those excursions, the returns always seemed a bit perilous, with the specter of being stuck for days on that bridge, in a concrete and barbed-wire limbo between the United States and Mexico.

El Paso continued to call to me long after I had grown. I decamped there for a summer in college, taking classes at Mother's old Texas College of Mines and Metallurgy, which was now Texas Western and has since been renamed for a third time as University of Texas at El Paso. I came again as a woman in my forties and my fifties, to talk to writers, stroll through art galleries, take in the city and the land. With my friend Adair Margo, I climbed the rugged trails of Mount Cristo Rey to the great cream lime-stone carving of Christ on the cross, which sits above what had been a favorite mule watering hole for the northern-bound Spanish conquista-dors. The last Sunday in October, devout religious pilgrims will crawl on their knees up the same rocky trails to demonstrate their fealty to God.

There remains something mystical about El Paso, built into a moun-tain pass that divides Mexico and Texas, sliced by the Rio Grande in its winding journey into the Gulf of Mexico. But perhaps other factors account for the city's magnetic pull. In 1971, a Texas biochemist declared the city's groundwater to be heavily fortified with lithium in its natural state. Some of my longtime El Paso friends say that people who move away invariably find themselves moving back. Because they're not happy anywhere else but in El Paso.

For much of my early childhood, I was on my way to becoming partially blind. I could not make out anything that was not directly in front of me. I could not see the line of the curb or down the sidewalk or over to the cor-ner. Shiny bikes, birds in trees, all were equally a blur. I finally got glasses in the second grade, and even then it was partly by accident. Midland pub-lic schools required their students to read an eye chart. When it was my turn, I could barely make out the biggest letters, and the school nurse sent an official letter home to mother, informing her that I had failed my eye exam. My mother berated herself for allowing me to walk around in this particular fog. She shook her head and said it should have been obvious to her. My mother is also extremely nearsighted. We have the same thing, progressive myopia. By her seventh-grade year, Mother's vision had so deteriorated that Grammee and Papa kept her out of school for a year and sent her to Arkansas, to live with Hal's old-maid sisters, Gertie and Kitty, and "rest" her eyes. The cure failed. Her glasses were as thick as bottles. Mine would be the same had I not been fitted for contacts at age thirteen.

I still remember leaving the eye doctor's office, my first pair of glasses perched awkwardly on my nose. And then I looked up. I was shocked to see individual leaves on the trees. I knew that trees had leaves, but I had not realized how distinct each one looked, even those of the squat mesquite that brushed over my head as I darted about those vacant lots on Estes Avenue. Midland suddenly came into focus on that sidewalk. But I think this partial blindness and the knowledge that one cracked lens could temporarily plunge me back into that narrow, myopic realm made me more cautious physically and less of a risk taker. When you do not know where edges begin and end, you are frequently surprised by what is hard or sharp.

My first school was Alyne Gray's Jack and Jill School, which she taught in her modest backyard inside a wooden lean-to shack, where the wind whistled right up against the wood. I started there when I was not quite five years old. It was Alyne's first year of running a school. Alyne's mother, Mrs. Odom, was a friend of Grandma Welch's in Lubbock. My mother recalls how Daddy had been instructed to look out for Alyne when he moved to Midland, and Alyne was told to look out for Harold Welch. They found each other when Mother introduced herself to Alyne across the fence alongside their first tiny home, before they moved to Estes Avenue. That was the shrunken world of Midland.

Alyne's husband died young, and the school was how she supported herself and her children, Jane and Robert. Daddy later built a new cinder-block school for her on a sandy patch along Garfield Street, in a newer part of town. Because the public schools didn't offer kindergarten, Jack and Jill was the first school for many Midland kids. I met Susie Marinis there among the paste and waxy crayons, and, a few years after me, Alyne would teach a smiling boy named Jebbie Bush.

Most kids left after one year, but because I was a November baby, I was too young to start first grade. I was five and three-quarters when September arrived, and the schools would not admit any five-year-olds into first grade. Susie was the same, having been born in late October, so we spent another year at Jack and Jill. When I was not yet seven, my parents enrolled me at North Elementary in the Midland public schools. There were, apparently, no rules about how old you had to be to enter the second grade.

As a result, I was always the youngest in my class, right up through college, when I graduated at age twenty-one, and I think I was a bit immature compared to the other kids, constantly trying to catch up and never quite succeeding. But I loved school. I adored my second-grade teacher, Mrs. Gnagy; I stayed in touch with her until she died. She and her husband rented a house from Mother and Daddy on that Estes Avenue block. Her husband worked as a geologist for Phillips Petroleum in Midland; he had fought in the war and then headed off to college in Kansas on the GI Bill. I don't know whether it was because she lived on our street or because I simply loved school—I loved the bright lead pencils and the thick practice paper and the readers and how letters and numbers would appear and then disappear across the vast blackboards—but I believed with all my second-grade heart that I was Mrs. Gnagy's favorite.

At recess, when the other kids were running on the dirt in their flat-bottomed canvas sneakers and leaping over whooshing jump ropes, I would stand with Mrs. Gnagy. She would wrap her arms around me, and I would lean against her. The other second-grade teacher, Mrs. McQuestin, would stand next to Mrs. Gnagy and hold her arms around another little girl, Gwyne Smith. Gwyne and I, nestled in the reassuring arms of these teachers, would look at each other while the two adults talked above us and the playground rang with the noise of races and bouncing balls.

I so wanted to be like Mrs. Gnagy, who was all of twenty-two and a newlywed when she gathered me in her arms. At home, I played school, lining up my dolls on the floor of my room for instruction and Scotch-taping pictures to my little mirror so that it would look like a classroom bulletin board. I taught my dolls writing and reading and solemnly held up picture books in front of their bright, painted eyes. I always wished that I had brothers or sisters who might sit at their imaginary desks for the lessons, but I happily made do with my dolls.

I was still very much a little girl. I sucked my thumb at night and in the afternoons, when we put our heads down on our desks to rest after lunch. I'd put in my thumb and twist my face away so Mrs. Gnagy wouldn't see and tell my mother. My parents tried everything to get me to stop sucking my thumb, direly explaining that it was riddled with all kinds of invisible germs. I responded by becoming something of an obsessive hand washer, holding up both hands to walk into the dining room and immediately rushing back to the sink if one of them so much as grazed a wall. Eventually they gave up and waited for me to outgrow it, which I did.

It was easy perhaps to be sad in Midland, sad from loss, sad from loneliness. "Terrible winds and a wonderful emptiness" were the painter Georgia O'Keeffe's double-edged words about the Texas desert plains, which I read years later, after I was grown. But in our home, where month after month, year after year, it might have been possible to feel sadness or at least an empty veil of loss, we were not sad. Every day, several times a day, my mother and I would hear the hum of the car engine and the slam of the door that announced Daddy was home. He invariably walked in whistling his favorite song, "Up a Lazy River," which was so catchy coming off his puckered lips that our resident mockingbird took up the tune. Along with the dust on his shoes, he always seemed to bring home a funny story about someone in town, not mean or malicious but simply funny, because Harold and Jenna Welch loved to laugh. They laughed at the kitchen table or chuckled in the den over some story Daddy had found in the newspaper. Daddy laughed when he ate hot chilies and jalapeños and his bald head began to sweat, and he would run his napkin through the last remaining strands of his perpetually thinning hair. And he laughed with his friends, many of whom he had known since they had grown up together in Lubbock.

Mother and Daddy had a wide circle of friends, from Daddy's buddies at Johnny's Bar-B-Q to Mother's bridge group and her ladies at church, where she taught Sunday school. Daddy wasn't much of a churchgoer, not because he was godless but because an hour was a bit too long for him to be without a lit cigarette in his hand. They had their couples friends too, whom they met for dinner parties, and it is that steady rhythm of friendship that I remember so completely from our lives back then.

We were happy in all our houses, especially in that brick one at the end of the block on Estes Avenue, with its step-down den that had been a garage until television came to Midland and Daddy converted it. The floor was a light red brick and on the hottest summer days still managed to remain cool. Mother had a low marble-top table made to give the room the air of early 1950s sophistication. We watched *Your Hit Parade* and Ed Sullivan on the black-and-white television. KMID-Midland was the only station, and it didn't come on the air until four o'clock. The very first show was *Two-Gun Playhouse,* and all the kids raced home from school to sit glued to the old western. KMID stopped broadcasting in the evening, when it signed off with "The Star-Spangled Banner" and a flag and then it dissolved to a test pattern. There was nothing but silence and snow until four the next afternoon.

Mother introduced me to literature in that house, starting with Golden Book stories about Snow White and Pinocchio. Suddenly I was transported. The curtain on my imagination lifted. We began *Little Women* when I was only seven years old. I listened curled up with her on the top of the guest room bed—the house had three bedrooms, but we only had use for two of them, so one was set aside untouched for guests—mesmerized by the lives of the four March girls. I can still remember the tears running down my cheeks when Beth died, while alongside me, Mother's eyes welled and her voice cracked as she read the story of this fragile, imaginary Victorian girl who would not live to the end of the novel.

When second grade was over, we moved again. Off the Estes Avenue block completely, away from the little Collins grocery just around the corner on Big Spring Street and the little toy store two storefronts down. I had spent hours gazing lovingly into its windows at a Tiny Tears doll, who looked right back at me with her bright marble eyes, until one Christmas she found her way into Santa's oversize sack. Our new house was on Princeton Avenue, with a covered carport at the end of the driveway and a giant red oak in the front yard, which Mother had imported all the way from Abilene. The tree was, for both of my parents, the height of extravagance, dug up and moved on a truck, but Mother wanted her full-grown tree, and Daddy was determined that she have it. As with all our other houses, my father had overseen the building of this one, but it was a fancier house, with a front hallway and picture windows and bits of decorative timber to offset the brick. My room was on the corner, looking out across the yard to the street and to whatever else lay beyond.

My mother set about fixing up what we called "the Big House." It had a turquoise refrigerator in the kitchen and bright turquoise Formica countertops. She picked out turquoise bed skirts for my twin beds and matching flowered coverlets. She kept the books for my father's house-building business, and she cooked. For most of her marriage, my mother made three full meals every day. Even before he began building houses, when Daddy had worked at CIT and wasn't on the road, he always came home for lunch.

Mother would be up at dawn each morning making coffee and eggs or pancakes. Then she would wash up and prepare lunch. At the end of the day, she cooked dinner. We ate mostly what would be considered Southern or rural food; Daddy's favorite meal was Mother's chicken-fried steak, a grainy cut of meat dipped in egg-and-flour batter and crisp-fried in bubbling oil, with cream gravy and homemade French fries on the side. Both Mother and Daddy had grown up in rural enough towns that the table was set by what was coming off the vine or out of the field. They both looked forward to the corn coming in each summer, and we loaded up on bags whenever we stopped in Lubbock or El Paso. They bought sweet, juicy Pecos cantaloupes, and some years, Daddy planted tomato vines. He also had an onion patch in the backyard because he liked to pull an onion or two for dinner. He grew squash, long and thin and a little bit tough because it never soaked up enough water, even with the hose, to swell up tender and plump. All summer, my mother made squash and chilies for lunch or supper. She called it a famous Texas recipe, but it was squash, green chilies, and Velveeta cheese baked together in a casserole. Or she would make fried squash. In high summer and early fall, we hardly ever ate anything out of a can.

My mother considered herself a dainty eater, and for her entire life she has been tiny and bird thin, but my dad liked everything, even the jar of pickled pigs' feet that he kept in the refrigerator. He would eat anchovies or smoked oysters on a cracker, and sometimes the raw ones as well. Once or twice, Johnny Hackney, who owned Johnny's Bar-B-Q, would order big barrels of oysters shipped on blocks of ice from the Gulf Coast. Daddy and Johnny and their friends would sit out on a back porch and eat oysters as fast as Big Daddy, who worked the grill at the Bar-B-Q, could shuck them. Mother wrinkled up her nose at the anchovies and the oysters, but I tried them all and loved most of them.

We ate out too. The fanciest restaurant in Midland was the Blue Star Inn, where they served delicacies like fried shrimp and grilled sirloin. But Daddy said that he loved his Jenna's cooking best of all. He wasn't like the other downtown men, who ate lunch out at a restaurant or ordered at the counter at Woolworth's. And so Mother would listen each day for his car to come humming up the street right around noon.

I had largely forgotten about those lunches until my wedding. When George and I got married, George was also working in downtown Midland. Daddy stood up at our rehearsal dinner the night before the wedding to give a toast. He ended it by looking at George with a quick wink and say-ing, "If you go home for lunch, make sure that when you go back to the office, you have on the same tie."

The main streets in Midland were named Wall Street and Texas and Broadway. From there, they were christened for distant states, like Ohio, Michigan, and Missouri, and also for some of the old ranching families, like the Cowdens and the Nobles. But gradually, as the town spread out into a city and men from the East began to drift in, the street names changed. First they were named for universities, like Princeton and Harvard, and then for the oil companies, Gulf, Humble, Shell, and Sinclair. And then, in the later boom years, when the crosshatch of streets pushed farther into old ranchlands and cotton fields, they had names like Boeing and Cessna, and eventually lofty English names, like Wellington and Keswick and Coventry, which graced subdivision cul-de-sacs.

We lived on Princeton Avenue now. Our neighbors were mostly com-pany and professional families, whose fathers put on ties to go downtown. Many were geologists and scientists and chemical engineers, men who had studied the science of oil. A few bankers wore suits. But even the roughnecks who worked on the wells in the fields and came home covered with grease didn't walk around in their heavy boots and Wrangler jeans when they came into Midland. The most you might see was the black oil under their nails, which were almost impossible to scrub clean.

People dressed up to go to church and to go out. At the Blue Star Inn, women wore dresses and did up their hair, while over at Johnny's Bar-B-Q, men wore jackets and ties to sit at the rough picnic tables covered with plastic cloths and drink from cold, dripping pitchers of ice tea. Midland remained a dry town. It wasn't legal to order a mixed drink at a restaurant with lunch or dinner. Johnny Hackney's friends circumvented the rule by wandering back into the Bar-B-Q's kitchen to pour their own drinks from a jug of vodka that Johnny kept in a cabinet.

Midcentury Midland was, however, far from a cultural wasteland. The Yucca Theater, which abutted Hogan's Folly, showcased musical acts before it was taken over by the movies. My mother remembers dancing to Guy Lombardo and his orchestra when they came through Midland on the train from Dallas and stopped for a night to play before moving on to El Paso. By the mid-1950s, Midland had its own symphony. But the city was small; it was a place of ice cream sundaes at the Borden dairy and Saturday morning pony rides around a nearby lot. My own little world didn't extend much beyond the same four blocks that I walked each morning to James Bowie Elementary School or the blistering hot metal swings, merry-go-round, and slide at the Ida Jo Moore Park.

During most of my childhood, drought paralyzed West Texas. I recall wind but very little rain. In a wet year, Midland averages fourteen inches. What few rainstorms we had became spectacular events, with water rushing down the streets in fast-moving torrents. Certain roads were built like natural arroyos, with dips in the middle to channel the runoff into the big parks, like A Street Park, which for the majority of its historical life had been a buffalo wallow and filled up, lakelike, when it rained. Then, at dusk, the low places would teem with frogs that had congregated in the damp. We heard their rhythmic croaking as we fell asleep. They were usually gone by dawn when the sun rose to bake the ground back to dryness. And every night, the cool air carried the piercing call of train whistles as miles of freight cars rolled past Midland on the rails.

I was a homebody even as a child. My mother enrolled me in ballet, piano, and Brownies, but I was happiest at school or at home. The absence of brothers and sisters had another side: it cemented the deep bonds between my parents and myself. We were a tightly knit unit of three. My parents took me out to dinner, took me driving. Our lives intertwined, and I wanted to be with them. I felt my greatest sense of contentment lying on the couch in our den. I had no desire to stray too far from home or from Mother and Daddy.

The summer when I was eight, Mother was pregnant with the baby who would have been my sister. The baby was not due until September, but on July 15, Mother went into labor. Daddy drove her to Midland Memorial, and I was sent to stay with Alyne Gray and her daughter, Jane. It was Alyne who told me that my sister had died, that no baby would be coming home.

Instead, I was the one who was going away. For months, Mother and Daddy had planned to send me to Camp Mitre Peak, a Girl Scout camp outside Alpine, Texas, where there were mountains, including the sixteen-hundred-foot-tall Mitre Peak, which looked like a giant arrowhead covered with green, scrubby brush. I left only a week or two after Mother lost my sister.

I was so homesick the feeling was almost crushing. Stuck in a completely unfamiliar place, I missed my parents dreadfully. Camp was nothing like being in El Paso; at night, there was no Grammee to hold my hand. I sent one letter home. I sat on my bunk and with my schoolgirl penmanship wrote to Mother and Daddy reminding them to pick me up on Saturday. When I addressed the envelope, I wrote "Estes Avenue," but forgot "Midland, Texas." The letter came back on Friday afternoon. The counselors gave it to me during mail call, and I sat holding it in my shaking hands. I was convinced that if my parents didn't get that letter, they wouldn't remember to pick me up the next morning. I envisioned spending days, perhaps another week, alone in my bunk under the shadow of the mountain. Sick with worry, I threw up, and the counselors put me to bed. The next morning, Mother and Daddy showed up exactly on time, and for years they would tell the story about how I started off running toward Daddy's side of the car and then stopped and hurriedly turned toward Mother's door, wanting so desperately to hug them both at once.

I went to Camp Mitre Peak again after seventh grade and adored it. But at age eight, I preferred home.

When I came through the door in the afternoon, I was greeted by the soft rustle of book pages and my mother, her feet propped up, book open on her lap. My mother loved to read. Her canon ranged from the traditional to the eclectic, writers like John Marquand and Somerset Maugham. She loved Willa Cather, especially *Death Comes for the Archbishop*. She read eagerly about the Southwest; it didn't matter whether the story was set in far West Texas or New Mexico or Arizona. She read books about anthropology, native peoples, and early explorers. She delved into naturalists, like Loren Eiseley. And she read to me, her voice weaving its spells of character, plot, and place, until I too yearned to decipher the fine black letters printed on the page. Once I did, I read with my friends, swapping well-thumbed copies of Cherry Ames, Student Nurse, and Nancy Drew with Georgia Todd, who owned the complete collection. We loved Nancy not for her independence or her car—we expected to have the same when we reached eighteen—but for the twists and turns of the mystery plots and the depictions of friendship. And, like me, Nancy was an only child making her way in the world.

We did not buy many books; instead, we borrowed from the Midland County Public Library, located inside the county courthouse, the biggest and most important building in the city. The courthouse sat in the center of downtown Midland, in a lush square with watered green grass. But the library was particularly interesting because of its location: the basement. All of the houses and many of the buildings I knew in Midland had no basements and hardly any stairs. To enter the cool, dark library, Mother and I had to walk down an entire flight of stairs. Each visit was exciting before we ever looked at the books.

If she wasn't reading, my mother wanted to be outside. Jenna Welch was nearly blind, left-handed, and woefully uncoordinated, but she loved nature. And she was an extremely knowledgeable self-taught naturalist. She remembered the name of every wildflower and was passionate about birds. Her fascination began when I was ten and she volunteered to be my Girl Scout leader. One of our requirements was to earn a bird badge. The best location for bird-watching in Midland, aside from Rose Acres, the euphemistic name given to the city's sewer ponds, where bird-watchers congregated despite the overwhelmingly noxious smell, was the yard of Ola Dublin Haynes, one of Midland's school librarians. She had let her place grow wild with scrub brush and prairie grass. We would stand silently with our binoculars, or sit Indian-style, and wait for the birds to swoop down and alight on the mesquite and prickly stubble. We were rarely disappointed; each year thousands of birds poured through Midland, which sits along one of the West's north-south migratory paths.

Mother began carrying binoculars in the car. On almost every long car trip when I was a teenager, the routine was the same. I would fall asleep, and Mother would gasp, "Look, there's a hawk" or "Did you see—it's a painted bunting!" and wake me up to see. I was invariably irritated, but the announcements took. Today I scan the trees for the swish of wings and am waiting for a screech owl to roost in the owl box nestled atop our live oak in the front yard.

Once my mother spotted a rare bird, a northern varied thrush, in our backyard. He had apparently been blown off course during a windstorm and had taken refuge in the trees. Mother identified it and then called her friends at the Mid-Nats, the Midland Naturalist Society. For weeks bird-watchers showed up at our front door, hoping to glimpse the bird and add it to their list. Come lunchtime, geologists and scientists would arrive and head into the kitchen with their sack lunches to sit at the Formica counter and wait for the elusive thrush. The few times it appeared, everyone in the room would jump up and hug each other and hug Mother, thrilled to have seen this small bluish gray bird, which resembles a robin. My dad would look around and shake his head over all the fuss, but he never minded driving Mother around with her binoculars to look for whatever might be there.

The sky, however, was another matter. Mother and I loved the sky. From almost as far back as I can remember, on a particularly spectacular summer night, Mother would gather a blanket and we would go outside

47

to lie on the ground and gaze up at the sky. The wool of the blanket would scratch at our arms and legs, and we could feel the prick of the hard, sturdy grass blades below.

In Midland, the sky sits overhead like a flawless dome, bowing up from the earth at the edge of each horizon. The land does not pitch or rise but remains perfectly flat, without bright lights or tall buildings to obscure our view. So complete was the darkness that all we saw were the stars and the inky blackness. Above us, the constellations hung like strands of Christmas lights waiting to be plucked, and I would lift my little-girl arms to try to touch the glowing orbs. Lying beside me on the blanket, my mother pointed out Orion, the Little Dipper, Cassiopeia, and the planets, the glowing pink of Venus or the distant fire of Jupiter, as her mother had done for her. And she would say, "Laura, look at the sky, because it won't look like this again for another year.

"Look up," she would say, "Laura, look up."

But I wasn't the only one gazing up at that all-encompassing sky. Amid baseball diamonds, backyard slides, and sandlots, another child was listening to the croak of frogs and watching for the stars. That boy was George W. Bush. My Midland childhood was his as well. We were the same age, and only about ten blocks separated our two homes, his on Ohio, mine on Princeton. My elementary school friends Mike Proctor and Robert McCleskey played catch with George; his dad, George H. W. Bush, coached the local Little League. The Bushes lived in Midland from the time George was three until the year 1959, but the closest he and I ever came to meeting was passing each other in the hallways of the seventh grade at San Jacinto Junior High.

By age twelve, I was old enough to ride my bike on a Saturday morning to the Rexall drugstore for a ham sandwich. But, like most twelve-year-old girls, I longed to do more grown-up things.

In Midland, our first escape came directly from Hollywood. For two hours in the plush seats and darkened rooms of the downtown movie houses, we were transported to Europe or back in time. The women were glamorous and the men dapper, everyone was a wit, and there was almost always a happy ending. We never imagined that the Wild West was actually a movable set on a back lot, that each looming mountain was the backside of the same Hollywood hill, or that the acres of picture-perfect New England snows were manufactured under blue California skies by giant ice machines. Our lives grew as large as those on the celluloid reels that filled the screen. We went to the movies nearly every weekend.

On Saturday afternoons, Mother would load my friends and me into the car and drive down to the Yucca Theater, where we would rush to the ticket line. The Yucca showed mostly family fare or westerns. But we vaguely knew there was more to Hollywood. Once, as soon as Mother had waved to us and driven out of sight, we raced around to the other downtown theater, the Ritz, to watch the film *Blue Denim*, about teenage pregnancy, a subject that was all but taboo in Midland. Carol Lynley, the star, played a fifteen-year-old girl. She herself was only seventeen.

Boys and girls paired off early in Midland. Before elementary school ended, a small frenzy had built around trading disks, flat circles engraved with our names. In the sixth grade, I was convinced that a boy was going to ask me to trade disks with him. After school, I dragged Mother to the Kruger Jewelry store to buy a gold-plated disk. He never asked. Another boy, Robert McCleskey, did invite me to the Yucca Theater to see *Gone With the Wind* and still remains one of our best friends.

By seventh grade, boys began calling for what we dubbed "Daddy dates." Girls sat in the backs of the cars with their adolescent escorts while the boys' fathers drove. I had one "Daddy date" after I turned thirteen, which not coincidentally was the year I traded in my thick glasses for hard contact lenses that sat right on top of my blue eyes. My date was Kevin O'Neill, whose brother Joe would be the one to introduce me to George W. Bush almost twenty years later. Kevin invited me to a dance, and his father, Mr. O'Neill, a wealthy oilman who had come to Midland from Philadelphia, drove us. By age fourteen, chaperoning parents became increasingly superfluous. Fourteen was the age when most Texas kids got their driver's licenses.

Regan Kimberlin was my best friend at San Jacinto Junior High, and she loved being behind the wheel. She had raven black hair, green eyes, and a throaty laugh, and she had attended almost every school in Midland, including second grade at Sam Houston Elementary with George. Regan's mother, Wanda, was on about the fifth of her seven marriages. She married and divorced Regan's dad two times. Indeed, Wanda believed in divorce almost as much as marriage, and she moved with each tying or untying of the knot. By the time Regan was in junior high, Wanda was married to Jerry Cooper, whom she would marry and divorce three times. We thought Jerry was the perfect stepfather. Jerry and Wanda had bought a red Thunderbird convertible for Jan, Regan's older sister, in the hope of persuading Jan to annul her hasty marriage to Mike Morse, who in the infinitely small world of Midland, was the son of Ann and Joe Morse, our next-door neighbors on Princeton Avenue. Jan ignored the car and stayed married to Mike, and Regan was given the keys to the Thunderbird. Regan had that Thunderbird longer than Jan had Mike. Regan first took it for a spin when we were still thirteen years old and in the eighth grade, before we got our official licenses. We used to drive around in that or in her mother's pink Nash Rambler, a stubby car that we nicknamed "the pink pig."

After we got our licenses, all of my friends went out driving. We drove to the three drive-in movie theaters that ringed Midland. Whoever was behind the wheel would pull over before we reached the entrance, and half of the crowd in the car would squeeze into the trunk to avoid paying the admission fee. After we parked, one of us would have to sneak out and open the trunk to release the stowaways. We drove to the drive-in restaurants, like Agnes's or A & W. Sometimes Regan and I headed out alone to Mr. X's, on the dicier south side of town, where they served taquitos, steak fingers, and fried chicken livers and where, as we grew older, we could smoke without being seen.

But if we wanted to be seen in Midland, we went to Agnes's. Friday and Saturday nights now consisted of trips to the movies and Cokes at Agnes's. Agnes herself was a strong, stocky West Texas woman with a broad back from bending over hot stoves and steel gray hair wrapped in a knot on top of her head. Once I watched her raise her hand and slap a boy across the cheek in the parking lot because she thought he was being smart-alecky. But every night Agnes's would fill with cars. No one ever got out; we sat in our seats and waited for the carhops and eased the wheels forward or back as new cars pulled up and old ones drove off. Sometimes we went twice in one night. When couples left, it was usually to go out in the country, to the dark, flat stretches of unpaved road past the city loop, to park and then head back, so they could tell their parents the truth, that they had just come from Agnes's.

We were lucky in Midland to have so many places to drive. In other, smaller West Texas towns, there were no drive-ins or movies. Night after night, restless kids cruised the town square, making endless loops around the local city hall and the courthouse.

No one ever thought we were too young to drive. At age thirteen, we attended driver's education classes in the San Jacinto Junior High auditorium to prepare for the written test. Some boys got cars when they turned fourteen, not because their parents were wealthy but because they worked at jobs after school. They had '57 Chevys and old Fords, whatever they found cheap or used. The rest of us simply borrowed from the garages of our parents.

Around Easter of my fourteenth year, my mother lost the last of her babies, another boy, this one too early even to name.

When he took my mother to the hospital, my father left her car keys for me. One evening, I carefully backed Mother's Ford Fairlane out of our driveway and drove down the side streets to Agnes's. I pulled in, placed my order, and then I had to move. That part I was not prepared for. I managed to get the car into reverse, only to back straight into a pole in the parking lot.

Chastened, I studied for my written test, making notes with my No. 2 pencils, and I practiced in the car with my mother. She took me to the one place near our house where the roads were guaranteed to be quiet, the Midland cemetery. I learned to accelerate, brake, and turn among the somber rows of crosses and polished headstones, where the paths were peaceful and the speeds slow, never once knowing what this place and a single automobile could mean for my own future.

At age fourteen, I, like everyone else, got my driver's license.

If we weren't driving, we were trying to figure out other ways to get out of our homes. Almost every weekend, I went to a slumber party. We were a gaggle of girls, Regan, my friends Peggy, Jan, Beverly, Cathie, and the twins, Sharon and Susan, and we thought we were sort of wild. In truth, we weren't wild at all. We wore loafers and bobby socks and dresses or skirts and blouses or sweater sets to school and Bermuda shorts and pants only on the weekends. Once, when Wanda moved Regan to Norman, Oklahoma, for a semester, Regan came back with four perfect wool skirts and sweaters that had been dyed to match. We were all very impressed. Girls, or at least my group of girls, started wearing lipstick in the seventh grade, but there were rules. Gwyne Smith's mother had decreed that the only appropriate color was Miss Ritz, a pale pink from Charles of the Ritz. My mother would never buy Charles of the Ritz lipstick, and certainly not for a seventh grader. I had a pink shade from the drugstore.

In the summers, Regan, Cathie, and I would sun ourselves by the pool at the Ranchland Hills Country Club, where Jerry Cooper belonged. Ranchland was a bit farther out, but the Midland Country Club was stricter. It wouldn't allow anyone by its pool who wasn't a member. My mother silently threw up her hands at our quest to turn our pale skin to ever-darker shades of bronze. She still drove with long sleeves and white gloves even when the temperature pierced one hundred degrees, to keep the sun from marking her hands and arms.

Girls in Midland didn't drink at all in high school. Boys only drank beer, when they could get it, which wasn't that often. But we did smoke, holding our cigarettes out the window and blowing out long, smooth streams of smoke, trying to look like 1960s movie stars. It seemed that everyone smoked back then, except for my mother. My dad smoked, and so did most of my parents' friends. Within twenty-five years, so many of the women would be dead, their lungs, larynxes, and hearts giving out one by one. By the time I was seventeen or eighteen, I was smoking in front of my parents, although once when my father found a cigarette pack in the clutch purse on my nightstand, I immediately swore that it belonged to my friend Cathie. I was adamant that it wasn't mine. As Khrushchev sparred with Kennedy and the world contemplated a nuclear missile exchange, we trailed around in pale gray clouds laced with nicotine.

Our parents' generation might have been glued to the radio for news and the somber-toned voice of Edward R. Murrow from London, but in Midland, the radio and later television were our gateways to music and our Edward was simply an Ed, Ed Sullivan. I was not quite ten when Elvis Presley first sang and shook on *The Ed Sullivan Show,* and I remember watching him at Gwyne's house. Her parents were out for the evening, and we had a babysitter. The two of us were alone in her den, and when Elvis got up and began to swivel his hips, we did too, shimmying as the King crooned and danced on the grainy black-and-white screen.

We were raised on rock 'n' roll, and the adults didn't complain. Buddy Holly was from Lubbock, and Roy Orbison was from another West Texas town, Wink, so we felt as if the music was almost homegrown. Late at night, after Mother and Daddy had gone to bed and all the local radio stations had signed off, I'd shut my door, prop open my school books, and listen to Wolfman Jack play hits out of Nuevo Laredo or tune in to KOMA Oklahoma City, whose signal carried across the skies at night on the AM radio, reaching as far away as Wyoming and the Dakotas in the north, or west to Arizona, on the cool, clear air.

I had some records, and I bought the Beatles' first American album when it was released, but Regan was the one with what we considered a priceless collection of 45s, which her mother boxed up and sold for pennies on the dollar at a garage sale once Regan was grown and gone.

To be truly daring, we snuck out of the house on sleepover nights. We would tiptoe out of a bedroom and quietly open the front door. The more daring kids might climb out a window and drop down—no one ever had a second-floor bedroom and at most you risked hitting a low bush. Then we would walk around the neighborhood streets in our pajamas under the faint glow of the streetlights. When we went to Peggy's house, we crossed over to the big Cowden Park, which had once been a buffalo wallow and now became a lake when it rained, with frogs that called to each other deep into the darkness.

Some girls snuck out of doors and windows to go to their boyfriends' houses, and some took their parents' cars as well. I never did any of that, although I did ride around one time with my friend Candy after she put her parents' car in neutral and rolled it out of the garage. She made it around the neighborhood on numerous nights until our friend Mike Jones opened the car door as we pulled into the driveway. Candy kept driving and smashed the car door into the side of the garage. The door closed on Mike's foot, and the garage wall left a huge dent in the door.

Candy sat there in total shock; until that moment she had always gotten the car home without a scratch.

My one foray backing into the pole at Agnes's at age thirteen had cured me of any desire to sneak our car out, and I was a classic only child who never wanted to disappoint Mother and Daddy. My biggest acts of teenage bravery were trotting along Midland's sidewalks in checked pajamas.

After San Jacinto Junior High, I should have attended Midland High, but instead I went to the brand-new high school, Robert E. Lee, because we had moved again. Every other school in Midland was named for a Texas hero or event, from Jim Bowie, Sam Houston, James Fannin, Mirabeau Lamar, Davy Crockett, William Travis, and Lorenzo de Zavala to San Jacinto and Alamo, for the famous battles against Mexico. Looking back, there were likely a lot of reprobates in the Texas group, but they seemed so much more distant from our own time and place. And of course, in Texas, they were venerated and then some. As John Steinbeck once mused, "Like most passionate nations Texas has its own history based on, but not limited by, facts." It is almost impossible to be raised in Texas and not know that Texas was once an independent nation. To make sure that no one in Midland forgot, we studied Texas history in the fourth grade and again for the whole of the seventh, and every morning, we crossed under our heroes' names emblazoned on the brick or concrete block of our school buildings. The only outside hero was George Washington Carver, whose name adorned the segregated high school where Midland's black students went. But now there was Robert E. Lee.

Midland had not existed during the Civil War, and it seemed both absurd and wrong to name a school for a Confederate commander in the year 1960. At the time, my mother told me that one school board member was adamant about calling it Robert E. Lee and with a shake of her head just let it go. And I did too. No one I knew protested; it was simply considered to be out of our hands. As kids, we lived in our own little world, where we could ride our bikes wherever we wanted and sneak out in our pajamas because Midland was a safe town and we were safe within its limits. Our parents were not afraid for us to dash outside the minute school was over and play until the front porch lights and streetlamps flickered on and it was time to come in and eat. We lived our lives in a kind of easy oblivion and ceded the important decisions to the adults.

At Lee, they played "Dixie" at the football games, and we were expected to sing when we heard the first chords. Our teams were called the Rebels, our annual was the Rebelee. But it bothered me. It bothered me from the moment I went.

I went to Lee because Daddy had sold our house. It wasn't even for sale. One afternoon, a real estate agent came to the front door and rang the bell. Daddy answered, and the woman asked if she could buy the house. She had a client who was willing to offer Daddy a very good price, and on the spot, Daddy said yes. It is the one time I remember Mother being upset and disappointed. She loved that house and did not want to leave, but we did. We packed up and moved to a spec house that Daddy had recently built on Hughes Street and then, a couple of years later, to another home over on Humble Avenue, the last house that Daddy ever built for us, our "nice" house.

It was in our nice house that one afternoon I answered a knock at the door. Standing on the front step were two men in suits. They held up their badges and said, "We're from the FBI." The next thing they asked was, "Is Harold Welch at home?" Daddy was taking a nap, and I was quite nervous to go wake him. But I did. The FBI men were in the process of "busting a bookie," as they put it, and they wanted to know if Daddy could come downtown and help identify him. Daddy shook his head. "No," he said. "I've only talked to him on the phone. I don't know what he looks like." The men thanked him politely and left. Betting itself apparently didn't bother them.

Our Humble Avenue house sat at the intersection of Humble and Lanham, but it was so quiet that if a car cruised down the street late at night, the low rumble of its engine would wake me from a sound sleep. On Humble, Regan and I spent a lot of time in my room, which stood at the end of the house, adjacent to the sidewalk and the street. At night, when the streetlights began to glow, we would prop open the window — the same one that blew in during a particularly fierce dust storm, spraying glass, sand, and grit all over my room — and our boyfriends would tiptoe along the side yard to stand on the grass and talk to us through the screen. One of my neighbors, Dick Taylor, preferred to shoot out the streetlight with his .22 gauge hunting rifle and then amble over in the dark to stand at the window and talk. Each time he shot it out, Mother would call the city and say, "You need to replace the streetlight, somebody else has shot it out." But it was only Dick with his .22. The city would put in a new light, and Dick would wait a week and then shoot it out again. My parents made no real effort to investigate; they liked Dick. And my mother was waging her own stealth battle with the lamppost. She had joined the Audubon Society and eagerly devoured its magazine and mailers, which were crusading against the pesticide DDT. Quietly around our blocks, bright yellow Ban DDT bumper stickers began appearing on utility poles and light posts. Mother was hardly in a position to turn Dick in. Still, I'm sure if I had ever crawled out that window, Mother and Daddy would have done far more than make another call to the city authorities.

But living on Humble Avenue meant that I was no longer in the Midland High School district, and from that, so much else changed.

All of Lee's home football games were held at the Midland High Stadium. I had been going to the Friday-night games since I was a fifth grader at Bowie. There was something thrilling about those Friday nights. Everyone went, parents and children, people whose children had long since moved away, even people with no children at all. It was football and Friday night in Midland. I would watch neighbors stream out of their houses and walk down the streets or more often see lines of cars snaking toward the parking lot. The stadium rose up out of the ground like a great bowl, and everyone had a place in it. Kids did not sit with their families; they sat with their school and their grade. The fifth and sixth graders from all the city's elementary schools sat in the bleachers on the elementary end in one end zone. The other end zone was reserved for the junior high students, in seventh, eighth, and ninth grades. The high schoolers sat together in the middle of the stadium; the adults sat around them. If anyone bothered to look down at either end zone, it seemed as if the whole stadium was levitating, because most of the kids didn't sit still, they spent the entire game jumping around and talking. The boys would race to the top row and pretend to leap off the top of the stadium or would flutter their arms and kick their legs as if they were about to fall off into the inky dark night. All around them, the girls had their eyes trained on the boys. I think Midland and Lee had good football teams all the years I was there, but I can't recall who won or lost each game.

By high school, the game watching changed. A boy might invite you to a game, but most girls hoped they would be dating a football player down on the field. If you were going with someone on the team, he would send you a big mum with his number on it; for Midland High, it was a big gold chrysanthemum with the player number twisted in purple pipe cleaners and adorned with long purple and gold ribbons. Lee High School players sent white mums with their numbers in maroon pipe cleaners and trails of maroon and white ribbons. Football players' girls pinned these chrysanthemums to their jackets or sweaters so everyone could see them. For several years, I dated a boy who played for Midland. He couldn't afford to send me a chrysanthemum for every game, but he did have one delivered for the big contests, and I pinned it on my clothes and then brought it home to wilt for months afterward on my bulletin board.

The biggest game was between Midland and Lee high schools at the end of the season, but otherwise on Friday nights, the two teams played the Odessa schools, Odessa Permian and Odessa High, and teams from San Angelo and Abilene and other towns in the district. The visiting teams would ride in big buses with convoys of cars, fans who came to cheer for their school.

Midland hardly ever has a fall. Occasionally, we would get just the right mix of rain and cool to turn the red oaks a bright, rich russet, but most of the time, summer with its shimmering heat would linger well past October. Then suddenly, around November 17, the cold would barrel in on a tight, hard wind, and the grass would freeze. There was very little in-between. But because Midland sits at the edge of the desert, the nights, even in the baking heat, would be cool. It was possible to actually feel cold when you went to a football game, sitting under that enormous, star-laced sky. The blazing stadium lights couldn't dim the vast display of stars overhead, an arc of light beaming back down upon us.

I loved school. I was a good student with good grades. I learned to write in a style that Mrs. Stallings, my senior English teacher, called the Dr. Guthrie style, after the sermons of Dr. Guthrie, the minister at our First Methodist Church. You stated your argument, found examples to support it, and then summed up your point all over again. I took mostly honors courses and earned five points for my grade point average if I made an A, four if I made a B. I was always in Honors English, where we read the early 1960s definition of the classics: *Jane Eyre, Ethan Frome,* Shakespeare's plays, Charles Dickens, and George Eliot's *Silas Marner.* But I loved to read books, all the time, in any class. During the hours we spent on math or science, I would perch my textbook on my desk to look particularly studious, while behind its thick cover I was hiding my latest book. In one case it was *Lady Chatterley's Lover,* which for 1963 Midland was quite risqué. Before I was out of junior high, I had devoured William Goldman's *The Temple of Gold* and Margaret Mitchell's *Gone with the Wind.* I looked for any opportunity to read. I also took a course that was reserved for the top students in the school called History of Western Thought. It was a philosophy course that started with Plato, and at the end of the school year we had to write a big paper, like a thesis. I loved it, reading Plato and Socrates and St. Augustine in the middle of West Texas.

I was not the most popular girl in high school, but I got asked to dances, which had moved from the San Jacinto Junior High cafeteria, where the dance committee would hang green and white crepe paper streamers from the ceiling and girls by the dozen would troop off to the bathroom or mill about at the edge of the linoleum floor, to the newly built youth centers adjacent to Lee or Midland High. They were real dances, with hired bands and couples twisting and turning on the dance floor. Before each dance, most boys sent a corsage of roses or gardenias, sometimes orchids if the date was very special. After the girls had worn them, they tacked the corsages to droop and dry on the bulletin boards that were staples in every bedroom and that held such other prized possessions as the folded-up paper notes that were passed in class and occasional pictures of friends. I pinned my dance corsages next to my shriveled gold football flowers.

⟳

Mother was the one who always thought "what if," and the "what if" invariably came back to the same thing, what if she and Daddy had never sold the big house on Princeton Avenue? What if we hadn't sold that house and had just stayed there? If we had stayed on Princeton, I would have gone to Midland High rather than Lee, and then in her mind everything would have been different. Everything was the night of November 6, 1963, two days after I had turned seventeen.

That night, I picked up the car keys and my purse. I stopped in the kitchen to tell Mother and Daddy good-bye. They were standing around the breakfast bar with some of their friends, the smoke drifting up in slow, lazy curls from the ends of four or five half-smoked cigarettes. I was smiling. Everything felt unbelievably light and happy, and someone called back, "Have fun." I walked through the utility room door as I had done hundreds of other times, pulled the car out of the driveway, and headed off down the smooth street to my friend Judy Dykes's house. She was one of my good high school friends; her dad had been a friend of Daddy's from Lubbock. We had made plans to go to the drive-in movies, though in typical seventeen-year-old fashion we hadn't bothered to look in the paper to see what was playing. We decided that we would drive by and see what was there. So I left Judy's house and headed to the loop, which back then was a little country road with no streetlights circling around Midland.

We talked as I drove along the pitch-black road. I knew in my mind that somewhere ahead was a right turn for Big Spring Street, where the drive-in theater was, because the loop almost dead-ended at Big Spring. Beyond the turn the asphalt stopped, and there was nothing more than a trail of unpaved dirt and dust. Most drivers turned right, toward town. I knew there was a turn, but where that turn was seemed very far away until suddenly, off in the middle of a field, I glimpsed a stop sign with the corner beam of my headlights. At that moment, I heard Judy's voice: "There's a stop sign." And I just couldn't stop. I was going along, a little below the speed limit, which was fifty-five miles an hour. The next thing I knew, I was in the intersection, and immediately in front of me was another car. It came rushing out of the darkness, and I was right upon it, without a second to turn the wheel. All I heard was the horrible sound of metal colliding, the catastrophic boom that occurs when two hard pieces of steel make contact.

The next thing I knew, I was rolling on the ground, in the dirt, holding my head. I had been thrown from the car with a force so great that I didn't even hit the asphalt on the road but was tossed clear over to the hard, dry ground alongside. In those awful seconds, the car door must have been flung open by the impact and my body rose in the air until gravity took over and I was pulled, hard and fast, back to earth. I have no memory of being thrown or of raising my hands to my head; it must have been an automatic reaction. Eventually, I stopped rolling and simply lay there, completely stunned. And then slowly Judy got out of the car, and I got up.

My face was banged up; I had a cut on my knee that bled in a long red gash, and my ankle was broken, although no one knew it until several days afterward. The doctors didn't find it in the emergency room. In the distance, I saw headlights, and someone else stopped. It was a family from Midland, and they came over and put their arms around Judy and me. We stood there, embraced by them. But I knew we were not the only ones in the crash. There was another car.

The whole time, I was praying that the person in the other car was alive too. In my mind, I was calling, "Please, God. Please, God. Please, God," over and over and over again. Then more cars pulled up, and someone must have gone for help, because eventually we heard the wail of sirens and glimpsed the rotating, flashing lights of ambulances and police cars.

One driver who arrived was a man I recognized, Bill Douglas, the father of my very good high school friend Mike. The Douglases lived up beyond the loop, in a small neighborhood about four long city blocks past that corner of Big Spring Street. We considered it almost a country neighborhood because there was nothing around the houses except the bottom tips of ranches and open land. But, on a quiet November night, that block of houses with their long, wide yards was close enough to hear a thunderous crash at the edge of Big Spring. And I saw Mr. Douglas lean over whomever had been in that other car.

Judy and I were waiting to get in one of the ambulances, and Judy kept saying to me, "I think that's the father of the person who was in the other car." And I said, "No, that couldn't be the father. That's Mr. Douglas."

I was still pleading with God as I lay in the emergency room, waiting for the doctors to stitch my knee. The lights were bright, and I could hear the scurrying of the nurses' flat-soled shoes on the floor, but no one was paying attention to Judy or to me because our injuries were cuts and bruises, scrapes and strains. I was still thinking, lying there, that Mike could not have been in that other car. And then, on the other side of the hospital curtain, I heard a woman start to cry, and I knew that it was Mrs. Douglas. But I couldn't stop asking God, over and over in my head, to please keep this other person alive.

It was Mother and Daddy who told me that Mike had been driving the other car, after I was home, in my own bed. But by then, I already heard the sounds of his parents' choked sobs ricocheting in the far recesses of my mind.

November 6 was a Wednesday, but we were out that night because Thursday was a school holiday. Mike was on his way into town for a date with Peggy, whose house backed up to Cowden Park, where the old buffalo wallow was, and where we would climb out the window and sneak around in our pajamas. He had dated Regan for a long time before that. He was a handsome boy with a beautiful smile, and he was a top athlete at Lee. He was not my boyfriend, although for a decade some in the press have claimed that he was. But for years, he was my very close friend. I have images of Mike in my home movies, the movies that Charlie White, who lived behind us on Estes Avenue, took every Christmas because the Whites owned a little movie camera. The Whites were good friends of Mike's parents, and that's how Mother and Daddy knew them, long before we were in high school. I can still see a gap-toothed Mike in at least one of those old Christmas movie reels, where years later, everything looks slightly tinged with blue or brown.

All through high school, Mike and I were good friends; we talked on the phone for hours, and Mike's circle of close friends included nearly all of my own. And so it was unbelievable to me that it was his car in that almost always empty intersection. It was a small car, a Corvair Monza, Detroit's version of a compact, economy car designed to compete with the Volkswagen Beetle. It was sporty and sleek, and it was also the car that Ralph Nader made famous in his book *Unsafe at Any Speed*. He claimed the car was unstable and prone to rollover accidents. A few years later, the

National Highway Traffic Safety Administration went so far as to investigate the Corvair's handling, but it didn't reach the same grim conclusions. I was driving my dad's much larger and heavier Chevy Impala. But none of that would ever ease the night of November 6. Not for me, and never for the Douglases.

So many lives were wrecked that night at that corner, which was known as a particularly dangerous place. Already that year, two other people had lost their lives in crashes where the loop met Big Spring Street. After Mike's death, the city did install a much bigger stop sign and posted warnings. But it was too late for us.

A dangerous intersection, a less than safe car, and me. I don't see well, I didn't ever see well, and maybe that played a part. Or perhaps it was simply dark, Judy and I were talking, and I was an inexperienced driver who got to a corner before I expected it.

I didn't have to tell anyone what happened. Every single person in Midland knew. Regan had been with Peggy at a school dance performance rehearsal, and then both had gone home to wait for their boyfriends. Regan was waiting for her boyfriend, John. Peggy was waiting for Mike. Regan's dad called her to say that I'd been in an accident, and Regan and John rushed to the hospital. By the time they arrived, I had already been sent home, so they drove to my house. They knew that Mike had died when they pulled up to our curb. My mother met them outside and told Regan that I didn't know Mike had been in the other car, so Regan and John sat with me as I lay in bed, with this horrible, unspoken truth hovering in the air. After they left, Mother and Daddy told me.

Immediately afterward, Mother and Daddy's friends showed up, and I'm sure it was the same at the Douglases'. Betty Hackney, Johnny's wife, came over and stood at the sink and washed dishes because so many people came and everyone brought something to eat or stopped to eat something. People from our church came. Mary White was at our house almost every day. All of Mother and Daddy's best friends came. The next morning Mother and Daddy and Mary and Charlie drove over to see the Douglases. I never knew what they said, and they never told me. I only knew that they had gone.

My friends were brokenhearted, but Regan and Jan, Candy, and a bunch of Mike's friends and my high school boyfriend, now a college freshman, came over to our house to sit with me. That is the amazing thing about Midland. So many people could be utterly devastated and could wish that this terrible thing had never happened, and they were and they did, but they still found it in their hearts to be supportive of me.

I did not go to the funeral. It was held that Saturday, November 9, at St. Mark's Methodist Church. I wanted to go, and I told Mother and Daddy that I wanted to. But they wanted me to stay home. No doubt they were trying to protect me, thinking that it would be too hard on me, and on the Douglases, if I were to attend. Whatever their reasons, I did not have a chance to decide. The next morning, no one rapped on my door to awaken me. When I finally opened my eyes, the service had started, and it was too late. So I didn't go, and I never contacted the Douglases. Like everyone else around me, I thought that they wouldn't want to see me, that there wasn't one thing that I could say to them that they would want to hear.

Pretty quickly no one mentioned the accident. My parents never brought it up. And neither did my friends, with the exception of Regan. I remember when the story of the crash appeared in the press during the 2000 presidential campaign, two of George's cousins, with whom we're very close, were shocked. I'd never told them. I didn't even get to tell my own daughters. A Texas Department of Public Safety officer on our protection detail did that when George was governor. He assumed they already knew.

But when one of Barbara's and Jenna's best friends committed suicide during their junior year of high school, I insisted that we go over right away to see his parents. I tried to do for them what I couldn't do for the Douglases.

Once I became a mother myself, I thought more about the Douglases. I began to understand how devastating their grief must be. On some level, only when I had children could I begin to comprehend the enormity for them of losing Mike. Only then, when I could imagine that it was Barbara or Jenna.

Looking back now, with the wisdom of another forty-five years, I know
that I should have gone to see the Douglases; I should have reached out
to them. At seventeen, I assumed that they would prefer I vanish, that I
would only remind them of their loss. But in retrospect, I think all of us—
not only me but all of Mike's friends—should have been more solicitous
of them. We weren't. We were so close to leaving Midland; in a few short
months we all went off to college. We did not grasp what a difference a
simple visit would make. But having friends now who have lost their own
children, as well as knowing the parents of Barbara's and Jenna's friends
who have died—the boy who was killed coming home from the Texas–
Oklahoma game their freshman year in college, the girl who died with
her date when their car skidded off the treacherous, winding roads heading back to Washington and Lee University in Virginia, the same little girl
who had shown Barbara and Jenna around school and had become their
first friend when we moved to Austin—I know from these parents that they
like being with Barbara and Jenna. Having their child's friends remember
them, and also remember the child they have lost, gives them another way
to remain connected to that adored child who is forever gone.

To them, those children will always be seventeen or eighteen years old,
a little bit older than I was in 1963. Their futures exist only in the ache of
imagination. I see that now, but I did not see it then.

In the aftermath, all I felt was guilty, very guilty. In fact, I still do. It is
a guilt I will carry for the rest of my life, far more visible to me than the
scar etched in the bump of my knee. At some point most people in these
situations come to make a mental peace with the fact that it was an accident. And that it cannot be changed. There is no great clock to unwind,
no choice that can somehow miraculously be made again.

But I can never absolve myself of the guilt. And the guilt isn't simply from Mike dying. The guilt is from all the implications, from the
way those few seconds spun out and enfolded so many other lives. The
reverberations seem to go on forever, like the ripples from an unsinkable
stone. There are the hard, inner circles wrapping around Mike's parents and Mike's sister, whose lives were changed and ruined. His parents
grieved until their deaths. And then there are the more distant ripples,
encompassing all of his friends and my friends. It is a grief that they had
as well.

Since I became a public person, I've gotten many letters—letters from strangers, from mothers, aunts, cousins, teachers, and friends—asking if I could write a note of encouragement to a young driver who had been in a terrible accident. Each time, I've answered. I've told them that, although you will never get over what happened, there will come a time in your life when you can move on. And I've always suggested that they talk to the people whom they love. Or that they speak to a counselor or a spiritual or pastoral adviser. Sometimes the letters are to kids in situations where someone was drinking, but a lot of them are just like I was, an inexperienced, seventeen-year-old driver who didn't have a good concept of where I was in town, who didn't know how far I'd gone in the dark or how close I was to the intersection.

But while I give this advice in my letters, I didn't do any of that. West Texas in 1963 was a time and a place where no one would have gotten a counselor. People in Midland did not think of psychologists or psychiatrists. I don't remember if our pastor, Dr. Guthrie, stopped by. He must have come to talk with Mother and Daddy. But I have no memory of it, no memory of anything but my own thoughts about that dark November evening.

Most of how I ultimately coped with the crash was by trying not to talk about it, not to think about it, to put it aside. Because there wasn't anything I could do. Even if I tried.

I lost my faith that November, lost it for many, many years. It was the first time that I had prayed to God for something, begged him for something, not the simple childhood wishing on a star but humbly begging for another human life. And it was as if no one heard. My begging, to my seventeen-year-old mind, had made no difference. The only answer was the sound of Mrs. Douglas's sobs on the other side of that thin emergency room curtain.

Over dinner one night my dear friend Jim Francis shared a story of a mutual friend. This man had lost his son to suicide. One day in the summer of 2009, he was sitting in a men's shop in Dallas trying on a pair of shoes when a small boy, a special needs boy, came racing up to him and nearly knocked him off the bench with a hug. The boy's mother hurried up, apologizing profusely, and pulled her son away, only to have the boy launch at the man again. As she started to apologize a second time, the father looked up at her and said, "Please don't apologize. It's been a long time since I've had a hug from a boy."

Jim cried as he told it. So did his wife, Debbie, and so did George and I. George, who lost his little sister Robin to the ravages of leukemia, and I, who will forever carry with me those four or five seconds on that blackened Midland road, and lovely Debbie and Jim, whose youngest son nearly drowned when he was two but who didn't die. He's in his thirties now, but mentally he is like a newborn baby. They have lived for thirty-four years with the grace of accepting, of not asking "why me?" of not seeking to blame, or becoming cynical, or being lulled into bitterness. Life's largest truth may be that everyone faces tragedy. Learning to accept those tragedies, learning to accept that life is riddled with events large and small, events that you may cause or that may happen to you, events that you can never control, is perhaps the hardest lesson of all. In that wrenching fact, I have faith that no one is ever alone.

In the months ahead, Lee was full of memorials for Mike. He was remembered in the school annual. His teammates picked out a little metal cannon to salute him in the school courtyard. At the end of the school year, Regan and a couple of Mike's friends went to visit his parents. Mike's mother asked them all to sign her copy of his annual, as they would have done had he been alive.

I stayed home from school for a week with my broken ankle and blackened eyes, but by mid-November, I was back at class. I walked the hallways with stiff tape wrapped around my ankle. Almost as soon as I returned, Kim Hammond, one of Mike's best friends, a boy who had been a pallbearer at his funeral, called and asked if he could nominate me for the Rebelee Court, which crowned the princesses and queens for Lee's senior program. (Midland High's homecoming court was called Catoico, for cattle, oil, and cotton, the three industries of Midland.) I said thank you and yes, although I felt about the farthest possible thing from a princess or a queen. It was a sweet gesture of unspoken forgiveness, and I have never forgotten. Quietly, I went back to my books. My mother started thinking about what might have happened if my father had never sold the Big House. My father worried about whether there had been anything unsafe about his Chevy Impala.

But I already knew that the "what ifs" are fruitless. It's a futile exercise to go through the "Oh, if I only hadn't done that, then that wouldn't have happened."

Two weeks and two days later, on November 22, President John F. Kennedy was riding in a preelection motorcade through Dallas when he raised his hand to wave to the crowd and a perfectly aimed bullet whistled through the air under that all-enveloping Texas sky.

Traveling Light

*As a fourth-grade teacher at
John F. Kennedy Elementary School,
Houston, Texas, 1970.*

We knew something was wrong the moment the wooden door with the glassed-in window closed and our teacher, Mr. Carter, walked to the front of the room. Standing there, slump-shouldered, with a catch in his voice, he uttered the unimaginable words, the President of the United States had been shot dead in Dallas. Most people can remember whatever quiet, mundane task they were doing on that day when they heard the news that John F. Kennedy had been assassinated. I was seventeen years old, sitting in my senior year History of Western Thought class at the precise moment when our own history shuddered and changed. I sat at my desk surrounded by the writings of some of the greatest minds that humanity has ever produced, and all I could feel was mute shock, utter horror, and a numbing disbelief. It was a Friday afternoon.

That Sunday, with the TV droning in the background, Daddy came rushing in the side door from the carport while Mother was fixing lunch to tell us that someone had shot Lee Harvey Oswald, Kennedy's assassin. The report had just come over the car radio. He stood there in the kitchen shaking his head and saying how tragic it was, because now no one would ever really know what had happened. There would always be speculation. We would never be certain of the truth.

For the rest of that day and the Monday following, I lay on the couch in our den and watched the entire presidential funeral ceremony, the inky mourning crepe looking somehow even blacker on the grain of the black-and-white TV. I was aching from Mike Douglas's death. Kennedy's assassination entwined itself with my own sense of tragedy until all I felt was a smothering sadness. I could never imagine meeting a president, but I had given Kennedy's book, *Profiles in Courage*, to my high school boyfriend for Christmas the previous year. Now I was watching President Kennedy's flag-draped coffin roll by.

My mother sat glued to the ceremonies as well. She would have seen Jackie Kennedy, her face obscured behind a voluminous black veil, and known that the first lady had already buried two babies, a stillborn girl and a premature boy, Patrick. That day, along with the country, she was burying her husband.

There is a story, told forty years later by one reporter, that at a single Midland restaurant, Luigi's, an Italian pizza and pasta place where the tables were covered in red and white checked cloths, lunchtime diners applauded when they heard the news of Kennedy's murder. I never heard that. Not at the time, not in the years afterward. Neither did any of my friends. The not so subtle implication behind the story was that Midland was fiercely conservative and more than a little racist, although many of the United States' greatest civil rights gains would come under a Texan, Lyndon Baines Johnson.

Certainly Midland in the early 1960s wasn't a racially integrated town. As in most of Texas, much of the South, and indeed the rest of the country, the schools were segregated, and there was an undercurrent of racism. The Midland of my early childhood had a few separate water fountains, each porcelain basin clearly marked "white" or "colored." But they were soon taken down. The prejudice that remained was subtler, a back-room or bridge-club type of prejudice, inflicted behind closed doors. No one burned crosses or scribbled epithets or deployed water cannons. And if some people spoke badly, most assuredly not everybody did. I never heard my parents talk in a racist way. When George once used a derogatory word that he had overheard, his mother smacked him for speaking "filth." In the early 1960s, there was a small African-American section in Midland but not yet a sizable Hispanic one. I didn't have any black friends, but I didn't have any way to make black friends, and they had no way to make friends with me.

And I always knew that on the horrible night of November 6, the first car that had stopped to help and the family that had come running up to wrap me in the protective cover of their arms was African-American.

Ultimately, it took federal intervention—starting with the 1954 Supreme Court ruling in *Brown v. Board of Education* and continuing through years of school closings, National Guard encounters, and federal marshals dispatched to open barred doors—to change the schools. Attitudes changed even more slowly, because this wasn't just how Midland was, it was how much of the United States was, even places that had once been bastions of abolition, like Boston. Change had to come from the top, not the bottom.

But little, isolated Midland was also more diverse than it appears to many of the people who find it so easy to condemn.

When it came to class, we were far more integrated than other parts of the country. Midland was a working-class town. Most of the people who made money in the oil business came from working-class roots. Quite a few of them had grown up with close to nothing. Even the men from wealthier families, like Mr. Bush or the Philadelphia-bred Mr. O'Neill, who had driven the car for my first "Daddy date" with his thirteen-year-old son, Kevin, had moved out to the West Texas plains determined to prove themselves. They didn't carry with them the trappings of moneyed East Coast homes. That kind of showmanship would not have sat well in midcentury Midland. The children of roughnecks and roustabouts went to the same schools and played on the same teams and were friends with the children of geologists and engineers and landmen and ranch owners, both those with oil leases on their properties and those with nothing but dry grassland. When people retract their noses ever so slightly at the mention of Midland, or West Texas more generally, I am reminded that there are many ways to denigrate a place or demean a person.

In the years that followed, my friends and I watched the civil rights movement unfold, and we embraced it. We had already learned not to judge a man or a woman based on the place that he or she called home.

And so, on those late November days, we watched and grieved in Midland as an Irish Catholic from Boston was buried at Arlington National Cemetery outside of Washington, D.C.

⌐⌐

It cost twenty-five dollars a semester to attend the Texas College of Mines and Metallurgy when my mother enrolled, in the fall of 1936. She waited until the night before final registration to ask her father for the money. It was a bleak seven years into the Great Depression, and twenty-five dollars was a significant sum. There were women who took jobs making sandwiches in soup kitchens just so they could be guaranteed one meal a day. Education was a luxury. My mother barely worked up the nerve to say anything. In the morning, Hal Hawkins handed over the twenty-five dollars, likely counted out in part in quarters, nickels, and other small change. After that, his daughter never asked him for school fees again.

When my mother went off to college, she could no longer afford to live at home and ride the bus some fourteen miles from the upper valley down to El Paso and back each evening, so she boarded with a family in town, taking care of their daughter in return for a room and food. The father worked for the Royal Dutch Shell oil company. Mother once chaperoned the little girl, Charlotte, all the way to New York on the train and then down the length of the East Coast on an oil company tanker—"the biggest ship I had ever seen in my life," she recalled—to Aruba. Charlotte's parents insisted that Mother pay her own way to New York, and she had to "scrounge" to gather enough to cover train fare. By 1938, she had dropped out of school altogether to earn her way in the world. My father had long since quit his own college in Lubbock.

But they never doubted that I would attend college. When I was in the second grade, my father proudly announced that he had bought an insurance policy designed to pay for my college when the time came. He walked into our brick house on Estes Avenue and said, "I bought this college plan for you." When I actually went to college, that little plan was worth only enough to cover one semester, but my parents were always determined that I have a college education. That was what so many of our parents in Midland wanted, a future beyond the best of what theirs had been.

And it was all the more remarkable that my father kept his promise. By the time I left Midland for Dallas, in 1964, an oil bust had struck. Some 4,500 people ultimately left the city. Homes went unsold or were foreclosed. My father did not build a single new house the entire time I was away at school.

After traversing what seemed like half the state of Texas with my parents looking at schools—the sprawling University of Texas campus in

Austin, Southwestern University in Georgetown, Texas, and all the way over to Sophie Newcomb in New Orleans—I chose Southern Methodist University in Dallas. By East Coast standards, it was a young school. The same year that it was founded, 1911, the venerable Yale University in Connecticut turned 210 years old. But SMU looked old. Its buildings were brick, and the centerpiece, Dallas Hall, had massive white columns that appeared to have stood in exactly that spot since the time of King George III. Unlike in the University of Texas system, many of SMU's students came from other states; it drew its applicants from up and down the corridors of the Midwest. And I liked the fact that it was in Dallas, home to my uncle Mark and city of innumerable visits, especially each fall to the Texas State Fair. I had first become enchanted with SMU in the seventh grade, when I read a biography of Doak Walker, SMU's legendary football running back—not at all an odd choice for a girl from Midland, where we breathed football each autumn. Walker won the Heisman Trophy in 1948; the Dallas Cotton Bowl used to be called "The House That Doak Built." But my girlish crush was not on the running back, it was on his campus, and I nurtured it for six years. I would also be going with a group of Midland girls, including Gwyne Smith, my friend from elementary school.

The fall of 1964 on college campuses around the country was not the spring of 1968 or 1969. Far from being hotbeds of radical activity, most schools were bastions of youthful irresponsibility, worlds of brimming punch bowls and the nervous social banter of night after night of sorority rush in antebellum-style houses that looked like backdrops for *Gone With the Wind*. In our dorm rooms and sororities, we had curfews, 10:00 P.M. on weekdays, midnight on weekends. House mothers came to do bed checks. Irresponsibility could occur only during preset hours. We dutifully followed the rules, having no sense of the seismic fault lines that trembled beneath our feet.

At SMU, the boys were clean-cut. The girls didn't wear pants, only dresses or skirts, which grazed the knee. The miniskirt was not invented until 1965, and it was worn in Great Britain first. I can still remember how daring it felt to wear jeans to class when I was a senior; I was the only one in denim in the entire seminar room. During my sophomore year, when I went to a Bob Dylan concert, I wore a little wool skirt suit that I had bought in El Paso the summer before with Mother at the Amen Wardy department store. My date wore a jacket and tie, and so did all the other boys around him. The crowd booed when, after the first half of the show, Dylan came back and reset the amplifiers to switch from folk music to hard rock 'n' roll. They wanted him to remain a folk singer. "The times they are a-changin'" didn't yet apply to North Texas.

I lived in the women's dorms in my first years and joined a sorority, Kappa Alpha Theta, in my second. My best friends were now a new orbit of girls, Jane Purucker and Bobbie Jo Ferguson from Kansas City, Janet Kinard from Abilene, Mary Brice from Snyder, Texas, a West Texas oil town far smaller than Midland, and Susan Englehart from Corpus Christi. I was only seventeen when I started college, at a time when many of the girls I knew aspired more to getting married than to attending their own university graduations. SMU was coed; it was not a suitcase school, like so many women's colleges of the time, where girls packed up and headed off each weekend to marathon excursions with boys, trying to make a good impression as the clock ticked down the seconds until Sunday afternoon. But we had girls who pined after loves on other campuses and hundreds of others who were searching for lifelong mates among the fraternity boys on our own.

In the beginning, I didn't know whether to be social or studious. I spent too many nights on dates at the El Toro Room, and my first-semester grades were embarrassing. Not since the fifth grade at Bowie Elementary, when I received a C in social studies, had I been so devastated. Back then, my pediatrician, Dr. Dorothy Wyvell, had ordered me to come home and lie down in the afternoons to recover from a bad cough. The result was that I missed weeks of social studies and ended up with a C. Worse than my own disappointment was the thought that I had failed Mother and Daddy. Now, eight years later, that failure was magnified. I called home, cried, and apologized. It was not just my own opportunity that I was squandering; it was theirs as well, the opportunity that they had given to their only daughter, out of love and without demands or strings. After that, I became, if not a model student, then certainly a very serious one. And I had one tremendous advantage. I had already studied many of the classics during my senior-year course in Western thought in Midland.

One of my favorite classes was a course in children's literature taught by Harryette Ehrhardt. Ironically, my mother had already studied children's literature in Midland when I was in junior high as part of the local college extension program. One night a week, while she headed off to discuss children's classics, I would fix dinner and silently roll my eyes. Now I saw that some of history's greatest writers had penned their best works for children. I was enchanted by the words of E. B. White, Madeleine L'Engle, the Brothers Grimm, and my childhood favorite, Laura Ingalls Wilder, and by the way Dr. Ehrhardt unraveled the layers upon layers of meaning in what others saw as merely whimsical turns of phrase. The class was demanding, and I was one of the few students to make an A. I already knew that I wanted to be a teacher.

Having a chosen profession was a rather new concept for women in the South. Women had always worked, doing the backbreaking labor of running a home, cooking, cleaning, hefting piles of sopping wet laundry onto the line to dry. And many women did work in jobs before they married or if they were widowed young. A few in Midland, like Mary White, worked for most of their married lives, although the oilmen whose offices they ran rarely promoted them beyond the typewriter and steno pool. Most girls, though, were schooled to dream of being wives and mothers. Their curious minds were largely self-taught—my brick-laying grandmother with her intricate garden or my mother with a book open in her dishwater-dry hands. When Betty Friedan published *The Feminine Mystique*, in 1963, their lives, my life, and those of my friends were not upended. What I see now in retrospect is that so many of my friends broke barriers not by intention but simply by doing.

With the exception of my uncle Mark, who had gone to medical school, I was the first person in my family to earn a university degree. And even Mark had not technically finished college. When he was accepted to medical school in Arkansas, he just left Texas Tech rather than spend another semester's tuition during the Depression. Mine was not an immigrant story, aside from Eva Louise LaMaire, but simply the story of families who had moved beyond the bare-bones life of small Arkansas and before that Mississippi and Kentucky farms, where families made do with a cow, a garden, and a clutch of chickens.

But in the mid-1960s, the present quickly became all-consuming.

At SMU, we stayed up late at night smoking cigarettes and engaging in discussions about the larger meaning of life, great debates without any final resolution. They were our own private versions of the heated debates being waged around us, debates that we watched, but sometimes with a bit of remove. When I entered SMU, the Vietnam War was not yet raging. America's ground war in the jungles did not begin until the spring of 1965. Even as the conflict escalated, SMU was not an early hotbed of antiwar protests, although the school did briefly have a chapter of Students for a Democratic Society. And boys I knew in Midland or at SMU were among those who enlisted or were drafted. One of our friends, Buddy Hensley, spent hours shirtless in the steamy Southeast Asian heat, filling giant barrels with the chemical defoliant Agent Orange; another, Mike Proctor, was a helicopter pilot. Both survived the war and remain our close friends. The only casualty I knew from Midland was Bob Zonne, the big brother of one of my high school classmates, Bill Zonne. Among our friends who fought, he was the one who did not make it home. His name is inscribed on the Wall in Washington, D.C.

What we felt much more keenly in the mid-sixties was the civil rights movement. In 1961, when I was just a high school sophomore, SMU students had already picketed local barbershops and movie theaters that practiced segregation, and even though SMU had few African-American students, the student body as a whole had voted strongly in support of a completely integrated campus, where all admissions would be color-blind. I was proud that SMU had the first African-American football player in the Southwest Conference, Jerry LeVias. In two years, he went from being pummeled on the field by other players long after the whistle had blown to winning the Fort Worth Kiwanis Club Award for Sportsmanship and becoming an all-American player in his senior year. When LeVias came to SMU, fellow coaches had told Coach Hayden Fry that they "would never allow" a black player on their team.

The civil rights cause gave us the words to talk about the racial divide that still stubbornly clung to our cities and towns, even our own homes. At last, I had a language to understand what I had intuitively known, that naming Lee High School in 1960 for a man who a century before, in 1861, chose his state of Virginia and his slaveholder ties over abolition while Midland's black students were still assigned to George Washington Carver High School was wrong. Suddenly everything was open for question: why my father's black friends were the men who worked the stove and the grill at Johnny's Bar-B-Q or why the only black women the rest of us knew were the ones who cleaned homes.

I was not a placard-waving protester. But the scenes from the Alabama marches or the riots that left Detroit and Newark in flames cemented my desire to do what I could, and that was to teach in an inner-city, minority school. I wanted to work with children who had been left out and, too often, left behind, simply because of the color of their skin. When I taught, I always asked to be placed in what were called "minority schools."

In 1964, when I arrived on the SMU campus, panicked students would ask the student health center, located only a few doors down from my dorm, for amphetamines to stay awake late to study for exams. One of my girlfriends even experimented with a California turnaround, what truckers used to stay awake on the road. She didn't sleep for three days. It was perhaps a frail line separating that kind of officially sanctioned self-medicating from the other, illegal drugs that would start to creep onto college campuses. By 1968, marijuana had arrived at SMU, although none of my Midland friends ever smoked pot. And the few girls at school who did try it would never admit it, in the same way that they would never reveal private details about their boyfriends. These were considered deep secrets, which girls kept to themselves alone.

Even if there was no "Summer of Love" at SMU, we did know that there was another world being unleashed beyond our white columns and redbrick walls. A few students played tracks from the Beatles' *Sgt. Pepper* or "Light My Fire" by Jim Morrison and the Doors, although at parties we danced to the sounds of what is now Motown but was then called "soul music," the Supremes, the Isley Brothers, and Cookie and the Cupcakes. Once, during my senior year, I was curious to see what real hippies looked like. My roommate, Jane, and I dressed in jeans and bare feet and hung beads from our necks. Then we headed off to Lee Park, one of the largest parks in Dallas and named for Robert E. Lee, to look for the fabled hippies. But there were none—instead, everyone else in the park turned to stare at us, imagining that we were the hippies who had come to commune with nature in the middle of the city.

One thing we did in our cute skirts and bubble hair, which we teased and sprayed and rolled on big, bristly rollers clamped tight with pins, was drink, even though we were underage. All the fraternity parties served alcohol, especially in lethal blends of spiked punch, and we drank, way too much, and smoked, even in class. By the early 1970s, our drinking would seem almost passé. By then, the drug culture had overwhelmed college life. Graduating in the South in 1968 put us just slightly ahead of the wave. But in time, alcohol would prove to be equally devastating for far too many of my friends.

At SMU, the wild boys were not the drunken fraternity brothers who would go on to become bankers and businessmen; they were the boys who drove motorcycles and who rebelled against anything that smacked of authority. Yet even they were not as freed from convention as it seemed. Chuck, the long-haired boy with the devil-may-care smile, who rode a motorcycle and dated Bobbie Jo, volunteered to go to Vietnam. Another of his biker friends once stole a suit, which he wore to his seminary interview for the Episcopal priesthood. He got in. But there was a James Dean–style restlessness that gripped our college years, a desire to throw off one by one the conventions of our parents and our grandparents. The gross injustices underpinning the need for the civil rights movement, the pat explanations that "certain groups had to earn their rights," in order to justify the sins of segregation, and subtle racism made many of the previous generations' values seem suspect and shallow. A few of the more vocal among us rejected everything.

Indeed, most of the class of 1968 had grown up during a period of unprecedented abundance. We had never known a great depression or a global war that ran hot rather than cold. Our parents' sacrifices had shielded us from these things. But now our own generational discontent had produced a highly combustible equation. I remember sitting in our sorority house on the last day of March 1968, when Lyndon Johnson announced that he would not run for reelection. We watched largely in silence; there was no collective gasp of regret.

At my commencement, just over a month after Martin Luther King was assassinated and a few weeks before another bullet felled Bobby Kennedy,

SMU's president, Willis Tate, implored students not to abandon rational thought and judgment, saying, "We live in a day when contagious hysteria and social pressures can completely anesthetize a person's ability to reason," and adding, "In times of rapid change, the old may be destroyed along with the decayed. There are some time-tested, eternal values."

Not everyone participated in the upheaval of the late 1960s. Many of the girls I knew, including most of my Midland friends, were getting on with the next phase of their lives. They had become engaged or had already returned home to their childhood churches for their weddings. I fully expected to be married by the end of my senior year. I thought about it whenever I caught sight of a beaming bride preparing to walk down the aisle under the serene cream spire of Perkins Chapel at the center of the SMU campus. I even dated a young medical student at the start of my senior year and assumed for a while that I would settle down with him. But I graduated with no ring on my left hand and no immediate prospects for one.

For my graduation gift, I wanted to see Europe. Midland was still firmly in the grip of an oil bust, so my parents looked for something affordable. The answer came in the form of my uncle Mark, who was taking his family on a fourteen-day trip, stopping in ten different countries. He invited me to come along. My cousin Mary Mark and I saw a huge swath of the continent at a rapid clip. What captivated me was the age of all the places, stones that had been quarried, cut, and laid over a millennium ago, sculpture carved by hands that could not imagine a wild grassland where Indians had pitched animal skin tents and stalked buffalo. I would look up and see stained glass that had already survived multiple wars before Midland even had a name or an old railroad boxcar to hold its mail.

My first job, if you could call it that, was making coffee for my parents in the pot at home—I got a nickel if I made coffee for Mother and Daddy every morning. I also set the table and made my bed, and I kept a little chart of all the chores that I had done, a kind of grade-school time clock, I suppose. My other bits of gainful employment were teaching swimming at the Midland public pool and working as a counselor at summer camps. One summer, Jane Gray and I opened our own three-hour morning camp, advertising it on mimeographed flyers and holding it in her mother's Jack and Jill school. Now I was about to set foot in a fourth-grade classroom, with nothing more to prepare me than a few months of practice teaching at one of Dallas's most elite elementary schools. Bradfield Elementary, where aspiring SMU teaching students went to practice, wasn't even in the Dallas Independent School District; it was in the separate city of Highland Park. My second-grade practice classroom did contain one surprise: the football legend Doak Walker's seven-year-old son. He was a shy boy; his parents had been divorced for several years. His quiet presence was a reminder that not even childhood idols remained unchanged; Doak Walker was no longer a young man charging toward the end zone, and I was no longer dreaming of college from the shelter of the seventh grade.

I had decided to remain in Dallas, at least for the moment. Susan, Janet, Bobbie Jo, and I rented a little postwar-style garden apartment amid a cluster of two-story brick buildings with white trim and stairs. Our building sat at the end of the block, only a few hundred yards from the train tracks. Susan used to dash across the rails to go visit her boyfriend, Mike, who lived on the other side. All I needed was a job, preferably a job that didn't involve a long drive. Ever since the accident, I preferred to cede the driving to friends like Regan, who loved being behind the wheel. I did not want a long commute, and I turned down jobs at two Dallas schools because they were too far away. Finally, the personnel director for the school system called back and said, "Well, Miss Welch, how about the school on your street?" And I said, "Oh, good, that will be perfect." So every morning, I walked to Longfellow Elementary, two blocks from my apartment.

Longfellow had been built amid large, gracious two-story homes that sat back from the roads on acres of manicured green lawns, but very few of the local residents sent their children there. Many were older people whose children had long since grown. But the well-to-do also largely avoided the Dallas Independent School District. Those who didn't settle in places like Highland Park sent their children to private academies instead. The students at Longfellow, a solid two-story, tan brick school, were bused in from other neighborhoods, close to downtown. Most came from a predominantly African-American neighborhood near the new Parkland Hospital, which had replaced the old redbrick building where John F. Kennedy was rushed after he was shot.

I loved my students. I was just twenty-one when I entered that fourth-grade classroom, and my students in so many ways taught me. I had only twenty in my class, a luxury at a time when many public schools had upwards of thirty or forty students in a single room. My classroom was on the first floor, with windows all along one side because there was no air-conditioning. We opened the glass and hoped for a breeze. It was in that school in the September heat, as sweat glued my blouse to my back, that I felt the physical demands of teaching, six hours or more on my feet, standing at the blackboard, on the recess blacktop, or in the cafeteria as students navigated the lunch lines and downed their meals. And I had to keep their attention, by myself, alone.

The realities of an elementary school classroom are far from the Hollywood romance of tweedy academics or wisecracking professors. The movies can condense an entire school career into a little over two hours. That doesn't take most teachers even through the morning. Teaching is, even for those who love it, at times isolating. It happens behind closed doors, one adult navigating the needs and complexities of twenty or more children, twenty or more entirely different personalities. We are not, in truth, so far removed from the days of the one-room schoolhouse. As much as teachers may talk to other faculty members, they don't go out to lunch or briefly laze by coffeepots or watercoolers. Elementary school teachers must calculate when their classrooms are subdued enough for them even to escape to the bathroom. But I never found it boring, and as I got my bearings, it became deeply rewarding.

My education degree had not prepared me, I quickly learned, to teach reading. Like many new teachers, I followed the textbook teacher guide provided by the school system. But that did little to make words and stories come alive. It was when I began a story hour after lunch that my passion quickly became the children's. We read books like *Where the Wild Things Are*, and the children would pretend that the characters had come alive in the classroom. We saved a space in the corner for a web for Charlotte, the famous spider in *Charlotte's Web*. Wilbur's pen was a nearby locker.

Bunnies lived in supply closets; monsters screeched on the blackboard. Every book came to life, and the children would gaze eager and wide-eyed, leaning forward as I turned each page. I had them write poems and created books of their poetry, each bound between two cardboard sheets and secured by a ribbon threaded through hand-punched holes. I would save up the funny things they said and call home to regale Mother and Daddy, who laughed at the other end of the phone.

Four decades later, the antics of my students would become the inspiration for my first book, a children's story, *Read All About It!*, which I penned with my daughter Jenna. Like me, Jenna would begin her career as a teacher in inner-city schools, hers in Washington and Baltimore. In *Read All About It!*, as in my first classroom in Longfellow, cherished storybook characters magically came to life.

By the end of that year, though, I was ready to leave Dallas. I had lived there for five years; most of my close college friends were now drifting off to other cities. And I had never lived outside of Texas. I was twenty-two and restless. My students were moving on to the next grade, and it seemed time for me to move as well. One of my roommates, Bobbie Jo, wanted to head east, to Boston, which to our imaginations seemed a world removed from the Texas and Kansas plains. She planned on getting a job at Filene's department store; I would just get a job. We hopped in my car and started across the country, stopping in Nashville and other spots to visit college friends. When we arrived in Boston, neither of us knew one single person to call or where to look for an apartment. After three days, we left, this time driving south to Washington, D.C.

In the nation's capital, we rented a cheap room at the YWCA and washed our clothes in the sink and hung them on lamps and curtain rods to dry. Bobbie Jo applied for a position at Garfinckel's department store. I went to Capitol Hill and interviewed with my local congressman. George Mahon had represented Midland since 1935. He was a lawyer from Lubbock who had been born in northern Louisiana. In 1969, he was almost seventy years old. I called his office and got an appointment.

One late July morning, I walked through the marble-halled warren of congressional offices, where earnest young men and women labored behind piles of paper on their desks. I sat down in a leather chair in Congressman Mahon's office, wearing my nice dress, my purse perched on my lap, as he looked over my résumé and asked me if I could type or take shorthand. I could barely type; I had taken a quick course during summer school but hadn't paid much attention. I didn't think that I needed to type because, in a burst of intellectual snobbery and a bit of feminism, I had decided that I wasn't going to be anyone's secretary, and I wasn't going to waste my high school class time on typing lessons. Congressman Mahon then asked me if my father would consider sending me to secretarial school to learn how to type professionally and take shorthand. I thought about what my father had already spent to send me to SMU and said no again. And Congressman Mahon gently suggested that, without being able to do either, I really wasn't qualified for a position in his office. Had I been a typist, however, in the summer of 1969, I might very well have become a congressional staffer in Washington.

Bobbie Jo decided to remain in Washington. Her boyfriend, Chuck, was in Vietnam, and she couldn't bear to spend the year in Texas, seeing her friends arm in arm, hand in hand. She wanted to, as she put it, "go into exile." I left her to board in a rooming house, with her job at Garfinckel's, and drove back to Texas, alone, driving for hours during the day and sleeping each night in neon-lit motels that dotted the highway. My SMU friend Janet Kinard had moved from Dallas to Houston. All summer, she had been calling and saying that she needed a roommate. I repacked and set off for Houston. When I got on the Katy Freeway bound for downtown, traffic came to a halt. A wrecked truck was blocking the freeway. People rolled down their windows and got out of their cars to sit on the roofs and the hoods because it was August and it was hot, that hot, humid air from the bayous and the Gulf of Mexico that hangs over Houston the way it does over the Mississippi Delta to the east. I sat on the roof of my car listening to people mill around and talk until the authorities had cleared the accident and we could move again. I hoped it wasn't some sort of an omen that, as I drove into Houston to begin the rest of my life, I got stuck on a freeway and waited for hours in the August sun.

Dallas was a newer city. As late as 1860, it had a mere 678 people. By that same year, Houston had briefly been the capital of Texas and was already sporting the beginnings of a port and a rail system, with more than four hundred miles of track laid in the surrounding ground. But over a century later, in 1969, Houston seemed younger and brasher. The city's buildings were a hodgepodge across the skyline. There were no zoning regulations, so it was possible to have a gleaming skyscraper on the lot next to a funny old house that had stood in that same spot for decades. I moved in with Janet and joined the ranks of young, professional women by getting a job at a brokerage house.

Prior to that job, my closest brush with high finance had been when I was around fifteen. One Saturday morning, Daddy put on his nicest suit and tie, Mother wore her best dress, I spent hours with spray and hard rollers to get my hair to billow up over my head, and we drove downtown to a photography studio for a formal family portrait. After he saw the pictures, Daddy smiled his big, broad grin and said, "I think I look like a Philadelphia banker." His idea of a Philadelphia banker came from the old black-and-white Katharine Hepburn movie *The Philadelphia Story*, but for someone from Lubbock, Texas, it was the look of success.

I, however, was not cut out to be a banker. I was dreadfully bored at the brokerage house and longed to return to the classroom. Within a couple of months, I was teaching again, taking over the class of a teacher who had left to have a baby. My school was the John F. Kennedy Elementary School; my class was the fourth grade, and our principal was Mrs. Gunnells.

At first, I hated it. I was starting in the middle of the school year, the classroom was in chaos, and after my sweet class in Dallas, I was unprepared for this group of nine-year-olds. My students were wild, screaming, talking back, hiding erasers, wadding up pieces of paper and lobbing them across the room. They were determined to see just how far they could push a new teacher. Every weekend, I would get the "Sunday sads"; I dreaded returning to my classroom on Monday morning. When I passed construction workers with their hard hats and lunch pails, I envied them. They did not have raucous children to deal with, particularly two rambunctious brothers, whom I thought of as the "dynamic duo." The older brother was in my class; his younger brother was a first grader. Whenever the first grader grew bored, he would sneak into my classroom, jump out from behind the desk, and scream, "Boo." All the children would laugh, and whatever tenuous control I had asserted to get them to pay attention would vanish all over again. Gradually I started to read the signs of restlessness and learned to spot the little brother before he reached the door. I would send one or both brothers on an errand to deliver a note or sharpen pencils, giving them a chance to get up and move around.

The Kennedy School sat on a busy commercial road; trucks, cars, and buses rattled outside the windows. The students, nearly all of whom were African-American, lived for the most part in small, run-down houses behind the school building on narrow side streets, which eventually dead-ended alongside warehouses and the train tracks. The houses were tiny and old; they had clapboard siding with peeling paint and loose asbestos shingles on the roofs. Parked in front were rusting cars, whose tire treads dug into the yards. Most of the parents worked, but there were few opportunities available to them. Poverty, lack of education, even alcohol abuse lurked behind too many doors.

It was only the mothers who came to school; the dads never did. Most of our students qualified for free lunch and a breakfast, if they got there early enough. For a few, these were often the only regular meals they had. They would arrive in the morning, bellies rumbling, and pile their plates with food. After lunch had passed, they endured the slow burn of hunger until the next day. I can't imagine how they navigated the holidays and weekends. One of my students was so hungry that he could not stay awake; he spent part of the day with his head resting on his desk. He was a talented artist, able to draw lovely and elaborate pictures. Once, his mother came to a meeting at school, and I gingerly mentioned that her son spent a lot of time sleeping at his desk. She told me very matter-of-factly that she left quite early in the morning, and the kids "just had to make it on their own." It was not her choice; there was just no alternative. I don't remember that she ever came back to school after that. We were used to partly empty back-to-school nights and the ghosts of parents who failed to sign the notes we dutifully sent home with their children. But in the early 1970s, teachers were not expected to reach into families' lives. We could only try to teach our students before they moved on. Corporal punishment was still in use in the Texas school system; I had seen it at

Longfellow. I could have spanked a hungry child or smacked his knuckles with a ruler, and the school would have been obligated to take my side.

There were some students we did help. At Longfellow, I had a petite girl who was constantly jumping up and down and trying to attract attention. Then we did the eye chart and found that she was just like me: partially blind. She was the way I would have been if I hadn't had glasses. I moved her to the front row, and the school nurse sent a note home saying that she needed glasses. Her mother refused to get them, but the nurse did not give up. Eventually, the child got glasses. And John F. Kennedy Elementary, despite the pressures of the neighborhood, was a well-run school. The faculty, white and African-American, was dedicated; many had taught for years. But too often at other city schools, teachers were put in rooms with twenty or more students and simply told "good luck." I've always been struck by how teachers were the last professionals to get phones on their desks, and how hard it has been for them to stay in contact with parents. Today, of course, they have e-mail and cell phones, but for years, parents and teachers in huge urban school districts coexisted in a perpetual state of mutual isolation.

Not all contact was good, however. Once a student's mother stormed into my classroom and yelled at me over something she thought had happened to her son. The entire class watched with their mouths hanging open. I was stunned, but Mrs. Gunnells, the principal, quickly came to my defense—she was very strict with the parents too. From the wild fourth grade, I moved to the second grade and had the younger brother of my dynamic duo, the little boy who had so loved sneaking in my classroom door. I stayed with that class for third grade, which meant more story time after lunch, but it also meant that every subject I was weak in, like math, my students were weak in too. They became very dependent on one adult, me. For much of their fourth-grade year, they told their new teacher, "We don't have to do that, because Miss Welch didn't say that we had to."

While I was figuring out how to be a teacher, I was also learning how to be a grown-up in Houston. I knew Houston from summer trips with Mother and Daddy. One of my college boyfriends had been from Houston, and even Regan's mom, Wanda, had moved there.

In our little apartment, Janet and I would host dinner parties and fix King Ranch chicken, a famous casserole of tortillas, cheese, chicken, and three different cans of soup. Janet's mother had sent her off with the Abilene Junior League cookbook, and we thought it was a good cookbook, since most recipes called for several cans of creamed soup. We hosted our dinner parties, inviting our boyfriends and their friends, with everyone crammed onto our few pieces of furniture, eating from plates perched on their laps. We went to the Athens Bar & Grill, an old Greek place along the ship channel. At the other scarred tables were sailors from the far corners of the world; their ships had docked in Houston. We drove to Austin for football games and headed west to Laredo, on the banks of the Rio Grande, one of the oldest border crossing points between the United States and Mexico. We went to bars to drink and restaurants for dinner, because there is only so much King Ranch chicken that anyone can eat. A couple of our friends had sailboats, and we would spend afternoons blowing about on the waters of the Gulf of Mexico, traversing the foul-smelling, oil-covered Houston ship channel to sail. Another close friend of mine from SMU had an old family beach house that we visited out on the barrier island of Galveston. It was built of weathered wood and sat up on stilts to give it a slim chance against the fierce hurricanes and blanketing tides that would periodically rip through.

In Houston, after my brief flirtation with working in a brokerage house, I dated a stockbroker while, one by one, my friends settled down. Regan, who had bounced from house to house and even from state to state during her growing up, was one of the first to say "I do," with Billy Gammon, who worked in his family's insurance business. Then Peggy married Ronnie Weiss, and Janet married Fred Heyne. Right after their wedding, Regan and Billy moved east, to New York, so he could train at a top insurance firm. In the fall of 1970, my stockbroker boyfriend invited me to New York, where he had meetings, and we went out to dinner with Regan and Billy. The next day, my boyfriend took Regan and me, in our fashionable miniskirted dresses, down to Wall Street. We walked onto one of the brokerage trading floors with him to get a glimpse of high finance. I saw a sea of desks and agitated men grabbing at ringing phones, until some guy yelled out, "Hey, who are the bimbos?"

We thought it was hilarious. Regan was a newlywed and newly pregnant. As for me, how many bimbos are able to moonlight as second-grade teachers and school librarians?

In Houston, I lived in the place for singles, the Chateaux Dijon, a sprawling, block-long apartment complex with several swimming pools and turrets rising on each side. With its sloping gray roof, it had pretensions of being a brown-brick Versailles. My suite was a revolving door of four roommates, including Jan Donnelly, one of my Midland friends, who moved home in 1972 to marry Joey O'Neill. One summer, I spent nearly every day at the pool reading the classics of Russian literature, traveling through the frigid, snow-laden novels of Tolstoy and Dostoyevsky in the swampy heat of Houston, where by midmorning you could break a sweat simply by stepping outside.

Reading and books were my passion, and I began to think seriously of enrolling in graduate school for library science. Also, as much as I loved Houston, I wanted a change. Like my parents moving from house to house, I had uncovered a similar restlessness, from teaching to setting off for the East Coast, moving to Houston, working in a brokerage house, going back to the classroom. I had so many options that I was seeking an anchor to ground myself. Here my married friends had it almost easier; they had already made their choices, and a quadrant of their lives was settled. I was determined to settle on a job, and I wanted to be surrounded by books.

I applied to the library science program at University of Texas and was accepted. But before I left for Austin, I wanted to take two of my favorite students from Kennedy to AstroWorld, an amusement park near the baseball stadium. My boyfriend, Ralph, and I arrived on a Saturday morning to pick them up. One of the boys was waiting, all dressed, with his sister; their mother obviously hoped that we couldn't resist an outing for the two of them. And we couldn't. We put both in the car and headed over to the other boy's house. He opened the door in his underwear and couldn't manage to get dressed while we were there. He was nine and going into fourth grade. We could hear his mother in the back of the house, but she never came to the door. I hugged him good-bye with an extra squeeze.

There were many kids like him. The disarray of their parents' lives repeatedly spilled over into their own.

Three decades later, in 2003, a couple of days before Christmas, the John F. Kennedy Elementary School found me again. I was sitting in a television studio in Washington, D.C., with the then host of NBC's *Meet the Press*, Tim Russert. We were taping his Christmas show, and the other guest for the morning was Caroline Kennedy, the daughter of the president. The red lights on the cameras were lit, and their giant eyes were swiveling just out of sight in the set when Tim announced, "In 1969 and the early 1970s, you taught at the John F. Kennedy School."

And I turned to Caroline Kennedy to say that I had once taught at a school named for her father.

My first apartment in Austin was a hand-me-down from my friend Bobbie Jo, who had come back to Texas after her year of self-imposed exile. She had left the world of department store retail to return to school to earn a graduate degree in education. Like me, she had spent that first year out of college teaching in Dallas.

The apartment was on the second floor of an old wood-frame house. I had to walk up a metal fire escape that groaned and clanged to reach it. Once when I stepped into a tiny storage space under the eves, my leg sank through the cheap Sheetrock into the apartment below. Bobbie Jo left behind a kitten from her cat's litter. I named her Dewey, for the Dewey decimal system, a library staple. My home was now two rooms, a living room in front, a bedroom in the back, and a slim pass-through kitchen in between. I painted the cabinets cobalt blue. My painting jobs were never as good upon completion as they were in my imagination. My furnishings were secondhand pieces from junk shops.

The library school was located in the Harry Ransom Center on the UT campus, a treasure trove of rare manuscripts from Shakespeare's First Folio to manuscripts by the Brontë sisters and John Keats and the page proofs from James Joyce's *Ulysses*. I was learning about the conservation of books in a place with some of the most beautiful pieces of literature in the world.

In January of 1973, the day after Richard Nixon was inaugurated for his second term, Lyndon Johnson died in his bed at his ranch. His flag-draped coffin was brought to lie in state at the Johnson Presidential Library on the UT campus. I was one of thousands who lined up to file past the casket of "our Texas president." One of my library professors had wept that day in class, saying, "President Johnson made it possible for me to get the money to go on to graduate school." Lady Bird Johnson and her daughters, Lynda and Luci, stood at the entrance, shaking hands with everyone who walked through that afternoon. I extended mine, never imagining that someday we would meet again.

After I got my degree, I returned to Houston. My plan was to work in a public library, which would have a far more extensive collection than a school. I envisioned working in the main, downtown branch, where I could help readers and researchers and where I might meet an eligible man on my lunch hour. I was offered a post in the Kashmere Gardens Neighborhood Library, in an African-American section of Houston, sandwiched between a rail line and an industrial building corridor. Instead of businessmen looking for mystery novels, I helped families find books, and as soon as school ended, we were overrun with children who had no place else safe to go; I was their de facto caregiver. I read stories and devised activities, and I began to visit the neighborhood elementary schools to lend them library books for their classrooms. When the library was quiet, I read. Inspired by my mother and Lady Bird Johnson's love of wildflowers, I devoured books about landscaping. I read every book in the library with advice about how to quit smoking, and I read stacks of literary classics. One of my library colleagues invited me to join her women's consciousness-raising group, and I did. We talked about sisterhood and read still more books, including *Sisterhood Is Powerful* and works by Betty Friedan and Germaine Greer.

But I missed Austin. I missed being able to gaze up at the edge of the Texas Hill Country, where at dusk the sun cast a violet crown around the rising land. I enjoyed Austin's small space, its lake and trails. And I missed working in a school. In the summer, I quit my job in Houston and returned to Austin, to a tiny apartment in another old, converted house near the downtown, and began applying for jobs. Regan and Billy had also moved to Austin from New York, and Regan and I slipped back into the easy flow of friendship that had been the compass of our teenage lives. Indeed, I was in Regan's house, borrowing her iron to press my skirts and watching television on the afternoon when Richard Nixon resigned the presidency.

Countless other afternoons, I would head to Regan and Billy's around five o'clock and watch as Regan cooked dinner; I really learned to cook in her kitchen. Billy often invited friends over, and we would eat and then I would head home. Other nights we wandered to Armadillo World Headquarters to hear country music or rock 'n' roll. Austin in those years billed itself as the anti-Nashville, showcasing music without the corporate side, and the Armadillo was the central symbol of its musical underground. Once, I took my parents to eat in the Armadillo's beer garden, where Daddy ran into Johnny Hackney's daughter, Mandy. The shocked look on her face told me that I was one of the few people to ever take their parents anywhere near the Armadillo World Headquarters.

I had a new job working in a library, this time as the school librarian for the Molly Dawson Elementary School, in a largely Hispanic neighborhood. Now my day was spent with children and books, and each class was my much-loved story hour. For many small children, there is a fine line between reality and fantasy, and it's easy for them to cross back and forth, just as little boys trot off to face imaginary bad guys in their Superman capes. Books and their stories help children do just that. I wanted these children, like the ones at John F. Kennedy, to dream of possibilities beyond their web of city blocks and brick school walls.

Unlike other urban schools during that era, Dawson was lucky enough to have music, art, and physical education teachers, along with a librarian, and we were the only educators who had a chance to work with every student in the school. But we went a step beyond that. Dawson's music teacher came up with the idea of applying for a special grant to develop and teach an entire interdisciplinary curriculum based on the nation's bicentennial. We taught our students about American history not simply with textbooks and time lines but through the music, art, and literature of the Revolutionary period. During gym, the students played Revolutionary-era games and learned colonial dances. We used grant money to take the children on field trips to the historic sites of Laredo and San Antonio. Many of our kids had barely been out of the confines of greater Austin.

My life had found its routine: work in Austin, visits to Midland a few times a year. Although while at Kennedy I had spent the summer of 1971 taking a University of California course in England, living in Oxford, where I studied the schools in Bath and Exeter and took quick jaunts out to the English countryside, now my summer vacations consisted of a week or two of visiting Mother and Daddy and trips around Texas to visit friends. I was back on the flat asphalt highway between Austin and Midland, bisecting the geography of Texas, the Big Empty, as it is often known. And I was thirty years old.

For at least a year, my friend Jan Donnelly's husband, Joey O'Neill, had been telling me that he wanted to introduce me to one of his friends. Jan had gone to Lee High School and had lived with me in Houston at the Chateaux Dijon. After spending a few years in San Francisco, Jan and Joey had come home to live in Midland. Joey was working in his dad's oil business, and his childhood friend George Bush was working as an oil landman, scouring county courthouse records for land that might be leased for drilling wells. Joey talked up George every time I stopped by to visit with Jan.

I was in no rush. I had a vague memory of George from the seventh grade, almost twenty years before. I knew that his dad had run for Senate and lost in 1970, when I first moved to Houston, and I assumed that George would be very interested in politics, while I was not.

It was late July, one of those high heat days when, come dusk, the sun had, as Willa Cather wrote, "left behind it a spent and exhausted world." I put on a blue sundress, drove the car around the corner, and walked up to the door of Jan and Joey's brown-brick town house. Even the roof was a cedar-shake brown. The cicadas were droning, and overlaying their vibrating wings was the steady whir of air conditioners to keep the baking-hot houses cool. Joey was at the grill. It was not some elaborate party; it was just the four of us—Jan, Joey, George, and me—sitting out back, eating hamburgers. We laughed and talked until it was nearly midnight. The next day, the phone rang. It was George saying, "Let's go play miniature golf." And so we did, with Jan and Joey tagging along as our chaperones.

The miniature golf course is one of the prettiest places in Midland. It was built among a veritable forest of old elm trees, which had grown tall and graceful even in the West Texas ground. We played golf under the stars and laughed again. Then I went back to Austin, and George started visiting on the weekends. Sometimes he would fly over on a Friday night, or he would drive, but he came every weekend, except for the very end of August, when he left for Maine to see his family. Bar Bush loves to tell the story that George spent exactly one day in Kennebunkport that summer. When he called my apartment, she says that "some guy answered, and he raced for a plane and flew right back down."

I returned to the library at Dawson and worked all through September. By the end of the month, George had asked me to marry him. We had been dating only six or seven weeks but our childhoods overlapped so completely and our worlds were so intertwined, it was as if we had known each other our whole lives. I loved how he made me laugh and his stead-fastness. I knew in my heart that he was the one. I looked at him and said yes. That Sunday night, when George arrived in Midland, he headed to Humble Avenue to speak to my parents. A week later, early on a Sunday morning, George and I drove to Houston for his niece Noelle's christening. Jeb and Columba Bush had a little house in Larchmont, a neighborhood just past the Chateaux Dijon. The senior Bushes and their good friends Susan and Jim Baker were already there. I said hello to the Bakers first, and then George took my hand and led me to meet his parents. He introduced me with the news that we were getting married.

After lunch at the Bushes' home, George's dad pulled out his pocket calendar and looked over each weekend that fall. In a few minutes, we had picked a wedding date: November 5, 1977, one day after my birthday, one day before the anniversary of the awful accident, and only about three weeks away. There was no time even to order printed wedding invitations. Mother wrote and addressed all of ours by hand.

I gave my two weeks' notice at Dawson and went wedding dress shopping with Regan in Austin. I had been in a number of large Texas weddings, where the brides wore long, white gowns and elaborate, lacy veils and had acres of bridesmaids. George and I wanted a very simple celebration. I bought my dress, an ivory silk skirt and blouse, at a store called Maharani's, where most of the clothing came from India or Afghanistan. I would carry a bouquet of gardenias and pin gardenias in my hair. We had no groomsmen or bridesmaids and invited only our immediate family and close friends, about seventy-five people, a very small wedding by Texas standards.

Far more nervous than either the bride or the groom were Jan and Joey O'Neill. Joey and Jan had dated for years before they got married. Neither had dreamed that their invitation to dinner would lead us to the altar in a mere three months. And perhaps it wouldn't have if Joey had introduced us when we were growing up in Midland, or when George and I had lived on opposite sides of the sprawling Chateaux Dijon in Houston, or at almost any other moment prior to that night. But at that particular moment, on that warm summer night, both of us were hoping to find someone. We were not looking for someone to date but for someone with whom to share life, for the rest of our lives. We both wanted children. We were ready to build an enduring future.

Those were the facts of our lives when we went to dinner that night. It was the right timing for both of us.

Of course, not everyone in Midland agreed.

As I was packing to leave Austin, Regan and Billy were selling their house. A week before the wedding, the mother of a friend of mine from Midland came to see Regan and Billy's house. She was thinking of buying it for her daughter. She didn't recognize Regan, but Regan recognized her and said, "We're going to be in Midland next weekend. We're going to Laura and George's wedding." And without a second's hesitation, this woman said to Regan, "Yes, can you imagine? The most eligible bachelor in Midland marrying the old maid of Midland?"

Regan was speechless. But I thought it was funny. After all, I am four months less two days younger than George.

The movers loaded up my few things. After the last box was stowed, my cat, Dewey, and I began the drive that I had never quite imagined making, back to live in Midland. Right outside of San Angelo, I came upon a few scattered trees lining the edge of the road. Now, on the verge of November, the frost had already settled on the land, and their leaves had fallen and blown away. Trunks and branches stood dark and empty against the sky. Suddenly, from one naked tree, a great mass of winged birds lifted up, feathers pulsing, air swirling as they rose. I slowed and watched in silence as they beat their migratory way south, then glanced back at the unremarkable tree that had extended its branches for rest and refuge. The sight was like a beautiful wedding gift on the long road toward home.

We were married on a Saturday morning at the First Methodist Church in Midland, the church I had gone to all my childhood, where I was baptized as a baby, where I had learned to sing in the choir, and where my mother still went every Sunday. Methodist weddings are brief, and ours was particularly so. There were no bridesmaids to add a few extra minutes as they walked down the aisle. It was perfect for the "old maid" and the "eligible bachelor." The rehearsal dinner had been held the night before in the windowless basement ballroom of the new Hilton Hotel. Bar and George Bush had hosted it, and the menu was chicken and rice. When dinner was served, my mother blanched. Our wedding reception was to be a post-ceremony luncheon at the Midland Racquet Club the next day, and Mother and the caterer had settled on chicken and rice. Mother and Bar had never thought to compare menus. The next morning, Mother called the caterer at the crack of dawn to see if something could be changed, pasta instead of rice, anything. But the meal was already in motion, so our guests ate chicken and rice all over again.

The morning after my thirty-first birthday, I stepped into the chapel on my father's arm. George was waiting at the altar. The night before, when George stood to give his toast, he'd wept. George and his father are deeply sentimental men. In years to come, to others, the cool remove of television would frequently obscure the depth of their caring, how much and how deeply their own hearts open. George Herbert Walker Bush didn't even try to give a toast. Only Bar spoke.

That morning the stained-glass windows sparkled with light, casting pretty patterns over the simple wooden chapel pews. It was, I later learned, exactly thirty-one steps down the aisle and into the rest of my life.

We chose the beaches of Cozumel, Mexico, for our honeymoon. We drove from our wedding luncheon to Mother and Daddy's house to pick up my bags. On the driveway, we posed for our last round of wedding photos. Mother was our photographer, and she was so nervous and near-sighted that she would hold up the camera, think she had taken a picture, and then hold it down toward the driveway to advance the film. When they were developed, all of our honeymoon departure photos were shots of the driveway and the tips of Mother's dainty feet.

We arrived at the Midland airport for our flight to Houston, only to find the entire Bush family—parents, brothers, and sister—plus all our guests from Houston waiting for the same afternoon plane. It looked as if the Bush entourage was following us all the way to Mexico for our honeymoon. But they disembarked when the plane landed in Houston. We went on to Mexico City and then the next morning to Cozumel, once a thriving Mayan enclave that for centuries was nearly deserted. Pirates sailed its waters, and Abraham Lincoln apparently toyed with the idea of purchasing it to serve as a home for freed slaves. In 1977, it was a quiet island resort. We rented a car and drove around the island, marveling at the ever-present iguanas, who clung to everything, including the bottoms of billboards. In the afternoons, we sat on the beach and drank margaritas. By about the third day, we were drinking Pepto-Bismol. The mid-November weather had turned, so we spent most of the rest of the time in bed—playing gin rummy. Thus did my marriage begin, with a deck of cards, playing a game that led my father to keep a couple of hundred dollars cash in his pocket in case he spotted one of his Midland friends ready to deal him in for a hand.

We returned home to George's new, single-story town house on Golf Course Road, a street named for Midland's first and now long-vanished golf course. George had furnished the house by trading oil leases with Charlie Knorr of Knorr's furniture. One lease had gotten him a brown leather couch. Otherwise, he hadn't done much; in his yard, a small forest of weeds had grown up as tall as the roofline. Indeed, George had hardly done his laundry at home. He used to go to Don and Susie Evans's home for dinner; Susie was Susie Marinis, my kindergarten friend and George's second-grade friend. As he ate, he would do his laundry in the big commercial machines on the first floor of their garden apartment complex.

But we were not destined to hang around home. A few months before

George and I met, Representative Mahon had announced his retirement from Congress after forty-four years in office. The seat was open, and George was trying to win it as a Republican. Politics was in his blood. His grandfather had been a U.S. senator, and his father had lost twice running statewide for the U.S. Senate in Texas. But from 1967 to 1971, George H. W. Bush had served two terms in the U.S. House of Representatives. Almost from the moment we arrived home, George and I hit the campaign trail, covering a big swath of West Texas.

We drove up and down the back roads and asphalt highways of the Texas panhandle, from Midland at the southern tip up to Plainview and Hereford in the north, with the New Mexican border running alongside. We spent nearly a year on the road, and in many ways the bonds of our marriage were cemented in the front seat of that Oldsmobile Cutlass. When George and I met, it was as if two parallel lives suddenly converged. Our childhood memories, the places we had known, even many of our friends overlapped. We were like the last two pieces of a puzzle, our similarities and contradictions sized to fit. George was boisterous and loved to talk, while I've always been quieter. And George came from a big family. It was an unexpected answer to my childish wishes on all those stars. On my side, George got to be the only son-in-law. But these layers of connections and commonalities forged a deeper, richer bond. We never worried that any long-buried fact about the other person would appear and surprise us. From the start, our marriage was built on a powerful foundation of trust. We had been cut, as it were, from the same solid Permian Basin stone. So we drove and we talked and we laughed and we dreamed in the front seat of George's Oldsmobile.

Campaigning in West Texas is an exercise in retail politics, shaking every hand, knocking on every door. Many mornings, we'd head off to small farm towns where a friend would host a coffee to meet the candidate and invite all of his or her neighbors. We'd arrive, the coffeepots would be set out, along with plates of one hundred home-baked chocolate chip cookies. The morning would pass, and just three or four people in pickup trucks would drop by. George and I would smile and eat through the mounds of cookies as fast as we could.

The Nineteenth Congressional District was a traditionally Democratic district, even if its voters had chosen Republicans for president for the last twenty-five years. Eisenhower and Nixon may have carried Midland, but Congressman Mahon was a Democrat, our governors and our state representatives were Democrats. Across the graphlike lines of its square-grid counties, the sheriffs, the county commissioners, the mayors, every local officeholder was a Democrat. Most people, including my parents, were registered Democrats, and the Democratic primary usually mattered more than the general election. As George H. W. Bush used to joke when he started the Republican Party in Midland in the 1950s, only three people voted in the Republican primary, Barbara Bush, himself, and a drunk Democrat who had wandered into the wrong side of the polling place.

George knew all of this. He has an amazing intuitive grasp of politics, not just the people aspect of it but the numbers, the vote totals that a candidate needed in each part of the district to win. He understood the science of politics in a way that was quite sophisticated for a candidate in 1978. But he had been working in politics for years. Beyond his dad's races, he'd handled Gerald Ford's presidential run in Midland County in 1976, and he had worked for candidates in Florida and Alabama. From the start, George knew that the numbers were stacked against him, but he also knew that the Nineteenth was a conservative district with an open seat. The election could be very close. It was a "what the heck, why not" run for George. We both knew that we could just as easily live in a Midland ranch house for the rest of our lives as we could move to a Georgetown town house, the kind of place where I imagined that all bright young congressmen and senators resided.

But first we had to make it through the primary.

Because the district was large and sparse, candidates went out to meet the people, and all five of the candidates, the two Democrats, Kent Hance and Morris Sheets, and the three Republicans—George, Jim Reece, and Joe Hickox—would cross paths almost every week. Most of the time it was at local forums, held on the lawns of the county courthouses, the same courthouses that teenage boys and girls would cruise past in endless circles on a Saturday night.

It was in one of these towns, Levelland, Texas, where the land lay every bit as flat as the name, that I gave my first speech, a few months after George's famous pledge to me that I would never have to give a speech. Not ever. It was the only promise he made to me that he ever broke.

George couldn't be at this particular candidate forum, so I went in his place and sat in a folding chair with all the other candidates in front of the courthouse. A local official introduced me, and I got up to give my speech. I planted myself behind the podium, grateful for the heavy, thick wood because my legs were shaking. And then I looked up. Everyone in the audience and even the other candidates were nodding their heads, encouraging me the entire time. When I finished speaking, I wasn't particularly eager to do it again, but it also wasn't nearly as bad as I had anticipated. In fact, it wasn't much different from reading a story to my students. People have an image of a librarian as someone who says, "Shh," but a children's librarian talks all the time and is constantly trying to engage students by reading and telling stories. Suddenly, all my old story hours had a very different use. Out on the campaign trail, I discovered that politics is really about people, and even though I was more reserved than George, I liked meeting the oilmen, the farmers, the moms, and the store owners. I wanted to be with them and listen to their stories.

During the long months before the primary, we got to know Kent Hance, the Democratic front-runner, who was funny and smart and understood in his bones that this was a rural district. Then George won his primary, and Kent won his. And the real hard-nosed politicking began. Kent launched an ad that said, "In 1961, when Kent Hance graduated from Dimmitt High School in the Nineteenth Congressional District, his opponent, George W. Bush, was attending Andover Academy in Massachusetts. In 1965, when Kent Hance graduated from Texas Tech, his opponent was at Yale University. And when Kent Hance graduated from the University of Texas Law School, his opponent—get this, folks—was attending Harvard. We don't need someone from the Northeast telling us what the problems are." Never mind that George had spent nearly half his life in Midland, he couldn't combat the ad. It was devastatingly effective.

On election night, George won 77 percent of the vote in Midland

County. He also won Ector and Andrews, the two other oil-producing counties in the district, but he lost in the cotton-farming sections. George knew he'd lost the race when the Lubbock vote came in. He had not won enough votes in that county. Overall, he lost to Kent Hance by some 6,600 ballots, or about 6 percent of all the votes cast. We were sad but not particularly disappointed. Whatever plans we'd made in our minds, we'd simply have to make new ones. It's a bit, I suppose, like breaking up with a boyfriend. When you are together, you map out your future with that person in your life. When you separate, every plan for that future is changed. But George and I still had each other. We were living in a town where nearly every voter had voted for George, where our friends were, and where my parents lived.

George went back to being a landman in the oil business, going to an office every day, and I began to set up our new home. It was 1979, my thirty-fourth year, and I had no strollers or baby buggies to park in our garage. I was hoping now, with the campaign behind us, all that would change.

Our lives in Midland moved along at much the same pace as our parents' had; men worked, women largely stayed home, and there were dinners out on Friday nights and dinner parties on Saturdays with our circle of friends, Susie and Don Evans, Jan and Joey O'Neill, and Penny and L. E. Sawyer, who had gone to Andover with George and had come to Midland to work in the oil industry. There were times, at first, when I missed campaigning, the thrill of setting off, just the two of us. When George came home and dropped his wet towels on the furniture, I had to remind myself of how terrific he'd been when he gave speeches. I came to overlook the fact that he also wasn't a great handyman around the house. With his usual single-minded focus, George set out to build his small oil business. He had gone from trading land leases to starting an exploration company of his own. But to drill wells, he needed capital, so as much as we were at home in Midland, we were also traveling to other parts of Texas, to New York, even to Scotland, so George could line up investors. And in just a few months, we were back to politics. George Herbert Walker Bush was running for president.

This time, though, I was on the periphery. George left to do some surrogate speaking, but once Ronald Reagan wrapped up the nomination, we returned to our lives in Midland. We didn't even bother to go to Detroit for the Republican convention. Instead, we were in New York. It was a weeknight, and George and I were having dinner with some investors at the "21" Club, waiting like everyone else for the official announcement that Ronald Reagan had selected former president Gerald Ford to be his vice president. Suddenly a couple of white-jacketed waiters muscled a television over to the corner where our group was sitting. The dial was turned to CBS. Correspondent Leslie Stahl reported that George H. W. Bush was Reagan's vice presidential pick. George leapt up from the table to call his dad, and then we raced back to the hotel and left at the crack of dawn the next morning to fly to Detroit. There wasn't a hotel room to be found; we slept on a rollaway in one of George's brothers' rooms. And suddenly, we were back on the campaign trail, this time stumping for Reagan and Bush.

Election night was November 4, my birthday, and we gathered in Houston. I went out to lunch with friends and then went to the Bushes' house on Indian Trail before the family drove to a big hotel ballroom for the results. Reagan-Bush won in a landslide. Days before, many commentators had predicted a second term for Jimmy Carter.

George and I and Regan and Billy and Donnie and Susie flew up to Washington for the inauguration. We sat on the inaugural platform at the back of the Capitol, gazing out at the Washington Monument in the distance as the oaths of office were recited. When the ceremony ended, we were ushered inside to a lunch amid the gleaming marble columns of Statuary Hall. Suddenly, I heard the U.S. Army Strings begin to play, their haunting violins unexpectedly surrounding us, and I gasped. Years later, at my own White House dinners, I would glance around to watch the enthralled expressions of our guests as a procession of strings magically appeared in the State Dining Room.

⌒

George and I now existed in that particularly strange netherworld of celebrity by association. In Midland, cars drove slowly past our house as locals pointed out "this is where Vice President Bush's son lives" to their out-of-town guests. We were vaguely "someone," the children of the famous, while I had the quiet ache of having no children of my own.

For some years now, the wedding invitations that had once crowded the mailbox had been replaced by shower invites and pink- or blue-beribboned baby announcements. I bought onesies and rattles, wrapped them in yellow paper, and delivered them to friends. I had done it with a happy wistfulness, believing that someday my time, my baby, would come. George and I had hoped that I would be pregnant by the end of his congressional run. Then we hoped it would be by the time his own father announced his presidential run, then by the presidential primaries, the convention, the general election. But each milestone came and went. The calendar advanced, and there was no baby.

The English language lacks the words to mourn an absence. For the loss of a parent, grandparent, spouse, child, or friend, we have all manner of words and phrases, some helpful, some not. Still, we are conditioned to say something, even if it is only "I am sorry for your loss." But for an absence, for someone who was never there at all, we are wordless to capture that particular emptiness. For those who deeply want children and are denied them, those missing babies hover like silent, ephemeral shadows over their lives. Who can describe the feel of a tiny hand that is never held?

In the fall of 1980, as the white-hot presidential race was drawing to a close, George and I decided to apply to the Gladney Home in Fort Worth to adopt a baby. We had friends from Midland who had been Gladney babies and other friends who had already adopted their own children from there. Janet and Fred Heyne's daughter and son were Gladney babies. In later years, Susie and Donnie Evans, Jan and Joey O'Neill, and then George's brother Marvin and his wife, Margaret, would all adopt one or more of their children from Gladney.

What became the Gladney Home began in 1887, when a trainload of abandoned children from the northeastern United States arrived in Fort Worth on what was called the "orphan train." Over 150,000 children rode those trains from the East Coast to the Southwest until 1929. Now we were hoping that someone else's child might find a place to be loved in our home. We filled out the paperwork. Mother snapped a photo of us along the fence line of our backyard, George in a brown corduroy jacket, me in a red sweater and pleated pants, our smiles strained but hopeful. Every time I come across that photo, it seems to say, "Please give this couple a baby."

At the same time as we were driving to Fort Worth for our Gladney interview and tour, I started to see Dr. Robert Franklin in Houston, Texas, for hormone treatments. In April of 1981, just as we were waiting for our home visit from Gladney, I discovered that I was pregnant.

I was anxious the entire time that I was pregnant. The memories of Mother's late miscarriages hung over me. And I was thirty-four years old, which in 1981 was considered old for a first-time mother. We had so longed for children and I was so superstitious about this pregnancy that I even avoided the baby aisle of the grocery store. The days and then the weeks passed, but I remained afraid to hope.

Dr. Franklin was also worried that I might miscarry, just as Mother had. The recommended treatment was cervical sutures. George and I headed to Houston for the procedure, our fingers interlaced, our hands clasped together, communicating in that one gesture every hope that we held for all the months to come. While we were in Houston, Dr. Franklin scheduled us for a sonogram, which was a relatively new technology and not at all routine. Our radiologist was a doctor named Srini Malini, and we watched her as she studied the incomprehensible flecks of white scoring the dark gray screen. At last she turned to look at us and said, "There are two babies." George's eyes and mine overflowed.

But Dr. Malini kept staring at the screen.

Her next words were "They are not cojoined." Both of us gasped; we had never envisioned such a thing. My mind began to race with questions, and I asked her to look to see if there were any heart defects, anything associated with Down syndrome. I had already decided against amniocentesis, because we didn't want to tempt the risk of miscarriage. And these were my babies. I would love them however they came. Dr. Malini looked very closely, and then she said, "They're beautiful babies," the words I had longed to hear.

We asked if she could tell whether they were boys or girls. She turned back to the machine and said, "I can tell that the top one is a girl, but I can't see the one underneath as well. I'm pretty sure she's a girl, but I'm not positive."

The next day I had the sutures, and I sat in my hospital bed that night watching the highlights of Prince Charles and Lady Diana's storybook wedding, dreaming of a happy ending of my own. George had a dozen roses delivered to my room and signed the card, "With love, from the father of twins."

When I first learned that I was pregnant, I had pictured two babies in my mind. My next thought was that it's greedy to want two babies, and I berated myself for even thinking such a thing. Now there were going to be two babies, if all went well. One of my friends in Midland was a midwife, and she told me that anyone pregnant with twins should lie down in the morning and again in the afternoon, and I did that. I took Lamaze lessons from my close friend Penny Slade-Sawyer, who was the mother of three boys. I went to the neighboring city of Odessa to see my obstetrician, Dr. Charles Stephens, every three weeks, and my father insisted upon driving me there each time. Then in early November, when I was barely seven months along, Dr. Stephens found the early signs of preeclampsia. My blood pressure was dangerously high. He looked at me with a worried face and said, "I'll never forgive myself if you don't get at least one baby." He wanted me to go to Houston or Dallas, where there were neonatal intensive care units, because he was sure the babies would be born prematurely and might need special care. I chose Baylor Hospital in Dallas because my uncle Mark was a doctor there and the neonatologist, Dr. Delores Carruth, was the mother of twins. George and I booked our flight.

In Dallas, I was admitted to the hospital and put on bed rest. I was determined to give the babies every possible day to develop and grow; I wanted them to have whatever chance I could give them. George was traveling between Dallas and Midland, tending to me, tending to his business, finishing his job as chairman of Midland's United Way charity campaign. But I was not lonely in my hospital room. Barbara Bush scheduled an event in Texas and came to see me, and so did my Dallas friends Pam Nelson and her husband, Bill, and Anne Johnson, the wife of Clay Johnson, one of George's longtime friends from Andover and Yale. Clay and Anne had seven-year-old twin boys of their own. Weldon and Robert visited me one day in my hospital room and soberly counseled, "We were premature and it wasn't that bad."

On November 24, George was back in Midland hosting the final

United Way luncheon when my Baylor doctor, James Boyd, called him and said, "You are going to have your babies tomorrow." George asked him, "Are you sure?" And Dr. Boyd said, "Yes, unless you want your wife's kidneys to fail." My blood pressure was too high, and it was dangerous to continue the pregnancy. George rushed back to Dallas, and at dawn the next morning, I was wheeled into the operating theater for a cesarean section. George was standing next to me as they delivered the babies. Barbara came first at five pounds, four ounces, and Jenna second at four pounds, twelve ounces. They were five weeks early.

We had chosen to name the girls after our mothers, and we did it alphabetically and democratically. The baby who arrived first would be Barbara, the second would be Jenna.

Word was out that the vice president's daughter-in-law would be giving birth at Baylor, and all the television stations from Dallas were waiting at the hospital. One cameraman brazenly walked up to the maternity ward. As I was being wheeled from the operating room, he stepped from behind a wall with his camera. I was swollen with edema from the toxemia and my failing kidneys, and now my postcesarean face was flashed on the local news. It was humiliating. And what was even worse was that I smiled, trying to be accommodating, rather than simply telling him to go away and leave me alone. News photographers snapped pictures of George and the babies so that papers across the country could run the photo with the caption "The vice president's latest grandchildren."

Our girls were here and healthy, and we were thrilled. The country music group the Oak Ridge Boys sent tiny pink sequined jackets. And the jazz great Lionel Hampton sent three vases of red roses to my room, one for me, one for Barbara, and one for Jenna, with a note saying, "Welcome to the world. Lionel Hampton."

And we welcomed them. They were, quite simply, the answer to all our prayers.

⌒

I never saw Dr. Malini after that one visit in Houston, when she showed us the first images of our girls. Then on July 18, 2005, George and I hosted an official dinner at the White House for the Indian prime minister, Mahmohan Singh, and his wife, Gursharan Kaur. The State Dining Room was transformed into an Indian garden, with overflowing vases of orange and red flowers, saffron-hued silk tablecloths, and miniature trumpeting elephants fashioned from hot pink and green mums and roses. For that dinner, one invitation was particularly precious to me. I invited Dr. Malini. When she came through the long receiving line wearing a stunning orange sari, George announced to the prime minister of India that she was the doctor who'd told us we were having twins, that she was the first doctor to see our babies. Dr. Malini laughed and said, "Yes, and I've honored patient confidentiality for all these years. I've never told anyone that I was the one who saw for the first time that you were going to have twins." I sat her at my table, and nothing made me happier than to see her beautiful smile all through dinner. It was such a small thing to give back to someone who had given us so much on that hot and anxious July afternoon.

A few days after the girls were born, Mother and Daddy flew into Dallas to see the babies. Uncle Mark stopped by, and Daddy told him that he was having shoulder pain. Mark immediately went on alert. "I just had a patient who died of lung cancer," he told him, "and his first symptom was shoulder pain. When was your last X-ray?" Daddy hadn't had a chest X-ray in a while. Uncle Mark hustled him off to Radiology. When the films came back, the radiologist didn't see anything, but Uncle Mark did. It was a tiny spot, the kind of shadow that perhaps only a brother would have seen. He pointed to it and asked the radiologist, "What about this?" I had just given birth to twins, and my father was being diagnosed with lung cancer. He and Mother headed back to Midland to pack for a long hospital stay. Daddy's only hope of beating the disease was if surgeons removed part of his lung.

Joey O'Neill's dad offered to send his private plane to pick George and me and the girls up when we were finally released from the hospital, in mid-December. It saved us a six-hour drive or a commercial flight with two premature babies. When the plane left Midland for Dallas, my mother and daddy were onboard. Daddy was coming to Baylor for his surgery; I was leaving to return home to Midland. I don't remember what we said to each other; I was too overwhelmed. Life and death were balanced on the span of those two aluminum wings.

George and I arrived home, and we were on our own. While I had been at Baylor, my friends had hosted a baby shower for me and had set up the nursery. I hadn't even decorated a room or shopped for baby clothes because I was afraid to prepare for a future that might not come to pass. Now I had armfuls of diapers and tiny clothes and bottles, and I was completely overwhelmed. George and I had no experience with babies, and suddenly we had two, who seemed to cry all the time. I longed for my own mother, but she was with Daddy, first in the hospital and then for his long convalescence at home. Friends came over to help set up our Christmas tree.

For months, I had secretly daydreamed of sitting under the Christmas tree with George and our two wonderful babies, like some storybook tableau. Instead, we were bleary-eyed and nervous, trying to soothe howling twins. Some nights, we put them in their cribs and literally ran to the other side of the house, hoping for an hour of quiet. Eventually, driven by exhaustion and inexperience, we hired a baby nurse to help us get up with the girls in the middle of the night and to give us a chance to ever so briefly leave the house. After the girls were in their cribs, we would take long walks around Midland in the chilly wintry darkness, arm in arm.

Christmas came and went, and we adjusted. We got the girls on a strict routine. We fed them both at the same time, even in the middle of the night. We put them down early, and they woke up early, and I had them nap in the mornings and afternoons. I believe very strongly in the importance of sleep for all children, but especially for premature babies, whose brains are still growing and developing. After the initial crying and the trauma of us trying to adjust to them and them simply trying to adjust to the world, both girls became happy babies. And George and I discovered a wonderful symmetry in having twins; there was always a baby for one of us to hold. Every morning before dawn, George would get up to make the coffee, as he had done from the start of our marriage; then he would go get the girls and carry them into our bed. We'd each hold a baby and drink our coffee while they drank their bottles, with the morning news droning quietly in the background. The start of the day was reserved for just the four of us. Those early mornings were some of the sweetest times of our lives.

In the afternoons, even in the frigid winters or broiling summers, I would push the girls in their stroller around the sidewalks of Midland. I adored those walks through the daytime quiet in the same neighborhood where my family's "Big House" had been, where each yard or square of sidewalk held a childhood memory of my own. At the end of our walks, we passed a large, frosted globe light planted atop a post on a neighbor's front lawn. One afternoon Barbara lifted up her little hand, pointed, and said, "Moon." We had been reading *Goodnight Moon* at bedtime, and she thought this white orb was the moon rising on her street.

I still worried, though. The doctors had told me that many premature babies have eye problems, so when they were around six months old, I took both girls to an eye specialist, who waved a penlight around the room and had them follow it with their eyes. He told me they were very alert girls, and I breathed a relieved sigh. They crawled early and walked by age one. But I still remember the couple of days when Barbara acted listless. I bundled her off to Dr. Dorothy Wyvell, who had been my pediatrician and who had treated the Bush children. Every child in Midland seemed to have been poked, prodded, and tongue-depressed by Dr. Wyvell. She had gray hair now, and she remained strikingly blunt. She did an exam, ordered some tests, and looked at me. "I know why you're worried," she said. "It's to be expected." With that, she pronounced Barbara fine. Dr. Wyvell was the one who had diagnosed George's little sister Robin's leukemia when she was three and had told Barbara and George Bush that there was nothing they could do but make her comfortable. Leukemia was fatal, Dr. Wyvell explained, and she would slip away in a matter of weeks. Robin spent most of the next six months in Sloan-Kettering in New York, pumped full of transfusions on the slim hope of a cure before she died.

At home, I bought a baby food grinder and made all the girls' meals from scratch. Later, when we went out to eat Mexican food on Friday nights, we would bring the girls, and they would sit in their high chairs eating beans and rice. After those years of living just the two of us, I was happy to have a home with baby toys strewn across the floor and crawling and toddling twins, exploring every nook and cranny of their world.

Daddy recovered from his surgery, and he and Mother began to drop by all the time to see the babies. Daddy's favorite time to arrive was right after lunch, just when I'd put the girls down for a nap. He would knock on the door, open it wide, and loudly call, "Laura, are the babies awake?" They invariably heard him, and once they could pull themselves up, they would be standing in their cribs beaming when their grandfather opened the door. He loved to hold them on his lap, their two little bald heads and his big one bent over together. We spent our Christmases with Mother and Daddy, and the girls clamored to go to Mother and Daddy's house on Halloween, to trick-or-treat there first. Mother brought pink-frosted cupcakes on Valentine's Day, and we set up Easter egg hunts. Barbara scoured the grass and bushes and found the most eggs. She was a young collector, with mounds of colored eggs clutched in her hands and pressed tightly against her chest. Jenna was our homebody. When we were selling the town house on Golf Course to move to a larger ranch-style house on Harvard Avenue, she got on her tricycle and pinned one prospective buyer inside our little concrete backyard. As fast as her feet could push, Jenna rode in tight circles around the woman's legs until she could hardly take a step. Jenna was determined to defend her home against intruders at all costs.

Both girls were early talkers. I would repeat to them, "Say 'Daddy,'" and "Daddy" was their first word, which thrilled George. I've long thought that it's a smart thing for mothers to do, to teach their children the word "Daddy" first.

George loved being a dad. He changed diapers when the girls were small. He got up at night to help feed them their bottles. He would come home and think of adventures. One night, when a rare Midland snow had started to fall and the girls had just turned three, he announced after dinner that we were going for a snow walk. We bundled the girls in their jackets and trooped off in the darkness, and as the snow shimmered under the glinting streetlights, we held up our faces to feel the flakes land one by one. And he loved to play with his daughters. Some weekends, we would head to Donnie and Susie Evans's house on Lake Travis outside of Austin, and the dads would play El Tigre with the kids at night, under the stars and the moon. The kids would run around the cedar brush and the dads—George, Donnie, and Charlie Younger, another good friend from Midland—would chase them and growl or roar. Somehow, the kids always managed to hide from or outwit El Tigre. Once, George, Donnie, and Charlie were creeping underneath the branches of live oaks when they spooked an owl that took off screeching into the air. That bird gave the three Tigres more of a scare than they ever gave the kids.

Another of our good friends, Mike Weiss, later told me that George had taught him how to play with his own kids. "My dad never played with me," he told me once. "George taught me how to be funny, how to have fun with them and have a good time."

Our lives in those years in Midland were centered on our family and our friends. Often, Mother and Daddy would come for dinner. I would call Mother late in the afternoon to see what she was cooking, and we would put our meals together around our little table. I remember one summer evening, working in the flower beds in our yard after the girls had gone to sleep, while the sun still hung low in the sky. George was sitting on the steps with the newspaper, and I thought to myself, This is the life. And it was.

For the first four years that George's dad was vice president, we rarely went to Washington. In the late spring of 1984, the Bushes came to Midland for a reelection rally for Reagan-Bush. We met their motorcade at the airport and rode in with the girls in the fleet of sleek black limousines. As we wound our way along the loop road, past the new acres of warehouses and strip mall buildings toward downtown Midland, cars slowed down and pulled over. Dozens of Midland drivers thought we were a funeral procession heading to the cemetery.

But that physical distance also meant that we were the outliers on the Bush family curve. We were not with them for Christmas, only for summer visits in Maine, with all the other cousins and meals for a small army of Bushes and wet beach towels strewn about the Kennebunkport house. George's parents had no time for drop-by visits to our home. Once, when the girls were two and a half, Bar Bush made a rare stop in Midland. Jenna and Barbara ran out of the house with their arms held out to greet her, calling "Ganny," the name all Bushes give their grandmothers, and she looked up at me and said with gratitude, "Thank you for teaching your girls to know me."

I always hoped I would have more babies. But I was thirty-five when the girls were born. The years unwound and it didn't happen. George never once said that he wanted more children. He never once said that he would have liked a son. He has always been thrilled with the two girls we got. We both are. But my heart was deep enough for more. There remained that twinge of what might have been.

Some 300 million years ago, the oceans overran much of the earth's land. The place I know as West Texas was nothing more than a vast floor at the bottom of the tepid Permian Sea. Slowly, over the millennia, the waters began to recede. Reefs and shell banks collapsed into dry ground. Twelve thousand feet of sand, limestone, and silica were left behind by the sea's ebb, collecting in what is known as the Permian Basin. Then the water swept in one last time. Clay and limestone, prehistoric boulders and debris were strewn across the valley, producing a long, continuous plain, with the remnants of this ancient sea floor buried underneath. And among the fossilized fish and shells and curious spiny creatures that once plumbed its depths, pools of oil and pockets of natural gas formed. The roughly 100,000 square miles of Permian Basin land in West Texas and New Mexico are thought to hold significant portions of the United States' oil and natural gas reserves. Midland, Texas, sits in the basin's geographic center. When oil was found, Midland was where the oilmen came.

The inhabitants of the Texas plains had long known about petroleum. They were not as resourceful as the ancient Egyptians, who covered their mummified bodies in pitch, or the Babylonians (who built their kingdom in what is now Iraq), who employed it to pave their streets. But occasionally native Indian tribes wandered past oil springs and tar pits; their healers and medicine men sometimes spread the black oozings over achy joints and sores on the skin in hope of a cure. The Indians taught the early settlers to do the same, and on the range, ground oil was used for lubricating wagon wheels.

Although the first Texas oil well was dug in 1866, only in 1901 did men succeed in finding an oil gusher. Midland's first oil boom occurred during the 1920s. It sputtered back to life partway through the Great Depression. The 1950s were its golden age, the 1960s its crash. But by the mid-1970s, Midland had begun to rebound. The Arab oil embargo and long gas lines sent oil companies flocking back to Midland. Cranes dotted the skyline, sleek glass buildings rose along the downtown streets, and by 1983 only three other cities in the entire state of Texas had built more office space than Midland. Money followed. From 1974 to 1981, Midland's bank deposits rose from $385 million to nearly $2 billion. The most successful oilmen bought private planes and Mercedeses or outsize Cadillacs. They teed off at the country club in the middle of a weekday afternoon and gambled outrageous sums on every hole. Their wives glittered with diamonds. There were ranches bought in other states, second homes, and jet rides for an afternoon of shopping in Dallas at Neiman Marcus. People planned spectacular parties and flew in the bands and the caterers. Rolls-Royce opened a Midland showroom. So many newcomers flocked to the city to get into the oil business that Midland literally ran out of room; it was impossible to find a vacant house.

George and I lived a life far removed from this extravagant wealth. Our biggest indulgence was a membership in the Midland Country Club, although George did earn enough that I had the luxury of being able to stay home with the girls.

Still, living in Midland in 1982 was like having drawn up a chair to a card game where the bettors at the table held a flush in every hand.

George started in the oil business as a landman. He had moved to Midland in 1975 after he graduated from Harvard Business School. He spent hours combing courthouse records to determine who owned the mineral rights on a particular tract of land, which could be leased for oil well drilling.

After he lost his 1978 congressional race, he started a small, independent oil exploration business, Arbusto Energy (*arbusto* is "bush" in Spanish). Independent oilmen find and drill new wells. When prices are high, the risks are good ones. In the early 1970s, a West Texas oil driller had a one in fifty shot of hitting a small oil field, a one in one thousand chance of striking a big one. But at the start of 1983, oil prices in Texas plunged.

A barrel of West Texas crude lost five dollars in a single week in January. As opposed to twenty-six or twenty-eight dollars a barrel, it was now just over nineteen. The Midland banks were the first to fail. George walked into First National Bank on the morning of its demise. Mr. Cowden, the descendent of one of Midland's first ranching families, was standing in the gray marble lobby pleading with his depositors not to withdraw their funds. His weathered face taut with emotion, he promised them, "Your money is safe here. Please don't take your money. Your money is safe." But the line of customers stretched across the lobby and down the block as people waited to cash out their holdings. By the time the final slip had been passed to a teller, the bank's last cent was all but gone. In a concluding touch of irony, First National, the largest independent bank in the state, had been chartered back in 1890, during the cattle days, after the devastating drought of 1886 and 1887. Cowboys who rode the range to round up what animals remained called it the "Great Die-off." Ranches were abandoned from the Rio Grande to the farthest reaches of the Great Plains. After that disaster, three Midlanders, including John Scharbauer, whose family later built the fancy downtown hotel, chartered a bank designed to see cattlemen through the "bad times." Slightly less than a hundred years later, Midland's First National would not survive this one.

George was anxious about the future of his own small company and his seven employees. He merged with another, larger company, Spectrum 7, in 1984. Oil prices briefly stabilized, then dropped again. We watched as drilling rigs went idle one by one. The top owners lost their vacation homes, their jets, even the desks and the few spanking-new computers that had been in their now-empty buildings. Moving trucks pulled up to downtown towers, and the contents of entire offices were carted out by burly men. The remnants of prosperity were bundled off to warehouses and sold for cents on the dollar at periodic public auctions. But it wasn't just the wealthy oilmen. Oil drilling is built on a scaffold of engineers, geologists, scientists, pipeline men, and roughnecks, pumpers, and roust-abouts out in the field. They were among the first to be let go. Families picked up and fled, houses sat for months, even years, unsold. I'd see the signs planted on lawns, or swinging forlornly from posts as I drove around. Friends, acquaintances, and stalwarts around Midland edged toward ruin. The "big oil" I knew were the people who worked at decent jobs, who bought homes, sent their children to school, prayed in church, and pushed their shopping carts down the supermarket aisle next to mine.

With that peculiar West Texas pluck, car bumpers sported stickers that read: "Please, Lord, let there be another boom. I promise I won't piss it away next time." George took a 25 percent pay cut, shaved whatever costs he could, and tried to hang on.

We had already been going to church since before the girls were born; it was where I felt, at last, the gentle embrace of faith again. Now some of our friends, like Don Evans and Don Jones, started a Wednesday-night Bible study for men. George was one of the first to begin attending.

One summer during college, I had a date with a boy in Midland. We'd gone downtown to see the Summer Mummers, the local theater group, perform, and he was driving me home. During the show, he had con-stantly refilled his frosted glass from a pitcher of beer. I had paid no atten-tion until we were in the car. His face was flushed, and his eyes shone like glass. He drove me back home without stopping at a single red light or slowing for a stop sign. We screeched through the streets of Midland, and I gripped my seat until my knuckles were white, and I could feel rivulets of sweat sliding down my skin. Whenever the engine slackened, I wondered if I could simply open the door and jump out, leaving him and the car to sail on alone. We made it to my front door, but I was shaking. Yet after I was back at SMU, I still got in cars with people who had been drinking, because that was just what everyone did.

Midland was a drinking town. After Prohibition was repealed, Midland County remained largely dry; residents repeatedly voted against allowing alcohol sales. But that only changed how people drank. Range-weary cow-boys drank; cattlemen, railroad men, oilmen coming in from the fields, all of them drank. But so did the operators, the engineers and scientists and geologists who came after that. For years, liquor and mixed drinks couldn't be served in restaurants, but private clubs could pour a drink straight from the bottle, so people joined clubs, especially country clubs, where their individual "bottles" could be kept in their lockers. Vodka, bourbon, scotch, gin, anything with a kick, came out, glass after glass. Those who didn't join clubs, like my father, simply drove to package stores at the county line and carried out their bottles in brown paper bags. At Johnny's Bar-B-Q, Daddy could pour his own drinks from Johnny's private stash in the kitchen.

All through my growing up, adults hosted dinner parties laced with cocktails and finished with nightcaps. More than once, men and women would weave their way from the hostess's front steps to their cars and drive home. My mother rarely drank, and certainly not to excess. She might nurse a Tom Collins through an evening. But my father drank every night. On the weekends, he and his buddies would watch football, betting on the games and mixing martinis or pouring generous fingers of bourbon. During the week, the downtown men usually ordered cocktails with their lunches behind the thick walls of the Petroleum Club.

Women drank too. I remember one girl I knew in high school who we all thought was wild and who had a bad reputation. Twenty years later, back in Midland, I was working on the high school reunion committee. She came and told us that throughout high school, her mother had been falling-down drunk in her house. But in Midland, no one talked about those things. Any escape had to be her own.

Two decades out, almost nothing had changed. We were wealthier than our parents, we were less frugal because none of us had been scarred by a depression, but we were living much the same lives—dinners out on Friday, dinner parties in on Saturday—and alcohol was part of each one.

On Fridays, we usually ate Mexican food, and the women drank margaritas and the men drank beer. On Saturdays, it was dinner at someone's home, usually a barbecue where everyone would bring something— appetizers, salads, desserts. And alcohol. There was wine, there was vodka, and there were mixed drinks, and we drank them. My father, who was retired, now liked to have a martini with lunch and a bourbon or two with dinner. George drank the three Bs, a bourbon before dinner, a beer with dinner, and then B & B, a sweet after-dinner drink. It was lethal, and it was completely accepted because that, or some version of it, was the drinking life of most men. At parties as the night deepened, the men grew louder, the cut of their jokes sharpened, and they laughed at everything. In many homes, the morning began with coffee and aspirin. George would go for a run. He is an incredibly disciplined athlete, and he ran every day, even at lunchtime in the summer, when the sun seemed to stand still atop Midland. He ran and he sweated out the dregs of the alcohol. But come nightfall, he'd pour another drink.

He didn't have three drinks every night; many times all he had was a beer. But when he'd poured enough, he could be a bore. Maybe it's funny when other people's husbands have had too much to drink at a party, but I didn't think it was funny when mine did. And I told him so. But I never said the line "It's either Jim Beam or me." That joke came much later. I was not going to leave George, and I wasn't going to let him leave me with twins. Our marriage was enduring, we loved each other, and we were two people who did not have divorce in our DNA. But I was disappointed. And I let him know that I thought he could be a better man.

In 1986, we planned a July trip to the Broadmoor in Colorado Springs to celebrate our fortieth birthdays, George's, mine, and Don and Susie Evans's. Jan and Joey O'Neill came, and so did our good friend Penny Slade-Sawyer. Neil Bush, George's younger brother who lived in Colorado, came too. The men played golf, and the women sunned by the pool. And on the last night, everyone, especially the men, ordered too much to drink at the bar. I heard the same toast repeated twenty times. I've joked that George quit the next day because he got the bar bill, but it was a combination of things. It was the fact of turning forty; it was the fact of his father being the vice president and the expectation that Mr. Bush would run for president. None of the Bush children ever wanted to do anything to embarrass their dad. But it was also having talked with Billy Graham the summer he turned thirty-nine, when we were visiting his parents in Maine, and it was joining that Wednesday-night Bible study in Midland, which fixed George's mind on a higher purpose. It was living through an oil bust when people we knew had lost everything and recognizing that failures are best met head-on, clear-eyed. And some of it was growing into being a father and a husband. There had been many drunken and half-drunken weekends, there was nothing particularly out of the ordinary about this one, except that it was one weekend too many. It was to be the last one.

When George decided that he was done with alcohol, he never complained, he just stopped drinking. And he was surprised by how quickly he felt better, by how great it is to wake up in the morning when you haven't had a drink the night before. He ran better, he read better. We had always taken books to bed and read at night, but George never read for very long. Now reading became a pleasure for him again.

We kept going to the same parties, but George would have a nonalcoholic beer. And gradually, many of our friends stopped or slowed their drinking, one after being stopped for drunken driving, another after a stay at the Betty Ford clinic. Others just put away their bottles and six-packs and moved on. One friend told me, after she had joined AA and progressed through the twelve steps to the one for making amends, that she had driven Barbara and Jenna to their art lessons after she had been drinking. I had seen her, waved to them as she got behind the wheel, and had never known. A few of the heaviest drinkers who didn't quit, women and men, are in their sixties now, and my heart breaks at how much they are struggling.

Years after George quit, as Mother and I sat talking one quiet afternoon, she turned and said that, unlike me, she had never thought to ask Daddy to stop drinking.

Although George H. W. Bush was in his second term as vice president, George and I had not been invited to a single state dinner. We read newspaper accounts of the Reagans' black-tie evenings, where the women wore long, shimmering gowns and strappy high heels and everyone toasted equally elegant foreign guests. Once, George's dad did ask, "Have y'all been invited to a state dinner?" And George and I both said no. He immediately promised that we would receive an invitation. Months passed. George finally said, "Dad, I thought we were going to be invited to a state dinner." He replied, "Oh no, I said a *steak* dinner." We all laughed and assumed that our invitation would never come as the Reagan administration ticked toward a close. Then, a lovely embossed envelope with the perfect pen-and-ink calligraphy arrived, inviting us to a state dinner at the White House. It was one of the last dinners that the Reagans held. And it was on the same day the movers were coming to our house to load our boxes and start on the journey up to Washington, D.C. George H. W. Bush, the man our children called Gampy, was going to run for president, and his campaign manager, Lee Atwater, had asked George to move to Washington to work on his father's race. We were leaving Midland.

I had been working with the movers for over a month to arrange everything. Traveling to Washington for the dinner would require two plane flights and considerable expense. It seemed impossible to change our dates and rearrange everything. I called the White House's social secretary to decline, and she made a surprised sound into the other end of the phone.

Indeed, during the first Reagan-Bush term, when George and I were invited to a Sunday-afternoon concert performed by Itzhak Perlman, we had decided to make a special trip to Washington. George packed his nicest suit; I had a fancy dress. We were both nervous about going to the White House. Inside, women gingerly picked their way along the slick marble stairs and halls. My eyes wandered, taking in the velvet and brocade and the heavy wooden tables and carved chairs, the high ceilings and glittering chandeliers, and the crush of far more elegantly dressed people in each room. We sat on gold banquet chairs that had been precisely arranged in rows across the East Room, with a special roped-off section for the most important dignitaries, and waited patiently in the receiving line to shake President and Mrs. Reagan's hands. When the military aides announced us, both George and I were speechless. We smiled and stayed mute, having no idea what to say. Now, after years of receiving lines, I'm grateful for the people who don't say anything except "I'm so happy to be here," and just keep moving. It can take hours for the president and the first lady to shake all those hands.

Before the movers came, we had a big yard sale. I sold off furniture, books, baby clothes and toys, almost anything that wasn't nailed down. Susie and Donnie Evans helped us tag everything, including the baby beds and baby

Me, about age three, in front of one of the houses
that Daddy built on Estes Avenue.

My mother, Jenna Louise Hawkins,
age ten, in Canutillo, Texas, near El Paso.

My father's first photo, taken in 1913,
when he was nearly one. With him are his
brother, Mark; father, Mark Anthony Welch;
and mother, Mary Lula Lane Welch.

My mother and her mother,
Jessie Laura Sherrard, dressed up
to visit El Paso.

My mother with her future husband,
Harold Welch, and her father,
Hal Hawkins.

The photo of my mother that my father
carried across Europe during World War II.

My father's photos from the Nazi death camp
at Nordhausen, which his unit helped liberate
in 1945. American GIs found five thousand bodies;
survivors often lay beside the dead. For years
we kept these photos in a cigar box. My father
never wanted to speak about Nordhausen.

My parents' wedding photo.
Daddy said the war caused him to lose his hair.

Mother holding me.

Me on Grandma Welch's lap. She was
a sturdy woman with heavy, lace-up shoes.

Reading with mother.

Our house on Princeton Avenue.

Me, about age twelve.

My high school graduation photo,
age seventeen. Born in November,
I was always the youngest in my class.

With my father and Marty
the dog by the Christmas tree
when I was a teacher in Houston.

George and me with his parents on our wedding day.
We had a small Saturday-morning wedding. (Frank Miller)

Having Jenna and Barbara
was the answer to our prayers.

My father with the girls.

Reading *'Twas the Night Before Christmas* in 1985.

Bar Bush casts a wary eye on Jenna during a 1984 Reagan-Bush rally in Midland. (White House photo)

The 1988 White House Easter Egg Roll. (White House photo)

Trick-or-treating on Gampy's 1988 campaign plane.
George and I made Jenna's costume. (White House photo)

Reading with the girls in Dallas. When they were born, George and I
loved that we each had a baby to hold. (Photo © Barbara Laing)

things that we had kept in storage for so long, and set it out on our front lawn. We were shedding our life of almost ten years. Some things we got rid of I wish I'd kept, like an old Ronald Reagan movie poster that we had framed. I don't know what possessed me to sell it, just the frenzy of divesting ourselves.

I've always traveled light; I look back on over thirty years of marriage, and aside from shelves of scrapbooks and books, we've accumulated startlingly few things. As we've moved, we've donated or given away many of our furniture pieces and rugs, even posters and paintings. I prefer to keep memories rather than things. Some of it is my dislike of clutter and its complications. Some of it comes from being a librarian, when I had to manage a collection. I had to catalog each piece, check bindings and repair tears; I culled the volumes, removing copies that had grown too tattered or worn. Every object had to pass through my fingertips. It has made me wary of the responsibility of too many things.

We set off for Washington with a small moving van and our Pontiac sedan and Chevy station wagon, leaving behind our friends and our home. I had never lived outside of Texas for more than a few weeks. I was forty-one years old. For more than twenty-five of those years, Midland had been my home; for more than twenty years, it had been George's. It was not just the pan-flat arid land that we were leaving behind with each mile of road but a way of being and of speaking. People in West Texas believe that they think differently, and to a large degree they do. There is a plainness to the way West Texas looks that translates into how people act and what they value. Those who live there are direct and blunt to the point of hurt sometimes. There is no time for artifice; it looks and sounds ridiculous amid the barren landscape. From the era of the first settlers, people or animals could freeze or starve or roast if debates went on too long or too many niceties were observed.

The West Texas plains were seared on each of us like an invisible brand. I am struck sometimes by the words spoken by Ten Bears, the Great Comanche war chief, as he pleaded with Abraham Lincoln's men not to force his people onto a reservation: "I was born upon the prairie, where the wind blew free, and there was nothing to break the light of the sun. I was born where there were no enclosures, and where everything drew a free breath." And how similar his words sound to the rougher-edged lament of the cattlemen—the same men who had driven the Comanches from their land. As he grew old, the Midland rancher W. C. Cochran wrote, "For anyone who loved God's own creation, it was a paradise on earth. . . . The hills and valleys abounded with deer, turkey, bear, and antelope. Bee trees were numerous and buffalo common. . . . Every old-timer cowman remembers these times. The wire fences took all the joy and thrill out of the cow business for the old boys, who remembered when they used to sit around camp and talk about who had the best horses and play a little ten cent ante when it was not their night to ride fifteen or twenty miles. Those good old days passed away with the coming of the wire fence."

Out on that range, people adapted to the land; the land contoured them, not the other way around.

We left Midland, but never truly left it behind. And it invariably found us. After George was elected governor, he chose as his official desk an old oak piece that had belonged to his father. He was sure it had been his dad's congressional desk, and George had a brass plaque made identifying it as the desk of Rep. George H. W. Bush. The desk was installed at the Texas Capitol, and when his father first saw it, he laughed. That desk had never been to Congress. A young oilman named George H. W. Bush had bought it for a hundred dollars, secondhand, on a sidewalk in downtown Midland.

I arrived in Washington a day early and headed for the vice president's residence, to spend one night before I was to move us into a town house that George and I had bought near American University. My good friend Lynn Munn flew up to help me move in. Lynn is the sort of person who makes sure every box is unpacked and every picture is hung before anyone goes to bed that first night. We were up at 6:00 A.M. I went to the bathroom to put in my contacts and promptly washed one down the drain. I shut off the water immediately and knew that the contact was probably caught in the trap. We called the Navy stewards who manage the vice president's residence. They said perhaps they could call a plumber or someone else to help later in the morning. Gampy heard all the commotion and, still in his bathrobe, went downstairs, got a wrench, came back up to the bathroom, and proceeded to take off the trap and rescue my contact. Lynn later said that any man who would take a sink trap off for his daughter-in-law at six in the morning without a word of complaint deserved to be president.

We moved into our town house, and George began working on the campaign. After his father lost the Iowa primary, George flew into D.C. exhausted and, dropping his bag in the hall, said, "Well, we may be going home soon. But just where is home?"

Gampy won New Hampshire, and we stayed. But we stayed on a bit like squatters, aware that every day was temporary, that November would come, and soon after, win or lose, we would return to Texas. We were tourists that year, visiting the Lincoln Memorial in the Friday night dark, heading across the Potomac to George Washington's Mount Vernon home on Saturdays. We ice-skated downtown with the girls, watching them spin and fall in the now vanished rink near the old Willard Hotel. Once Jenna spun and crashed into a wall in front of a reporter for *The Dallas Morning News*. The girls were five years old when we arrived, and I enrolled them in the local public school, Horace Mann Elementary, where their teacher was Ms. Davis, an African-American woman from Midland, Texas. We walked to school each morning, past the cherry blossoms and the dogwoods and the flowering trees that leafed out each spring.

Many of our Texas friends came to visit and brought their children, and George and I would chauffeur them around for weekend tours, until we knew the monuments and memorials and the Mount Vernon gardens almost as well as the cross streets in Midland. Because Gampy, as vice president, was also president of the Senate, we regularly toured the Capitol and ate in the Senate Dining Room, where prices seemed to have frozen circa 1962 and where my father, during a visit, gladly reached for the check. We even got that coveted state dinner invitation to an evening in honor of President Chaim Herzog of Israel. But what was more unexpected for George and me was the relationship we formed with his parents amid the whirling chaos of a presidential campaign.

When I married George, I had thought that I would be embraced by his mother every bit as much as he was embraced by mine. I had planned on being more a daughter than a daughter-in-law, but Barbara Bush had five children of her own. She was their defender first. What I came to see ultimately as our bond was that we both loved George, and the depth of our love was what we had in common. Beyond that, we had little contact. I saw her during those harried Maine vacations, when the onslaught of adult children, their spouses and companions, and then their children often drove her to distraction—she is only partially kidding when she says that, when all else fails, follow the directions on the aspirin bottle: take two and keep away from children. I look back now through album photographs, at everyone grouped together, smiling gamely for the camera, and someone always looks as if he or she is about to cry. In a number of photos, the person on the verge of tears is Bar.

But from the start, she was also ferociously tart-tongued. She's never shied away from saying what she thinks, right up through Gampy's jump out of an airplane on his eighty-fifth birthday, in June of 2009. He was set to land on the lawn next to St. Ann's Church in Kennebunkport, and Bar said, "If the jump doesn't go well, it will be convenient. We can wheel him straight into his eternal resting place." I was with Bar in the mid-1990s when people would come up to us in a store or a restaurant in Kennebunkport and say, "I know you," thinking they'd met her somewhere, and her response was "No, you don't. You don't know me." She's even managed to insult nearly all of my friends with one or another perfectly timed acerbic comment. Once, one of them, Lois Betts, called her on it, and Bar was truly chagrined.

After our wedding had passed, I barely heard from Bar, until 6:30 one weekday morning a few weeks after George's losing campaign. His brother Neil had moved to Midland to help out on the race and, when the election ended, had returned to Houston, leaving most of his belongings behind. Now Neil was off to graduate school, and Bar wanted me to collect Neil's things, box them up, and ship them to Houston. With that, she was off the phone. I had my marching orders, and I was fuming as I drove around locating Neil's things in the places he had stayed, as well as rounding up big boxes from the supermarket. There were no pack-and-ship stores back then. I gathered, folded, and boxed everything, and carted it all to the bus station, irritation washing over me. Of course, here I was, the girl who had longed for brothers and sisters, who had always vowed that I would never be like my friends and complain about a sibling, and now I was doing precisely that.

So I was a bit apprehensive about moving to Washington, where we would be living within walking distance of the senior Bushes and George would effectively be working for his dad.

But a decade after my marriage, Bar Bush and I finally got to know each other. We both loved reading and shared our favorite books. One morning, just as I had finished reading a review of a new art exhibition at the National Museum of Women in the Arts, my phone rang. It was Bar, who had just read the same review and wanted to rush down and see it. By 9:00 A.M., we were out the door, en route to the gallery. And Sundays became our family days. No matter how frenzied the campaign trail, both Bushes made sure that they were home together in the vice president's residence each Sunday afternoon. George and the girls and I would walk over for Sunday lunch. After years apart, George's parents got to know their son as an adult, and we had a window of time for us to be a small family, two people from each generation. The girls got to know their grandparents not as flickering images on a TV screen but as people who loved them. Gampy pushed them in a wooden swing hung from a tree on the grounds, and on rare nights off, he and Bar volunteered to babysit. At last, I saw Bar for who she is, a funny, warm woman and a mother who is devoted to her husband and her children. Away from that overflowing Maine summer house and the conventions and inaugurations, those high-profile, high-pitched events where Gampy's political career was on the line, Bar and I came to know and love each other.

We still had plenty of high-profile events to come. The entire family gathered for the Republican convention in New Orleans, where Jenna and Barbara had the most fun swimming in the big hotel pool and watching *Ghostbusters* on the hotel television. That fall, we all hit the campaign trail. The girls and I joined Gampy for one trip on Halloween. In between plane stops, the crew cued scary music over the loudspeaker, and Barbara was dressed as a vampire, Jenna as a pack of Juicy Fruit gum. They trick-or-treated down the aisles among the unprepared press corps, who dug into their pockets to hand out pennies, pieces of gum, and a stray Life Saver or Cert for their sacks.

After eight years of Reagan-Bush, it was now George H. W. Bush at the top alone. Gampy won his election. I remember Jeb Bush saying a year or two later, "How great is this country, that it could elect a man as fine as our dad to be its president?"

For George and me, it was time to find a new place to call home.

⌁

When we married, George could recite the lineup from leading major-league baseball teams circa 1950. He can still do it today. His great-uncle had been a part owner of the Mets, and while George worked in oil, he had dreamed in baseball. One of his favorite movies was *Brewster McCloud*, simply because the lead character lived in an apartment in the walls of the Houston Astrodome. One evening, he burst into our house in Midland and announced that the Astros were for sale for $17 million. But George couldn't trade oil leases for the Astros the way he had for furniture, and what he had to trade wouldn't have gotten us much beyond a couple of pairs of season tickets. His baseball dreams were lived over the airwaves, and the Astros tortured us from the sidelines. When they made the play-offs, George would race home from work and we'd sit on our bed and watch the Astros raise our hopes and then dash them, inning after inning, game by game. Growing up in Midland, I did not follow baseball all that much; my father had bet on football, and for years, Texas didn't have its own baseball teams. People rooted for Chicago or St. Louis, franchises in other places. But my dad did take me to watch the Lee High School team when it made the state championships in Austin, and baseball games were a kind of background music to our life in Midland. In the sweltering summer heat, there was always a radio humming in a corner with the game. But it was with George that I learned to love the intricacies of baseball.

One of George's partners in the oil business was a man named Bill DeWitt, whose family had owned the Cincinnati Reds back when owning a baseball team was more of a mom-and-pop business. When George and Bill got together, they would spin a world in which they owned a baseball team and could sit in the stands to cheer for it. Like Kevin Costner in the middle of those rows of Iowa corn, they had their own little field of dreams.

When the Texas Rangers came up for sale in the late fall of 1988, Bill DeWitt was on the phone.

Suddenly, he and George were putting together a group to buy the team, and we were moving to Dallas. It wasn't politics; it was sports and a game we now both loved. The first thing I put in my desk calendar each year was a list of the Texas Rangers' home games, and we sat in the stands for nearly every one.

There is a loveliness to baseball that is only found in a stadium, that never quite conveys across the coaxial cables and pixels of a television screen. In a world of hyperspeeds, the game is long and slow and methodical until some explosive hit sends the players on the field into utter pandemonium and brings the crowd to its feet. And baseball was one of the few activities that could draw us outside in the summer. Dallas summers are woven out of crushing heat, weeks of one-hundred-plus-degree days that begin cooking the concrete the first minute after sunrise. Except for those brave or robust enough to work outside, most of the city moves among air-conditioned homes, cars, and office buildings, where the climate is always a preset seventy-two degrees. Baseball forces a person to confront the elements and the weather; it forced us into nature. And at night, under the floodlights, sometimes a brief touch of cool would descend, and the innings would drift past us as we sat behind the batter's box. I could talk to George, talk to the people sitting around us, and watch the game. In the stands, we cemented rich friendships with our partners, Rusty and Deedie Rose, Tom and Susanne Schieffer, Roland and Lois Betts, Tom and Andi Bernstein, and our cousins Craig and Debbie Stapleton. In the summers, I loved to take the girls. Often, by the seventh inning, they would retreat to an unsold suite above, and when the sounds of "Cotton-Eyed Joe" came over the loudspeaker for the seventh-inning stretch, I would turn and look up at them, holding hands and dancing the two-step in that empty box.

Those nights were like prolonged exhalations, as we looked out on the grass and the mound and the sandy baselines.

George was passionate about getting more fans to the games. He spent the off-seasons traveling to small Texas towns to talk to local chambers of commerce and Rotary clubs, to make the Rangers their home team. The Rangers put George's face on a baseball card, and little boys asked him to sign their cards, and George would always say, "Where are you from?" waiting to hear Plano or Corsicana, or Waco, or Texarkana, but they almost always answered "Texas." They were just Texans.

I settled into Dallas life, decorating our three-bedroom ranch house with a little converted garage for guests in the back. My days were filled with the girls and their friends and activities. I devoted hours to Preston Hollow Elementary School, which Barbara and Jenna attended, signing up for the PTA and driving car pool with other moms on the surrounding streets. The parents of our daughters' friends became our good friends as well. We spent our Sunday mornings worshiping at Highland Park United Methodist Church, at the edge of the SMU campus and where I had once taught a Sunday school class during college. I volunteered to help my friend Nancy Brinker with fund-raising for the Susan G. Komen Breast Cancer Foundation. For several years, I chaired the invitation committee for her annual luncheon gala in Dallas, which was probably the easiest job in the organization because attendance at the lunch was so coveted that people RSVPed for it long before we mailed any invitations. I was also invited to serve on the Dallas Zoological Society and Aquarium board and the Friends of the Dallas Public Library.

Yet while we lived a very regular day-to-day life in Dallas, our eyes were never far from George's dad in Washington. George was assigned a Secret Service detail; we spent Christmas in the woods of Camp David, and our names were now on the guest lists for lofty state occasions. But for the family of a president, there is another side. In August of 1990, the Iraqi president, Saddam Hussein, invaded Kuwait. George's dad had suddenly become a wartime president. We agonized for him. I can remember standing clammy and afraid in my kitchen, cooking dinner as the television showed President Bush announcing that he was sending troops to Saudi Arabia in response to the Iraqi invasion. We saw his lined and weary face at Christmas. Not long after, the media reported that the U.S. military was shipping tens of thousands of body bags to the Middle East. Even the quick victory and the Iraqi army's capitulation in Kuwait did not dim the private agonies he had faced sending young men and women into combat in harsh, unforgiving sands halfway across the world.

After the Gulf War, Gampy was wildly popular. But the conflict had taken a toll. That spring, like Bar before him, he would develop Graves' disease, a thyroid condition. They both wondered if it was caused by some contaminant at the aging vice president's house. Gampy's mother was in faltering health, and he had a primary challenger in Pat Buchanan.

The Democrats nominated the young Arkansas governor, Bill Clinton. But that was not the only opposition. The Texas billionaire Ross Perot joined the race as an independent. The epicenter of his campaign was Dallas. Perot opened a campaign office in an empty savings and loan building on a corner of Northwest Highway, directly in the line of sight from George's office. George would look out his window and see people we knew, people who were our friends and his dad's friends, walking into Ross Perot's building. He watched them walk in and essentially abandon his dad.

Day after day, we saw George's father mocked and mischaracterized until we couldn't recognize the man we knew. Even the ballpark was not immune. It had always been the one place that was not political. But during the fall campaign, when we came to sit in the front row by the batter's box, someone on the other side of the field dropped a painted sheet over the infield wall with nasty comments about President Bush. An usher removed it, but the damage had been done. That moment was a harbinger of other, larger things.

With the vote split three ways, in November 1992, Bill Clinton was elected the forty-second president of the United States.

We had our last Christmas at the White House. Aside from a quick trip to visit George's brother Marvin or his sister, Doro, I did not expect to see Washington again. George signed up for the January 24 Houston Marathon. As the District of Columbia swept up after the Clinton inaugural revels, he was one of five thousand runners looping around Houston. When the marathon was over, a new thought began to jell in his mind: the Texas governor's race. The election was more than twenty months away. He announced his candidacy in November of that same year, 1993. It was almost a mirror of his father's race. Ann Richards, the incumbent governor, was extremely popular. George was something of a known name but a political unknown. But he believed she was vulnerable. He based his campaign on education. I listened, and I believed in him. From the moment he raised it with me, I never doubted that he would win.

As painful as it was for his family, George H. W. Bush's loss had finally freed his own children to say what they thought and to go after their own objectives. George's brother Jeb was running to be governor of Florida. Both brothers had uphill battles in their election races, but both believed deeply in the responsibility of public service and were also fascinated with politics and public policy. And both were going into the family business. They were interested in politics because they so admired their father, and politics had been his vocation. Just as some sons follow their dads into medicine or carpentry or business, they were following their father into his main profession, public service and political office.

Now, in addition to Rangers home games, our lives were fixed on the lodestar of the Southwest Airlines flight schedule, from the first breakneck race of wheels along the tarmac toward takeoff in the morning to the last screech of rubber and reverse thrust at night. George was campaigning all over Texas, but because many of the events were in the day and so much of the travel involved flying, he was usually home for dinner, lending a refreshing bit of normalcy to our lives. To reach the smaller towns, he flew on a twin-engine King Air plane with four seats, one of which was a bench. The final seat in the back doubled as the plane's toilet, and after George received the nomination, that was where staffers or Texas state troopers had to sit on the cramped flights that leapt and dove amid the frequent turbulence. I did events as well, speaking to women's groups all around Dallas and sometimes joining George on the statewide hops. And when I wasn't his surrogate, I was the mother of two eleven-year-old girls, with their myriad of activities, friends, and preadolescent dramas. All the while, back in Midland, my father was slowly dying.

In the winter of 1974, Johnny's Bar-B-Q had developed a leak in the roof. Daddy climbed up a rickety ladder to see if Johnny could pour a concrete roof, and when he stepped back on the ladder to come down, it gave way. Daddy fell and broke his ankle so badly that the doctor on call at the Midland hospital told him he would heal faster if the foot and ankle were amputated because the ankle is such a low circulation point and difficult to mend. Daddy kept the foot, and it did heal, but his leg was never the same. Seven years later, he had the lung surgery, and a few years after that, the doctors found a second spot on his other lobe, so he had another operation, although this time they didn't need to remove so much lung.

He quit smoking then, but I can still remember the day when he waited in the car while Mother, Jenna, Barbara, and I went to do an errand at a shopping center in Dallas. We came out and found him dozing, and as he slept, his fingers had drifted up to his shirt pocket and were trying to lift out an imaginary cigarette. He was dreaming of his tobacco and of the feel of the paper roll poised at the edge of his hand.

Mother and Daddy still came to see us all those years. They flew up to Washington or over to Dallas, where they stayed in our little guesthouse out back. On one of their last visits, I was standing at my kitchen sink, where the window gazed across our square of fenced backyard, and I saw them slowly making their way in from the guesthouse. I watched as, at the exact same moment, both of their faces lifted toward the sky. Grinning, laughing, they turned to each other, eyes catching, and then they looked up again. They were happy. No sadness ever unraveled their happiness. In the tiniest thing, they could find joy. That morning it was our cat, Cowboy, who had climbed up on our roof. And they entered the kitchen smiling.

What Mother noticed first was that Daddy could no longer fill out the bank deposit slips. He got all kinds of small checks—$1.50 royalties from an interest in some West Texas well, a rent check from a bus station that he had built in Odessa—stacks of checks for minuscule amounts, which were of great comfort to a man from the Depression. And he had always enjoyed going to the bank and depositing them, until the paperwork became unmanageable. He would stare at the lines on the forms, a look of confusion washing over his face. Mother began to make the deposits for him. Then, one day, Daddy walked in the house, set his car keys on the table, and announced that he was not going to drive again. He quit forever that afternoon. For years his greatest fear had been that he would hit someone else's child. He would not risk that for a few more outings behind the wheel. But now, all the driving fell to my mother. If she did not take him out, he would not leave the house. She resigned from her ladies' bridge club, which met in the afternoons, and began to ferry my father around, just as he had done with her on all those Sunday drives and the expeditions to watch birds, her binoculars in her hands. She drove him to Midland's indoor mall, where they could walk undisturbed. She drove him to Johnny's to see his friends. And then he began to fall.

He would get up and start to walk, but it was no longer a walk, it was a rickety shuffle, as if the electrical impulses in his brain had begun to misfire. He would move a few steps, and then, instead of going forward, he would start to back up. Then he would topple back onto the ground. He was a large man and Mother was tiny, and she had a very hard time getting him up. Sometimes, she would call her neighbor across the street, and Trey would come, wrap his arms around Daddy's torso, and pull him off the floor. Gradually, he began falling so often that she had to call the local fire station at the very end of the street and ask the firemen to come to lift him up. And she was afraid to take him places because she was scared that he would fall. Their world shrank as Daddy became more and more housebound. Friends visited. They came to Daddy when he could no longer come to them. That is one of the luxuries of living a long time in a small town.

We never got a diagnosis of Alzheimer's or a specific form of cognitive failing. But we saw his mind erode. Once, he asked Barbara to get him some "B & Bs." He meant M&Ms, but he kept saying "B & Bs." In her ten-year-old way, she understood him and came out with the brown bag of bright candy just the same. He also started sleeping a lot, getting up to have his coffee and his breakfast, now minus the cigarette, and then heading back to bed. But he never gave up his drink at night.

When my mother took Daddy to the doctor, one of the questions on the cognition test was "Who is the president?" And my father, who had been a Democrat for years, answered, "Some joker from Arkansas." The doctor looked at Mother with a small smile and then asked, "Who was the last president?" And Daddy had no idea, even though it was George H. W. Bush, my father-in-law. I thought then, months before George announced that he was running for governor of Texas, how fleeting all of this is—our memories, our moments—how four years in the White House and the millions of still photos and tens of thousands of hours of videotape that accumulate from the highest levels of a political career can just vanish amid the death of brain cells. George H. W. Bush was one of the most recognized men on the planet in the year 1990, and now, three years later, my own father forgets my father-in-law.

My mother was fortunate that she was able to hire help. Friends and acquaintances would call with the name of someone who had assisted one of their relatives, and so she found a man to come in each morning to help Daddy bathe and dress and then had other people who came through during the day, especially to help her if he fell. Barbara and Jenna went out to visit that last summer. In the past, they had gone individually for a week at a time, to get to be the only granddaughter, and the one who stayed home was, ever so briefly, our only child. But this time they went together. Daddy still knew who they were, but so many other things had slipped out of his grasp.

In the middle of that same summer, after we'd packed Barbara and Jenna off to Camp Longhorn, George and I ducked out to a lunchtime matinee movie, *Forrest Gump*. Just as we were pulling into the parking lot of the theater, the phone rang in the car—it seems almost quaint to recall those big car phones now, when most of us walk around with BlackBerries hooked to our hips. One of the campaign staffers was on the line telling George that Ann Richards had just called him a jerk. "Some jerk" were her exact words at a rally in Texarkana. George rolled his eyes, shrugged his shoulders, and we went in to watch Tom Hanks on the big screen. Although it was shocking at the time, and it didn't help Governor Richards, I look back now and find it pretty tame mud that she slung.

The campaign's pace accelerated as we neared the big televised debate, which most observers thought that George had won. As Election Day drew near, I found myself barnstorming around the state with Bar and Nolan Ryan, one of the great pitchers for the Rangers. We'd bounce from small town to small town in that cramped King Air plane, landing on tiny asphalt strips. Nolan finally leaned over and said, "Barbara, you've got on two different earrings." Bar pulled them off her ears, gave them a glance, said, "They sure are," then stuck them back on and wore them for the rest of the day.

On Election Day, George donned his lucky tie, and we headed off to vote at Hillcrest High School in Dallas. He had his Department of Public

Laura Bush

Safety detail and an army of photographers and cameramen trailing him. He had everything but his wallet, with his voter registration card and driver's license; it was sitting on the bureau in our bedroom. He hustled back to retrieve his wallet, and then the officials waved him into the booth. And standing there as we entered the polling place was Kim Hammond, the boy who had been a pallbearer for Mike Douglas and then had nominated me for the Rebelee Court in Midland, and who had also played Little League baseball with George. I went over and hugged him. He was now a Dallas police corporal.

That night in Austin, George won his race, while his brother Jeb lost a hard-fought vote in Florida to the incumbent governor, Lawton Chiles. Six years after we had arrived in Dallas, we were packing to move into the Governor's Mansion, one of the oldest homes in all of Texas. The house was a grand antebellum design, but our actual private living space was a modest upstairs apartment, small enough that I had to leave many of our things behind; the den furniture would fit, but not the pieces from our living room. The cost of storing our possessions for four years was more than they were worth, so I gave away books to the Dallas Public Library, just as I had done in Midland. I gave away furniture and clothes. Barbara's room in the new house had once been a sleeping porch and had enough space only for a narrow daybed. We managed to squeeze a double bed in Jenna's room but little else.

After the election, Rita Clements, whose husband had served as governor before Ann Richards, invited me to lunch in Dallas. We sat at our quiet table in Café Pacific, amid the starched linens and solicitous waiters, and she gave me a tutorial on the Governor's Mansion, which had been built even before Sam Houston was the governor of the state of Texas. She reviewed the house, the staff, and the things I would need to know as first lady of Texas, including her advice not to accept any invitations to events where I would not be the speaker. At the end of our lunch, as the coffee cooled in our cups, she withdrew a small piece of paper from her purse. On it, she had written a single name, and she held it up, saying simply, "I do not recommend this person as an employee in the Governor's Mansion." She never spoke the person's name, and as soon as

I had read the paper, she crumpled it up and tucked it away in her bag. I was struck by her exceptional discretion, but fortunately for me, by the time George and I arrived in the Governor's Mansion, the employee in question had retired.

I suddenly had to buy clothes, inaugural clothes and first lady of Texas clothes. I have never been much of a clothes fanatic. The closest things I have to a uniform are jeans or slacks, a cotton shirt, and flats. But I was no longer going to be on the political stage as a daughter-in-law, the smallest possible bit of background scenery for my father-in-law. I would be standing next to George, and I wanted to dress my best. I went to a Dallas designer, Michael Faircloth, to make a red suit for the inauguration. As I recall now, there were at least thirty other red suits in attendance that January day, including several worn by my Dallas friends.

But before the inauguration, before we moved our reluctant, newly turned thirteen-year-old seventh graders to Austin and to an entirely new school, we went home to Midland for Thanksgiving with Mother and Daddy. By this point, it was very difficult for Daddy even to leave the house. Mother and Daddy's world rarely extended beyond those few rooms on Humble Avenue that Daddy had built just over thirty years before. Mother was back in the kitchen, amid the Formica counters. We were sitting in the living room, with its familiar green upholstery and the glass-top coffee table, when Daddy turned to me and said, "Who's that?" I looked over to where his head was pointing, took a breath, and replied, "That's my husband, Daddy. That's George Bush." And Daddy turned to me and said in an incredulous voice, "You married George Bush?" "Yes." Then he laughed, his big, deep-throated laugh, and said, "I think I'll ask him for a loan."

Inauguration Day was cool and damp. George's family was all there, but Mother had come alone. We didn't know how we could ever get Daddy safely around the Capitol, or how she would manage when I was up on the platform with George. Then, when I arrived, amid the crowd gathered at the Capitol, I saw a wheelchair at the edge of the family and dignitary section. Sitting in the chair was an elderly man, the close and dear relative who had raised Lieutenant Governor Bob Bullock from the time he was a little boy. The Bullock family had gotten him there and had hired someone to push the chair, and my heart sank. We had not thought to do the same for Daddy, so that this boy from Lubbock might see his only daughter and his son-in-law become the first lady and governor of Texas. We had left him home, with a helper and the television. When Mother returned, he told her, "You're so lucky. You're so lucky that you got to go."

Three months later, in late April, George and I were standing on the grounds of the Alamo as part of the historic site's annual pilgrimage, a pilgrimage they've held since 1925, in which, after a muted procession, a floral wreath is laid and the names of the Alamo's defenders are solemnly read from inside the mission's stone walls. My new chief of staff, Andi Ball, came running up with the news that my father had collapsed and been rushed to the hospital. Mother had called the Governor's Mansion, which had located someone on my Department of Public Safety security detail, who had called Andi. I raced to the airport and boarded the next Southwest Airlines flight to Midland.

Daddy had already been under the care of hospice, which provided tremendous comfort to my mother and to him. My dear friend Elaine Magruder, a fifth-generation rancher, had brought hospice to Midland in 1980 with members of her Episcopal church and later helped start hospice in Vietnam. But on that afternoon, the hospice nurse had already come and gone. Mother was getting something in the kitchen, and Daddy's aide was feeding him some soup when suddenly she shrieked. Mother came running to find that Daddy had collapsed. Hospice was closed; the aide was overwrought, and Mother later said that she panicked and dialed 911. The paramedics came, with their tackle boxes of syringes and oxygen, and resuscitated him. He had a pulse, but by the time the ambulance reached the hospital, his veins had collapsed. They couldn't get an IV into his arm. He was unconscious, and his eyes did not open again. He lived five more days before starvation and dehydration took him, early in the morning on April 29, 1995. I spent those days with Mother in his hospital room. We held his hand, we talked to him, we planned his funeral and wrote his obituary, the words never coming close to capturing the man. George and the girls flew in to tell him good-bye. Mother said later that she would never have forgiven herself for dialing 911 if they had brought Daddy back and he had lingered in pain. He had a living will. But he seemed not to be suffering until the last breath departed from his lungs.

Mother had borne the burden of caring for Daddy, but even she did not realize what a burden it had been. The constant vigilance of caregiving had left her feeling almost physically ill. It took a full year for the sense of weight to be lifted from her shoulders, for her own well-being to return. Then she set about tenderly caring for the house Daddy had built for her, painting, reupholstering the chairs, replacing the drapes and the cracked kitchen counters, fixing the myriad of things that had gone unrepaired because it was just too much disruption to have a painter or a handyman come into the house while Daddy was in decline.

Looking back now, I see other things I wish we had done. Daddy always loved music. As a boy, he had taken violin lessons, and he used to be teased as he rode his bicycle through Lubbock with his violin tucked under his arm. Daddy would get off his bicycle, fight whoever had mocked him, and then go on to his lesson. He loved Glenn Miller, Glen Campbell, and Jerry Jeff Walker's "London Homesick Blues," and I wish we had played more music for him during those last few years. Brain researchers say that songs are imprinted in our memories longer than many other things.

Alzheimer's and dementia more broadly are called "the long good-bye," but to my mind, they are the sad good-bye. So often, as with our family, we don't say good-bye when we can. We don't recognize that moment when the person we love still knows enough, still comprehends enough to hear our words and to answer them. We miss that moment, and it never comes again. My mother has said that just as a person's joints grow old, so does the brain. And today, my conversations with my mother have changed. Now they are reduced to simple talk about the present moment; I cannot ask her what happened an hour ago or this morning. A recent MRI of her brain shows that the temporal lobe has shrunk; there is only a gray pall where the bright fluorescents that delineate a healthy mind should be on the diagnostic screen. The image reads like the results of an X-ray for a broken arm, except that this is broken irrevocably. Her brain cells have literally died first.

When I heard those results, a deep grief washed over me. Her mind will never heal. It is too late for it ever to be again as it was. Too late for both of us.

⁓

Daddy's funeral was on a Monday. Later that week, I was back in Austin. My days were crowded; I did not have too much time to dwell on memories until Christmas, when we played our home movies of the girls as babies and Daddy's face and arms flashed across the frames.

And for years afterward, even now, I would dream of Daddy. And in my dreams, he is well.

⁓

In Austin, I no longer drove. My nearly brand-new minivan stayed parked in a downtown garage for over a year until I sold it—the grounds of the Governor's Mansion hadn't been designed to include a parking spot. For security reasons, car-pool duties now belonged to the DPS agents who ferried the girls to school. They heard the banter and the secrets that were traded in the backseat mornings and afternoons. I was relegated to a wave good-bye.

When I first went to look at the Governor's Mansion and saw the two small rooms for the girls, my heart sank, and I said, "Oh, I don't know what they'll do when they have friends spend the night." The house manager smiled and said, "The Sam Houston Bedroom!" The bedroom, with its massive four-poster mahogany bed that Houston had ordered when he became governor of Texas, back in 1859, would be perfect for a group of teenage girls. And that was where their friends stayed. I never did tell the girls that Houston's five-year-old son had locked members of the legislature in their chambers and hid the key. Governor Houston threatened him with a whipping, but still no key appeared. Only when he promised to have him arrested did Andrew Jackson Houston deliver the key to free the legislators, and his father was later overheard to say that his son had bested him at controlling the legislature. I figured we didn't want to try to top that.

The Texas Governor's Mansion is the fourth oldest continuously occupied governor's home in the nation and the oldest gubernatorial residence west of the Mississippi River. Even its dust seemed to be laced with history. The house itself is a large Greek Revival structure, built of buff-colored bricks fired from a clay pit on the Colorado River. The governor who chose the design was Elisha M. Pease, who had grown up in Hartford, Connecticut. The house's façade had elaborate scroll columns rising two stories, but it was also in some ways a thoroughly Texas house, with wide hallways running front to back to catch a bit of a breeze in the brutal summers—Austin sits between Dallas and Houston. Like my grandparents' old orange house, this house was a foursquare design, two rooms off each side of the central hall. But here the ceilings were high, sixteen feet downstairs and thirteen upstairs, with the kitchen and a set of what were once called servants' quarters built at the rear.

Governor Pease had to cart in his own furniture to fill the place, and his wife, who had lived in Connecticut during the construction, lamented how the sun and heat had parched the grass to brown and killed the corn planted in their new garden. But governors lived there from then on, as the city of Austin grew up around them. Inside, Sam Houston, who had fought so hard to make Texas part of the United States, all but wore grooves in the wide plank floors, pacing at night over his decision to resign the governorship rather than sign an oath of loyalty to the Confederacy, as Texas's state legislature had decreed. Along the grand, sweeping staircase leading to the second floor, the banister is covered with nail holes, from the successful efforts of another governor, James Stephen Hogg, to prevent his four children from sliding down the great, slick stair rail. Those children also kept a menagerie of dogs, cats, squirrels, raccoons, and exotic birds in and out of the mansion.

By the time George and I arrived, most of the rooms in the house were unalterable. The only place where we might choose the colors or furnishings was the small family quarters upstairs. The downstairs public rooms, which some 24,000 tourists walked through on tours each year, were set in mustard and blue and red, with heavy drapes and a priceless collection of early American antiques, many of them collected by Governor Bill and Rita Clements and their friends in Dallas. The rules of the Friends of the Governor's Mansion decree that nothing can be changed. In fact, far less can be done to alter the Texas governor's home decor than to modify the rooms in the White House.

I set about making our upstairs rooms into a home as I listened to the buzz and tramp of the tourists below, and people craned their necks to see if we were indeed there. Once, when Barbara was home sick from school, a tour group paused in the garden right below her window. The guide pointed out our cat, Cowboy, and then mentioned our dog, Spot, but couldn't remember the name of Barbara's cat, and I knew she wanted to call out her window, "My cat's name is India." In our own space, I painted the walls a soft gray.

Three months after the inauguration, the Texas State Capitol was rededicated after a lengthy restoration. I was tasked to be master of ceremonies for the event, held outside on the soaring front steps. Former governor Ann Richards was seated next to me, and as George was speaking, she told me that she had always wanted to add closets to the apartments and proceeded to draw a blueprint of her closet design for me on the back of a speakers' program. I did build the closets, although not exactly as she had specified. We had a tiny kitchen upstairs and only a small space to eat. We ate most of our meals in the family dining room on the first floor, with a chef to cook for us. It was probably a relief to George and the girls. When I was the cook, I could make it through about four nights of dinners. By the fifth, we had to eat out.

We were not totally unprepared for gubernatorial life, and not simply because George's dad had reached the presidency. Every newly elected governor and his spouse are invited to attend something called "governors' school," held by the National Governors Association before inauguration. We got a tutorial in the basics of state life. Our school was in West Virginia, and the most candid comments invariably came from the sitting governors' wives. One told us, "If your state troopers will drive you, be sure to let them. If you get into a fender bender," she added, "it will be front-page news. If your trooper does, it will be a note in the metro news section."

Twelve days after George was sworn in, we were back at the White House, for our first official National Governors Association meeting and a black-tie evening hosted by Bill and Hillary Clinton. Stepping into the gleaming hallways, we had a sense of nostalgia for the four years there, as well as the comfort of seeing ushers and butlers who had always been so welcoming. There were reminders too of the awkward intricacies of larger political life. That first year, at the White House luncheon for the governors' spouses, I was seated next to Rhea Chiles, wife of the Florida governor, Lawton Chiles, who had narrowly defeated Jeb Bush in a very tough race the previous fall. Whether the seating was intentional or accidental, Rhea and I were forced to make polite conversation as elegant china plates were silently placed and then, after many minutes, briskly whisked away.

Ann Richards was not married when she was governor, so there had been no first spouse in Texas for four years. I had a small office in the new underground space behind the Capitol building, which was across the street from the governor's residence. My space was a collection of three rooms with tan walls: first, a small, boxy office with my desk; second, a narrow sitting area, where I placed a couch from our Dallas den that hadn't fit in the governor's residence; and finally a workspace for the only person on my staff, Andi Ball. Xerox machines hummed down the hall, and staffers strode past carrying paper stacks, meeting agendas, and binders stuffed with the business of Texas. But what was my business? First ladies have innumerable events to attend—luncheons, dinners, occasions to make remarks for worthy causes—but small talk has never been my forte. Rita Clements, the state's most recent first lady, had a long list of accomplishments in her chosen causes: volunteerism, education, historic preservation, and tourism. Where would my mark be made?

Some of my duties were prescribed, like the annual Texas Historical Commission's Main Street Program, for which I traveled to small towns with Jan Bullock, wife of the lieutenant governor; she had taken over some of the ceremonial responsibilities during Governor Richards's term. Jan and I would walk past the solemn courthouses and along the newly restored Main Streets, where the 1940s and '50s false fronts had been pulled down and the old glass-front shops had been restored. On the streets, we could almost hear the clomp of horses' hooves or the sputter of Model T's or even the soft hum of brightly waxed tail fins passing down the street. Here, life before the interstate was preserved.

But others were causes that I could make my own. I started with art, collecting posters from major Texas museums and displaying them, framed, in an adjacent state office building so the corridors could have Robert Rauschenbergs, Georgia O'Keeffes, Richard Avedons, and other works to enhance their sparse monochromatic walls. I held exhibitions of Texas artists near my office in the new section of the Capitol, painters and sculptors, abstract and representational, women and men. And Nelda Laney, wife of Pete Laney, the Speaker of the Texas House, Jan Bullock, and I searched for historic Texas art that we could add to the Capitol.

The issue of education was a logical choice. I convened a summit on early childhood development and brain research, inviting top experts from around the nation to discuss the importance of reading from infancy and family literacy as ways to prepare students for learning years before they were enrolled in school. We discussed the latest brain science, unlocking the pathways for how small children learn, the connections their eager minds can make between sounds and symbols. We explored the ways that their physical environment—what they eat, how they play, what they do with the adults around them—molds their school years and their lifelong learning. I remembered my kids all those years ago at Longfellow and John F. Kennedy and Dawson and wondered how their lives might have been different if they had come through the school doors ahead rather than behind. This was my contribution to George's sweeping education reforms, which he enacted with Bob Bullock and Pete Laney. The summit helped convince legislators to create reading readiness programs for preschoolers and, for the first time, to add to the federal Head Start program.

I had, I suppose, an affinity for difficult causes. I made Texas's Department of Family and Protective Services one of my issues, working to support the caseworkers who investigate child abuse and neglect, who rise at 2:00 A.M. to answer a police phone call telling them a child or a family of children must be removed from their home. I had begun working with CPS when we lived in Dallas, helping with the Adopt-A-Caseworker program through an organization called Community Partners, which was started by several of my friends. Caseworkers would literally have children in their arms as they tried to find clothing, food, medicine, diapers, anything that a child removed from a house might need. Many of the caseworkers, who earned meager salaries, were spending their own money to buy these necessities. In Dallas, we started a Rainbow Room, a true haven inside the CPS building, where caseworkers could find anything from clothing to car seats, coloring books, and crayons, whatever they needed to assist families in dire financial straits and children who had been left dirty, hungry, and horribly neglected. The room was a welcoming place, furnished by the Dallas-based Container Store, which put up bright Elfa shelves and bins.

In Austin, I helped establish Rainbow Rooms statewide. I remember meeting one caseworker in Jefferson County, a woman named Dana Stamps, who had removed an abused boy from his home on his sixth birthday. Toys from the Rainbow Room became his only gifts, pajamas, underwear, and a set of clothes his only clean things to wear.

Some months after George became governor, an El Paso writer named Robert Skimin made an appointment to see me in my office. He told me that he had attended a state book festival in Kentucky and that he had always wanted Texas to have its own book festival, adding, "You would be the perfect person to start it, since you were a librarian." I was intrigued, and I called my friend Regan Gammon to ask her what she thought. She loved the idea and immediately had a suggestion about who should help organize it, Mary Margaret Farabee. I started making calls. We gathered a committee of book lovers and authors. We asked to hold the book festival inside the Capitol, where only legislative business was allowed, and we got permission. To sell our authors' books, we erected enormous tents on the streets outside, with authors signing their books and cashiers ringing up whatever was sold. Any monies we raised were to be donated to Texas public libraries. And authors wanted to come. Larry McMurtry, of *Lonesome Dove* fame, told a story about how his hometown of Archer City, Texas, did not have a public library, until he helped start one with some of his book profits. The playwright Larry L. King said that when he was growing up poor in Midland, the public library had saved him. His childhood forays into the works of Mark Twain had led him to dream of telling stories rather than roughnecking it in the oil fields.

But even after all the authors said yes, I was anxious. Weeks before the event, I lay awake at night and worried: what if the weather turned bad, what if the encampment of white tents blew over? The same weekend, Austin was hosting a beer festival and a gun and knife show. One newspaper article quoted an "unnamed" author as saying, "Great. Everyone'll be drunk and armed." I was worried that no one would come.

We hosted a reception for the festival's black-tie gala at the mansion, with all the writers, including Kinky Friedman, who came in his big black hat and big black coat, and chewed on a matted cigar. The next morning, television crews arrived at daybreak to start broadcasting promotional interviews for the festival, and when George walked downstairs, Kinky was there again, wearing his same undertakeresque attire, even with the same cigar clenched between his teeth, talking to the camera. George was convinced that Kinky had spent the night stretched over the silk-upholstered settee in the living room.

The festival opened in the House Chamber, and then the authors fanned out to read in various committee rooms around the Capitol. Outside the House Chamber, as the events were getting under way, a jackhammer was ripping up the ground. I flagged down someone to tell the construction crew to stop, but then I began to worry about all the other things we had forgotten. My head started to pound, and I slipped back across the street to the Governor's Mansion and got into bed. I was sure the whole festival was going to be a bust and people would leave as soon as they had arrived. Regan and another friend of mine, Pam Nelson, came over to the house and found me. They excitedly told me, "The festival is going great. Come back." So I got up, redressed, and raced back across to the Capitol. It was standing room only to listen to the authors in the committee rooms, and there were long lines in the tents. I bought the books of the authors who weren't selling many copies and walked around. Over the weekend, nearly fifteen thousand people came to the first annual Texas Book Festival. In its first fourteen seasons, the festival has given over $2.3 million to Texas libraries.

The next year, the University of Texas Humanities Research Center loaned the book festival its priceless copy of the Gutenberg Bible to be displayed under special glass inside the Capitol's Seal Court. Late on Sunday afternoon, as the festival was drawing to a close, I was walking through a balcony above. For an instant, I looked down. Three uniformed Texas DPS officers were clustered around the display, bent over the Gutenberg's pages. In the middle of Texas, they could gaze upon the first book to be printed on a printing press in Europe, the book that took reading out of the finely articulated, hand-copied vellum of high-walled monasteries and began to make it a democratic pleasure.

Even though George was the governor of the second largest state in the nation, I had considerable freedom as his wife. And there was a great normalcy to my life in Austin. A couple of nights after dinner, Regan and Billy and I would walk over to stand at Antone's to listen to Bobby "Blue" Bland, just as we'd always done. Many mornings, I would walk south on Colorado Street and around Austin's Town Lake (now renamed for Lady Bird Johnson) with my friend Nancy Weiss. I stood in line alone for coffee in the Capitol cafeteria or for stamps at the post office, and when people caught sight of my DPS detail in the statehouse, they swiveled their heads about, looking for the famous person who must be somewhere about the room. Barbara and Jenna love to tell the story of the time we were standing in a checkout line at Walmart in Athens, Texas, near our little weekend getaway lake house, and a woman kept staring at me. Finally, she said, "I think I know you," and I replied, "I'm Laura Bush," as if, the girls liked to point out, of course she would know who I was. Her answer was "No, guess not."

Even our family life held on to normalcy. The four of us ate dinner together most nights, and George routinely helped the girls type and proofread their term papers. When ninth grade came, Barbara and Jenna opted to go to Austin's large, downtown public high school.

The second year of George's term was also the year of George's and my fiftieth birthdays. I've never liked surprises. I was so shocked by a surprise wedding shower in Austin that it was at least a half hour before I could actually begin to enjoy the party. But George loves them. So I planned a surprise birthday party for him at the Governor's Mansion. I invited his childhood friends, school friends from Andover and Yale, friends from Midland, the familiar and the long-lost. The morning of the party, George and I set out to pick up the girls from Camp Longhorn. When we got home, he could see the tent and the tables going up on the lawn, so I handed him the party invitation, but I didn't say who was coming. We celebrated under the stars with heaps of dripping barbecue, and lots of toasts. Then the lieutenant governor, Bob Bullock, stood up. Bob, a Democrat, toasted George as "the man who will be the next president of the United States." It was July of 1996. George hadn't even been reelected governor. But by the following year, talk had turned to the presidency.

I waited before I weighed in, because I knew both sides of what that decision would entail.

In 1993, George H. W. Bush had been invited to Kuwait to be thanked by the nation for liberating them from Saddam Hussein. He and Barbara invited Marvin and Neil Bush, as well as Jeb's wife, Columba, and me to go along. On the way home from Kuwait, we stopped in France to see President François Mitterrand, who escorted us all through the recently opened Euro Disney, the Disneyland of Europe, a far cry from my California visit after a night spent in a sparse roadside motel. This time too I had "siblings." We rode on Space Mountain; we tried the famous rides and attractions. But at one point during the afternoon, I was walking ahead with Marvin and Neil, and I turned around. Behind us was the threesome of Gampy, Ganny, and Mitterrand. But they seemed larger than life, the way celebrities, when one sees them in person, look like the animation of a thousand paparazzi stills. In that instant, Gampy, Ganny, and Mitterrand appeared as fantastical as movie stars ambling through Euro Disney. And they were every bit as recognizable.

While as the years lengthened, their prominence might dim, but they would still never sit in a restaurant or a café or an airline seat and pass unrecognized. There was no chance for them to be anonymous again.

One Hundred and Thirty-two Rooms

With Spot and Barney at the White House.
(White House photo)

The Governor's Mansion in Austin has a small lawn and simple gardens. The place itself is hemmed in by a cross-section of city streets, pinning it to its urban spot amid blocks of stone office fronts and the slow progression of glinting high-rises. On the morning of March 2, 1999, a state staffer placed two white metal lawn chairs in the garden, and others hung a small rope to hold back the crush of television cameras, photographers, and reporters who had come to hear George announce that he was forming an exploratory committee to consider making a presidential run. The press corps is often referred to as a gaggle, as in a "gaggle of geese," but that hardly conveys the strange divide between the press and the "principal." What most video images and stills never capture is the sight of the candidate on one side and the crush of the media on the other, with their voice recorders, boom mikes, and cameras poised to capture his every movement and his every word.

The announcement of an exploratory committee was, we both knew, the same as an official declaration. As George himself said, only "a giant thud, a huge yawn," or the discovery that "it was my mother they were interested in" could derail his presidential train.

I sat beside George, smiling. But I had been late to sign on to his decision to run. Politics had turned ugly during his dad's 1992 race with Bill Clinton. I had watched political opponents and the media draw the most hideous caricatures of George H. W. Bush until I barely recognized my own father-in-law. I believed in my George, I love him, and I knew he would be a great president. It was the process in which I had far less faith.

My escape and at moments my salvation from this particular trail was to come in the form of nearly sixteen hundred acres of blackland prairie in an extended finger of the Texas Hill Country, a ranch near a town named Crawford.

My childhood fantasies of El Paso ranchland had matured into a dream of a quiet frame house on the banks of the Guadalupe or the Medina River, where a slow, gradual lawn dipped down to gurgling river waters or a meandering feeder creek. I imagined children or grandchildren playing in its currents and the soft rustle of branches from clusters of sturdy cypress trees rooted to its banks.

In late February of 1998, George and I went to look at a plot of land in north-central Texas, almost dead center between Austin and Dallas. It was flat tall-grass prairie, the bits of flinty range where generations of farmers and ranchers had eked out life with their livestock. The soil had been plowed generations ago and sowed with rich feed grasses, like kleingrass and coastal Bermuda, a spiky green blend that spreads in dense mats across the ground. Ten acres are enough to graze a full-grown cow in the high summer. All around us as we drove, the land stretched out, not frying-pan flat like Midland, but with subtle dips and rises. Uncounted millennia of natural events, from torrential floods to crippling droughts and fast-moving fires, and the migration of ancient bison, were silently recorded along its contours and folds. Amid the fields and pastures, there were fence lines and tree breaks and a healthy breeze, but nothing to distinguish this spot from thousands of other working farms and ranches across the Texas landscape.

Then George drove me in. In the back, the grassland abruptly sheared away into seven box canyons, their walls covered in steep limestone worn down from water and ancient geological upheaval. Thousands of years of erosion had left jutting bits of giant rock, some of which the rain, sun, and wind have chiseled away, until their features resemble the noses, eyes, and lips of Easter Island's silent Moai figures. Here, instead of gazing out upon an island, with the white-capped Pacific at their back, they stand watch over the brush and fallen branches. Below, when there is rain, the creek water runs. In centuries past, the Tonkawa Indian warriors rested and watered their horses in this part of the Bosque River and horse thieves hid their bounty along the winding canyon bottoms.

This back edge was what old-time ranchers call "sorry land," uncleared, untamed, a tangle of brambles and overhanging limbs. Much of it was impassable. We could only hike to the top ledge and look down. It was rugged and stark. For George, it was love at first sight. I was far less smitten.

Two months later, the following April, I was driving with Regan and the rest of my Austin garden club to an event in Fort Worth. We were heading up Interstate 35, and the land alongside was swollen with green grass shoots and carpeted with bluebonnets and other wildflowers, bright and plump from drenching spring rains. As I watched the grasses and the flowers bend in the wind, I realized that this was exactly the section of Texas where the Crawford ranch was, and that the blooming land was beautiful. We had money from the sale of the Texas Rangers baseball team. I called George from the car and said, "Let's buy it."

By August, the land was ours. Scattered around the front half of the sixteen hundred acres were a small 1940s farmhouse, which faced two diesel storage tanks and a tractor shed; a livestock barn; and a few other outbuildings. It was a working ranch; the same family had raised livestock on that spot for four generations, coming out to stake and settle when this part of Texas was still a place that drew jostling wagon trains and weary pioneers. From its rear windows, the ranch's little farmhouse overlooked the grassland and the herd. The same work boots had crossed its threshold at dawn and again at dusk year after year.

After George won his reelection race for Texas governor in November of 1998, with 68 percent of the vote statewide, I started work on the modest six-room house, painting the clapboard siding green, updating the small kitchen, and refurbishing the three tiny bedrooms. Later, on another part of the property, away from the grazing lands and closer to the steep canyons, we planned to build a real ranch house with a two-bedroom guesthouse alongside, but until that house became a reality, we needed a livable home where we could stay.

Then my eyes turned to the grassland. In 1999, as George was weighing his presidential run, I embarked on a prairie restoration. I found a native-grass expert, Michael Williams, and we began by planting native grasses along a strip at the edge of the old cattle watering hole that we were making into a small lake. The wild and rangy grasses took, so we searched for other spots where we could expand the grassland. We planted on a rise above the pond, and in early 2001 we turned our attention to a vacant pasture. Michael devised a plan of plowing up the nonnative grasses. Then in spots we sprayed the fallow soil with small bits of herbicide to kill a few stubborn sprigs of coastal Bermuda and Johnson grass whose roots clung to the soil even after the plow's metal blades had sliced and scored the earth. Finally, after four years of plowing and spraying, only the loamy ground remained. Michael seeded the land with native seeds from a tiny remnant of an intact prairie. We covered forty acres with seed, and in our final year of seeding, 2007, the rains came, fifty-six inches of them. The grasses took, and the prairie returned. We then began adding another forty acres of native prairie grassland. Susan Rieff, head of the Lady Bird Johnson Wildflower Center, has noted that our little project is the largest private, completely native prairie restoration in all of Texas. I feel a twinge of sadness when I think of the millions of acres across West Texas that were once alive with tall prairie. Big bluestem, Indian grass, and switchgrass have vanished from the landscape as thoroughly as the thundering buffalo herds.

The rhythm of a national campaign is the rhythm of the air, of planes pulling away from the ground as everything below recedes. Our first official flight of the 2000 presidential campaign was a June 1999 trip to Iowa. We left the Austin airport on a TWA charter plane that had been christened *Great Expectations.*

We touched down in Cedar Rapids and headed for a country barbecue, past the rolling farmland turned emerald and gold by the sun and dotted with old, white-painted farmhouses and red barns pressed against their stout silos of grain. In countless small ways, the iconic images that we have of so many regions of the nation are in fact true; rural Iowa is on certain afternoons a Grant Wood painting come to life, the layers of landscape, the geometric curves of the hills, the thin slices of valley, all resting against the flat backdrop of blue sky.

In a presidential campaign, the candidates, their spouses, and their staffs come to know three states—Iowa, New Hampshire, and South Carolina— with surprising intimacy, because of the early primaries and caucuses and the amount of time and resources devoted to each of those states. I soon recognized the corners of the rectangular grid streets of Des Moines and the glittering lights of its suspension bridge, which straddles a river where the Moingonas Indians once built burial mounds for their dead. George and I and our staff came to know the tangy taste of Iowa pork barbecue, as opposed to the spicy taste of Texas beef, and we could smell the sweet corn ripening in the fields. Although Des Moines was founded as a fort, Iowa for generations has been a largely pacifist state, without major military bases, unlike Colorado or Texas or Virginia or even California, which have vast military installations and defense industries. Like their land, the people are plainspoken and direct, solid in the questions that they ask and the stories that they tell. And, as I had during George's ancient race for Congress across West Texas, I loved listening to their stories. The difference now was that the clock was tighter; there was always another event, another school visit, or another speech. When I was on the road, I lived under the shadow of the schedule—arrivals, handshakes, greetings, remarks, questions and answers, and the quick dashes to the local airport as we headed on to the next stop and town. That tapestry formed the outlines of our days.

Campaigning for office is like running a marathon, day after day. You wake in darkness and sleep when the local news anchors are just signing off. You sleep in motels and hotel chains, on a hard pillow one night and a soft one the next. Or you sleep upright on the plane itself. Your life is packed between the two sides of a suitcase. Bar Bush once spoke to a group of Motel 6 owners and told them that people think she has Ritz-Carlton written all over her, but in fact, she's spent far more nights in a Motel 6. To be on the trail requires tremendous physical and emotional stamina and energy. It helps to have solid, robust health, which is what I have. George and his father have their athleticism to carry them through; Bar also has extraordinary stamina. Even the press sometimes has it easier than the candidates. If a reporter catches the flu, he or she can hop off the trail for a day or two to recover. But not the candidate. If George or I got that same flu, we couldn't get off; we had to keep traveling to every event. I think even now of the senior Bushes standing next to Kitty Dukakis, wife of Michael Dukakis, who ran against Gampy in 1988, and how she always seemed so frail and wan.

This constant life on the road meant that I missed things too. I missed Barbara and Jenna's high school senior homecoming ceremony. At half-time, during the big school football game, Barbara was going to be crowned homecoming queen, but she didn't know it. Austin High had called me that afternoon to tell me in secret, so that I could be there. Instead, we were heading for the airport. The only person I told was George's personal aide and our dear friend, Israel "Izzy" Hernandez, who had been with George and our family since 1992. Izzy tried to get her to dress up, but Barbara went off to the game wearing flip-flops.

But we always came home. Not simply to the Governor's Mansion, which was temporary, but to the land of Prairie Chapel Ranch, which we named for the tiny, historic chapel down the road. (George's first suggestion had been the Lazy L. Ranch.) In 1999, on the recommendation of my friend Deedie Rose, George and I selected David Heymann, associate dean of the undergraduate architecture school at the University of Texas at Austin, to design what would become our new ranch house. On Saturdays, we drove out with David and walked the property, imagining. David's gift was siting a home where it would have the best views, the best breezes, the best flood of sunlight. One afternoon we paused in view of the cattle tank, the low, flooded spot where the ranchers had watered their herd, the same damp place that we wanted to dig out to build a little lake for fishing. Along a small rise stood a cluster of large, old live oaks and cedar elms. There was just enough space to situate the house in the middle of those gnarled trees. And we did. We lost only one small tree, which we tried to move, but its roots had spread wide and shallow over the limestone shelf that lies hidden underneath the soil. In David's vision, every window of the house would frame a live oak or a cedar elm.

Then came the design. On our visits, David would hammer stakes into the ground. We would stand and imagine each room and feel the ruffle of the wind. The house itself is split, in the style of old Texas ranch houses, with a breezeway—or what they used to call a dogtrot—running through the center. When early Texans built a house, they would have a covered porch open to the breeze, so they could work there in the heat of the day, with the prevailing winds drawing through to provide some cool.

Our own entry hall has wide screens to capture the wind, and doors that open into the living room to usher through the breeze. I wanted the house to be low and to fit into the landscape. It was only when the house was nearly finished that my friend Peggy Weiss came to look at it and observed that what we'd built looked "like a Midland house." And it was, only a single story and following the ground, just like the houses Daddy used to build.

It was never designed to be a big house. It's less than four thousand square feet, with three bedrooms, one for us, one for Barbara, and one for Jenna. There's a small library, a sitting room off the girls' bedrooms, a kitchen, and a living room and dining room combined. We wanted the house not simply to fit into the landscape but to be of the landscape, so we used Lueders limestone from a quarry that was about forty miles away, and we chose the top and bottom pieces of the quarry cuts, the ones with streaks of color. Those are considered the discard pieces because most builders want only the creamy white centers. But the leftovers are feathered with warm streaks of ocher and rose and look like the burnished tips of prairie grasses. We used a local builder called Heritage Homestead for everything. When we wanted a cantilevered porch roof without columns that would obscure the view, they knew just how to engineer it.

Because water and power are always precious and scarce on the range, we also built the house to conserve whatever we could. A sloping metal roof of galvanized tin shunts rainwater into a giant underground cistern to irrigate the property. Even the water from our showers is recycled and saved. Our heat is geothermal, from pipes dug three hundred feet into the ground, where the temperature is a constant sixty-seven degrees. We have a heat pump to circulate the water, warming it in the winter, cooling it in the summer, when it comes from the sun-baked ground. The floors are poured concrete or wide plank wood, and we did not build a single stair. We want to live at that ranch when we are in our walkers and our wheelchairs, should that day ever come.

As the presidential primary season unfolded in 2000, slab was being poured and walls were taking form. We were building for the rest of our lives.

I had what some might consider an advantage: George and I had been in national campaigns before, four of them in total, two vice presidential, two presidential. We had leapfrogged up the Mississippi River, from New Orleans to St. Louis to Dubuque, over the course of three weekends. I had stood for hours at rallies and conventions, I knew the feel of sitting on hastily arranged hotel banquet chairs for a speech or the echoey roar of a civic center auditorium, or the slick treads of school gymnasiums, their gleaming, varnished floors itching not for political events but for basketball. But all those years, I had always managed to duck the spotlight as a daughter-in-law. Now this was our race, to win or lose. I frequently traveled with George, but I also made some swings of my own, including up to Michigan in the already chilly mid-November weather. I visited an elementary school, then walked around the quaint Bavarian-style town of Frankenmuth, with its half-timber architecture, home to the world's largest Christmas store, and saw the struggling industrial city of Saginaw. That night, the sky lit up with a meteor shower, and Andi Ball and I and my DPS agents gathered up blankets and lay out on the ground beneath the chill sky to catch a glimpse of the distant sparks of falling stars.

It was in Michigan again that I lost my contact lenses in my hotel room before a speech and spent what seemed like an hour blindly crawling around on my knees, feeling the rough carpet for the hard plastic case. At last, Andi located them behind the chest, where they had slipped during the night. After that, we started carrying spares.

When George won in Iowa, we packed up and headed for a bruising campaign amid the snows of New Hampshire, where we made lifelong friends. We had a core group who trekked to every rally. Some had known Gampy when he was running, but many were just our friends, like Senator Judd Gregg and his wife, Kathy. Senator John McCain won the New Hampshire contest, but the next morning, we were in South Carolina, shaking hands and asking for votes.

I was in Providence, Rhode Island, in March when the *Star* tabloid published a story about the 1963 car crash. The car accident was not a secret; all of my old friends knew about it, as did just about all of Midland. But up to now, it had been part of my private life. Except that there is no private life for a presidential candidate or his or her spouse. Now the accident was fodder for the national media, and for several days reporters hollered questions at me wherever I went. But then the next piece of news pushed my past out of the headlines. My life veered from rallies, school visits, and speeches to the angst of two teenage daughters trying to decide on which college to go to. Barbara selected Yale, in part because she would be the fourth generation of the Bush family, and the first female, to attend. Jenna had her heart set on the University of Texas at Austin. As she told me when she went to visit a North Carolina school, "I wish I could make myself go here, but I can't." She was overjoyed when her acceptance letter came from Austin.

They were graduating high school with a father who was the governor and who was now the Republican presidential nominee. We had traded our Texas Department of Public Safety detail for Secret Service. We drove in motorcades with flashing lights and sirens, traffic shunted to one side. Days and weeks collapsed into a blur, rather like the towns and countryside we passed, moving at warp speed outside the window. Our advance team, the small group of people who manage each campaign stop, would be on the road for months at a time, traveling across the country to preview and organize the events, speeches, and rallies. They did laundry in local Laundromats, and when the seasons changed, their families boxed up and shipped a fresh set of clothes.

In the late summer, George invited Dick Cheney to the ranch. Dick had been a longtime Wyoming congressman and Gampy's secretary of defense during the Gulf War. George liked Dick's thoughtful, measured demeanor and had asked Dick to head up his vice presidential search. I had long liked and admired his wife, Lynne, who had overseen the National Endowment for the Humanities and is an accomplished scholar and author in her own right.

Dick arrived with crisp file folders and sheaves of paper covering each possible vice presidential pick. But the more the two men spoke, the more George began to think that Dick himself was the best partner and candidate. He possessed the perfect combination of experience in Congress and the executive branch, and he had that clear, plainspoken, unruffled style of the West, which appealed to us as Texans. He liked to laugh and was funny, smart, and devoted to his wife, his daughters, and his grandchildren. Underneath, though, Dick had what George and I would call a quiet strength. As their meetings drew to a close, George asked Dick to be his running mate. He agreed, and there were so many times when we were both glad that Dick Cheney was the nation's vice president.

Our family summer gathering consisted of getting together at the Republican convention in Philadelphia, where the organizers dropped the confetti when I was introduced and a heavy layer of ripped paper covered every teleprompter screen below me on the floor. Only one side of one screen was still slightly visible beneath the red, white, and blue. I had to rotate my eyes sideways to catch a glimpse of my speech.

There were some things that I insisted upon during the campaign. I insisted upon leaving the trail to move the girls into their new schools.

When she was a sophomore in high school, Jenna had asked me to reserve a space for her at the Hardin House, a private dorm at the University of Texas in Austin. Even when I was heading to college, Miss Hardin's, as it was then known, was the place for young UT coeds to live. Jenna would live with two other girls in one room—they had all made their reservations together. We arrived and promptly went out to buy bed risers so that we could slide the storage boxes packed with Jenna's clothes underneath her bed frame—the other girls were doing the same. I thought of my own move-in day at SMU, when Mother and Daddy had dropped me off, remembering our spacious rooms with their tiny closets and my own wardrobe, which barely took up half of the space. My suitcase and a couple of boxes had fit neatly in the car trunk. I could still picture my parents' bemused faces as a girl from Corpus Christi arrived with an entire trailer of her things hitched up to the back of a large Cadillac.

I left Jenna with her friends and headed up to New Haven for Barbara.

Barbara had already spent a week camping in the wilderness as part of Yale's outdoor orientation program, which she adored. She arrived for move-in desperate for a shower, but first we had to get her things up the narrow, Gothic-style stairways of Yale's centuries-old dorm. We spent what seemed like hours navigating the turns and dark stairwells, and then came the negotiations with her new roommate over who would get the bottom bunk. A half hour of my negotiating prowess resulted in Barbara's sleeping on the top bunk all year.

With the girls in school, I was gone from my empty nest as well, back out on the campaign trail full-time.

The first presidential debate was to be held in Boston on October 3, at the University of Massachusetts. When we arrived at the airport, Al Gore's Air Force Two was already parked on the runway, looking large and imposing. I've always found presidential debates to be particularly nerve-racking. When Gampy was running in 1988, George and his youngest brother, Marvin, who lived outside Washington, D.C., were so nervous during the first debate that they couldn't bear to watch it. They went to the movies instead. Then every few minutes, they walked out to the theater lobby to call home from the pay phone and check on how things were going. After about an hour of that, they gave up and drove back to our house. I spent one of Gampy's presidential debates in bed with the covers pulled up to my eyes. I always politely turned down any invites to debate parties, with their uncorked wine bottles and platters of mini quiches and hot hors d'oeuvres. And now I had to sit, composed and almost expressionless, while George debated Al Gore. After what had happened to Gampy in 1992, when he had looked at his watch once during a debate with Bill Clinton, I was afraid even to check the time. Afterward, I walked up onto the stage to greet everyone. Bar had reminded me to be sure to walk over and shake hands with the opposing candidate and his wife.

George had gone into the evening trailing in the polls, but his focused answers, combined with Al Gore's grimaces and audible sighs, changed the dynamic of the race. George is quick-witted—during the primaries, when he had been asked about his biggest mistake, he said trading the baseball legend Sammy Sosa. I recall another primary debate question in Des Moines; the moderator asked, What political philosopher do you identify with most? I could almost see the other candidates' mental wheels turning—Do I say, John Locke, or Teddy Roosevelt, or Ronald Reagan?— and then George answered, "Christ, because he changed my heart." Some of the media and pundits were shocked, but to be in that room was to feel everyone else groping to follow George's lead.

By the time the third debate was over, George was ten points ahead in the polls. Now, as the days ticked down, we were trying to cover as many states and as much of the country as possible before the election. The attacks grew nastier, the tone sharper.

On October 23, I was flying to Wisconsin with Bar, Lynne Cheney, and Cindy McCain, when suddenly the oxygen masks dropped down. The pilot told us it was just a precaution because we were experiencing cabin pressure problems. The masks and the warning were enough for most of us to feel light-headed, whether or not we were in any danger of running out of air. The plane ended up making an emergency landing in Tulsa, Oklahoma. That flight was an apt metaphor for this last leg of the campaign. Neither side wanted to run out of air before November 7.

Five days before the election, the story broke that George had been arrested for a DUI, driving under the influence, in Maine before we were married. He had never discussed it publicly, although George had told me about it before we wed, and he had alluded to it once when he ran for governor. Actually, in some ways, what he said about those years was worse. He uttered the line "When I was young and irresponsible, I was young and irresponsible," which always made people think that he had been wilder than he ever really was. George's dad had been in politics since before George entered Yale. He knew the stakes; he knew he should never do anything illegal, never do anything that might disgrace his father. His whole family knew it. And what's more, none of them ever wanted to. But now, in an election where character was a key issue, the last four days were being devoted to questions about George's character. I called the girls at school before they heard the news from someone else. The polls showed that George's three-to-five-point lead had collapsed into nearly a dead heat.

Election night for a candidate's wife is largely about supporting your spouse. There are no speeches to give, no questions to answer. It is a mime performance of waves and gestures, and on your face, the look of radiant relief at victory or brave composure at defeat. I had chosen a royal blue suit to carry me through from dinner to the returns and whatever lay beyond.

In the final thirty-six hours, we had barnstormed from Florida through Texas, finally touching down in Austin so we could go back home to the governor's residence and get up the next morning to vote. Election night, we were slated to eat dinner at one of Ronnie and Peggy Weiss's restaurants, the Shoreline Grill. The tables were set, appetizers were ready, but before 7:00 P.M., we got the news that Florida was being called for Gore, along with Michigan. George and I got up from the table and left for the Governor's Mansion. Jeb came back shortly afterward and began furiously working the phones. When the first election call was made, the polls had not even closed in the Florida panhandle, which is in a separate time zone, one hour earlier than the rest of the state. Voter News Service had made their prediction based on the morning's and afternoon's exit polls.

The family gathered in our tiny upstairs rooms at the Governor's Mansion. The night was dark and rainy. Bar Bush was sitting on the sofa with a needlepoint canvas and a pair of earphones, listening to a Sandra Brown novel. She stitched and listened, stitched and listened as the minutes dragged by. I went into the kitchen to make coffee and unload and reload the dishwasher as mugs and glasses were filled and refilled. Then, a little after 9:00 P.M. Texas time, the networks retracted their calls.

At a little after 1:00 A.M., Florida was re-called for George. George stepped into the hallway to review his acceptance speech; the cars were waiting to take us over to the rain-soaked Capitol, and our supporters began leaving their hotels to line the grounds. Many of our best friends from around the country had flown in for the night. Thousands more people were already waiting for the man they thought would be the president-elect to arrive.

Then, at about 1:30 in the morning, 2:30 on the East Coast, Al Gore phoned to congratulate George and concede. The election was truly over. George hugged me, hugged his parents and his brother. My mother was on the verge of tears.

Our celebration lasted about twenty minutes. One by one the networks announced that Florida was again too close to call. An hour after his first phone call, Al Gore called George back to retract his concession. There was not to be an election night after all.

I looked around our small living room. Everyone was exhausted. After years of being on the road almost every night of every week, of working so incredibly hard, there was to be no resolution this night. I walked over to George, wrapped my arm around him, and said, "Bushie, would you rather win or go to bed?" He looked at me, laughed, and said, "Go to bed." Sometime after 3:00 A.M., after Don Evans, George's campaign chair, had gone out to speak to the press and our supporters in Austin, to tell them that he believed "when it's all said and done, we will prevail," I finally sent everyone off to their hotel rooms or their homes for what little sleep they could get. We assumed things would look different in the morning. We had no way of knowing that our election night would not end for another thirty-five days.

I look back on that recount period as endless and simultaneously brief. I ate, I walked, I read, but where and what I'm no longer entirely sure. George would grill chicken or steaks in the little barbecue pit at the back of the clapboard house on our ranch; I fixed tuna salad for lunch, including for Walter Isaacson, then of *Time* magazine, when he flew down with his wife to interview George. Most of the details, though, long ago eroded away, so that all that my mind retains are the barest outlines. Almost the entire time, we stayed at either the governor's residence or the ranch, detached and consumed, almost as one is with an ICU patient, looking for signs in the green-tinged monitors and their endless data streams, waiting for that decisive turn. The final Florida vote totals from election night had George leading Al Gore by over one thousand votes. Then the recounts began. I also had the Texas Book Festival to oversee the very next weekend.

When we'd picked the festival date, no one thought that we would be stuck in a strange kind of limbo, not knowing whether we would be staying in Austin or moving to Washington. I hastily redid my speech with the Texas writer Steve Harrigan to include some jokes about the unfinished election; I hosted the festival and the black-tie events, and like the tick-tock of a metronome, the counting continued. George and I left for the ranch, where at least we could look up at the sky and breathe. As with everything else that November, our new house, which was supposed to be finished by Christmas, was behind schedule. I watched the workmen, hoping I could will them to finish. The giant TV trucks followed us. Their satellite antennas pivoted like science-fiction creatures as they beamed footage of the coarse, sapped fall grasses and our neighbor's barn and hay pile. Back in Austin, correspondents did their stand-ups within full view of the Governor's Mansion, their klieg lights blazing on the sidewalks.

When we returned to Austin, there were protesters on the streets, but most of them were backing George. We saw the golfer Ben Crenshaw and his wife, Julie, pushing their little baby in a stroller and holding up signs of support. Many of our closest friends were walking around the Governor's Mansion with signs too. In Washington, Doro, George's sister, joined the protesters outside the vice president's residence.

But we also knew the vice president's house from George's dad, and I could imagine the Gores being cooped up in there, high on the hill, waiting, just as we were.

There was nothing to do but wait. On November 7, we already thought we had won. In the weeks that followed, George was still winning every recount. Al Gore did have the lead in the popular vote, but that is not how our presidential system works. Presidents are elected based on winning state electoral votes. If the popular vote decided who won, then each side and each candidate would have employed a very different strategy. We, for example, would have tried to turn out as many votes as possible among the 12 million registered voters in Texas. Four years later, when George won reelection by more than 3 million votes nationwide, John Kerry's campaign briefly considered a postelection legal challenge in Ohio, to try to win its electoral votes.

But for this election, it was now up to the lawyers and the courts. The ultimate decision was out of our hands. Like a baseball batter in the ninth inning of game seven of the World Series, we had learned to tune out all the extraneous noise. We did not hear the cheers or the taunts; there was only us, and the whoosh of the ball and the crack of the wood. Then, on December 12, election 2000 finally came to an end. The Supreme Court issued two decisions. The first was a 7–2 ruling that the manual Florida vote recount had violated the equal protection clause of the Constitution because not all ballots were treated alike in all Florida counties. Some counties recorded unperforated punch ballots as votes while others designated them as nonvotes. There was no uniform standard. On what the appropriate remedy to recount should be, the ruling was much closer. By a 5–4 decision, the justices ruled that there was no fair way to recount all the votes yet again and allow Florida to participate in the Electoral

College. The current vote count would stand. George was declared the winner. Months later, when most of the major media outlets conducted their own series of recounts, he still won.

The next night, Al Gore addressed the nation, and then George did the same from the Texas Capitol. George was now president-elect. We had survived the previous weeks by living in what we called "our Zen mode." Now, although George and his staff had been working on a possible presidential transition since before the election—as had Al Gore—I personally had less than five weeks, half the usual time, to prepare for an inauguration and the start of George's four-year presidential term.

~

We had last lived in Washington, D.C., thirteen years earlier, when George had come up to work on his father's presidential campaign. Then, as we drove around the city in our family station wagon, official motorcades would occasionally pass us. One evening in particular, we were in our car when George realized that a small motorcade was coming up from behind. He slowed down, sure we would know whoever was in the vehicle, most likely Secretary of State George Shultz. As we coasted and waited for the entourage to pass us, a Secret Service bullhorn blared, "Texas, move along." We, of course, had Texas plates on our car, and the procession wanted us to hurry up and get out of the way. Now we were the ones who would be riding in official motorcades.

On December 18, I returned to Washington. I had a new title, First Lady–Designate, and I was going to be shown the White House by Senator-elect Hillary Rodham Clinton. I knew the White House from Bar and Gampy's four years; I had slept under the high carved headboard and heavy covers in the Lincoln Bedroom. In the last six years, the Clintons had also hosted us for official governors association dinners. But that morning, as I waited at the ornate, gilded Mayflower Hotel for word that Hillary Clinton was ready for us to depart for the White House, there was a profound difference. My visit this time was rather like the walk-through of a house on the morning before settlement, except that a president and his wife do not own the White House. It is the American people's house. I would inhabit it, like Dolley Madison and Mary Todd Lincoln and Eleanor Roosevelt and Bess Truman, like Jackie Kennedy, Lady Bird

Johnson, Nancy Reagan, Barbara Bush, and the other women before me. I would care for it, and perhaps leave a little something of myself behind.

Hillary Clinton was waiting for us on the South Portico. With plans to move out and to assume her role in the Senate, she had been running late that morning, but in the press reports, I was the one who was chided for tardiness and for my clothes. That's the struggle with trying to find news when you have twenty cameras trained on two women greeting each other at a doorway for a private tea. What seems most interesting is often mostly wrong. I do remember that when my big, black car pulled up and the Secret Service agents appeared, they couldn't open the car doors. The agents tugged on the handles while we stayed stuck inside, smiling gamely, and Hillary stood, waiting awkwardly. Finally, someone figured out how to release the locks.

Once I stepped out, Hillary was gracious and forthcoming. There is a particular kinship that develops between the spouses of political leaders. I had it with many of the governors' wives, and I would continue to have it with former first ladies and the wives of many foreign leaders. There was a similarity and at times a strangeness to our shared circumstances that created an instant bond. It is a kinship I felt regardless of political persuasion, and I felt it that morning at the double-door entrance to the South Portico with Hillary, as she began our tour of the public house and the private living quarters and offered me her very candid advice. She even told me that, if she had it to do all over again, she would not have had an office in the West Wing, that she seldom used it after the healthcare debate ended. And I do know many women who wonder to this day why it is still referred to as Hillary's healthcare plan, rather than the Clinton healthcare plan, when it was done under the auspices of her husband, the president.

Hillary gave me another piece of heartfelt advice. She told me not to turn down invitations to unique or special events. In the late winter of 1995, Jackie Kennedy had called Hillary to invite her and her daughter, Chelsea, to the ballet in New York. Chelsea was in school; Hillary had a full schedule, and, feeling pressed, she declined. In May, Jackie died of cancer. Hillary said that she had long regretted her choice to stay home and wanted me to know that story so that I would not do the same.

Joined by Chelsea, Hillary led me through the lower level, sharing with me her fond recollections of the parties they had hosted in the Palm

Room, the glassed-in conservatory that divides the formal White House from the West Wing. It was a brief tour through their public and private lives, a whirlwind of parties arranged in the Blue Room, the Red Room, and the Green Room, until I could almost glimpse the elegantly set tables and the banquet chairs. But when we went up to the State Floor, both Hillary and I had forgotten about the public tours. She opened the door to lead me through the formal state rooms, and we caught sight of a large tour group. She quickly shut the door, but not before some very surprised tourists got a good look at the outgoing and incoming first ladies.

We moved upstairs to the family quarters, where at one point Chelsea said, "Mom, tell Mrs. Bush about the tomato plants," and Hillary led me out on the parapet off the third floor, where each spring they set out pots of tomato plants, because "you just can't get good tomatoes." I nodded my head and smiled and thought, Tomatoes? You can't get good tomatoes at the White House? But George and I also grew pots of tomatoes on the parapet.

Hillary was thinking about her own future and how much she wanted to buy a house of her own in Washington, saying that "men keep saying to me, 'You're going to be a senator, just rent something, and you can find something later.' But," she told me, "that doesn't work on my time line. I need to be moved into a new house. I need to have a house." And I understood her completely. If I had been Hillary, I would not have wanted to wait until after I was in the Senate to find my home.

We were standing in the first lady's dressing room when Hillary paused and remembered something that Barbara Bush had shown her, eight years before. "Your mother-in-law stood right here and told me that from this window you can see straight down into the Rose Garden and also over to the Oval Office, and you can watch what's going on."

I did look out that window many times over the years, out to the Rose Garden and around the grounds, always careful to stand just inside the frame so that no one would spot me. If George was doing an event in the Rose Garden, I could see it from the window and live on television at the same time.

I finished that day by interviewing potential staff members for my new East Wing office at the White House. The last candidate had four legs and was ten weeks old. He was a Scottish terrier puppy, born to a dog owned by New Jersey governor Christie Todd Whitman, and, of course, I fell in love. I had seen his puppy pictures on November 4, my birthday, when George and I were in New Jersey on the last leg of the campaign trail. George hadn't gotten me a gift, and Christie Whitman suggested a puppy. Our D.C. interview sealed the deal. Barney flew back with me to Austin the next day to join our animal family. We already had a springer spaniel, Spot, one of the six puppies born to Bar's dog, Millie, in 1989, when she lived in the White House. Spot was the runt of the litter, and I can still recall Barbara and Jenna proudly taking their new puppy and their grandmother, simultaneously, to first-grade show 'n' tell in Dallas. Afterward, the principal of Preston Hollow Elementary, Susie Oliphant, had the children line the halls so that Jenna, Barbara, Bar, and Spot could walk past the whole school.

All our animals in Dallas were named for Texas Rangers baseball players. Spot got her name in honor of the infielder Scott Fletcher, Barbara's favorite player. Of course, the Rangers almost immediately traded Scott. Our cat was named after Ruben Sierra, whose nickname, El Indio, gave Kitty her name, La India. And at times, I would look at our pets and remember our girls and our lives, the family that we were beyond the White House walls.

For the move to the White House, I packed our clothes, family photos, and a single piece of furniture, a chest of drawers that had belonged to George's grandmother, which I thought would fit perfectly in my dressing room. We didn't send another thing. I knew from Bar that the White House has a huge and exquisite collection of furniture and art, and that we would leave office with an entirely new book collection, titles given to us by authors, publishers, and friends. For the trip to Washington, our possessions took up less than one very small moving van. The rest I planned to send to our ranch, and the incoming governor, Rick Perry, and his wife, Anita, very kindly waited to move into the Governor's Mansion until our home was ready, so that the movers could transport our furniture directly to Crawford.

I do regret now that in those hectic days I never sat down with Anita, the new first lady of Texas, to give her much of the same helpful advice that Rita Clements had given me. I never had a chance to walk her through everything, from the house to the responsibilities; there just wasn't time. Our good friend Jeanne Johnson Phillips was overseeing the inaugural festivities, and I was being asked to decide on programs, a prayer service, an authors' event, and of course, clothes. I had not looked at or contemplated an inaugural wardrobe for me or for the girls before the election was decided. Now I had barely one month to be dressed, not simply for the inauguration and the night of balls but for the three days of events surrounding them. And clothes are a big part of being first lady, dating back all the way to Martha Washington and Dolley Madison. The Dallas designer Michael Faircloth made me a deep turquoise outfit for the inaugural and a red lace gown with Austrian crystals for the inaugural night. But I had to have more gowns and outfits for other inaugural events, and I bought two other long dresses, one champagne, one deep teal, as well as two suits and a cranberry-colored dress. Jenna and Barbara bought inaugural ceremony outfits designed by Lela Rose, the daughter of our good Dallas friends Rusty and Deedie Rose; she also made their gowns for the Texas Black Tie & Boots Ball the night before. For their official inaugural night ball gowns, they chose designs by Susan Dell of Austin, a strapless beaded black gown for Jenna and a V-neck silk and chiffon beaded currant gown for Barbara.

We arrived in Washington, D.C., and stayed, as all presidents-elect do, in the historic Blair House across the street from the White House, the same home where we had stayed with Gampy in 1988. When I went to the Lincoln Memorial for a concert to open the inaugural festivities, my place on the platform was next to the spot marked "President-elect."

Inauguration Eve began early in the morning with a series of interviews at Blair House, including a sit-down with Katie Couric, then of NBC's *Today* show. Toward the end of our conversation, she said to me, "You appear to be a very traditional woman. Is that a fair characterization?" It was slightly better than the other perennial interview question, "Are you going to be Hillary Clinton or Barbara Bush?" as if the first lady's role was like hand-me-down shoes and I had to choose between two previously worn pairs.

But there was, from the start, an underlying assumption on the part of the press that I would be someone else when I assumed the role of first lady, that I would not, under any circumstances, simply be myself.

As I had done when George was sworn in as governor of Texas, I planned an event to celebrate authors. This was to be my "first lady" inaugural party. I was much more interested in listening to Stephen Ambrose discuss history or Mary Higgins Clark and Carol Higgins Clark talk about plotting a mystery or having Stanley Crouch and the Texas author Steve Harrigan discuss literature than I was in attending another large luncheon or party; and to me, an afternoon with authors was as glamorous as a high-heeled, long-gown ball. The Cheneys sat in the front row, along with Bar and Gampy and my mother and George, who introduced me by saying, "Her love for books is real, her love for children is real, and my love for her is real." Then I walked onto a stage decorated to look like a library, and before a crowd of more than three thousand, I spoke of my passion for literature, saying, "Our country's authors have helped forge the American identity, create its memory, and define and reinforce our national consciousness," adding, "Books have done what humans rarely do, convince us to put down the remote control."

Inauguration Day dawned cold and rainy, but to George and me, the morning was beautiful. We began with a church service at the nearby St. John's Episcopal Church. The creamy yellow building held its first service in 1816; its nearly one-thousand-pound steeple bell was cast by Paul Revere's son. Every president since James Madison has worshiped there; pew fifty-four is designated as the President's Pew. St. John's became our Washington church while we were at the White House; it was where we had attended services in 1988, when George had been working on his father's presidential campaign.

Listening to the sermon and the prayers provided our last moments for tranquil reflection. From St. John's, we would be whisked from event to event; each second of our day would be accounted for, and the clock was unyielding.

After the service, we drove straight across Pennsylvania Avenue to the White House, where Bill and Hillary Clinton were waiting to greet us for the traditional coffee. The Cheneys came, as did Al and Tipper Gore.

Then we departed in our motorcade for the Capitol, George and Bill Clinton riding in the president's car, and Hillary and me following behind. As we chatted on the short drive, I thought of how, in most cases, a first lady's departure day is the start of her retirement. For Hillary, it was the beginning of her own career. And nearly two years after George had held his press conference in the garden of the Texas Governor's Mansion, he was going to be sworn in as the forty-third president of the United States, and only the second presidential son to hold the office himself. History would now record John Adams and John Quincy Adams and George H. W. Bush and George W. Bush.

As we rode up Pennsylvania Avenue, I saw a collection of protesters, waving placards and calling George's election illegitimate. Until that moment, I had thought that once a winner was formally declared, the postelection rancor would die down, that everyone would move on. But in the years to come, we found that, for some, the bitterness remained.

There is no grand entrance to be made for the outgoing president and his incoming successor. We entered through a side door at the Capitol into a rather ordinary hallway, distinguished only by two moderately sized gilded eagles perched at the top of each wall. From there, it was off to an interior room to wait. Outside, invited guests and spectators had been gathering for hours, even with the rain. Now, with the noon hour approaching, it was George's time. We began our walk, the same basic route that I had taken for Gampy's inaugurals and through the spaces where we had strolled with friends on all those weekend tours. We crossed the sturdy crypt, built to support the soaring dome of the Capitol Rotunda. Lynne Cheney was my companion; George, as the incoming president, would be the last to take his place on the podium. From the crypt, we climbed the stairs to the magnificent Rotunda, ringed by statues and enormous paintings of Revolutionary War scenes, the landing of the Pilgrims, the discovery of the Mississippi, and the baptism of Pocahontas. We passed them all as if in a blur; there was barely time to glance up at the fresco in the dome, painted to glorify George Washington.

George had wanted to use Washington's Bible, the same Bible that his father had used in 1989, for the bicentennial of George Washington's inauguration as the nation's first president. The Washington Bible had been specially transported under Masonic guard from New York to

Washington. But we also had a Bush family Bible on hand, the same one that George had used when he was sworn in as governor of Texas, in case the weather turned bad. In the end, we would use both, the Bush Bible laid on top of Washington's, both closed to protect them from the damp, and the continuity of our national past resting beneath George's hands.

As we left the Rotunda, we walked down a steep set of stairs in a very ordinary hallway, no decorations, just wide-cut, gray stone blocks bathed in darkness, except for the blinding array of television lights waiting to illuminate us as we descended. But from the small doorway, Washington, D.C., was spread before us, the vast expanse of the Mall, the tall, spare point of the Washington Monument, the wide colonnade of the Lincoln Memorial, and the blocks of hard granite buildings lining the avenues. Their edges were soft, as if in a dream, because a cool mist had settled over the city. And even though I had seen the exact same view three other times, on this day, that sight, for those few seconds, was uniquely ours.

I tried to savor it all—the oath of office, the inaugural address, the military band, the friends and family who had come to share the day. For me, the inauguration is the thing of beauty, the scene that will last when all others have faded away.

After the ceremony, back inside, George paused at the bottom of the staircase leading up to the Rotunda and tried to hug me and the girls and his parents, but there was a clock to be kept, and the Senate staffers who oversee the inaugural events were urging us on. We walked the Clintons out to the limousine that would carry them to Andrews Air Force Base, where they would depart for their new home in Chappaqua, not far from New York City. Then we returned for the inaugural luncheon in Statuary Hall, the semicircular room with the wide, marble Corinthian columns quarried from along the Potomac River. It was here that the U.S. House of Representatives had met for nearly forty years, where John Quincy Adams supposedly used the room's echoey acoustics to eavesdrop on his fellow congressmen, and where he also eventually collapsed at his desk. In this room too, John Quincy Adams, James Madison, James Monroe, and Andrew Jackson were inaugurated as president, and the Marquis de Lafayette became the first foreign dignitary to address the U.S. Congress.

This afternoon, I sat next to Senator Mitch McConnell, the Republican senator from Kentucky, who had overseen the inaugural events, and we talked about the intricacies of planning the ceremony. I looked out upon the other tables, catching site of Jenna and Barbara at their first inaugural lunch and at all our own good friends scattered about the room.

Surrounding us were the statues of prominent Americans from many states. We gazed out upon marble carvings of Ethan Allen, the Green Mountain Boy from Vermont; Robert Fulton, who invented the steamship; and also Sam Houston, whose statue had been carved by the Austin artist Elisabet Ney. She had called him one of "my wild boys."

George and I left the lunch so that he could review the troops, and then we began the trip down Pennsylvania Avenue to commence the inaugural parade.

Barbara and Jenna were halfway through their freshman year of college. I had told them to be careful of what they wore on their feet. Inaugural festivities require a lot of climbing stone staircases, standing on marble floors, standing in general, and then sitting in a chilly reviewing stand to watch all the wonderfully enthusiastic floats, performers, and bands from every state in the nation pass. They, of course, chose stiletto-heeled boots, and by the time they got to the Capitol, they were ready to take them off.

After the parade, where both the Midland and Lee high school bands performed, as well as the marching bands from my alma maters, the University of Texas at Austin and Southern Methodist University, there was a brief period to rest and eat a small dinner before we began dressing for the round of inaugural balls. The unbelievably efficient White House ushers and staff had removed the Clintons' possessions — Bill Clinton had told us that morning that, by the end, he was packing simply by pulling out drawers and dumping their contents into boxes. Then the staff unpacked all our clothes and arranged our rooms; even our photographs were out on display. The transfer of families is a choreographic masterpiece, done with exceptional speed.

By now, my feet hurt, but I squeezed them into my shoes. It was painful almost from the first step. One of my friends from Midland later wrote that she saw women wearing tennis shoes under their long evening dresses, and that our good friend Dr. Charlie Younger had lent blue surgery covers to protect everyone's shoes and feet from the cold and wet. Some of our close friends couldn't get rides back to their hotels after the balls; they rode D.C.'s subway system, the Metro, in their tuxes, ball gowns, and high heels.

We had eight balls; the Clintons had held fourteen just four years before. "Ball" is almost a misnomer for some of these events, which are held in convention centers and hotel ballrooms with cash bars and are more like cattle calls, where there is barely space to turn around and no place to sit down. People wait all evening for the president and first lady and also the vice president and his wife to walk in on a great stage. Each moment is like a scene from a play, with eight nearly identical performances in a single night. The inaugural organizers recite the same introduction; the president speaks; and the new first couple dances the same dance to the same music, waves, and departs for another ball in another part of town. The fun was actually getting to visit with whoever was riding with us to the next ball. We had Condi Rice and her date in our limo a couple of times; and also George's campaign chair, Don Evans, and his wife, Susie, old Midland friends; and Mercer and Gabby Reynolds, who had helped plan the inauguration. We told jokes and laughed as the motorcade rolled through the city that was now our home.

For the next inaugural in 2005, I chose my shoes with what I thought was more care, but they were dyed to match my dress, and they must have shrunk during the dyeing process. That night, I distinctly remember walking from ball to ball through the underground corridors of the Washington Convention Center in my bare, aching feet, carrying my shoes in my hand.

But I loved watching George dance with Jenna and Barbara at the Texas-Wyoming Ball, and I loved that the people who had worked so long and hard for us had a chance to celebrate as well. Our theme was "Celebrating America's Spirit Together." It was not, however, a late night for the new president. We were home before midnight, quite a change from the previous administration, which relished late nights. Bill and Hillary had not wanted to miss more than a few minutes of their last day in the White House, even watching a movie in the movie theater at 2:30 A.M. The fun of that night left them so tired that when Barbara, Jenna, and I glanced over at Bill during George's inaugural address, he was dozing.

As we pulled back inside the White House grounds a few minutes before midnight, George, who was already famous for his early bedtimes, joked to our Secret Service detail, "This is going to be new for you." And the agent in the front laughed and said, "Yeah, I'm going to say to my wife, 'Guess what, honey? I'm home!'"

That night, as we lay in bed, the entire White House upstairs residence was packed. George's parents were down the hall in the Queens' Bedroom, named for all the royal guests who had stayed in it. My mother was sleeping in another guest room, Jenna and Barbara were in their rooms, and every other space was filled with George's siblings and their families, a total of twenty-three relatives, some spending the night on rollaway cots. But having everyone with us was like the sigh of relief I would breathe back in Texas when I heard the door open late at night and I knew the girls were home and headed for bed. That inaugural night, I drifted off to sleep knowing that everyone we loved was safe, tucked in together under this one, remarkable roof.

The next morning, Sunday, we attended the traditional inaugural prayer service, decreed by Congress and held since the first swearing in of George Washington. It was now at the National Cathedral and was a beautiful interfaith collection of music, prayers, and verse. The Navy Sea Chanters and Larry Gatlin both sang in the musical prelude, and the service ended with a chorus of "America the Beautiful." We returned to the White House for a brunch with all of our friends. I was expecting to sit around and listen to their funny stories of the inauguration, like the blue surgical booties and the tennis sneakers, to hear about what they did, what parties they went to, who they saw. Instead, we were mobbed by our own friends, who wanted to snap pictures of us with their families and children. It was like being at an official event all over again. Our friends flew home, and George and I went to work, he to the Oval Office and I to my space in the East Wing. It was years before I got to hear all their stories.

I was grateful for the days we had already spent in the White House with Ganny and Gampy. Parts of it are warrens of rooms and alcoves and doorways; there are 132 rooms housed inside its walls. At first, my assistant, Sarah Moss, who worked in an upstairs office in the residence, would get lost just trying to find the elevator foyer. I might not be entirely certain of what I was going to do as first lady, but at least right away, I could find the elevator.

As for George, he was shocked when two members of the residence staff, Sam Sutton and Fidel Medina, introduced themselves to him as the president's valets. George took his dad aside and said, "I don't think I need a valet." Gampy smiled and told him, "Don't worry, you'll get used to it."

My first project found me on my first workday morning at the White House. I was coming down the elevator into the ground-floor Cross Hall as George's close political advisor Karl Rove was walking toward the West Wing with Dick Moe, head of the National Trust for Historic Preservation. The National Trust designates and protects many of our nation's most treasured landmarks. I introduced myself and said that I was interested in historical preservation and wanted to continue Hillary Clinton's work on Save America's Treasures, a federal program that had begun in 1998 to protect our country's leading historical landmarks and artifacts. Its first project had been the restoration of the 1812 Star-Spangled Banner. Dick was familiar with the work George had done in Texas to save and preserve the state's historic county courthouses.

I became the honorary chair of Save America's Treasures, and two years later launched a complementary initiative, Preserve America, which encourages every community to protect its unique historic assets. My co-chair at Preserve America was John Nau, a friend from Texas who is deeply interested in preservation and who had worked to protect battlefields and other important sites from the Civil War. Over George's two terms, more than six hundred communities in all fifty states and the U.S. Virgin Islands were officially designated as Preserve America Communities.

But my first priority was the White House itself. I knew what a remarkable collection of art and furniture the White House had, exceptional pieces by many of America's best furniture makers, pieces that had been owned by other presidents, even a collection of campaign bandannas from Andrew Jackson's run for the presidency. I was eager to start making the White House residence our home. Ken Blasingame, an artist and decorator, and my longtime friend, came to help me make the private rooms into a home for our family. Along with James Powell, an antiques expert from Austin, Ken searched the special, climate-controlled facility that stores the White House collection to look for furniture from past administrations that would be appropriate for each room.

Each new arrival to the White House finds the residence furnished in the style of his predecessor. Many rooms remain unchanged from administration to administration. The Clintons and the Bushes had kept the black lacquer Chinese screen that Nancy Reagan's much-loved decorator, Ted Graber, had installed in the long, cavernous upstairs Cross Hall. I kept the cheerful, light fabric that the Clintons had used to cover the walls of the small family dining room upstairs.

I set up the girls' rooms first, painting the walls a soft aqua and installing two double beds in each, so that they could have friends sleep over, as they had done in Austin. Many nights during college breaks and summer vacations we had eight girls crowded into the two rooms. In Barbara's room, I hung a loaned portrait of identical twins. My next project was the Treaty Room.

The Treaty Room is quite literally that, a room where the peace protocol to end the Spanish-American War was signed in 1898 and where President John F. Kennedy had signed the Partial Nuclear Test Ban Treaty some seven weeks before he died. President Grant had used it as his cabinet room, and the room had the original Grant administration cabinet desk, with eight drawers, one for each cabinet member, plus the president. After the West Wing was built, the Treaty Room was intermittently used as a private presidential study. George's father had used it as his upstairs office, and I knew George would like to do the same. Most nights, after we ate dinner, he would head to the Treaty Room to read his nightly briefing papers and make phone calls. I painted the walls cream and brought over Grant's original sofa and two chairs from the White House collection. I wasn't as excited by a room full of Victorian furniture once I saw it arranged, but George said, "I love having Grant's furniture." He did indeed. There is something special about knowing that a previous president has used that same furniture in that very same room. George would gaze up at the famous George P. Healy painting *The Peacemakers*, depicting Lincoln meeting with his generals Grant and Sherman, and Admiral Porter, at the end of the Civil War, and he would sense the history that had already happened here. There is a unique continuity to knowing your predecessors have walked these halls, have written on these tables, have sat in these chairs. And a particular comfort as well. We both felt that comfort in the rooms of the White House.

For our first week in the White House, I also had my friend Lynn Munn in residence. Lynn had helped me move into so many homes, but this time she had stayed in Washington because her husband, Bill, had suffered a heart attack early Sunday morning after the inauguration. She and her daughter, Kelly, and son-in-law, Tom, spent their days at George Washington University Hospital with Bill, but at night they came to stay with us until Bill was well enough to fly back home to Midland.

In mid-February, I was back in Texas. Our ranch house in Crawford was close to completion, and I had another move to oversee. I had to unpack our books, hang our pictures, and stock the cabinets in the kitchen. And I needed to look at the house with a different eye, for how we would entertain foreign leaders in our newly completed home.

We'd already had our first request: Tony and Cherie Blair were coming to visit at the end of February, and Cherie was hoping to be invited to our ranch in Crawford because she had already been to the White House and Camp David with the Clintons. But our guesthouse next to the main ranch house remained unfinished, so we invited them to be our first international guests at Camp David instead.

Nestled in the Catoctin Mountains of Maryland, Camp David has been a presidential retreat since the time of Franklin Roosevelt, who called it Shangri-La; President Dwight Eisenhower renamed it for his grandson, David. Camp David is a nickname for Naval Support Facility Thurmont, and it is an active naval base. Marines and Navy sailors work and often live on the grounds. The camp itself spans 180 acres, and the presidential section consists of a series of comfortable cabins tucked among the trees and connected by winding paths. Franklin Roosevelt met with Winston Churchill at Camp David, Ronald Reagan had invited Margaret Thatcher, and Gampy had hosted John Major.

Camp David is a far more intimate setting than the White House. It is a place where you can get to know another leader without the crush of a roomful of a hundred or so invited guests and an hour or more of receiving lines, with their jumble of announced names, quick pleasantries, and official photos, which are all but required for formal White House entertaining. It is a real treat to show off the White House in its full splendor to visiting heads of state or government, to introduce them to celebrities and other famous Americans. But entertaining at a place like Camp David, or later our ranch, was far more relaxed and casual. A visit to Camp David is more like a visit to someone's weekend place. And it cements a different friendship than simply having a fancy event amid gleaming silver and glittering chandeliers. We could visit with our guests over coffee at breakfast, or have dinner and then watch a movie; for the Blairs, it was *Meet the Parents*. Leaders who came to visit us at the White House stayed across the street at Blair House and invariably showed up at night on the front steps in black tie.

I was a bit nervous about meeting the Blairs. I knew what close friends they had been with Bill and Hillary Clinton, and I wondered how we would get along. The British tabloids didn't help. CLASH OF CHERIE AND DUBYA'S COWGIRL headlined *The Daily Record*, FROSTY FORECAST AS OUR MODERN MUM MEETS BUSH'S LITTLE WOMAN AT SUMMIT. The Brits were convinced that it would be torture for Cherie Blair to sit down and have a meal alone with me while George and Tony got to know each other. "Laura is a cookie-baking homemaker," they wrote, "dull, mumsy, and old-fashioned." At least with the British press, one never needs to say "Tell us what you really think."

But Cherie Blair and I did hit it off when we had our private lunch in Aspen Lodge, the president's cabin, while George and Tony Blair and their staffs had a working afternoon at Laurel, the main lodge. Cherie is funny and smart, and we talked about our families; her oldest children and Jenna and Barbara are close in age. We enjoyed talking about topics like women's issues and improving women's health, although what I liked most about our friendship was the intimacy of it, rather like two busy mothers catching up over coffee. Cherie is a wonderful reader, and we shared a love of books, and more than a few favorite authors. She was particularly attuned to the challenges of being an American first lady. In England, the prime minister's wife has no official title and few official responsibilities. Cherie was proud of having kept her day job as a barrister in the British courts.

Early on, George apologized to the Blairs that we couldn't have them to the ranch—because the final work wouldn't be complete until March. The only thing I felt bad about on this visit was that I don't think the Blairs, Cherie especially, were all that keen on pets. We, of course, had ferried Kitty, Barney, and Spot to Camp David. I asked Cherie if they had any animals, and she paused and answered, "Well, we had a gerbil. Once."

The day that the Blairs arrived, I had spent part of the morning with Oprah Winfrey. There was tremendous curiosity about me as the new first lady, and although I hadn't really done anything yet, reporters from across the country wanted me to sit for interviews. *The Washington Post, Good Morning America*, the Texas papers, *Harper's Bazaar, People*, Reuters, the list was long and growing. I was waiting upstairs for Oprah, who arrived with her best friend and business partner, Gayle King, but before they were escorted to the upper level, George passed by with Condoleezza Rice, his national security advisor, and Colin Powell, his secretary of state. My staff later told me that Oprah was speechless at meeting them. For the first time, the two individuals tasked with overseeing U.S. foreign policy were African-American. Gayle King had to give Oprah a little poke to remind her to talk. And I thought later, what a wonderful moment, to have this crossroads of success in the people's house that was, at the founding of the nation, built by the labor of unknown and unrecognized slaves.

While we hit the ground running, there were a few mishaps. Saturday afternoon after the Blairs departed we helicoptered back to the White House to prepare for the National Governors Association meeting, which George and I had attended for six years while Bill Clinton was in office. Now it was our turn to play host. Sunday night was the opening dinner. During their years, the Clintons had invited many of their gubernatorial friends to spend the night at the White House. We were planning on doing the same for some of our Republican governor friends, including George Pataki of New York and John Engler of Michigan. George and I waited for our overnight guests to arrive. Time passed, and no one appeared. Finally, George turned to me and said, "Well, what did they say when you invited them?"

"When *I* invited them? I thought you did it," I replied. Neither of us had told our staffs to invite anyone; each assumed that the other had taken care of it. At eight o'clock, Jeb and Columba Bush did show up. Jeb was the governor of Florida, and he had called us to see if he could spend the night while he was in town.

In March, I began my education initiatives in earnest. I started out wanting to replicate some of my most successful Texas projects on a national scale. I made school visits to highlight innovative educational programs and started planning an early childhood cognitive development conference to be held in Washington that summer. My other chief focus was teacher recruitment, positive ways to entice more people to work in our nation's schools and classrooms. I began by working with two programs, Teach for America and Troops to Teachers, which encourages members of the military who are retiring from the service to go into teaching. In less than ten years, it had sent almost four thousand troops into teaching. George wanted to boost the program's funding from $3 million to $30 million to help more men and women in uniform find a second career in the classroom. At a Troops to Teachers event at the San Diego Naval Station, I spoke before almost a thousand sailors and Marines and toured the USS *Shiloh*, a ballistic missile defense cruiser, as well as the USS *Decatur*, a destroyer, while the air rushed off the water and the waves broke around their hulls.

And there was another idea that I wanted to initiate, a National Book Festival, to be held in partnership with the Library of Congress, to bring some of the nation's leading authors to Washington and, with the help of cable television's C-SPAN, carry their words to the country at large. I had seen the overwhelming success of the Texas Book Festival, and I believed that it could have even more meaning on a national scale. The Library of Congress would be the perfect co-sponsor and a perfect venue to celebrate authors and promote reading and literacy.

By now, my official duties were in full swing. My chief of staff, the scheduler, and I held near daily meetings to review the hundreds of requests that came to the White House. But we were proactive; my policy director, Anne Heiligenstein, looked for opportunities where I could high-light education issues. My calendar was crowded with official and cour-tesy duties, like attending the opening of the Washington, D.C., Cherry Blossom Festival on April 9 with the Japanese ambassador. And when George met with a male head of state in the Oval Office, I frequently hosted his wife for coffee. Suzanne Mubarak, the first lady of Egypt, who was a longtime friend of Bar Bush's, was one of my first guests; Bar had shown Suzanne the photos of the girls when they were newborns. Queen Rania of Jordan came to the White House, as did King Juan Carlos and Queen Sofia of Spain. I needed to master the finer points of protocol that dictated whether I should address a sovereign as Your Highness or Your Majesty. Queen Elizabeth of England and King Abdullah of Saudi Arabia are both "Your Majesty," but the legion of crown princes and princesses around the world are called "Your Highness," or sometimes "Your Royal Highness." It's rather amusing that, more than 225 years after the United States declared its independence from the monarchy of Great Britain, American presidents and their spouses pore over protocol briefing books to ensure that they do not make a misstep in addressing foreign royalty.

Indeed, a coffee at the White House is a highly elaborate affair, involv-ing briefing books and protocol notes, as well as carefully selected china, coffee blends, and refreshments. It included not simply me and my guest but ambassadors' wives and staff members murmuring in the background. Some of the wives who came were so nervous either about meeting me or about being in the White House that they read their carefully scripted con-versation points off preprinted note cards folded in their hands or perched on their laps. But often these events turned into highly personal visits, in which the wives of other heads of state and I could talk about our lives, our families, and the challenges of balancing public needs with maintain-ing a private life at home. We were diverse women thrown together by circumstance, but we found much common ground in the way of shared experiences.

For Easter, we went to the ranch. It was the first time we had spent the night in our new home, and George was thrilled to stand in the finished rooms that we had imagined and planned together for so long. As with any new house, there were windows without coverings and beds without comforters and sheets, but at last our own home was complete. We were up for sunrise services at the Canaan Baptist Church down the road, and the world that morning had the tranquil sense of being at peace. Mother came back with us to Washington, and three nights later, we went to the Holocaust Memorial Museum on the eve of the Day of Remembrance for the Holocaust. Joining us were Don Etra, one of George's best friends from Yale, and his wife, Paula, and Tom and Andi Bernstein, who had been among our co-owners of the Texas Rangers. George had appointed Don and Tom to serve on the Holocaust museum board.

The museum is only minutes from the White House, tucked in between the Department of Agriculture and the Bureau of Engraving and Printing. Yet behind its brick and granite walls is a testament to overwhelming evil, evil planned and perpetrated by some of the most advanced minds in human history. We walked past a cattle car that had carried Jews and others along rail lines to the death camps; we saw piles of unlaced shoes from Majdanek, reconstructed barracks from Auschwitz, the implements of the crematoriums, the crayon drawings of children who were gassed and burned to ash at Theresienstadt.

The next morning, George, Mother, and I were in the Capitol Rotunda for the ceremonies to mark the Day of Remembrance. We watched as flags from each American military unit that had liberated the Nazi death camps were carried in. Mother and I waited, side by side, trying to remember which flag and which unit was Daddy's. Then suddenly we saw it, the Timberwolf flag, with its signature wolf, head up, mouth open, as if in full howl. And we both burst into tears. All those years, we had kept his photographs tucked away in that box, but they were so small, and this horror was so large.

For that moment, as we stood watching that flag and remembering, Daddy was with us.

Then George spoke. "When we remember the Holocaust and to whom it happened," he said, "we must also remember where it happened. It didn't happen in some remote or unfamiliar place; it happened right in the middle of the Western world. Trains carrying men, women, and children in cattle cars departed from Paris and Vienna, Frankfurt and

Warsaw. And the orders came not from crude and uneducated men, but from men who regarded themselves as cultured and well-schooled, modern and even forward-looking. They had all the outward traits of cultured men—except for conscience. Their crimes show the world that evil can slip in and blend in, amid the most civilized of surroundings. In the end, only conscience can stop it, and moral discernment and decency and tolerance. These can never be assured in any time or in any society. They must always be taught."

We felt such overwhelming sadness that day, yet we felt safe. On that morning, we never contemplated the face of other evils that might slip in.

One of the invitations that crossed my desk that spring was for the opening of the Metropolitan Museum of Art's exhibition of Jacqueline Kennedy's dresses. I said yes. The invitation offered the option of bringing guests, so I asked Regan and her daughter, Lara, and Barbara to join me. We arrived at the museum and were met in the receiving line by Anna Wintour, the editor of *Vogue*, as well as the designer Oscar de la Renta and Caroline Kennedy. It was my first-ever New York designer affair. The last time I had seen Caroline Kennedy was at the opening of the George H. W. Bush Presidential Library in 1997. I remember that, amid the sea of Carters, Fords, Clintons, and Bushes, she was standing there alone. So I went over and introduced myself, and we began talking. She was just a few weeks shy of turning forty then, eight years older than her mother was when she assumed the title of First Lady of the United States. At thirty-one, Jackie Kennedy was such a young woman when her husband became president, yet she left a rich legacy in decorating and conserving the White House. For me, the most moving story was her last project: the Oval Office. While the president and first lady were on a pre-Thanksgiving trip, the White House staff had installed her newly chosen curtains and other furnishings. The trip that Jackie and John F. Kennedy made was to Dallas. Before she returned to the White House, as a widow, the staff removed the new decor, restoring the Oval Office to the way President Kennedy had left it, the one thing in the home that could still be returned to the way it had been.

After the receiving line, we had to ascend the museum's grand marble staircase to reach the exhibition. Someone had cleverly lined the staircase with violinists and, I believe, a few trumpeters. Orchestra members stretched the entire way up. But it was a bit too clever. There was no way to grab on to the handrail. So there I was, holding up my gown and climbing these stairs, hoping that I wouldn't step on my dress and thinking, Please don't trip and fall. And later I heard that women in their long gowns did tumble on the marble stairs. It was instructive to me, though. I never lined the marble White House stairs with anyone, so that all guests could easily grasp the handrail.

We were guided through the collection by Hamish Bowles, the impeccably groomed *Vogue* contributor. I gazed at the dark red bouclé day dress that Jackie Kennedy had worn to give the television tour of the White House, which Americans saw only in black and white, as well as her crepe silk evening gowns and apricot silk dresses. When we came to her inaugural clothes, Hamish said, "This is what one should wear to inaugurations, pearl gray. It isn't turquoise blue or something like that."

I loved Jackie Kennedy's clothes because they were the clothes I had grown up seeing as a young woman. I remember a classic pink coat that I bought at Neiman Marcus when I was at SMU, which I kept tucked away in paper for years, hoping Barbara or Jenna might want it when they were grown. But there is something different about seeing another first lady's clothes on display. I knew my inaugural gown would be joining the gown collection at the Smithsonian, but there is more to it than that. There is the strange knowledge that how you look will be critiqued and that what you wear will likely end up on display. Nancy Reagan told me a few years ago that when the Ronald Reagan Presidential Library put together a showing of her clothes, it became the most visited exhibit in the entire library. She laughed when she said it, adding, "You know, those clothes that I was always criticized for?"

I was like all first ladies in that I wanted to look good. I knew how interested the public and the press are in what first ladies wear. Like the women before me, I wanted to look elegant, to appear my best at events here and abroad, and not to glance back later at White House photos and silently cringe. I really felt for Hillary Clinton, who spent years having the press write nasty things about her hairstyles. It unnerved me enough that I paid with our own money for someone to come to the White House and blow-dry my hair almost every morning, just so I could try to avoid a bad hair day. But while some first ladies are genuinely interested in fashion, I'm not one who follows each new season's trends; I have been wearing the same suits, sweaters, and slacks for years. Jackie Kennedy is always going to be more stylish. She was from a part of the country and a part of society that cultivated a certain style and manner. East Coast elegance was exotically enchanting but also out of reach to sweater-set girls in Midland.

The daily hair blow-dries were just one of the monetary costs of living in the White House. Most Americans may not realize that presidents and their families are responsible for their personal costs while they reside at 1600 Pennsylvania Avenue, and that George and I paid for ours out of our own pockets. The presidential room, as it were, is covered, but not the board. The house we had to live in was spectacular. We had luxuries that we could not have afforded in our private life, such as an exquisite home and furnishings, a full staff, a chef, and a fully staffed weekend retreat at Camp David. Presidents and their families are fortunately not responsible for a White House mortgage or the White House utility bills, and it is more than fair that they pay for personal items like every American household.

George and I covered the costs for our own food each month—breakfast, lunch, and dinner at the White House and at Camp David—and if the girls came home or we had friends to dinner or guests who stayed overnight, we were billed for their food as well. We paid for our dry cleaning and outside laundry, and if we hosted a private party, as we did when George's parents celebrated their sixtieth wedding anniversary, we paid the expenses ourselves, including the hourly wages for the waiters and servers and the setup and cleanup crews, who needed to receive time and a half if the party was held after 5:00 P.M. We did ask the Republican National Committee to pay for the White House Christmas parties, including the holiday parties for the press, and outside nonprofits sometimes assumed the costs of other events. The Ford's Theatre Society generously used its own funds to help cover White House celebrations of

Abraham Lincoln's birthday or the awarding of the Lincoln Prize. Every month, though, we received an itemized bill for our living and personal expenses at the White House.

But there were some costs that I was not prepared for. I was amazed by the sheer number of designer clothes that I was expected to buy, like the women before me, to meet the fashion expectations for a first lady. After our first year in the White House, our accountant said to George, "It costs a lot to be president," and he was referring mainly to my clothes. Of course, I recycled most of my wardrobe, wearing the same dress to the White House correspondents' dinner in the spring and then again to the Congressional Ball in December, but heavily photographed occasions, like state dinners or the annual Kennedy Center honors, required new gowns each time.

There were times when the recycling went too far. One Sunday morning, I arrived at Fox News for an interview with Chris Wallace. Looking around at the photos in the greenroom, I saw that I had worn the exact same suit to my last interview with Chris. Quickly, I exchanged tops with my press secretary, so that it would seem as if I had a bit more wardrobe variety. To look my best abroad, I employed a hairdresser to accompany me on overseas trips, and if I needed professional makeup for a state event or a television interview, I paid for that as well. Today, I like to flip through home decorating magazines while I dry my own hair.

On Friday, April 27, George and I were at our ranch after having spent most of the day in Austin for the dedication of the Bob Bullock Texas State History Museum. The next day, we would return to Washington for the White House Correspondents' Association dinner. It was early on Saturday morning when the phone rang. Jenna was on the line, in tears. She had been cited the night before for ordering drinks in a bar in Austin and being underage with a fake ID. By the time Jenna called us, nothing we could have said would have made her feel any worse, but we still gave her a stern talk. Her picture was splashed across the television and newspapers; she would be part of local news film footage and the slightly blurry image at the end of a photographer's long-range telephoto lens. When George had been sworn in, I had asked the press to keep the girls out of the public eye, much as they had done with Chelsea Clinton. But Jenna had put herself in the news. We told her that this would be a lesson, and one that she had learned the hard way. Her friends might do something wrong and not make headlines, but she did not have that luxury.

Almost immediately a warm note of encouragement arrived for Jenna and Barbara from Luci Johnson, who shared with them the advice that her own mother, Lady Bird, gave to her and Lynda: "Don't do anything that you wouldn't want to read about on the front page of *The New York Times*, because if you do, it will be." Cherie Blair also sent me a sympathetic note. The year before, her sixteen-year-old son, Euan, had had his own embarrassing run-in with the law, although enduring the British tabloids had proven to be a far worse punishment than a formal police caution.

That night in Austin was just dumb, in the way that so many nineteen-year-olds are dumb. I remember a line from *The No. 1 Ladies' Detective Agency*, a series of novels by Alexander McCall Smith, in which his main character, Precious Ramotswe, says, "Twenty-one-year-olds are so stupid. And there are so many of them."

To her credit, Jenna rose to the occasion. She quit going to clubs and other places in downtown Austin. And for years, I've talked to both Barbara and Jenna about the risks of alcohol. Their father quit drinking; my father overdrank; and I've warned both of them about the perils of alcohol, saying, "Nothing good ever happens when you are drunk."

But what bothered me long after the incident was over was the image left behind in the public mind, that Barbara and Jenna were party girls. We never considered using publicists to shape their image, as some prominent figures and celebrities do. We wanted them to live their lives as privately and as normally as possible. I tried to slip away to Austin to see Jenna's sorority show skits, which were put on by the girls for their moms. And I went to visit both girls at school during the year, coming in to do what all college moms do, help them clean their dorm rooms, make a quick run to Bed Bath & Beyond for a lamp or towels or a laundry bag. Most of the snippets that ended up on the news were nothing like our daughters. Many were just plain wrong. Otherwise, Jenna would not have chosen to work with AIDS sufferers in Central America or to teach, and Barbara would not be devoting herself to public health in Africa. But that is the baggage that comes with public life; there are no "private" mistakes. I accepted it and moved on, and they did the same.

In the way that ancient astronomical calendars measured time by the passage of the seasons, the movement of the moon, the seeding of the soil, the culling of the harvest, the presidential calendar is governed by summitry. There are the NATO summits, the Summits of the Americas; the Asia-Pacific Economic Cooperation summits; the G8 meetings; and the United States–European Union summits, all of which rotate locations, usually abroad. Then there are the visits to call on allies, to build relationships with other leaders, to engage other corners of the world. We would pass in and out of a country in a day or even a single afternoon. The flights were invariably overnight, and the expectation was that we would arrive looking perfectly rested and impeccably groomed. Our luggage and the bags of our aides made their own convoy; our vehicles traveled with us in the bellies of cargo planes.

Summer 2001 began with what would become the familiar whirlwind of travel, five countries in five days in June, first to Spain, where we called on the king and queen, and where I visited the Prado Museum with Ana Botella de Aznar, the wife of Spain's prime minister. Afterward, we went to the National Library, where the curators displayed drawings by Leonardo da Vinci, original editions of the classic novel *Don Quixote*, and early Spanish maps of Texas. From there, it was a stop in Belgium for the NATO Summit, and a tour of a market, a church, and a university library, then a NATO spouses' lunch, an interview for the CBS *Early Show*, then on to a meeting at the Brussels American School, as well as a visit with Belgium's King Albert II and Queen Paola at the Laeken Palace. The following morning, we were on our way to Sweden, where George joined the US-EU Summit while I toured a children's center and then a botanical garden. Late in the afternoon, we met with His Majesty King Carl XVI Gustaf and Her Majesty Queen Silvia, as well as Her Royal Highness Crown Princess Victoria. The Swedish monarchy is one of the oldest in the world; Sweden has crowned kings for over one thousand years. We were introduced surrounded by the tapestry-covered walls of the six-hundred-room Royal Palace; I learned that the king and queen had nine other royal residences scattered around Stockholm. Meanwhile, on the streets, poster-wielding and face-painted anti-globalization protesters were out in force, condemning international corporations and international financial institutions, and a few protesting George. The protests did not die down after we left. Three demonstrators throwing cobblestones and other objects were shot by Swedish riot police, but the protesters never got close to any of the continent's leaders, and by the time they had turned violent, we were long gone.

From the gilded chairs and high-ceilinged palaces of European royalty, I flew to Warsaw, Poland. I met First Lady Jolanta Kwaśniewska, and together we toured a children's hospital. Then, after lunch, I went to the Lauder Kindergarten, opened by the American cosmetics magnate and philanthropist Ronald Lauder to educate children of the few Jewish families who had survived the Holocaust and had returned to or somehow remained in Warsaw. All the children were blond, and Ron Lauder quietly said to me, "This is why their families escaped. They were the ones who were able to blend in." As I left, the children gathered and sang "Deep in the Heart of Texas," with a sweet overlay of Polish accents. My next stop was the Nożyk Synagogue. The only one in Warsaw to survive World War II, it stood within the walls of another property, almost hidden. Unlike the four hundred other synagogues in the city, Nożyk was left because the Nazis stabled their horses inside it and piled its floors and corners with feed. After the synagogue came an orphanage. I met with a group of eighteen- to twenty-year-olds who were about to leave their dormitory-style rooms and begin life on their own, with no family to call or come home to. The children were thin and sad, and they barely spoke as we sat inside the old building and its spartan rooms. I told them about how nervous I had been when I started my first teaching job, in the hope that they might find some small comfort in that.

As the afternoon drew to a close, I joined George at a ceremony for the Warsaw Ghetto Memorial, where some 400,000 Jews were fenced in like cattle behind barbed wire and then were deported to death camps or finally slaughtered by Nazi guns and flamethrowers that were shot into basements and sewers until entire blocks became infernos. At day's end, George delivered an address with the president; then it was a quick change into black-tie evening clothes for cocktails, a receiving line, and a formal state dinner.

After those few days, the crush of images was almost too much to absorb, from glittering fairy-tale palaces to the depths of human despair.

And we still had a meeting with U.S. Embassy staff the next morning, as well as a wreath-laying ceremony to commemorate the Warsaw Uprising before flying on to Slovenia. While George had his first face-to-face meeting with Russian president Vladimir Putin and invited him to our ranch, I was whisked off for lunch at the Grand Hotel Toplice, a favorite of the staff of Yugoslavia's old dictator, Marshal Tito, and then a boat ride over to a small island that houses the Assumption of Mary Pilgrimage Church, overlooking Bled's deep, blue lake, which had been carved out by the last of the thick Ice Age glaciers as they retreated from the lower reaches of Europe. I walked up the famous ninety-nine steps rising from the base of the island. Tradition is that, on their wedding day, grooms carry their brides up the steps to the church for the ceremony. When I arrived, there was a wedding in progress, and the bride rushed forward to embrace me, saying this was the best day of her life. I watched costumed folk-life dancers and rang the bell of wishes. Three more brides and grooms were waiting for us as we entered the church. As we left, people lined the sides of the road to wave. In central Europe, where the nations lived under decades of harsh Soviet domination during the Cold War, many of the citizens are deeply pro-American. Like that bride, they always welcomed me with open arms.

Those five days in Europe captured the routine of nearly all our travels, packed days with nations anxious to display their particular beauties and treasures, while others shared their struggles to face the dark episodes of their past.

Back at the White House, by late June, the Rose Garden was in full bloom. Designed like an eighteenth-century garden, it has neatly arrayed beds and borders. Tulips, daffodils, and flowering trees bloom in the spring, and by summer, the fragrance of roses fills the air. I watched the lines of tourists gather outside in the mornings in the rising heat to be led on tours of the public rooms, and I began to look for ways to showcase distinctive American arts inside the White House. On June 29, George and I hosted a White House celebration for Black Music Month, featuring Debbie Allen as the master of ceremonies and performances by the Four Tops and James Brown. Lionel Hampton, who had sent those beautiful rose bouquets to celebrate Barbara's and Jenna's births, bravely came, even though strokes and illness had shrunk him down to little more than skin.

For July 4, I at last successfully surprised George for his birthday. We had spent the day in Pennsylvania with Governor Tom and Michele Ridge. When the four of us returned to the White House, Gary Walters, the head usher, told George there was a sample of his new rug for the Oval Office in the State Dining Room and asked would he like to see it? George said yes, and as we stepped in, the word "Surprise" was being shouted by many of our closest friends. I did the same party every year after that, always on July 4, with fried chicken, deviled eggs, corn bread, all classic picnic and barbecue staples.

The White House pastry chef, Roland Mesnier, made George a cake in the shape of a baseball. It poured rain during dinner but cleared just in time for us to watch the Independence Day fireworks light up the Mall.

In mid-July, we were in Air Force One, high aloft the Atlantic, headed for our first visit to England. Queen Elizabeth and Prince Philip had invited us for a luncheon at Buckingham Palace, on perfectly pressed linens and china emblazoned with the royal coat of arms. Then we helicoptered over to meet Tony and Cherie Blair at Chequers, the sixteenth-century summer home of England's prime ministers.

We had hosted the Blairs at Camp David; now they wanted to show us the same comfort in return. Chequers sits on grounds that have been recorded in history since Roman times; the name of the original estate was inscribed in the Domesday Book of 1086. Its name likely comes from a twelfth-century British landholder who was an official of the King's Exchequer. Its house is a medium-size redbrick Tudor mansion completed in 1565, fifty-five years before the Pilgrims landed at Plymouth Rock. Inside, Cherie showed me a ring that belonged to the first Queen Elizabeth and a table used by the French emperor Napoleon during his exile.

Despite its formal pedigree, our evening at Chequers was very casual. The Blairs' children were there, along with one of their school friends, and Barbara had joined us with one of her school friends. The kids peppered everyone with questions, and it was a fast-moving conversation, covering everything from the merits of missile defense—George being the primary defender and Cherie the skeptic—to capital punishment. On that issue, the American president and the British prime minister's wife, a human rights lawyer, were on vastly different planes. But the debate was cordial. Cherie says no one, left or right, can claim that George doesn't have a very good sense of humor.

When it was over and we all began making our way upstairs, I overheard the Blairs' oldest son, Euan, saying to Cherie, "Give the man a break, Mother."

From England, our next stop was Italy, for George to attend the G8 Summit, a meeting of the eight leading industrialized countries, where we also had an audience with the Pope in his summer residence, Castel Gandolfo, and then on to Pristina, Kosovo, where Italian peacekeepers advised our staff not to walk on the grass adjacent to the airport runway because not all the land mines had been removed. Kosovo was, at that moment in July, the global hot spot where some seven thousand U.S. troops had been deployed two years before as part of a NATO force that had arrived after prolonged and bloody fighting between the Kosovo Liberation Army and Serbia. It was the last of the Balkan crises. Because we were entering what was considered a combat zone, the Secret Service insisted that we wear flak jackets for the ride on Marine One to the U.S. base named Camp Bondsteel. I dedicated an education center that was being named for me and toured the base before George addressed the troops, and we had lunch in the base's mess. In Kosovo, half the population being guarded by our soldiers was under the age of twenty-five. At that moment, aside from an incident in the spring when China had detained and interrogated the twenty-four-person crew from a Navy surveillance plane, the Balkans claimed the lion's share of international attention. So on that bright summer day, we had helicoptered into what everyone assumed were the front lines of the world's most prominent war.

By the end of the summer, I was finally hitting my stride in the White House. I had hosted my long-planned conference at Georgetown University on early childhood cognitive development; my pet project, the National Book Festival, was scheduled to debut on Saturday, September 8; and we had gotten away to our ranch in August, with George bringing his senior staff and all the White House work along. Whenever George traveled, even to Camp David, the chief of staff or the chief's deputy almost always came. Now, in addition to the barn and the tractor shed and the green clapboard house, the U.S. government had put a prefab house on our ranchlands for the military aides, the White House doctor, and other members of the staff who accompany the president. National Security Advisor Condi Rice frequently joined us; she had been coming to the ranch since before the election, and we had even named one of our hills Balkan Hill in her honor. On a hike, she was discussing the finer points of Balkan policy with George, never getting winded while she climbed the steep rise. Now her preferred place to stay was the green clapboard house.

At the ranch, there were briefings each morning, teleconferences, and piles of papers. Being President of the United States does not include an allowance for vacation days. George never took a full day off. There was little difference between being in Washington and being in Crawford, except that I could hike the trails we were building and could step out the door into the fresh air without trailing down hallways and having a phalanx of Secret Service agents filing behind. In the White House, I could walk each morning along the corridors from the residence to my offices in the East Wing. Most of the events we hosted and the entertaining we did, even simple coffees, were inside the White House itself, and unless I took Barney and Spot for a walk, it was possible to spend several days without ever venturing outside. At our ranch, from first light, the outside found us.

As September 2001 opened, I was reviewing my upcoming briefing before the Senate Education Committee on the findings of the early childhood cognitive development conference, readying events for the book festival, preparing for the official inaugural gown presentation at the Smithsonian, and overseeing plans for our first state dinner, in honor of Mexico's president, Vicente Fox. State dinner guests are selected by the president, the State Department, and the National Security Council. We had a particular interest in inviting Mexico because of trade and border issues. George wanted to establish a strong working relationship with our closest neighbor to the south.

I was not nervous before my own wedding—there were no jitters or cold palms then—but I was anxious now. A state dinner is far more intricate, an elaborate display of hundreds of moving parts, from guest lists to menus, which require an advance tasting, to table seatings, arrival protocols, and choices of linens, flowers, china, and silver, even the champagnes and wines. And traditionally all of this falls under the purview of the White House Social Office, working with the Office of the First Lady. If the four-hour evening is flawless, it is only because of the hundreds of hours that have been invested beforehand. No detail is too small. My dress of red lace over hot pink silk had been custom-made by Arnold Scaasi, bright colors in honor of the bright tones of Mexico. Cathy Fenton, the social secretary, who had worked for both Nancy Reagan and Barbara Bush, and Nancy Clarke, the longtime White House florist, created tablescapes of white hydrangeas, lilies, and roses interspersed with limes as another nod to Mexico. The arrival ceremony in the morning included a full twenty-one-gun salute and a review of the troops. Afterward, we escorted the Foxes to the balcony off the Blue Room, and surrounded by overflowing pots of red geraniums, we watched a fireworks display light up the sky above the Washington Monument.

The next day, Marta Fox and I flew to Chicago to tour an exhibition surveying two hundred years of Latino art in the United States at the city's Terra Museum of American Art. Many of the contemporary Latin American artists whose work was featured joined us, and it was a wonderful day of art and culture and beauty. The Foxes departed the next morning, as I began final preparations for the National Book Festival, which was set to open that weekend.

On Friday night, we held a gala for the festival at the Library of Congress, before the official day of author events. Dr. James Billington, the Librarian of Congress, introduced me. As the back of the stage opened, I walked out in a blue Arnold Scaasi dress, with sheer chiffon and a short underskirt. The crowd gasped, and I felt as if this was my official debut as first lady. Not quite nine months after George took office, I was now doing what I loved, finding my place in the world of Washington and beyond.

Goodness in the Land
of the Living

With George at the Pentagon, October 11, 2001.

(White House photo)

Tuesday morning, September 11, was sunny and warm, the sky a brilliant cerulean blue. The day before, I had hosted a lunch for Janette Howard, wife of the Australian prime minister, while George met with her husband, John. My friends who had come for the National Book Festival had all flown home, and even George was gone, in Florida for a school visit. George H. W. Bush and Bar had spent the night, but they had already left at 7:00 A.M. to catch an early flight. And I had what I considered a big day planned. I was set to arrive at the Capitol at 9:15 to brief the Senate Education Committee, chaired by Edward M. Kennedy, on the findings of the early childhood development conference that I'd held in July. In the afternoon, we were hosting the entire Congress and their families for the annual Congressional Picnic. The South Lawn of the White House was already covered with picnic tables awaiting their fluttering cloths, and Tom Perini from Buffalo Gap, Texas, was setting up his chuckwagons. Our entertainment would be old-fashioned square dancing and Texas swing music by Ray Benson and his classic band, Asleep at the Wheel.

I finished dressing in silence, going over my statement again in my mind. I was very nervous about appearing before a Senate committee and having news cameras trained on me. Had the TV been turned on, I might have heard the first fleeting report of a plane hitting the North Tower of the World Trade Center at the tip of Manhattan as I walked out the door to the elevator. Instead, it was the head of my Secret Service detail, Ron Sprinkle, who leaned over and whispered the news in my ear as I entered the car a few minutes after 9:00 A.M. for the ride to the Russell Senate Office Building, adjacent to the Capitol. Andi Ball, now my chief of staff at the White House; Domestic Policy Advisor Margaret Spellings; and I speculated about what could have happened: a small plane, a Cessna perhaps, running into one of those massive towers on this perfect September morning. We wondered too if Hillary Clinton might decide not to attend the committee briefing, since the World Trade Center was in New York. We were driving up Pennsylvania Avenue when word came that the South Tower had been hit. The car fell silent; we sat in mute disbelief. One plane might be a strange accident; two planes were clearly an attack. I thought about George and wondered if the Secret Service had already hustled him to the motorcade and begun the race to Air Force One to return home. Two minutes later, at 9:16 A.M., we pulled up at the entrance to the Russell Building. In the time it had taken to drive the less than two miles between the White House and the Capitol, the world as I knew it had irrevocably changed.

Senator Kennedy was waiting to greet me, according to plan. We both knew when we met that the towers had been hit and, without a word being spoken, knew that there would be no briefing that morning. Together, we walked the short distance to his office. He began by presenting me with a limited-edition print; it was a vase of bright daffodils, a copy of a painting he had created for his wife, Victoria, and given to her on their wedding day. The print was inscribed to me and dated September 11, 2001.

An old television was turned on in a corner of the room, and I glanced over to see the plumes of smoke billowing from the Twin Towers. Senator Kennedy kept his eyes averted from the screen. Instead he led me on a tour of his office, pointing out various pictures, furniture, pieces of memorabilia, even a framed note that his brother Jack had sent to their mother when he was a child, in which he wrote, "Teddy is getting fat." The senator, who would outlive all his brothers by more than forty years, laughed at the note as he showed it to me, still finding it amusing.

All the while, I kept glancing over at the glowing television screen. My skin was starting to crawl, I wanted to leave, to find out what was going on, to process what I was seeing, but I felt trapped in an endless cycle of pleasantries. It did not occur to me to say, "Senator Kennedy, what about the towers?" I simply followed his lead, and he may have feared that if we actually began to contemplate what had happened in New York, I might dissolve into tears.

Senator Judd Gregg of New Hampshire, the ranking Republican on the committee and one of our very good friends in the Senate—Judd had played Al Gore for George during mock debates at the ranch the previous fall—was also designated to escort me to the committee room, and he arrived just as I was completing the tour. Senator Kennedy invited us to sit on the couches, and he continued chatting about anything other than the horrific images unfolding on the tiny screen across the room. I looked around his shoulder but could see very little, and I was still trying to pay attention to him and the thread of his conversation. It seemed completely unreal, sitting in this elegant, sunlit office as an immense tragedy unfolded. We sat as human beings driven by smoke, flame, and searing heat jumped from the tops of the Twin Towers to end their lives and as firemen in full gear began the climb up the towers' stairs.

I have often wondered if the small talk that morning was Ted Kennedy's defense mechanism, if after so much tragedy—the combat death of his oldest brother in World War II, the assassinations of his brothers Jack and Robert, and the deaths of nephews, including John Jr., whose body he identified when it was pulled from the cold, dark waters off Martha's Vineyard—if after all of those things, he simply could not look upon another grievous tragedy.

At about 9:45, after George had made a brief statement to the nation, which we watched, clustered around a small television that was perched on the receptionist's desk, Ted Kennedy, Judd Gregg, and I walked out to tell reporters that my briefing had been postponed. I said, "You heard from the president this morning, and Senator Kennedy and Senator Gregg and I both join his statement in saying that our hearts and our prayers go out to the victims of this act of terrorism, and that our support goes to the rescue workers. And all of our prayers are with everyone there right now." As I turned to exit, Laurence McQuillan of *USA Today* asked a question. "Mrs. Bush, you know, children are kind of struck by all this. Is there a message you could tell to the nation's—" I didn't even wait for him to finish but began, "Well, parents need to reassure their children everywhere in our country that they're safe."

As we walked out of the briefing room, the cell phone of my advance man, John Meyers, rang. A friend told him that CNN was reporting that an airplane had crashed into the Pentagon. Within minutes, the order would be given to evacuate the White House and the Capitol.

I walked back to Senator Kennedy's office and then began moving quickly toward the stairs, to reach my car to return to the White House. Suddenly, the lead Secret Service agent turned to me and my staff and said that we needed to head to the basement immediately. We took off at a run; Judd Gregg suggested his private office, which was in the lower level and was an interior room. The Secret Service then told John that they were waiting for an Emergency Response Team to reach the Capitol. The team would take me, but my staff would be left behind. Overhearing the conversation, I turned back and said, "No, everyone is coming." We entered Judd's office, where I tried to call Barbara and Jenna, and Judd tried to call his daughter, who was in New York. Then we sat and talked quietly about our families and our worries for them, and the overwhelming shock we both felt.

Sometime after 10:00 A.M., when the entire Capitol was being emptied, when White House staffers had fled barefoot and sobbing through the heavy iron gates with Secret Service agents shouting at them to "Run, run!" my agents collected me. They now included an additional Secret Service detail and an Emergency Response Team, dressed in black tactical clothing like a SWAT force and moving with guns drawn. As we raced through the dim hallways of the Russell Building, past panicked staffers emptying from their offices, the ERT team shouted "GET BACK" and covered my every move with their guns. We reached the underground entrance; the doors on the motorcade slammed shut, and we sped off. The Secret Service had decided to take me temporarily to their headquarters, located in a nondescript federal office building a few blocks from the White House. Following the Oklahoma City bombing, their offices had been reinforced to survive a large-scale blast. Outside our convoy windows, the city streets were clogged with people evacuating their workplaces and trying to reach their own homes.

By the time I had reached my motorcade, Flight 93 had crashed in a

Pennsylvania field and the west side of the Pentagon had begun to collapse. Judd Gregg walked alone to the underground Senate parking garage and retrieved his car, the last one left there. He pulled out of the garage and headed home, across the Fourteenth Street Bridge and past the Pentagon, thick with smoke and flame.

In the intervening years, Judd and I, and many others, were left to contemplate what if Flight 93 had not been forced down by its passengers into an empty field; what if, shortly after 10:00 A.M., it had reached the Capitol Dome?

We arrived at the Secret Service building via an underground entrance and were escorted first to the director's office and then belowground to a windowless conference room with blank walls and a mustard yellow table. A large display screen with a constant TV feed took up most of one wall. Walking through the hallways, I saw a sign emblazoned with the emergency number 9-1-1. Had the terrorists thought about our iconic number when they picked this date and planned an emergency so overwhelming? For a while, I sat in a small area off the conference room, silently watching the images on television. I watched the replay as the South Tower of the World Trade Center roared with sound and then collapsed into a silent gray plume, offering my personal prayer to God to receive the victims with open arms. The North Tower had given way, live in front of my eyes, sending some 1,500 souls and 110 stories of gypsum and concrete buckling to the ground.

So much happened during those terrible hours at the tip of Manhattan. That morning, as the people who worked in the towers descended, water from the sprinkler system was racing down the darkened stairwells. With their feet soaked, for some the greatest fear was that when they reached the bottom, the rushing water would be too high and they would be drowned. A few walked to safety under a canopy of skylights covered with the bodies of those who had jumped. Over two hundred people jumped to escape the heat, smoke, and flames. I was told that Father Mychal Judge, the chaplain for the New York City Fire Department, who had come to offer

aid, comfort, and last rites, was killed that morning by the body of someone who had, in desperation, hurled himself from the upper floors of one
of those towers.

The early expectation was for horrific numbers of deaths. Manhattan
emergency rooms and hospitals as far away as Dallas were placed on Code
Red, expecting to receive airlifted survivors. Some fifty thousand people
worked inside the towers; on a beautiful day, as many as eighty thousand
tourists would visit an observation deck on the South Tower's 107th floor,
where the vistas stretched for fifty miles. Had those hijacked planes struck
the towers thirty or forty or fifty minutes later, the final toll might well have
been in the tens of thousands.

Inside Secret Service headquarters, I asked my staff to call their families, and I called the girls, who had been whisked away by Secret Service
agents to secure locations. In Austin, Jenna had been awakened by an
agent pounding on her dorm door. In her room at Yale, Barbara had heard
another student sobbing uncontrollably a few doors down. Then I called
my mother, because I wanted her to know that I was safe and I wanted so
much to hear the sound of her voice. And I tried to reach George, but my
calls could not get through; John Meyers, my advance man, promised to
keep trying. I did know from the Secret Service that George had taken off
from Florida, safe on board Air Force One. I knew my daughters and my
mother were safe. But beyond that, everything was chaos. I was told that
Barbara Olson, wife of Solicitor General Ted Olson, had been aboard
the plane that hit the Pentagon. At one point, we also received word that
Camp David had been attacked and hit. I began thinking of all the people
who would have been there, like Bob Williams, the chaplain. Another
report had a plane crashing into our ranch in Crawford. It got so that we
were living in five-minute increments, wondering if a new plane would
emerge from the sky and hit a target. All of us in that basement conference room and many more in the Secret Service building were relying on
rumors and on whatever news came from the announcers on television.
When there were reports of more errant planes or other targets, it was
almost impossible not to believe them.

George had tried to call me from Air Force One. It is stunning now to think that our "state-of-the-art" communications would not allow him to complete a phone call to Secret Service headquarters, or me to reach him on Air Force One. On my second call from the secure line, our third attempt, I was finally able to contact the plane, a little before twelve noon. I was grateful just to hear his voice, to know that he was all right, and to tell him the girls were fine. From the way he spoke, I could hear how starkly his presidency had been transformed.

We remained in that drab conference room for hours, eventually turning off the repetitive horror of the images on the television. Inside, I felt a grief, a loss, a mourning like I had never known.

A few blocks away, in the Chrysler offices near Pennsylvania Avenue, a group of White House senior staff began to gather. After the evacuation, some of those who were new to Washington had been wandering, dazed and shaken, in nearby Lafayette Park. By midafternoon, seventy staff members had congregated inside this office building, attempting to resume work, while Secret Service agents stood in the lobby and forbade anyone without a White House pass from entering. Key presidential and national security staff and Vice President Cheney were still sealed away in the small underground emergency center deep below the White House.

As the skies and streets grew silent, there was a debate over what to do with George and what to do with me. The Secret Service detail told me to be prepared to leave Washington for several days at least. My assistant, Sarah Moss, was sent into the White House to gather some of my clothes. John Meyers accompanied her to retrieve Spot, Barney, and Kitty.

Then we got word that the president was returning to Washington. I would be staying as well. Late in the afternoon, I spoke to George again. At 6:30 we got in a Secret Service caravan to drive to the White House. I gazed out the window; the city had taken on the cast of an abandoned movie set: the sun was shining, but the streets were deserted. We could not see a person on the sidewalk or any vehicles driving on the street. There was no sound at all except for the roll of our wheels over the ground.

We drove at full throttle through the gate, and the agents hopped out. Heavily armed men in black swarmed over the grounds. Before I got out, one of my agents, Dave Saunders, who had been driving, turned around and said, "Mrs. Bush, I'm so sorry. I'm so sorry." He said it with the greatest of concern and a hint of emotion in his voice. He knew what this day meant for us.

I was hustled inside and downstairs through a pair of big steel doors that closed behind me with a loud hiss, forming an airtight seal. I was now in one of the unfinished subterranean hallways underneath the White House, heading for the PEOC, the Presidential Emergency Operations Center, built for President Franklin Roosevelt during World War II. We walked along old tile floors with pipes hanging from the ceiling and all kinds of mechanical equipment. The PEOC is designed to be a command center during emergencies, with televisions, phones, and communications facilities.

I was ushered into the conference room adjacent to the PEOC's nerve center. It's a small room with a large table. National Security Advisor Condi Rice, Counselor to the President Karen Hughes, Deputy Chief of Staff Josh Bolten, and Dick and Lynne Cheney were already there, where they had been since the morning. Lynne, whose agents had brought her to the White House just after the first attack, came over and hugged me. Then she said quietly into my ear, "The plane that hit the Pentagon circled the White House first."

I felt a shiver vibrate down my spine. Unlike the major monuments and even the leading government buildings in Washington, the White House sits low to the ground. It is a three-story building, tucked away in a downward slope toward the Potomac. When the White House was first built, visitors complained about the putrid scent rising from the river and the swampy grounds nearby. From the air, the White House is hard to see and hard to reach. A plane could circle it and find no plausible approach. And that is what Lynne Cheney told me had happened that morning, a little past 9:30, before Flight 77 crossed the river and thundered into the Pentagon.

At 7:10 that night, George strode into the PEOC. Early that afternoon, he had conducted a secure videoconference from Offutt Air Force Base in Nebraska with the CIA and FBI directors, as well as the military Joint Chiefs of Staff and the vice president and his national security staff, giving instructions and getting briefings on the latest information. Over the objections of the Secret Service, he had insisted upon returning home. We hugged and talked with the Cheneys a bit. Then the Secret Service detail suggested that we spend the night there, belowground. They showed us the bed, a foldout that looked like it had been installed when FDR was president. George and I stared at it, and we both said no, George adding, "We're not going to sleep down here. We're going to go upstairs and you can get us if something happens." He said, "I've got to get sleep, in our own bed." George was preparing to speak to the nation from the Oval Office, to reassure everyone and to show that the president was safely back in Washington, ready to respond.

By 7:30 we were on our way up to the residence. I have no memory of having eaten dinner—George may have eaten on the plane. He tried to call the girls as soon as we were upstairs but couldn't reach them. Barbara called back close to 8:00 P.M., and then George left to make remarks to the nation.

We did finally climb into our own bed that night, exhausted and emotionally drained. Outside the doors of the residence, the Secret Service detail stood in their usual posts. I fell asleep, but it was a light, fitful rest, and I could feel George staring into the darkness beside me. Then I heard a man screaming as he ran, "Mr. President, Mr. President, you've got to get up. The White House is under attack."

We jumped up, and I grabbed a robe and stuck my feet into my slippers, but I didn't stop to put in my contacts. George grabbed Barney; I grabbed Kitty. With Spot trailing behind, we started walking down to the PEOC. George had wanted to take the elevator, but the agents didn't think it was safe, so we had to descend flight after flight of stairs, to the state floor, then the ground floor, and below, while I held George's hand because I couldn't see anything. My heart was pounding, and all I could do was count stairwell landings, trying to count off in my mind how many more floors we had to go. When we reached the PEOC, I saw the outline of a military sergeant unfolding the ancient hideaway bed and putting on some sheets.

At that moment, another agent ran up to us and said, "Mr. President, it's one of our own." The plane was ours.

For months afterward at night, in bed, we'd hear the military jets thundering overhead, traveling so fast that the ground below quivered and shook. They would make one pass and then, three or five minutes later, make another low-flying loop. I would fall asleep to the roar of the fighters in the skies, hearing in my mind those words, "one of our own." There was a quiet security in that, in knowing that we slept beneath the watchful cover of our own.

Waking the next morning, I had the sensation of knowing before my eyes opened that something terrible had happened, something beyond comprehension, and I wondered for a brief instant if it had all been a dream. Then I saw George, and I knew, knew that yesterday would be with us, each day, for all of our days to come.

I put on a simple black shirt and gray slacks and went down to meet my staff. With the exception of Andi Ball and a few others, who were in their fifties, most were twenty-two or twenty-three years old. For many, it was their first adult job. Nearly all had been told yesterday to run for their lives and had literally kicked off their high heels and fled from the East Wing out the asphalt path toward Pennsylvania Avenue. Now they were being asked to come back to work in a building that everyone considered a target and for a presidency and a country that would be at war. That morning, they passed piles of strollers scattered across the lawn, left behind by tourists who had grabbed their children and fled the White House grounds.

In the days that followed, plans were made to clear the street-side offices of the Eisenhower Executive Office Building, next to the White House, where much of the presidential and vice presidential staff worked. The building sits against a narrow sidewalk along a main cross street, and there were fears of a car or truck bomb pulling alongside and detonating. Pennsylvania Avenue in front of the White House had been closed since the Clinton administration. Huge concrete barriers had been erected to keep traffic from moving past the president's home.

I wanted to start by reassuring my staff. The night before, I had asked Kathleene Card, a Methodist minister who is married to Andy Card, George's chief of staff, to come in to speak. She tried to quiet their fears.

But it was difficult. It was difficult to awaken in this new world. We were all still moving on adrenaline, but with an overlay of anxiety. Would today bring something worse?

After the latest security briefings, George left the White House for the Pentagon to inspect the damage. I traveled north through Washington to Walter Reed Army Medical Center, where many of the injured from the Pentagon were being treated. I visited with the patients and spoke to the doctors and nurses. Those in the military understood that this was only the first wave. Walter Reed would no longer just be a place for veterans, or for active-duty troops to recover from severe training injuries, or for the few casualties from Kosovo. It would be transformed into the closest thing to a combat hospital on U.S. soil, ministering to the brutally injured from the coming war. And they knew that we were at war. George knew it too, had known it instantly, but for me, the realization was more gradual and the ramifications of just what war meant more elusive. Even when we knew that it was Osama bin Laden from the remote reaches of Afghanistan who was behind 9-11, I was still focused on the day-to-day needs of people here at home. How could I help them?

That afternoon, White House staffers lined up in the Indian Treaty Room in the Eisenhower Executive Office Building to give blood. Already, overseas, American embassies were choked with flowers. By week's end, millions of people had paused for moments of silence; over 100,000 came to stand in remembrance in Ottawa, on Canada's Parliament Hill. Truck drivers stopped and blew their horns in unison all over Poland. In Berlin, 200,000 Germans marched in support of the United States. Israel, Ireland, South Korea, and many other countries held national days of mourning. In Great Britain, at Buckingham Palace, the queen's band played our national anthem during its changing of the guard, while in Paris, the newspaper *Le Monde* headlined WE ARE ALL AMERICANS.

The next morning, September 13, I had been asked to appear on all the major morning television shows. What I could think to offer were words of comfort, both to parents for their children and for the nation at large. I had already written two letters, one for middle and high school students and one for kids still in elementary school, about the tragedy. To the youngest children, I wrote, "When sad or frightening things happen, all of us have an opportunity to become better people by thinking about others. . . . Be kind to each other, take care of each other, and show your love for each other." And that is what I saw, in the footage showing the faces of rescue workers at the World Trade Center and the Pentagon, in the eyes of the burned and injured Pentagon soldiers at Walter Reed and Washington Hospital Center, in the people who brought food to grieving neighbors and those who simply sat and grieved with them. I could feel us joined together as a nation.

Some of the worst victims of the Pentagon attack had been brought to Washington Hospital Center, which has a state-of-the-art burn unit. On Thursday afternoon, George and I went to visit them. I was the first to enter the room of Lieutenant Colonel Brian Birdwell, who had suffered severe burns on his hands and his back. He was covered in white gauze. His wife was at his side, where she had been since he was brought to the hospital. I spoke with both of them, hugged her, and then said that "someone else" was waiting to see them. George walked into the room. He asked Lieutenant Colonel Birdwell how he was doing and told the Birdwells that he was very proud of them both. "You are my heroes," he said, and then George raised his hand to salute the injured soldier on the bed. For almost half a minute, Lieutenant Colonel Birdwell worked to move his heavily bandaged hand to his head to return the salute. George would not break his salute until after the soldier was finished with his own. In the military, there is no higher sign of respect than for an injured officer to be saluted first by his commander. Then George hugged Mrs. Birdwell.

At the World Trade Center, we still didn't know exactly how many were dead—initial reports had been in the tens of thousands—or if anyone else might be found alive.

George had chosen Friday as a national day of prayer and remembrance for the victims of the 9-11 attacks, and we had scheduled a memorial service at Washington's National Cathedral, where less than nine months before George and I had gone for the wonderful celebratory prayer service on the day after his inauguration. There would be private family memorials in communities across the Northeast and in scattered spots around the rest of the country. But this was a time for all of us to mourn as a nation. I had selected a variety of speakers, Reverend Billy Graham to preach, Rabbi Joshua Haberman to read from the Book of Lamentations, and Imam Muzammil Siddiqi to offer verses from the Koran. Even Reverend Graham said he could not, to his own satisfaction, answer the question of why God would allow such tragedy and suffering. He added that he just had to accept that God "is a God of love and mercy and compassion in the midst of suffering." When George spoke, he said, "We are here in the middle hour of our grief." He recalled those who died, having begun "their day at a desk or in an airport, busy with life." And he remembered the rescuers, "the ones whom death found running up the stairs and into the fires to help others." After the service, George flew north to visit the remains of the Twin Towers. When he returned, he told me of the incredible heart of the rescue workers and of the posters and homemade signs plastered across posts and buildings, made by people searching for missing family and friends in that week of hope. Those were the images we reflected on that night, people holding out every last shred of faith that the ones they loved might have been spared from this tragedy. Because we knew by then that it was not to be. The bodies of some had been consumed by an ocean of fire and ash, and their resting places were the wind, the river, and building niches across Manhattan.

We spent that Friday night and Saturday cloistered away at Camp David with key cabinet members and the national security team. George was convening a council of war. On Saturday evening, after a day of intense meetings, Condi Rice, the daughter of a Presbyterian minister, took a seat at the Camp David piano and began to play hymns. As she played, Attorney General John Ashcroft encouraged us all to join him and sing. With intelligence being analyzed and plans under way, on Sunday, we returned somberly to Washington.

For over a month, I had planned a small dinner at the White House that Sunday to celebrate the wedding anniversary of Debra and Alan Dunn, friends of ours from Gampy's 1988 presidential run. George had read at their wedding ten years before. I decided to keep the evening. I knew that George was consumed, almost every waking hour, with responding to the attacks, and for an hour or two, I wanted to change the subject, to give him a chance to briefly refocus and be surrounded by friends. There were seven couples, and we all chatted, but our guests had driven through largely deserted streets to a White House that was heavily secured and fortified. It was even slightly disconcerting for some of them to be within our walls. The threat was too new and too raw. But we lived with that low-level anxiety all the time, and would do so for years to come. It was almost 9:00 P.M. when George walked onto the South Lawn with the last of our guests to take Spot out. Above, a plane roared. George and everyone else looked up, and George asked, "Is that supposed to be there?" That is the question we asked about every plane, every noise. As the engine rush grew fainter, George lowered his gaze and said quietly, "I'm fighting an enemy that I can't see."

At noontime the next day, Monday, I flew to Shanksville, Pennsylvania, for a memorial for the victims of Flight 93, which had been bravely forced down by some of its passengers before it reached Washington, D.C. Whenever I visited Shanksville or later Manhattan, or almost anywhere in the Northeast, people would hand me prayer or memorial cards that they had made for their loved ones. Some families held out bracelets that they had engraved with the names of those they had lost. These items were given with such reverence to me and also to George, and we were careful to collect each one. I kept one card with the photo of a twenty-five-year-old, raven-haired girl, on my mirror. Suzanne was her name; her mother had handed it to me along a rope line, where people gathered so that we might shake their hands or say a quick word. I never knew Suzanne's last name; I only knew that she had died in one of the towers. I kept her photo tucked in my mirror frame at the White House until January 20, 2009. Every day I looked at her beautiful, young face. And in the mornings after 9-11, I longed to hold my own daughters in my arms.

The leaves were already turning in the rural Pennsylvania southwest when Governor Tom Ridge and I drove to the memorial service at the crash site. We stood alongside the field where the plane had plummeted to the ground; the trees at the edge of the woods were blackened from the fireball that had enveloped this small spot of earth. It was windy, and we stood under a tent while the families lit candles in honor of their loved ones. The flames flickered as the air swirled by. It was not a place of orderly white crosses and Stars of David, like the green fields above the beaches of Normandy in France. It was a crater in the ground, a mark that time and weather would erode until perhaps the land would lie almost flat again. This would always be the last resting spot for their loved ones.

When it was my turn to speak, I said, "America is learning the names, but you know the people. And you are the ones they thought of in the last moments of life. You are the ones they called, and prayed to see again. You are the ones they loved. A poet wrote, 'Love knows not its own depths until the hour of parting.' The loved ones we remember today knew—even in those horrible moments—that they were not truly alone, because your love was with them."

As we left Shanksville, my staff and I had our arms filled with pages of notes and reflections from children whose school building had been within earshot of the crash site, who had felt the earth shudder and who had heard the ground and woods convulse in flames.

For the one-week anniversary of 9-11, I flew to Chicago to tape Oprah Winfrey's talk show. Then, on September 20, as the initial estimates of the dead at the World Trade Center passed six thousand, George prepared to address a joint session of Congress, the nation, and the world. British prime minister Tony Blair flew in from London to visit the World Trade Center site and then came to Washington to stand alongside us. We had a private dinner at the White House and drove over to the Capitol. The sergeants at arms for the House and the Senate met us at the door, and I was escorted to a small waiting room off the gallery. But unlike at the State of the Union, now I was not alone; Tony Blair was waiting with me. Inside the gallery, we were joined by Tom Ridge, as well as New York mayor Rudy Giuliani and Governor George Pataki. We had invited a group of hero guests, representatives of the New York fire and police departments and the Port Authority, as well as the U.S. Army and Navy, and Lisa Beamer, the pregnant widow of Todd Beamer, one of the passengers on board Flight 93. Vice President Cheney was absent from his customary spot behind the podium and was spending the night in a secure location because of fears of a mass attack on the Capitol. I listened as my husband gave the Taliban rulers of Afghanistan the first of a series of ultimatums, including surrender Osama bin Laden or face military retribution, and as he recalled how Republicans and Democrats, senators and representatives, had come together on the steps of the Capitol to sing "God Bless America."

I was always nervous when George spoke before Congress, but on this night, with all that was at stake, having Tony Blair, Tom Ridge, Rudy Giuliani, and George Pataki surrounding me was a great comfort.

Both George and I find the presence of close friends and the people we love comforting. Our whole married life, though, we have been comforted most by each other. Being nearby was how in those days, weeks, and months we reassured each other. We do not have to speak; ours is a language not just of words but of a shared presence. We take comfort simply from knowing that the other one is in the room. We are anchored to each other. And if it is my nature to be calm, it is also George's to steady and buoy me. We are two symbiotic souls.

I was anxious, but I was never fearful. And I received so many forms of unsolicited comfort. My old roommate from Houston, Janet Heyne, told me on the phone that "the whole time you've been in Washington, I've been so glad that I wasn't you and that I didn't have to do what you're doing." She went on, "Now I'm jealous for the first time because you can do something after this horrible tragedy." And I *could* do things, things that could make a difference. That was my solace, even as the roar of Air Force fighter planes flying cover patrols echoed through the walls and Secret Service details conducted new rounds of evacuations because there were reports of a truck bomb waiting to detonate on a nearby street.

That weekend, September 21, our girls came home. They flew on commercial airplanes that had just begun returning to the skies. We went to Camp David for Saturday night and spent Sunday afternoon at the White House, basking in the sunshine. I was so grateful just to hold them in my arms again. Monday brought a meeting at the White House with family members and friends of the victims of Flight 93. I read their stories in the customary White House briefing binders prepared beforehand, but there is almost no way to be "briefed" on such a visit. Passenger Thomas Burnett had called his wife, Deena, four times from Flight 93. In the fourth call, he said, "I know we're all going to die—there's three of us who are going to do something about it. I love you, honey." Jeremy Glick also managed to phone his wife, Lyzbeth. After they spoke, she gave the phone to her father, who heard the final screams before the connection went dead. The GTE phone operator Lisa Jefferson heard Todd Beamer's final words, "Are you ready, guys? Let's roll." Flight attendant Sandy Bradshaw had called her husband, Phil, and told him that they were gathering hot water and were going to rush the hijackers. He heard men on the plane nearby whispering the Twenty-third Psalm, "Yea, though I walk through the valley of the shadow of death, I will fear no evil: For thou art with me." Then his wife said, "Everyone's running to first class. I've got to go. Bye." In the Blue Room, under the portraits of Presidents Thomas Jefferson and James Monroe, George and I shook hands and embraced their families, and the families of the other passengers and crew members who gave their lives on that bright blue morning.

In the evening, I joined Senator Kennedy on the stage of the Kennedy Center for a concert in remembrance of 9-11. The next morning, I was on a government plane, bound for New York City.

Manhattan from the air looks doll-size, a perfect expanse of individual buildings rising from the island. With no way to build out, the city built up, until the thousands of building tops have meshed together to create a kind of aerial terrain, gleaming mountains of steel and glass high-rises, shadowy valleys of tenements and brownstones. And now, at the tip, a cataclysm. We circled the still smoldering wreckage where the Twin Towers had been, before landing in Newark, New Jersey, and traveling into the city.

My first stop was Madison Square Garden, where I was scheduled to address three thousand of the city's Learning Leaders, a nearly ten-thousand-strong volunteer school corps—larger than the U.S. Peace Corps—composed of specially trained parents, retirees, college students, businesspeople, and senior citizens who donate their time to New York City students and schools. My role was to help encourage them to return to their schools and classrooms because the city's children were in desperate need. My friend Andi Bernstein, who had been one of our co-owners of the Texas Rangers and whose husband was the business partner of one of George's oldest friends, had asked me to come. From Madison Square Garden, the motorcade headed south to one of the city's elementary schools, P.S. 41. That day, P.S. 41 was more than a school packed to bursting. It was a refuge, as it had been for the last fifteen days.

On the morning of 9-11, students at another school, P.S. 234, an elementary school for grades pre-K through fifth, were on their playground four blocks from the Twin Towers. They heard the thunderous crash and saw the first plane hit. Other children, already in their classrooms, where windows were open to let in the air on that bright, fresh fall morning, caught sight of the North Tower engulfed in flames.

Within minutes of the attack, many parents had rushed to the school to pick up their children, but as the streets clogged with evacuees and emergency vehicles racing south, 150 students remained behind. The school's principal, Anna Switzer, herded them, their teachers, and a few parents inside. Before the South Tower fell, Switzer and her teachers lined up the students, ages five to eleven, in a single file and told them to hold hands. They stepped out of the building into the ash and smoke. Some looked up and watched as men and women flung themselves from the upper floors of the towers, their bodies passing through the billowing flames. One child said, "The birds are on fire."

Running, some being carried, others being pulled, they moved north. Moments later, the air rumbled and the South Tower fell. The torrent of dust blotted out all signs of sky and sun. Students and teachers at the front of the line kept going north. Switzer grabbed those at the rear and raced back into the school's basement. "The day turned into night, and we ran for our lives," she later recalled. At first, Switzer did not know if her caravan of students and teachers who had left survived. They did, walking and running about a mile and a half north to the sheltering brick walls of P.S. 41.

Not only were many of the P.S. 234 students forced from their school but their families also had to abandon their homes for weeks or even months. Staff, parents, and children in both schools, P.S. 41 and 234, had friends who had died.

With rescue workers using the school building and the Trade Center site still aflame, the P.S. 234 children and teachers were sharing the classrooms at P.S. 41; two sets of students and two teachers were crowded into each room. I was there that morning to try to comfort them. I spoke to the children, and I read the storybook *I Love You, Little One* while, in the back of the classroom, teachers wept into their hands.

Governor George Pataki's wife, Libby, had joined me at the school. Now we were on our way to Engine Company 54 and Ladder Company 4 in lower Manhattan. The fire battalion had lost fifteen firefighters. The sidewalk in front had become a makeshift memorial of candles, notes, and flowers. The flowers were stacked one bouquet on top of another, creating a slowly fading mound. We placed our own fresh bouquets of sunflowers on the sidewalk and went inside to meet the men who remained. They were the ones who hadn't been on duty that day, who had been somewhere else when their friends suited up and raced south, climbing the stairs of the North Tower in full gear, including helmets and oxygen tanks, and wearing the locator devices that are designed to chirp so firefighters who fall in the dark can be found. I think sometimes of all those chirpers that suddenly went silent.

Inside the firehouse, the men were grieving. Unlike the grief of the teachers, which was laced with fear and uncertainty for the future, this was a very different grief—raw, aching, and angry.

The next week, on October 2, George and I went out to dinner in Washington, D.C., with Mayor Anthony Williams and his wife, Diane, at Morton's, a steakhouse. Across the country, people had stopped going to shopping malls and to restaurants. They had stopped flying on airplanes and staying in hotels. No one could promise them that other strikes would not come. But now, in addition to all the fears of another terror attack, George was concerned that the economy would spiral into a full-blown crisis. We had already been in a recession from the bursting of the dot-com bubble. He did not want the specter of more people losing their jobs, of storefronts being boarded up and businesses going bankrupt. It's not a large gesture for a president to go out to dinner, but we hoped that by doing so we might encourage other Americans. It was why George wanted them to shop, to fly on commercial airlines, and to travel again—those were all ways to bolster business. If the terrorists had succeeded in undermining our economy too, they would have scored a double blow.

The White House was abuzz with foreign leaders arriving for meetings with George. They came for Oval Office sit-downs and for small working lunches and dinners, at times with their spouses. On September 28, I hosted Jordan's Queen Rania for a coffee while her husband, King Abdullah, talked terrorism and security with George. In all, over the next six months, more than twenty-five foreign leaders would fly to Washington to meet with George, and he would keep in near constant touch with others by phone. I also wanted to invite friends over. As the blistering intensity of the early days continued unabated, I felt very strongly that every so often George needed an hour or two to clear his mind, or at least to have the distraction and the comfort of longtime friends. From before dawn each morning, he was reading threat assessments and reviewing retaliation options. I wanted him to have a few brief moments of respite. So our friends came: Penny Slade-Sawyer, who had been one of our good friends when we moved back to Midland and who now lived in Northern Virginia, as well as Joan and Jim Doty, whom we had met in 1988 during Gampy's campaign, and other friends scattered around Washington. At the start of October, our longtime friends from Lubbock, Mike and Nancy Weiss, came for a few days. We took immeasurable comfort in seeing all of them.

On Friday, October 5, we traveled to Camp David with Mike and Nancy. We had known them since George's race for Congress back in 1978. Mike was an accountant who had been George's Lubbock County chairman for the campaign; the two had met in the back of a men's clothing store when George had dropped by to introduce himself and shake hands. Mike had supported George on every run since, even moving to Austin to help George set up the Texas budget office, and Nancy and I had spent count-

George H. W. Bush tears up as George W. Bush becomes Governor of Texas in 1995.

Election night 2000. Loading the dishwasher in our kitchen as we wait.

Walking in the 2001 inaugural parade.
(Eric Draper/White House photo)

Dressed for the inaugural balls. George, who wakes at 5:00 A.M., had us home before midnight.
(Paul Morse/White House photo)

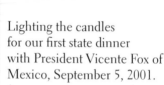

Lighting the candles for our first state dinner with President Vicente Fox of Mexico, September 5, 2001.
(Eric Draper/White House photo)

Welcoming book lovers to the first National Book Festival on September 8, 2001. I launched the festival with Jim Billington, the Librarian of Congress.
(Moreen Ishikawa/White House photo)

With senators Ted Kennedy and Judd Gregg on September 11, 2001, in Senator Kennedy's office. I was on Capitol Hill to brief the Senate Education Committee. (Moreen Ishikawa/ White House photo)

Speaking to the press on 9-11. (White House photo)

In the Presidential Emergency Operations Center below the White House, listening to George after his return from Florida on 9-11. (Eric Draper/White House photo)

Laying flowers with New York's first lady Libby Pataki in tribute to fallen New York City firefighters outside of Engine Company 54 and Ladder Company 4 in lower Manhattan. (Moreen Ishikawa/White House photo)

Guest teaching in Newark, New Jersey, October 2001. The girl on my lap whispered to me, "Did you hear about the buildings?" (Moreen Ishikawa/White House photo)

Breakfast at our dining room table with Vladimir Putin and Lyudmila Putina during their November 2001 visit to our ranch in Texas. (Eric Draper/ White House photo)

Lighting the Christmas tree in Rockefeller Center with Mayor Rudy Giuliani, and Al Roker and Ann Curry of NBC News. (Susan Sterner/ White House photo)

Representing the United States at the United Nations for International Women's Day in March 2002, alongside UN Secretary-General Kofi Annan. (Susan Sterner/White House photo)

Flying with Jenna from Paris to Prague. I love traveling with my daughters and seeing destinations through their eyes. (Susan Sterner/White House photo)

A service of remembrance at St. John's Church to mark the first anniversary of 9-11. (Eric Draper/White House photo)

Leaving the Diplomatic Reception Room after saying good night to the Czech president Václav Havel and his wife, Dagmar, in 2002.
(Paul Morse/White House photo)

Greeting female teachers from Afghanistan. I admired their bravery after years of oppression, and I longed to make my own visit to their nation.
(Susan Sterner/White House photo)

Laying a rose at Auschwitz, the infamous Nazi death camp in 2003.
(White House photo)

Standing in the Door of No Return on Gorée Island, Senegal, a monument to remember the hideous Atlantic slave trade. (Tina Hager/White House photo)

Visiting the wounded at Walter Reed Army Medical Center. George and I often went together to visit the wounded or those who had lost loved ones. I always knew when he had gone alone. A special grief shone in his eyes. Here, with Staff Sergeant Chester Duncan. (White House photo)

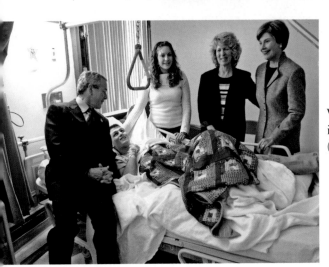

With Specialist Aaron Bugg in November of 2004. (White House photo)

Sharing a laugh at the 2005 Black Tie & Boots Inaugural Ball. (Eric Draper/White House photo)

George taking the oath of office, administered by Chief Justice William Rehnquist. (Susan Sterner/White House photo)

The official 2005 inaugural family portrait, which my mother missed. Everyone pictured is part of the extended Bush family. (Eric Draper/White House photo)

less mornings walking around the city's lake trails. They were with us to lend their companionship and friendship, but as we ate our meals or took brief walks at the edge of the Catoctin Mountains, George knew what was to come. I knew as well. He spent most of the weekend closeted with his staff, and in the evening, when we were alone, he talked about sending our forces into combat. I knew how anxious he was; along with the fears of more terrorism, he now had the added worry of the safety of our own troops. There was no precedent for this type of war and for what would have to be done. But he and I said nothing about it to Mike and Nancy.

On Sunday morning, on our return to Washington, we stopped at the National Fallen Firefighters Memorial in Emmitsburg, Maryland, to honor firefighters who had died during the year. Over three hundred firefighters had perished on 9-11. When we landed at the White House, George left to prepare for his remarks to the nation. I took Mike and Nancy upstairs, into our bedroom, and told them: at one o'clock that afternoon, George was going to announce the first round of bomb and missile strikes against the Taliban rulers in Afghanistan. He would speak from the Treaty Room, the place where other presidents had pursued peace, with the Washington Monument and Jefferson Memorial rising in the background. A few doors down, technicians were adjusting the lights and checking the audio feed, and George was reading his speech a final time. I turned on the television and got in bed; Nancy and Mike drew up chairs beside me, although Nancy later told me that she felt like getting in bed too.

George's voice was steady as he spoke, but I knew the consequences. Twenty-six days after 9-11, my husband was formally announcing military action. The Taliban had ignored every ultimatum. "The battle is now joined on many fronts. We will not waver, we will not tire, we will not falter, and we will not fail," he said. Less than two hours before, American and British forces had launched the first strikes on the cities of Kabul and Kandahar. Missiles and bombs would be followed by drops of food, medicine, and transistor radios that were tuned to a message broadcast for the people of Afghanistan. George had been given update reports on the military plans since before we boarded Marine One that morning. "Peace and freedom will prevail," he said as we watched him on the television screen.

In our system of government, while Congress is the body that can officially declare war, presidents are the ones who make the ultimate call to send our troops into battle. My father-in-law had done it at the start of 1991; four presidents—John F. Kennedy, Lyndon Johnson, Richard Nixon, and Gerald Ford—had presided over a single war: Vietnam. After two years of Nazi aggression in Europe, Franklin Roosevelt took the country to war against Japan and then Germany in 1941. Harry Truman had the Korean War, although it was undeclared, and every post–World War II president through George H. W. Bush had faced the nuclear specter of the Cold War. The history lessons are easy; what is hard to find are the words to convey my emotions when my husband had to commit precious American lives to combat. In his speech, George spoke of a letter he had received from a fourth-grade girl whose father was in the military. "As much as I don't want my dad to fight," she wrote, "I'm willing to give him to you." I pictured the faces of the sailors and Marines on the cruisers in San Diego, where I had gone for my first Troops to Teachers event, six months ago; I thought of the Navy personnel who sat alongside us in the chapel at Camp David; I thought of the faces of the men and women in uniform who had met us at the Pentagon, of the injured at Walter Reed. They were people with names, with hometowns, with parents, spouses, and families, and they were willing to give themselves and their lives so that other dads and moms going to work on a quiet, late-summer morning might never know terror again.

For months, I would lie in bed at night or wake in the darkness and think of our troops, think of them sleeping on cold, hard ground beneath the unforgiving Afghan winds, and feel guilty that I had a warm room and a warm bed while they risked everything. At Camp David, on that first Sunday morning after 9-11, our chaplain, Navy Lieutenant Bob Williams, had selected as the scripture reading Psalm 27, "I shall see the goodness of the Lord in the land of the living." I knew that goodness wore camouflage and khaki; it wore Army green, Navy white, Marine tan, and Air Force blue.

The first anthrax-laced letters were mailed from Princeton, New Jersey, on September 18, 2001. Four were addressed to major New York City media companies, including to the NBC News anchorman Tom Brokaw; a fifth letter arrived at the offices of American Media, a tabloid newspaper and magazine company in Florida. The Florida letter killed a photo editor and nearly killed a mail room employee. Robert Stevens died on October 5, two days before George gave the final order for attacks to begin on the Taliban. Then, on October 12, five days after our air strikes began, an assistant to Tom Brokaw tested positive for skin anthrax, an infection marked by sores or boils that can spread to the bloodstream if left untreated. Anthrax was found at ABC and CBS news, as well as the *New York Post*, and each news organization had at least one employee with a confirmed case of skin anthrax. On October 15, the anthrax reached Washington, D.C. Contaminated letters had been sent to Senators Tom Daschle and Patrick Leahy. The Hart Senate Office Building was evacuated and shut down, and all mail, including all mail to the White House, was quarantined. But no one thought to close the post office that had processed the mail. Two employees at the Brentwood postal facility, Thomas Morris Jr. and Joseph Curseen Jr., would die from inhaled anthrax; two others would fall ill but, after prolonged treatment with antibiotics, would recover. The entire mail facility, along with the Hart Building, would be sealed shut while chlorine gas was pumped in to kill any remaining bacteria. October was the month of anthrax. Suddenly, threats seemed no longer confined to the sky; they were coming from all directions.

The White House was now literally cut off. Any letter or package being sent was entombed in an off-site facility. Letters could not reach us, not even ones from fourth-grade girls. It was impossible to send any kind of envelope to the White House grounds. For years, the mail sat in sacks, unopened and waiting to be irradiated. Even the finished art by Adrian Martinez that we had chosen back in the hot months of summer to adorn our holiday card vanished for three years inside those mail sacks. Hallmark had mailed it back, along with the final proof for the card. They had to rush to create another proof, and the president of Hallmark met me on the tarmac of the airport in Waco, Texas, during a stopover so I could approve the proof before the final printing began.

The mail was the last severed link to much of the outside world. During the spring and summer, after we had moved in, I would occasionally sit in my small, private upstairs office and gaze out at the lines of tourists streaming through the White House doors, people who had waited in line for hours to see the East Room, the State Dining Room, the Blue, Red, and Green rooms. But since September 12, the doors had been closed. There were no tours; the grounds were deserted except for the clusters of sharpshooters who paced the roof and patrolled among the trees. I grew accustomed to heavily armed men in black combat gear walking in through the doors from the Rose Garden and bomb-sniffing dogs making their rounds in the previously placid corridors of the East Wing. Sharpshooters hung out the windows of our convoys, and helicopters hovered above our destinations. The flak jackets that we had worn for the trip into Kosovo seemed like a quaint memory; we were now living with danger all around us, so that every errant sound, every fast-moving plane made me lift my eyes to scan the sky.

Inside the White House, the stillness was almost deafening. Gone now was the tan and brown folding screen that had been routinely spread across the ground-floor Cross Hall, allowing the president or me, or anyone else coming from the upstairs residence, to pass through the corridor unseen by tour groups or other visitors. In this emptiness, there was no longer any need for a protective screen.

⌒

When George and I were visiting the Blairs at Chequers the previous summer, Gary Walters, the head White House usher, had called to tell me that painters and plasterers had found a false wall in the large upstairs Cross Hall in the residence. The Cross Hall had not had a new coat of paint since the Reagan administration. The White House walls are plaster with canvas stretched on top, so this time when they repainted they removed the canvas to repair the plaster, and at the entry to the Yellow Oval Room found bookshelves dating from Truman's term that had been covered, probably by Jackie Kennedy. The shelves emerged, looking freshly painted and perfectly preserved, although no one on the staff had known that they were there. They also discovered delicately carved shells in niches above two doors along the hallway. The White House is a home that gives up its secrets one by one.

Although it was George Washington who chose the site for the White House, the first president to live inside its walls was John Adams. But little of the Adams era survives; the house was torched by the British in 1814, during the War of 1812, and had to be rebuilt. Its first major renovation was by Theodore Roosevelt, who tore down great glass conservatories erected to grow fruits and flowers for the first family and built the West Wing offices in 1902. He also transformed the ground floor from a cooking and laundry area with bedrooms for White House servants and staff, including a separate room for the fireman who manned the house's enormous furnace, into receiving and reception rooms for the president and his guests. By 1948, the house's interior was so fragile it was in danger of collapsing. Harry and Bess Truman moved across the street to Blair House, and the building was gutted down to its original brick walls and completely rebuilt. Jackie Kennedy updated many of the interior decorations and made changes to the family living quarters, and subsequent first ladies have added their own personal touches, transforming carpeting and wall and window coverings, moving furniture, and adding art.

But above all, the White House is a living, breathing place; even in the public rooms, there is always some flux. The Green Room, now a formal sitting room on the State Floor, began as a bedchamber and then a breakfast room for Thomas Jefferson; James Monroe made it into a card parlor. Many commentators hated its various iterations of green color, particularly Andrew Jackson's. Only in 1962 did Jackie Kennedy select its well-known waterfall green silk wall coverings. The State Dining Room was originally Thomas Jefferson's office, and even after it became a dining room, Theodore Roosevelt hung large mounted moose heads on its walls. The Map Room, which we frequently used as a waiting place for formal receiving lines, was the room where FDR monitored the progress of U.S. forces during World War II. Before that, it had housed Woodrow Wilson's billiard table. I knew whatever I did was temporary; it was merely to keep and care for the house. Other administrations would make changes of their own.

When we first arrived, I had set about redoing the girls' rooms and the Treaty Room (in the residence). But that was only the start. The White House is a home, but a home that accommodates more than 100,000 people a year. Hundreds alone came for small events upstairs in our residence quarters. Butlers, maintenance staff, and White House staff and employees also walk across the carpets and hallways, because it is a place of business as well as a residence. And it is an old, historic home, making the need to refurbish almost constant. Painters literally walk around with cans and brushes, constantly touching up scuff marks, streaks, and nicks on the walls.

So it was a strange incongruity that, as the White House was being emptied of all but essential personnel, I was going room by room to see what was in need of repair.

When my father-in-law was president, Bar and I would walk the house some nights, in the quiet dark, switching on lights, exploring the Red, Green, and Blue rooms in a kind of perfect stillness, wondering who else had, on other nights, also walked there. For days after we moved in, I found that each room in the residence reminded me of Bar and Gampy, of some moment or memory that we had made during their four years.

Indeed, despite its museumlike atmosphere, the White House remains a home. Until the Kennedys arrived, many presidential families did most of their living downstairs, amid the vintage furnishings. They ate their meals in the old Family Dining Room, a small, square space that abuts the large State Dining Room. George would sometimes host working lunches and dinners for foreign leaders there; otherwise, it is a quasi-storage room used to plate the food for official dinners and other functions.

The upstairs, until the time of Theodore Roosevelt, had housed the president's office space—the famous Lincoln Bedroom actually served as Lincoln's office; his aides occupied a room across the hall, and visitors congregated in a small sitting area in between. Just a doorway away from the offices was the corridor for the family bedrooms. Our room was the traditional first lady's bedroom, while the president's bedroom was our sitting room. Not until Gerald and Betty Ford took up residence at the White House did the custom of a separate presidential bedroom officially end. Before that, a host of American presidents—from Abraham Lincoln to Woodrow Wilson, Calvin Coolidge, Franklin Roosevelt, Harry Truman, Eisenhower, Kennedy, Johnson, and Nixon—chose separate but usually adjoining rooms for themselves and their wives.

I decorated our room in a soothing blend of pale celadon green and cream, covering the walls, headboard, and curtains in a fabric designed by Peter Fasano, with wide, round tables by the bedside to hold books for reading. George's table was stacked with history books. We were at home in the past almost everywhere we turned.

Jenna's room had also been the bedroom for Caroline Kennedy, who liked to creep down the massive marble staircase nearby and peek at her parents' guests through the balusters, as well as for Lynda Bird Johnson, and Chelsea Clinton, and President Taft's sons, Robert and Charles, while Barbara's room next door had rested the sleepy heads of John F. Kennedy Jr., Luci Johnson, Tricia Nixon, and Amy Carter. The room that Jackie Kennedy had designated as the upstairs presidential dining room was once the bedroom where Alice Roosevelt, Teddy Roosevelt's daughter, remembered having her appendix removed. By the late 1940s, the room's floor was so unsound that a leg of Margaret Truman's piano broke through the boards.

Over time, the upstairs residence became a collection of sitting and guest rooms. In 1902, Theodore Roosevelt's large family necessitated going up into the attic, which had its dusty spaces partitioned to create a few new, small bedrooms. Calvin and Grace Coolidge oversaw the replacement of the White House roof in 1927, building in the process an entire finished third floor, which was enlarged and redone by Harry and Bess Truman. Married presidential children, including the Fords' and the Carters', made their Washington homes in suites of rooms up there, and Hillary Clinton's mother and my mother were most at home in a third-floor room tucked under the eaves.

Under doctor's orders to get out of the Oval Office during the middle of the day as World War II raged, FDR would eat lunch in the third-floor "sky parlor" added by Grace Coolidge. The Trumans transformed it into a rectangular solarium. President Eisenhower liked to barbecue on the parapet outside when he and Mamie weren't eating their dinner on TV trays downstairs in the West Sitting Hall, sitting side by side, each watching his or her own television. Mamie preferred *I Love Lucy*, while Ike chose westerns. Both did sometimes watch the news. The solarium was also the room where Lynda and Luci Johnson entertained their teenage friends and where Caroline Kennedy for a while had a tiny, private preschool and an at times solitary playroom. And over the years, it became a favorite place for male guests and sometimes presidents to smoke cigars.

Each room that I entered had a history, each piece of furniture a past, whether it was the antique English canopy bed that had been finished in 1775, a year before American independence, or the table and bookcase made from the original 1817 wood used to finish the White House roof after British troops had set it aflame, or the collection of framed silhouettes, including one of President John Tyler that had survived a shipwreck in the English Channel. And it was not just the intimacies of the daily lives of other first families that we felt as the years passed, but their private sufferings that were also contained within these walls.

Every day I walked by the room where Willie Lincoln had died in February of 1862 after a two-week battle with a typhoidlike illness, probably contracted from contaminated water in a nearby canal, water that was drunk at the White House and a canal where children played. Mary Todd Lincoln spent hours at his bedside as he was plied with everything from Peruvian bark to beef tea. The night that he took sick, the Lincolns were hosting a party in the East Room. The orchestra strains rose up to the room as Willie's parents scurried back and forth between his bedside and their guests. The last ones departed late into the night, and as their coaches clattered off, Willie's fever was rising. After his death, Mary Todd Lincoln refused ever again to enter that room, or the Green Room, where his body had been embalmed. The Lincoln biographer Carl Sandburg would write that there were thirty-one rooms in the White House, but Lincoln was not at home in any of them. And Willie Lincoln was not the only child to die while residing in the White House.

The Coolidges lost their sixteen-year-old son, Calvin Jr., to blood poisoning, or septicemia, in July of 1924. He had developed an infected blister after playing one of his favorite sports, tennis, on the rear grounds of the White House. The Coolidges stayed at their son's bedside, but doctors could offer them nothing. "When he was suffering, he begged me to help him, but I could not," Coolidge later wrote. On July 4, as workers were readying the White House grounds for celebrations and fireworks, Calvin Jr. was rushed to Walter Reed. He died three days later. Coolidge openly wept in the Oval Office and later said that if he had not been president, his son would not have suffered a raised blister playing lawn tennis on the South Grounds. Jackie Kennedy had lost an infant son just three and a half months before her husband was assassinated. And three first ladies—Letitia Tyler, Caroline Harrison, and Ellen Wilson—died while they lived in the White House. Presidents suffered too. After his own stroke, Woodrow Wilson, his left side paralyzed and barely able to write his name, retreated to the East Room, where with curtains drawn, he spent hours watching the flickering reels of silent films lent by a local theater. He was just sixty-three years old.

I was always aware of the brave faces that other families had placed on their personal tragedies and on the way that the demands of the White House gave no time for grief, even less for reflection. "The funeral is a very solemn affair," wrote William Stoddard, an aide to President Lincoln about Willie's funeral in the East Room, where cabinet secretaries, senators, ambassadors, and soldiers choked back tears. "But it cannot be permitted to interfere overmuch with work. The burden is increased rather than laid aside."

Five days after American and British fighters began strikes on the Taliban's strongholds, as additional U.S. Special Forces readied themselves to enter the bleak, mountainous Afghanistan terrain on the backs of horses, weapons slung over their sides, I accompanied George to the Pentagon for a service to mark the one-month anniversary of 9-11. We traveled across the Potomac over streets that had been cleared and sealed off to form an almost perfect security bubble. There could be no more casual breaches of the perimeter. We were in a constant state of vigilance, always saving some awareness for wherever we were standing. This morning was no different, except for the addition of an F-16 fighter cover, flying low and close above the Pentagon.

The hijacked plane had penetrated the entire outer ring, and a good portion of the river side of the building was charred with layers of thick, black soot. But what lingered for weeks, even after the cranes had arrived and the debris began to be collected, was a fierce smell, the noxious, deep scent of burning jet fuel, building materials, and human remains. It was a smell that burned the throat and stung the nostrils, a smell so strong that even commuters in closed subway cars racing underneath the World Trade Center site inhaled it for months after 9-11. And it remained at the Pentagon. We looked at the gouge in the building, and I looked into the somber faces of the men and women who were embarking upon a war.

Before fifteen thousand people, George spoke of a wound to the building that would not be forgotten but that would be repaired. In an overwhelming bit of irony, it was on September 11, 1941, that construction on the Pentagon had first begun. As the cameras clicked, both of us had tears in our eyes.

I felt the grief again at a memorial service sponsored by Elayne Bennett's Best Friends organization for three exceptional eleven-year-old Washington, D.C., students who were on Flight 77 with their teacher, bound for a special National Geographic program on California's Channel Islands. So many lives lost, each one exceptional to someone.

On October 16, five weeks after the attacks, I was attempting to return my official life to a regular routine. I had committed months before to teach in different schools across the country for Teach for America Week, highlighting the program and its efforts to get bright and eager college graduates into some of the nation's toughest classrooms. Teach for America recruits commit to spending two years teaching in public schools in low-income communities. During Teach for America Week, professionals from all across the country spend an hour teaching children in public school classrooms.

There are those who dismiss school visits as photo ops, but there is so much more to them than that. There is a chance to connect with the students and the teachers, to convey how much they are valued. And every school that I visited was thoroughly vetted, so being selected was a significant badge of honor. Many of the schools I saw were in rough areas; they were not wealthy schools, even though the districts had rushed to spruce them up. George and I always noted that we could smell the coats of new paint before we even stepped through the doorways. But paint couldn't camouflage rusty pipes, ancient bathrooms, and dilapidated desks. Or the neighborhoods that I saw on the drives in—graffiti-covered walls, stray bullet holes, abandoned buildings, and makeshift cardboard where glass windows should have been. There were piles of trash, chain-link fences around asphalt blacktops, and hardly anything green, such as a patch of grass to play on.

That week, I was scheduled to teach in Washington, D.C.; Baltimore, Maryland; Atlanta, Georgia; and Baton Rouge, Louisiana. My second stop was the South Seventeenth Street Elementary School in Newark, New Jersey, where I was to teach a kindergarten class. South Seventeenth Street

Elementary was similar to the John F. Kennedy Elementary School in Houston; 453 of its 537 students were eligible for free and reduced-price lunch, and the majority of them were African-American. Mark Williams, the kindergarten teacher, had graduated from college just over a year before. He had painted a bright mural on his classroom walls.

I spoke to the students and read a story. At one point, a little girl snuggled up next to me and tugged on my arm to whisper in my ear. I bent my head and listened to her hushed, solemn voice. "Did you hear," she asked, "about the buildings?" I very slowly nodded my head. "The bad men knocked them down and all the people died," she said, and then asked, "What do you think about what happened?" I wrapped my arms around her and said, "I'm sad." And she nodded and said, "I'm sad too."

In Baton Rouge, on the morning of October 19, I taught at the Eden Park Elementary School, and then, instead of flying directly back to D.C., I made a stop at the ranch. George had left for China for the Asia-Pacific Economic Cooperation Summit. He had wanted to decline, but the Chinese were determined that the event go forward and had made elaborate plans to host the Pacific Rim nations, so he made the trip. When he arrived, he called me to say that all of Shanghai was a ghost town. The Chinese had cleared it out for the conference; almost 16 million people had been moved. With George away, I did not want to spend the weekend in the White House alone. I invited my good friend Debbie Francis to spend Saturday night at the ranch with me. We were sitting in the living room after dinner, having a glass of wine and talking, when my Secret Service agents burst in. They had received warning of an impending attack on our ranch. I was shocked. When I didn't immediately leave the house, the agents told us to turn off all the lights, and they moved the convoy of blast-proof vehicles into the driveway so we could run to the road if necessary. Debbie and I sat in the pitch black and kept talking, although I'm sure for her it must have seemed unnerving to sit in total darkness before we made our way to bed, where we would try to sleep, waiting for an attack that never came.

There were many such warnings, whispered in my ear when I was at an event or even sitting on a sofa in the White House residence, having a quick cup of coffee with a friend. I would be told of a suspicious plane or vehicle or other concern. One time, when Barbara and Jenna were home on a spring break and we were sitting in the living room with some of their friends, we heard the agents' footsteps pounding down the hall. They raced in and told us that we had to go to the bunker. Everyone jumped up and started running down the hallway to the long, slick marble stairs. Panting, we made it the three long flights down. Then word came that it was only a stray plane that had violated the protected airspace.

We had another evacuation incident in the spring of 2005, when Nancy Reagan was staying with us to attend a lunch that I was hosting in her honor. Again, the agents appeared to hustle us down to the bunker, but this time I insisted on taking the elevator. I was not going to make Nancy Reagan walk down three steep flights of marble stairs. So we dropped in our elevator cage to the subterranean bunker. After we arrived, fighter jets intercepted the plane. It was a pilot from Pennsylvania who had mistakenly strayed into the restricted airspace. Months after the incident, he ran into someone I knew and said, "Please tell Mrs. Bush that I am so sorry."

But there was no way of knowing which threats were accidents and which were real. We grew used to dashing down to the bunker, to always being a bit more aware. It came with our new lives.

George read the daily threat assessments, the pages upon pages of worrisome plots, activities, and chatter. He didn't bring it all home, but he brought enough that I could see the lines cut deeper in his face and could hear him next to me lying awake at night, his mind still working.

But whatever our private anxieties, our public lives required us to go on. Just three days after the ranch scare, I visited the National Gallery to tour its new exhibition of Renaissance art, featuring a portrait by Leonardo da Vinci.

It is hard to recall now just how empty parts of the nation were in the months after 9-11, especially museums, movie theaters, malls, restaurants, and hotels. Washington, D.C., hotels were all but vacant. There was a collective unease about large public spaces, and one of the things that mattered most was interrupting that cycle of fear. I walked through the National Gallery of Art with its charming and smart director, Rusty Powell, and the exhibition's wonderful curator, Russell Sale. Over the years, I would visit many exhibitions in Washington, usually quietly, just to take in the beauty and power of the creations. In a time of destruction, art reminds us of the ennobling impulses that exist in human beings, the desire to create, to beautify, to build, to educate, and to make something that will last for generations. Art and artists are among our bulwarks against ruthless terrorists who would fashion bombs or commandeer and crash planes. Art reminds us too that time passes and things change; peace may not always be permanent, but neither is war. On that morning, going to this museum, I brought the press with me. If I was unafraid to go, perhaps others would begin to feel the same. And I remember the gratitude of Rusty Powell and Russell Sale, for the simple effort of my coming. "You just can't know," they said, "what it meant for a first lady to come to the museum at all, and then to come so soon after 9-11."

But there were still moments when fear crept in.

On Monday, October 29, a second national terror alert was issued. The FBI announced that it expected terror strikes against the United States, either at home or abroad. Among the most specific warnings, the CIA believed that al Qaeda had plans to attack a nuclear facility with a hijacked aircraft. The next day, we were back in New York City.

George had been asked to throw out the first pitch at the opening New York home game of the World Series, where the Yankees were playing the Arizona Diamondbacks. Barbara came down from Yale to be with me, and we were perched in the box of George Steinbrenner, the Yankees' owner. George would be walking onto the field alone. He would stride from the dugout to the empty mound and stand with no agents beside him and a packed crowd filling every seat in the stands. George was focused on his pitch. Under the stadium, as George was warming up, the Yankees star Derek Jeter had already asked him if he was going to throw from the mound. As George worried about throwing a strike, I was worried about far more. Every entry point had metal detectors; bomb-sniffing dogs roamed the grounds, and sharpshooters took up positions on the roof. Evacuation information flashed across the scoreboard as both teams began batting practice. The official start to the evening was a phalanx of fighter jets flying overhead, after which we all observed a moment of silence to honor the fallen and our troops. The flag that snapped in the air was one recovered from the wreckage at Ground Zero, where buried fires were still smoking. It was partially torn and missing twelve stars.

I smiled and watched as my husband raised his arm and hurled the ball straight into the grooved leather of the catcher's mitt. I heard the chants of "USA, USA, USA," but inside my heart was racing, my hands were cold, and my mind was wondering, What if? It was the same feeling that followed me when I glanced at pro football stadiums packed for weekend games or when we began planning the 2002 National Book Festival. For a long time afterward, I would look up at the sky and wonder, Are we going to see something else? Every night, I went to bed wondering, What will tomorrow bring?

The next day, Halloween, we met at the White House with the families of the two postal workers who had died the previous week in the anthrax attacks. Joseph Curseen was forty-seven and had spent fifteen years with the post office. Thomas Morris was fifty-five and had been a postal employee for twenty-eight years. Both left behind wives and children. They had merely been in a place that had processed infected mail bound for the Capitol. Unspoken in the room, as we shook hands with the postmaster general, was the question of whether there would be more such envelopes in the weeks and months to come. Anthrax had already been found at a remote White House mail site, and on Monday, after the new threat assessment, the Secret Service had locked down all the gates at the White House.

The fall deepened, and more foreign leaders came. Over the course of six days, the presidents of Nigeria and Algeria, Jacques Chirac of France, and Tony Blair flew to Washington to meet with George. But I was focused on another significant meeting: Vladimir Putin and Lyudmila Putina were about to become our first official guests at the ranch. They were heading to New York for the United Nations General Assembly meeting and then to visit us. I still didn't have all my furniture for the guesthouse — I was frantically borrowing some from my friend and decorator Ken Blasingame. And the day I flew to the ranch to finish the preparations, I first had to give a speech before three hundred journalists sitting amid a sea of banquet tables and starched white cloths at the National Press Club in downtown Washington.

The Secret Service advance team had arrived hours beforehand, walking the hallways with a bomb-sniffing dog. My speech was originally going to be about education, but it was now about something more, about the country I had found after 9-11. I told of seeing flags waving in front of almost every home and building up and down the streets of Chicago when I arrived a week after 9-11 to tape a television interview with Oprah Winfrey, and of the memorial service at the Pentagon, where a single woman stood up to wave her flag during the singing of the "Battle Hymn of the Republic," and how we all stood after that, waving our flags and singing, tears filling our eyes. I told about the women from a Jewish synagogue outside Washington, D.C., who volunteered to shop for Muslim women who were afraid to go out on their own, and about the woman in New York who called her rabbi a few days before she was set to give birth and told him that she wanted to name her child after a World Trade Center victim who didn't have a child of his own. She said good-bye by telling Rabbi Joseph Potasnik, "I promise that I will try to have more children because I know there are so many more names." I told of an art student who signed up to join the military and of hundreds of Washington, D.C., students whose families can't afford to buy lunch but who pinched pennies to give me $173.64 for the Afghan Children's Fund. I spoke of children in Southern California who in early October, before the anthrax attacks, raised $85.75 for Afghan children at their sidewalk lemonade stand and sent the money to the White House, with a letter to the president signed "Your citizens."

If we set aside one day to honor each victim of 9-11, it would take us nearly a decade to complete our tribute. There were, at final count, 2,973 innocent dead from that morning. I closed by saying, "Americans are willing to fight and die for our freedoms, but more importantly, we are willing to live for them." And when I look back now at that fall, for all the worry and the darkness, I do still see, as the Psalmist said, so much goodness in the land of the living.

~~~

In sixth grade, our big class project was to write a country report. I painstakingly copied mine into a green notebook, with a green and gold compass that my mother helped me design to decorate the cover. My research came from the encyclopedia, what all elementary school students in Midland used back then. At home, we didn't have a set of leather-bound *Britannicas* or *World Books*; Mother and Daddy hadn't wanted to spend the money on them. Instead, our encyclopedia set came from the grocery store. Mother "earned" it one volume at a time as part of a special promotion; whenever she spent a certain amount of money at the store, she received a coupon good for one or two volumes.

The moment I got the assignment, I decided to pick a country that sounded completely exotic and remote compared to anything I knew in Midland, Texas. Our teacher, Mr. Bain, told us to look at a map of the world, and I ran my finger around and picked the crossing point for the ancient Silk Road. And so my sixth-grade country report was on Afghanistan, a nation I never thought that I would encounter again.

The Afghanistan I wrote about in 1957 was very different from the one the United States was confronting in 2001. For thousands of years, it has been a land of high mountain ranges, sweeping desert, and remote green valleys, where goats and sheep grazed and orchards were planted. Landlocked, it was never totally isolated. Trade routes between West and East snaked across its harsh terrain. Nomadic peoples from the Mongolian steppes used its corridors to push east toward Persia or south to India, and it was invaded from the west as well. Alexander the Great conquered Afghanistan in 329 B.C. on his way to India; Arab armies came in the 600s; and Genghis Khan left a trail of carnage in 1219. In the 1300s, Tamerlane made Afghanistan part of his Central Asian empire. Afghanistan became its own confluence of cultures—Persian, Turkic Central Asian, and Indo-Persian—along what would become the Pakistani border. It was tribal and diverse, and repeatedly caught between other empires. In the nineteenth century, the British and the Russians used Afghanistan as a wedge between their two dominions. In the mid–twentieth century, as I was writing my sixth-grade report, Afghanistan was a pawn between the Soviet Union and the Americans in the Cold War. It was technically a nonaligned nation, and its king and prime minister were hoping to benefit from playing one side against the other. From 1955 to 1957, the United States gave Afghanistan more than $30 million in economic aid. The following year, the Afghan prime minister came to Washington, D.C., and addressed both the House of Representatives and the Senate. But by 1960, the Russians had given $300 million in economic aid to Afghanistan, and its prime minister was meeting with Nikita Khrushchev. After that, the United States largely ceded Afghanistan to Russia's sphere of influence and began looking to other nations arrayed across the vast, global Cold War chessboard.

But this period was notable in other ways, particularly for women. In 1959 Afghanistan formally abolished the requirement that women wear a veil and a chadri, a shroudlike head-to-toe covering. By 1965 women were allowed to vote in national assembly elections, and soon after a woman was made the minister of public health. Women became teachers and doctors and ran businesses; eventually 40 percent worked in paying jobs. They played sports, watched movies, wore skirts and heels, and the few well-to-do copied the fashions in Tehran.

Then in the early 1970s, a severe drought hit. Crops failed, and much of the country's sheep population, a key source of meat, perished. Hunger was rampant, and as many as eighty thousand people died of starvation before international food aid could reach them. From there came coups and then the overthrow of the government. A communist faction took control, but the Soviet Union was still not pleased, and in December of 1979, Soviet troops invaded Afghanistan. Jimmy Carter announced a U.S. boycott of the 1980 Moscow Summer Olympics in protest, and no American athletes participated.

United States– and Middle Eastern–backed Afghan mujahideen fighters drove the Soviets out ten years later, after the country had been largely left in ruins and 1.5 million Afghans had been killed. Five years later, in 1994, as George was running against Ann Richards for Texas governor, some of those mujahideen regrouped, found fresh recruits, and became the Taliban.

Like most of America, I didn't pay much attention to the Taliban and Afghanistan in the 1990s, although some women did, among them Mavis Leno, wife of the comedian Jay Leno, who made the repression of women in Afghanistan her personal cause. But in the weeks after September 11, what I learned horrified me. Starting in 1994, when they came to power over swaths of Afghanistan, the Taliban imposed a brand of sharia law never before seen in the modern Muslim world. They shut down girls' schools and banned women from working outside their homes. They destroyed television sets, banned dancing and music because it "creates a strain in the mind and hampers the study of Islam." They required men to grow long beards and women to cover themselves in the heaviest and most restrictive style of burka. Women, they decreed, should be neither seen nor heard; otherwise they would tempt men and lead them away from the path of Islam.

When the Taliban seized Kabul, they closed the university. Ten thousand students, including four thousand women, could no longer study. Schools for boys suffered too, because the majority of teachers were women. By December of 1998, UNICEF reported that in Afghanistan nine out of every ten girls and two out of every three boys could no longer attend school. Then the religious police began to patrol the streets, beating women who might venture out alone, beating women who were not dressed properly, beating women who so much as laughed out loud. Women were ordered not to wear shoes that made noise. The Taliban closed female bathhouses and hair salons.

The repercussions for an already impoverished country were staggering. After half a decade of Taliban rule, 70 percent of the Afghan people were malnourished, one in four children would not live past the age of five, and mothers routinely died in childbirth. Old was age forty-five.

The more I read, in books and briefing papers, and the more I listened to Condi Rice, to George, and to others, the more heartbroken I became. It was late, very late, but after years of repression, the United States needed to speak out on behalf of these women. And we needed to do more than talk; we needed to reach out and help them.

I became passionate about the women of Afghanistan and their children, children who had been scarred not just by sharia law but by the near constant violence of Taliban attacks and civil war. According to reports from UNICEF, almost three-quarters of the children in Kabul had lost a family member during the years of conflict. Half of the children in the capital had watched someone be killed by a rocket or artillery, and many more had witnessed corpses and dismembered body parts scattered along city streets. Most no longer trusted adults, and most did not expect to survive themselves. On November 17, George was slated to give his weekly presidential radio address on conditions in Afghanistan, and his longtime advisor and now Counselor to the President Karen Hughes raised the idea that I speak for part of it. Karen had been with us since George's early days as governor. We valued her counsel, her creative thought, and her years of unselfish service. Her bright spirits made her a dear friend as well.

George responded, "Why not have Laura give all of it?" And so I was slated to be the first first lady to give a full presidential radio address, and I was to tape it on November 15, the same day that Vladimir Putin and Lyudmila Putina would be leaving our Crawford ranch after their upcoming visit.

The Putins were arriving in Washington, D.C., on the morning of November 13, the day that the U.S. ally, the Afghan Northern Alliance, captured Kabul as Taliban fighters fled in pickup trucks. George and President Putin were scheduled to have a working lunch in the White House's old Family Dining Room, on the first floor. I was hosting Lyudmila for a smaller lunch in the second-floor dining room. After lunch, we left for Andrews Air Force Base and Texas. The Putins would join us at the ranch the following afternoon after a stop in Houston.

My staff, Cathy Fenton, our social secretary, and I had arranged the decorations. Outside, we had strung lights through the branches of the old live oaks, and in the dogtrot, we'd arranged round tables with orange cloths and pumpkin and hydrangea centerpieces. Tom Perini and his team would be barbecuing out of the backs of old-time covered chuckwagons. Everything was ready by noon. The Putins were scheduled to land at the ranch at 3:05 P.M. By one o'clock, it was raining; two hours later, the Putins got off Marine One in the middle of a thunderstorm. Our ranch is in one of the most arid parts of the country, and it rained almost the entire visit. George spent forty-five minutes driving President Putin around the ranch in our pickup truck, and fortunately they never got stuck in the mud. Rain blew through the screens to our porch, where we were to have cocktails before dinner. The staff was frantically moving tables and hunting for umbrellas minutes before we had to start greeting the guests. The cowboys cooked in the rain, and the cowboy band the Ranchhands played on the covered porch. The Putins walked from the guesthouse in the downpour.

We started the meal with fried catfish and corn bread and then mesquite-grilled beef tenderloin, plus a birthday cake for Condi Rice. I had invited twenty people, all of whom we thought a Russian head of state might be interested in meeting, including ranch owners, athletes, and our friend the pianist Van Cliburn, who was the first person to win the prestigious International Tchaikovsky Competition in 1958, at the height of the Cold War. He gave a toast to Putin in Russian. I seated the Russian president next to Alice Carrington, one of the heirs to the famous King Ranch in Texas. The Putins thought we had a large ranch at 1,600 acres. Then President Putin asked Alice how big the King Ranch is, and she told him 825,000 acres. The funniest part for me, after all my protocol briefings and binders, was that in Texas it's considered a real faux pas to ask someone how big their ranch is. But it was a perfectly natural question for the head of state of the largest nation in the world.

Jenna came up from Austin. She speaks Spanish, and I sat her next to Lyudmila Putina, who does not speak English but does speak Spanish.

The rain finally abated during dinner, and afterward, we walked outside to have coffee around a crackling bonfire. Vladimir Putin struck up a conversation with Don Evans, the commerce secretary, over the fire pit. Putin said, "You have such a short history. You only have two hundred years of history and look how far you have come. How have you done it?" We forget that Russian history dates back well over a thousand years, with centuries of czars and dynasties. Donnie looked at him and said the answer is simple, freedom, democracy. "Here in the U.S.," he added, "people are free to run their own lives."

To us, it was a very simple statement of the fundamentals of American life, but George and I and the rest of the administration were never under any illusions about how hard a concept that is for the most powerful in Russia to grasp.

For the remaining seven years, whenever George was scheduled to meet with Vladimir Putin, leaders from around the world would start calling the White House weeks in advance. First it would be the Baltic countries, then the Balkan ones. Nation after nation wanted George to deliver messages for them. Even Tony Blair would call and say, "You've got to tell this to Vladimir." George would go to the meeting with a string of messages from others. And he would have a few of his own as well.

Both here and in Russia, he repeatedly chided Putin for cracking down on the press, telling the Russian president that his country had to have a free press, that a free press is essential for a democracy. "You need to have an independent press," George would tell him. And Putin would invariably reply, "Well, you control your press." George would shake his head and say, "No, Vladimir, I don't. I wish sometimes that I could control them, but I can't. They are free to say whatever they want. In our country, the press is free to write terrible things about me, and I can't do anything about it."

But Russia is a country without those traditions, and with no memory of them, and many in Russia believed that the U.S. government did control our press. In fact, following a summit meeting, one of the first questions George got from a Russian newsman essentially was, How can you complain to President Putin about the Russian press when you fired Dan Rather?

George worked hard to reach out to Putin in spite of the philosophical divide between them. The next morning at the ranch, the four of us had breakfast and then headed into Crawford, so the two presidents could make remarks to the press at the local high school. First-grade students had hung a banner that read "Howdy, Russian President Putin." Having world leaders visit our private home forged relationships; it helped to make it possible for George to deliver all those messages to Putin for so many years. And we quickly discovered that leaders from all over the world wanted to come to Crawford. When George invited Chinese president Jiang Zemin to "come and visit America," President Jiang indicated that George had invited him to be a guest at our ranch. A few months later, he arrived at our door. We entertained fifteen foreign leaders among the live oaks and wild grasses of Crawford.

After lunch, the Putins departed, and I walked over to our old green clapboard house to tape the president's weekly radio address. I had spent hours editing the draft of the address and going over every nuance with Karen Hughes. I was a little bit nervous, but I was also proud to be able to say something on behalf of the women of Afghanistan, who were threatened with having their fingernails pulled out if they wore so much as a coat of nail polish. I spoke of the Taliban's "degradation" of women and children, forcing them to live lives of poverty, poor health, and illiteracy. "The plight of women and children in Afghanistan is a matter of deliberate human cruelty, carried out by those who seek to intimidate and control. Civilized people throughout the world are speaking out in horror—not only because our hearts break for the women and children in Afghanistan, but also because in Afghanistan we see the world the terrorists would like to impose on the rest of us." I wanted the address to be strong, because we needed to speak strongly. But I also wondered if anyone would be listening.

On Sunday, the day after the address aired, I spent the afternoon in Austin with Jenna, doing all those mother-daughter things that I loved doing with my girls as they grew, including shopping. We stopped in the cosmetics section at one of the big department stores, and the women working behind the counter said something I never expected. They all said, "Thank you so much. Thank you so much for speaking for Afghan women." I was stunned. And for the first time, I realized the degree to which I had a unique forum as first lady. People would pay attention to what I said. I had always known that intellectually, but now I realized it emotionally.

When I had put on the headphones and bent over the microphone to read the address, I had thought of those Afghan women, weighed down under their burkas, with nothing more than tiny mesh slits to uncover their eyes, hidden away from the world and having the world hidden away from them. They were truly powerless. At that moment, it was not that I found my voice. Instead, it was as if my voice had found me.

"Grand Mama Laura"

Upstairs in the private White House residence.
(Tina Hager/White House photo)

The eighty-one-foot-tall, eight-ton Norway spruce that towered over Rockefeller Center had arrived on November 9, strapped to a specially designed trailer, with a full police escort. The tree, donated by the Tornabene family of Wayne, New Jersey, required a giant crane to hoist it onto a steel platform located just behind the golden statue of Prometheus, overlooking the plaza's famed ice rink. For days the tree was encased in scaffolding as twenty-four electricians draped five miles of colored lights, thirty thousand red, white, and blue bulbs to be wrapped around its limbs and boughs. All that remained was for the giant evergreen to be lit.

But even Andy Tornabene, who had grown up in Queens and from whose backyard the tree came, at one point had doubted that New York would light any holiday tree this year.

As I made my way into the city just after dusk on November 28, I could sense the security corridor from blocks away, the sky blue NYPD street barricades, the phalanx of uniformed officers ringing Rockefeller Center, the mass of steel pens to hold back spectators, and the near total absence of traffic, as the usual sea of yellow cabs and shiny cars was shunted to far-off cross streets and distant avenues. New York still lived under an umbrella of fresh alerts; periodically, police and antiterror task forces would surround Grand Central or Penn Station. There were visibly armed National Guard soldiers walking through the airports and along the commuter rail platforms. A mournful silence seemed to reverberate through the city. The people were fewer, the sounds were quieter, the streets less brilliant and more subdued.

Mayor Giuliani was waiting for me in the holding area, and there we stayed until given the signal to make our way outside. As I stood alongside

New York's fire and police commissioners, and the performers, all of us cast brief wary glances up at the night sky. The tree-lighting ceremony was designed to honor the rescue workers and the victims of the 9-11 attacks, and some of their relatives and friends were there. One hundred thousand people filled the streets between Fifth and Sixth avenues. They came for hope; many had tears in their eyes. "America loves New York," I said, adding, "President Bush and I wish for all Americans a happy holiday season and a New Year filled with peace." Then, together, at 8:56 P.M., while television cameras beamed the signal live across the country, Rudy Giuliani and I held our breath ever so slightly and flipped on the lights. That night, the only sounds we heard in return were the cheers and applause from the crowd.

Three days before, the United States had suffered its first casualty in Afghanistan. Johnny Michael Spann was killed during a riot by Taliban prisoners who launched an attack in the courtyard of a medieval fortress that had been commandeered to serve as a twenty-first-century jail. On that same day, more than seven hundred Marines set up camp in the desert south of the remaining Taliban stronghold of Kandahar. The Taliban leader, Mullah Mohammed Omar, was calling on his forces to "fight to the death."

I had slowly started watching television again. In the first weeks after 9-11, the television had been a constant drone at night as I waited in the residence for George. For the most part, the news was a repetition of that initial horror. And we lived with threat assessments more disturbing than any ever spoken on the air. By October, to try to sleep at night, I kept the sets turned off. Finally, on November 12, I turned the TV on to catch up on the news before the Putins arrived. The first images I saw were of a horrible plane crash in Queens, an Airbus that had accidentally gone down just after takeoff. Two hundred and sixty passengers died, along with five people on the ground. I stared at the screen, numb, tears welling in my eyes. It was as if I were being transported back to September all over again. And I knew that for the families of these dead and the dead from 9-11, the ache would be harder, the missing greater as the holiday season began.

I had chosen the theme for the White House's Christmas, "Home for the Holidays," back in the humid heat of summer, when everything was lush and green. Now that theme had a far greater meaning, for those who had lost loved ones, for those whose loved ones would be fighting overseas, and for the nation as a whole. One of the White House trees was decorated with snowflakes from third graders who attended school at the various military bases scattered around Washington, D.C. Carpenters, plumbers, and electricians who worked in the White House had built eighteen miniature replicas of former presidents' homes. Using original floor plans, they re-created John and John Quincy Adams's Peacefield, Lyndon Johnson's ranch, James Madison's Montpelier, George Washington's Mount Vernon, Ulysses S. Grant's and Abraham Lincoln's Illinois homes, and Woodrow Wilson's birthplace in Staunton, Virginia. Our pastry chef, Roland Mesnier, made a gingerbread house based on the original White House of 1800, before British troops attacked the city and the house burned practically to the ground. We also asked the nation's governors to select local artisans to create handmade ornaments representing a special historic home or structure in each state, using shades of white. We received cut-paper sculptures, fabric, and leather to adorn the Blue Room tree. One ornament was a little cotton cloud from which the Twin Towers rose, as if they had been transported whole to Heaven.

The other trees scattered through the rooms and halls were draped in lights and frosted with shimmering snow. That season, the White House had the quality of stillness after a snow. Almost no one was allowed inside to see the decorations. On Monday, December 3, the threat assessments arriving in the West Wing were so great that George placed the entire nation on high alert for possible terrorist strikes. The Secret Service insisted that all public tours be canceled. Some of the guests we invited to White House Christmas parties turned us down; many were still too afraid to fly or to visit a city where terrorists had struck. I wore a red dress and walked cameras through the rooms for a video of the decor.

With the absence of visitors, we worked on expanding the virtual White House, and in addition to the television special, the White House communications office created the "Barney Cam," a specially mounted camera that followed Barney and Spot through the decorated rooms and the grounds. Each year at Christmastime we debuted the footage for the young patients at Washington's Children's National Medical Center. One of our press aides, Jeanie Mamo, became an expert at launching bright plastic Christmas balls around the East Room, which Barney chased, slipping and sliding across the glossy waxed floors. In subsequent seasons, we developed more elaborate story lines and included celebrity guests. One Barney Cam video ended with Kitty serenely sitting on my lap. Unlike our canines, she steadfastly refused to mug for the camera.

On December 10, we hosted the White House's first-ever Hanukkah party, which I had begun to plan in August. The Jewish Museum in New York lent us a century-old menorah for the candle lighting, and we had a catered kosher buffet. That holiday season and all others to come, we took special pride in two sets of parties, one for the Secret Service and their families—I loved watching year after year as new babies appeared and children grew older—and our final party of the season, for the residence staff. They were the ones who showed us every small kindness, who cared for us, who came to serve under every condition, and we are grateful for their generosity and constant, unflagging goodwill.

On December 22, when the last holiday party had ended and the last hand had been shaken, at just before 8:30 in the morning, the Olympic torch arrived at the White House on its way to the Winter Olympics in Salt Lake City. We watched the torchbearer, Elizabeth Anderson Howell, whose husband, Brady, had been killed on 9-11 at the Pentagon, carry the flame up the Southeast Drive. She handed her torch to George, who dipped it into the Olympic cauldron, setting it alive with fire. "We pray for peace and comfort for you and your family," he said, before dipping a second, unlit torch into the cauldron and handing it ablaze to Eric Jones, a George Washington University student who, on the morning of 9-11, left campus and headed for the Pentagon. He spent four days helping with the rescue efforts there before driving to New York to do the same for ten days at the still burning remains of the World Trade Center. Eric had been among those to carry the tattered Marine Corps flag out of the Pentagon debris. We watched as he strode down the drive and off the White House grounds. He and Elizabeth represented the best of our country.

A few hours later, Richard Reid would attempt to detonate a bomb onboard a Paris to Miami flight as it raced above the dark waters of the Atlantic. Inside the sole of his shoe was a sophisticated explosive capable of blowing a hole in the plane's fuselage. He was lighting a match when a flight attendant caught him and screamed to the passengers to pass her "water, contact solution, anything you have!" After he had been subdued, passengers offered up their belts as restraints and a doctor on board injected Reid with Valium. We remained on high alert as U.S. troops and Afghan forces battled against enemy fighters in the mountains around Tora Bora, and remnants of the Taliban found sanctuary in the tribal areas of Pakistan.

And we waited for the coming of 2002. Our official holiday card was a serene still life depicting a corner of the residence, painted by Adrian Martinez, who had grown up in poverty in Washington, D.C., and had found refuge in the art of the Smithsonian museums. Inside, we wrote, "May the New Year bring peace on Earth."

Since early October, the former Pennsylvania governor Tom Ridge had been working in the West Wing as chief of Homeland Security. His office was a tiny, windowless room with a desk. There was barely enough space for two full-size chairs. The West Wing had become a nerve center for terror watches, and the December watch was now extended through the February Winter Olympics. News reports would soon describe the fighting in Afghanistan as "winding down," as *Time* magazine put it on February 16. The worry now was other terror cells around the world. And there was still the unanswered question of what had happened to Osama bin Laden.

Inside the White House, I was stuck in a kind of limbo. We had difficulty planning events because of the great uncertainty of the security situation. We would plan cultural or education activities, and just as the invitations were being finalized, the Secret Service or someone on the West Wing staff would say no. We hosted a salute to gospel music in February, and a few White House tours resumed, for prescreened student groups and members of the military and veterans. Otherwise, except for official visitors and the constant stream of heads of state and their spouses, the entry gates remained locked and the house quiet.

We did manage to have a formal unveiling of George's finished Oval

Office for the fabric and rug makers and the donors who had helped us redecorate this remarkable room. There were new drapes and new beige and ivory damask sofas, three in total, in case someone spilled coffee on one and the staff had to replace it in a hurry. There was a new pale wool rug, with a sunburst pattern featuring the presidential seal, because George had wanted the room to say, "An optimistic man works here." Adorning the rounded room's walls and niches were paintings and bronzes, including a bust of Sir Winston Churchill loaned to George by the British government. To hang in full view of his desk, George chose the portraits of his two most revered presidents, George Washington, who had created the American presidency, and Abraham Lincoln, who had saved it. George did not hang a portrait of the president he loved the most; that image, of his dad, was, he said, "imprinted on my heart."

While the Oval Office's windows face toward the iconic monuments of Washington, for its remaining walls, we selected images of Texas. On the east and north walls, we hung three paintings by the early Texas artist Julian Onderdonk, a field of Texas bluebonnets, a prickly pear cactus in bloom, and a scene of the old Alamo and its plaza, crowded with local women at their stalls, selling hot, red chilies at dusk, all lent by Texas museums. The fourth painting was a Tom Lea image of the Rio Grande. Tom had been our friend for years, and in his 2000 convention speech, George had quoted Tom's words. Tom wrote that he and his wife "live on the east side of the mountain. It is the sunrise side, not the sunset side. It is the side to see the day that is coming . . . not the side to see the day that is gone."

"Americans," George added, "live on the sunrise side of the mountain. We are ready for the day to come."

A fifth painting was loaned by our longtime friend Joey O'Neill, who had introduced us. Painted by W. H. D. Koerner and entitled *A Charge to Keep*, it shows a lone horseman charging up a steep and rough trail. Joey's father had given it to Joey and Jan as a wedding gift. After hearing the famous Charles Wesley hymn "A Charge to Keep I Have" sung at George's gubernatorial inaugural in 1995, Joey had loaned George the painting to hang in his Texas governor's office.

George had chosen to use the *Resolute* desk, given to President Rutherford B. Hayes by Queen Victoria. In May of 1854, the British ship

HMS *Resolute* became trapped in Arctic ice and was abandoned by its captain. An American whaling vessel found and rescued the ship in 1855, whereupon Congress purchased the *Resolute*, had it refitted, and returned it to Queen Victoria as a gift of peace. When the ship was decommissioned in 1879, the queen requested that a desk be fashioned from its timbers and sent to the American president. Queen Victoria had it inscribed with a plaque, noting that the piece was "a memorial of the courtesy and loving kindness" of the Americans. Franklin Roosevelt asked that a panel be added to the desk to hide his wheelchair, but the panel arrived only after his death. Harry Truman installed it anyway. John F. Kennedy was the first president to place the desk in the Oval Office, and his toddler son, JFK Jr., would play underneath. Later Ronald Reagan and Bill Clinton spent their working hours in the West Wing at the *Resolute* desk.

Facing south and surrounded by windows, the Oval Office is bathed in light even on cloudy days. The first time Vladimir Putin walked in and saw that brilliant south light spilling through the windows, he said simply, "My God." The room itself is not palatial, like the offices of many leaders in other countries. It is a modest, human-size room, and surprising in its simplicity. The longest point is just over thirty-five feet; at eighteen feet, the ceiling is barely higher than in the Texas Governor's Mansion. At least once, a foreign head of state came through and afterward was heard to complain, "I thought I was going to see the Oval Office." When told that he had, his expression turned incredulous. "But it is so small."

At the end of January, I finally returned to the Senate to give my education briefing to Senator Kennedy's committee. It was two weeks after George had signed the landmark No Child Left Behind Act, which Democrats Ted Kennedy and Rep. George Miller and Republicans Judd Gregg and Rep. John Boehner had shepherded through Congress with the help of Education Secretary Rod Paige and George's Domestic Policy advisor, Margaret Spellings, in the previous session. I thought back to what Ted Kennedy had written on the daffodil print he had given me that September morning, "To the First Lady of Education, whose impressive leadership is enabling millions of American children to dance with the daffodils! Your friend Ted Kennedy Sept. 11, 2001." I was still able to visit schools and to highlight innovative educational programs, but now we were a nation at war. When I finally donated my inaugural gown, coat, purse, and shoes to the Smithsonian's National Museum of American History for its first lady exhibit on January 20, a year to the day since George had been sworn in, it seemed as if that glittery red dress had been worn by a woman who existed in another era.

Three days later, on January 23, Daniel Pearl, the South Asia bureau chief for *The Wall Street Journal*, was kidnapped in Karachi, Pakistan. He was investigating ties between the shoe bomber, Richard Reid, al Qaeda, and Pakistan's Inter-Services Intelligence.

The kidnappers e-mailed photos of Danny, hunched and holding up a newspaper, with a gun pointed to his head. They claimed that he was working for the CIA, and they demanded that Pakistani terror detainees be freed and that the United States ship disputed F-16 fighter jets to Pakistan's government. For weeks, Danny's wife and American and Pakistani agents scoured the country searching for him. But it was too late.

On February 1, Danny Pearl's captors had slit his throat and then sliced off his head. Only on February 21 did we learn the grisly truth. American FBI agents, posing as journalists, obtained a video in which Danny Pearl confirmed that he was "a Jewish American." The video continued with a longer list of the captors' demands, and then, nearly two minutes in, it showed the beheading in full, gruesome detail. The final scene was of a captor holding up Danny's severed head by its hair. The video ended with the words "And if our demands are not met, this scene shall be repeated again and again."

The man who would later confess to beheading Daniel Pearl is Khalid Sheikh Mohammed, who also claims to be the mastermind behind the attacks of 9-11.

Among those whom Danny left behind were his parents, Ruth and Judea, and his wife, Mariane, who was six months pregnant with their first child.

As we waited for news of Danny Pearl, I invited a couple to the White House who had lost their son on September 11. Sharon and Kenneth Ambrose's son, Paul, a doctor with the U.S. Public Health Service, had been on board the flight that crashed into the Pentagon. I had heard about Paul not long after 9-11 from our longtime Midland friend Penny Slade-Sawyer, who now worked with the Public Health Service. She said that in Paul the service had lost one of its brightest stars. But it was the message from his parents that truly broke my heart. In clusters of suburbs across New York, New Jersey, Connecticut, Massachusetts, and around Washington, D.C., there were hundreds of families devastated by grief. But in some small measure of comfort, they were not alone. The Ambroses were the only family in all of West Virginia who had lost someone in the horror of 9-11. In their particular grief, they knew no one else who could truly understand. On February 7, the Ambroses came to the White House. Over coffee we sat and talked about Paul, about his life and his dreams. I listened to their words of love and loss. They had already suffered the death of another son. Paul was their one remaining child. Long after they left, I thought about them and that depth of sadness. And I thought of all the parents who now wondered what could happen to their children when they did something as routine as board a plane.

I turned to books for comfort. The quietest part of my day was always late afternoon, when my official schedule was finished but George was still at work in the Oval Office. I no longer ran errands, the way I had in Texas. In Dallas, by four o'clock I would have been pushing my cart around the supermarket aisle, trying to come up with something to fix for dinner. I would be waiting for the girls to return; I would be rushing to pick something up at the dry cleaners, or driving car pool, or taking Barbara and Jenna to a lesson or an activity. In Austin, when the girls were in high school, I would go to a game or a practice or be around to make sure that they did their homework. Every moment would be accounted for until bedtime, when I could finally take a breath. Now, those pre-evening hours had become the emptiest.

I thought about Nancy Reagan, lying down late one afternoon to rest after breast cancer surgery and learning that her mother had died. Ronald Reagan opened the door and told her; he had gotten the word first.

Day after day, as the afternoon waned and darkness settled over Washington, D.C., I would read, newer works, such as Leif Enger's *Peace*

Like a River; histories, such as Jay Winik's *April 1865*; or classics, such as Willa Cather's *Death Comes for the Archbishop*, just as my mother had done all those years ago in Midland when I would come home and find her with a book in her hands. I read as I waited for George to arrive for dinner, and I was grateful to have words to keep me company.

I looked too for ways to bring words and writers into the White House, hosting symposiums on authors such as Mark Twain or on schools of literature, including the Harlem Renaissance. We gathered literary figures and scholars in the East Room and invited students and teachers from local schools. It was a chance to discuss some of the most powerful works in the American past and the writers who speak to all of us through the humanity of their characters. Our guest lists were limited, but we made sure the events were televised around the nation via C-SPAN.

And I looked for ways to help the women and children of Afghanistan.

At the time, there were 10 million children in Afghanistan; one in three was an orphan; one in four would not live to see a fifth birthday, and more Afghan mothers died in childbirth than mothers in almost any other part of the world. On October 12, 2001, George had announced the creation of America's Fund for Afghan Children. He asked children across the United States to donate one dollar to help the children of Afghanistan. The response was overwhelming. In less than four years, the program would raise more than $11 million. Thousands of those donations were sadly "lost" for years in the bags of potentially anthrax-contaminated White House mail.

By early December, though, the fund was sending humanitarian aid. The world is full of suffering peoples and nations, but in the harsh, remote hills and plains of Afghanistan, the deprivation has been particularly cruel. Afghanistan was a place where children came of age barefoot and where many of them could not imagine something as simple as a bright, soft plastic ball. In a Red Cross warehouse in New Windsor, Maryland, George and I saw the first-aid pallets. Bundled together were winter coats and tents and ten thousand individual gift parcels, which included wool socks, knit hats, soap, pencils, paper, and inflatable balls. FedEx had offered to ship the packages free of charge to Germany, where they would be loaded onto U.S. military transport planes, flown to Turkmenistan, and then trucked across the border into Northern Afghanistan. The formidable logistics were a reminder of how isolated this region and its people are.

On December 12, at a special ceremony at the National Museum of Women in the Arts, where I had once loved to stroll through exhibitions with Bar, George signed into law the Afghan Women and Children Relief Act of 2001 to provide health and education assistance to women and children in Afghanistan. One woman in attendance was known only as Farida. She had come to the United States as a refugee in 2000. She was a former aid worker who had tried to promote basic human rights for women. Even with the Taliban being driven from power, she was afraid to use her full name.

I had already seen that wary-eyed fear firsthand in late November of 2001, when I hosted a group of Afghan women for coffee.

Melanne Verveer, Hillary Clinton's White House chief of staff and now head of the organization Vital Voices, had phoned Andi Ball, my chief of staff, to say that eleven Afghan exiles, some living in the United States, some living overseas, were arriving in Washington. Would I consider meeting with them? I immediately said yes and invited them to the White House. I still remember the women's amazement at being welcomed into the home of presidents. Inside Afghanistan, under the Taliban, they had been banned from almost all government buildings and public places. We gathered in the Diplomatic Reception Room, which until Teddy Roosevelt's time had housed the White House's massive coal furnace. During the Depression and World War II, it would become the iconic scene of Franklin Roosevelt's fireside chats. Jackie Kennedy had installed the room's fanciful French wallpaper, printed in 1834, depicting scenes from early America, including Niagara Falls and Boston Harbor. I watched the women's eyes move across the walls, taking everything in.

In speaking to reporters, I said that I hoped "one principle of that new government will be human rights, and that includes the rights of women and children." And I hoped that the new Afghan government, then being formed at a special gathering of Afghan nationals and exiles in Bonn, Germany, would "include everyone." I wanted women to have seats at the table and every Afghan child, girls as well as boys, to be offered an education.

Most of these women had served as aid workers, trying to improve life for the millions of others left behind. One, Mary Chopan Alamshahi, a nurse-practitioner who now lived in exile in California, thanked me for "giving voice to us" in the November 17 presidential radio address. "The entire world listened," she said, as her words caught with emotion.

Not everyone was quite so willing to let my voice be my own. Writing in *Newsweek* after the White House event, reporter Martha Brant said, "If I had closed my eyes, I could have sworn it was Hillary Clinton talking."

On January 28, Hamid Karzai, Afghanistan's new interim leader, came to Washington to meet with George at the White House. Before he left, I gave him an inscribed children's English dictionary, to emphasize the importance of education.

On March 8, I was at the United Nations in New York for International Women's Day. The UN's glass tower rises like a glittery monument to postwar optimism. But inside, it is old. The once state-of-the-art linoleum floors are worn with age, the back hallways drab and industrial. The escalators that cart people between floors look like relics from another era; ironically, the Pentagon has similar metal escalators linking its floors. Newer, high-gloss models can be found in almost any shopping mall.

As I walked beneath the flags of the member nations, I hoped that today's UN would not forget Afghanistan's women and children. Hamid Karzai had already signed a Declaration of the Essential Rights of Afghan Women, legally granting women equality with men. But a sizable gap remained between paper pledges and people's lives. Everyone knew it would take years to undo the damage wrought by the vicious gender apartheid of the Taliban.

The morning began with a simple coffee in one of the building's reception rooms, with stunning views of New York's East River. Nane Annan, wife of UN Secretary-General Kofi Annan, orchestrated an impromptu receiving line; I stood and smiled alongside international luminaries, including Jordan's Queen Noor. Then it was on to the conference, with six hundred attendees. My chair was marked as the lead seat of the U.S. delegation. Not until that moment did I realize that I was, on that morning, representing my country at the United Nations.

I spoke of the U.S. government's commitment to aiding the people of Afghanistan and the more than $4 million donated so far by American children to help the children of Afghanistan. American aid workers were doggedly helping Afghan refugees return home and helping the country's widows, devastated after twenty-three years of fighting, support their families. Some of our contributions were bags of wheat for the twenty-one women-owned bakeries in Kabul. Those bakeries fed over one-quarter of the city's population. I spoke too of helping to educate the children of Afghanistan. "When you give children books and an education, you give them the ability to imagine a future of opportunity, equality, and justice," I said. My favorite line in the speech was a quotation from Farahnaz Nazir, the founder of the Afghanistan Women's Association, who said, "Society is like a bird. It has two wings. And a bird cannot fly if one wing is broken."

We would help bind that broken wing.

My next stop was P.S. 234, the school in lower Manhattan where children had witnessed the horror of the attacks on the Twin Towers from just four blocks away. I had first met many of the students and teachers at the end of September, when they were crowded inside another school, P.S. 41. The students had returned to their original building in early February, once the smoldering fires had finally been extinguished and the worst of the air pollution had cleared. School officials conservatively estimated that at least 5 percent of the students were still suffering from severe emotional trauma. The number was probably far higher. Many children were terrified of getting on an airplane or riding the subway. Low-flying helicopters and planes or sudden loud noises would leave them shaken and in tears. I listened to these ten- and eleven-year-olds and thought of them, like me, still anxiously scanning the skies.

On March 23, school was set to resume in Afghanistan. For most girls, after nearly eight years of Taliban rule, it would be their first time in a classroom. The Red Cross had already shipped more than one thousand school kits, with supplies for forty thousand children, to Kabul to be distributed on opening day. George and I helped assemble more kits alongside students at Samuel W. Tucker Elementary School in Alexandria, Virginia. But that was only the beginning of the needs. Children, especially girls, were in dire need of school uniforms; those who attended school in ordinary street or house clothes often felt shame. Most Afghans, though, had little more than a needle or thread to sew. Working with Vital Voices, we shipped several thousand manual sewing machines across the Pakistani border—the old foot-pedal style that my grandmother had used, since much of the country lacked any form of electricity. And we sent fabric, yards and yards, enough to outfit 3 million children. The Liz Claiborne company alone donated a half million yards of material. For the barefoot, we received shoes from Bass, New Balance, Sebago, and Timberland. The Sara Lee Corporation paid for socks. L.L.Bean donated shoes, jackets, and blankets. Walmart and General Motors gave money to help offset costs. It was, for me, a moment of real pride to see the generosity of these companies and their employees to people in a place half a world away, a place that had given refuge to the plotters of the worst civilian attack in our history.

And other companies came forward to meet other needs. When I met with Afghan judges who told me that they could not even type court records, that every court document had to be laboriously copied by hand, I asked my office to approach the Dell Computer Corporation and Microsoft. The two companies donated computers, software, and printers to bring a bit of modernity to Afghanistan's judicial system. Time and again, Americans from all walks of life gave, and they did so with open hearts.

In New York and Washington, the scars from the previous fall were slower to heal. Secretary of Defense Donald Rumsfeld and his wife, Joyce, spent many hours helping the families of those killed and wounded in the attacks of 9-11. They followed the progress of the burn victims, helped when other concerns arose, and did not forget to be encouraging. When plans began for a memorial on the Pentagon grounds to honor those who had perished that September morning, Don and Joyce quietly became one of the memorial's largest donors. Another couple who generously gave were Sharon and Kenneth Ambrose, whose son, Paul, the public health doctor, had been on board the hijacked plane. In the months that followed, I wrote to them several times and told them that they remained in my prayers.

That spring, Cherie Blair got her wish, a visit to our ranch in Crawford. She and Tony came in early April with her mother and their two youngest children, as the final stop on a holiday for her family in the United States. That was one of the remarkable things to me about other national leaders and their spouses, the freedom they have to go on holidays, often abroad. Presidents of the United States must get away inside one compound or another, whether it is a rented retreat on Martha's Vineyard, as the Clintons had chosen, or the privacy of their own homes, Crawford for me and George, Kennebunkport for Gampy and Bar, or their California ranch for Ronald and Nancy Reagan.

At our ranch, after dinner, Tony Blair borrowed a guitar and strummed and sang along with the San Antonio band Daddy Rabbit. During the day, we braved a pouring rain to drive across the rugged grounds in George's pickup. Most of all, we enjoyed each other's company. During our final lunch, George and Cherie managed to have another of their good-natured back-and-forths. This time, she was urging him to agree to make the United States a participant in the newly created International Criminal Court, designed to prosecute genocide, war crimes, and crimes against humanity. (The United States, India, China, and Indonesia are among the nations that have not ratified it, citing concerns about sovereignty.) George ran down the driveway as Tony and Cherie were driving off to get in the last word. He joked that Cherie's persistence must have been the reason Bill Clinton had considered signing the document in the first place. But for George and Tony, these couple of days at Crawford had been deeply serious. With the Taliban for now beaten back in Afghanistan, they were looking toward the threat from another country, Iraq, where American and British intelligence, and indeed nearly every intelligence agency in Europe, told them that Saddam Hussein was sitting on a massive stockpile of weapons of mass destruction.

The Blairs departed for London, and so did I, for the funeral of the Queen Mother, who had died just before their visit. I was designated to lead the U.S. delegation, which included the prominent Texas ranch owners Anne and Tobin Armstrong. Anne had been ambassador to the British Court of St. James's under Gerald Ford. The world bade the Queen Mother farewell beneath the glorious Gothic arches and stained glass of Westminster Abbey. Cars had been banned from the nearby streets; there was only the clop of horses' hooves, pipers playing haunting notes, and the thump of the funeral drum. It was a scene from another time and place, from a century so very far from our own.

When I returned to Washington, my first meeting was about the Christmas holidays. At the White House, Christmas preparations begin in April, from choosing an artist for the card to planning the themes and events. It takes over half a year to organize the three weeks in December during which George and I would often host two events in a single evening and shake well over nine thousand hands.

But even as we planned, we did not know what the future would hold. On April 25, Crown Prince Abdullah of Saudi Arabia came to Crawford to meet with George. I had overseen plans for the lunch. "No pork products, no flesh of scavenger animals, birds, or fish, including shellfish," advised Don Ensenat, Chief of Protocol. "All meat should be cooked until well-done." So we served barbecued beef ribs, and I made myself scarce on other parts of the ranch after the arrival ceremony. Women did not travel with the crown prince. Condi Rice, our national security advisor, would be the sole woman in attendance. Those were the customs in the prince's part of the world.

I was also preparing for my own trip, fifteen days through Europe, starting in Paris with a speech to the Organization for Economic Cooperation and Development's 2002 Global Forum on Education. Jenna was coming with me. Four days before we left, in Kaspiysk, part of Russia's Dagestan republic, land mines placed by the side of the road had exploded, killing forty-three civilians, seventeen of them children who had gathered to watch a parade in remembrance of World War II. The bombers were Chechen terrorists. I tore up much of my prepared speech as we flew over the Atlantic. Instead of the expected lines about the importance of education, I called on parents and teachers to teach their children to respect all human life, and I told the world that it needed to condemn bombings like that in Dagestan, and other recent ones in Pakistan and Israel. "Every parent, every teacher, every leader has a responsibility to condemn the terrible tragedy of children blowing themselves up to kill others." I added that "prosperity cannot follow peace without educated women and children." It is a simple idea, but it lies at the heart of so much suffering in the world. And I was reminded of exactly what ignorance breeds during the balance of my days in Paris.

The following morning I toured the Guimet Museum's exhibition "One Thousand Years of Afghan Art." The museum's curators had begun the exhibition months before 9-11, when the Taliban leader Mullah Omar ordered the destruction of the two giant Bamiyan Buddhas that had been carved into majestic sandstone cliffs less than 150 miles northwest of Kabul, in a valley region of central Afghanistan that lay at a crossroads of east-west trade routes along the once-fabled Silk Road. The Bamiyan Buddhas were shockingly dynamited in February of 2001, after inhabiting their niches for almost fifteen hundred years. They had been the largest examples of standing Buddha carvings in the world and had been designated by UNESCO, the United Nation's Educational, Scientific, and Cultural Organization, as a World Heritage site. Now they lay in a pile of rubble.

At the Paris museum, curators had meticulously created replicas of these ancient statues. Displayed alongside were other priceless artifacts from Afghan history, which had been lent from museums and private holdings across Europe. I gazed upon intricate bronze buckets from the year 700, the dawn of the nation's Muslim era, as well as delicate ivory figures and a carved foot of Zeus, all that remained of a statue painstakingly sculpted in the third century B.C. Daring Afghan curators had rescued some of the rarest objects, smuggling them out of the country in the backs of trucks or on horseback after the Taliban looted Kabul's art museum in the mid-1990s. Gazing around the rooms, I wondered about a regime so determined to destroy everything of beauty from its nation's past and about the Taliban's deep hatred of any culture outside its own.

I made another stop in Paris, one so private that it was not listed on my official schedule. Without the press or most of the staff, Jenna and I made our way to the small flat where Mariane Pearl, Danny Pearl's widow, was staying. It was a modest place, with a bit of a student feel, reminding me for a minute of my little walk-up all those years ago in Austin.

Mariane was less than two weeks away from giving birth to their son, and what should have been a buoyant, slightly anxious time was instead framed with sadness. There would be no father for Adam, no husband beside Mariane. I thought of the pregnant wives of the firemen and other victims on 9-11, how some had asked their lost husbands' brothers or friends to be with them at their baby's birth. But Mariane was alone. We talked. I asked her about her experiences and what we might learn, and I told her that she would be welcome in the United States if she chose to come. I thought that in a city like New York there would be others who might comprehend her unique pain.

On May 16, as I left Paris, Danny's body was found on the outskirts of Karachi. A week later, the day before her son was born, Mariane received an e-mail that had been intended for another recipient. In its mechanically spaced electronic letters, the terse dispatch described how, after his throat had been slit and he had been beheaded, Danny's body was cut into ten parts, then dumped in a shallow grave.

When Adam Pearl was born, both George and Jacques Chirac called Mariane with good wishes. Her heart, she later said, was so heavy that she could barely speak.

From Paris I flew to Budapest, where the focus of my stop was women and disease. In my first few hours on the ground, I met with Hungary's president and first lady, Ferenc and Dalma Mádl, and Prime Minister Viktor Orbán, lunched with women leaders, many of whom were struggling to establish themselves in their nation's traditionally patriarchical society, and at night attended the opera *Madame Butterfly*, sitting in the gold-trimmed president's box. The opera was in Italian, the subtitles were in Hungarian, and my exhausted staff fell asleep.

The American ambassador to Hungary was my good friend from Dallas, Nancy Brinker, who had become a breast cancer activist after her sister, Susan Komen, died at age thirty-six from the disease. Hungary has the fourth highest death rate from breast cancer in Eastern Europe, and Nancy made it her personal mission to improve cancer screening rates and care for women. Together we visited an oncology clinic where the nurses in their starched white caps reminded me of my childhood Cherry Ames books. I spoke with and tried to comfort women who were days away from major cancer surgery and who were terrified. By October of 2002, Nancy had convinced the reluctant Hungarian government to put aside its fear that pink was the color of homosexuality. Pink ribbons for breast cancer awareness began to appear, and the Hungarians lit bridges linking the city halves of Buda and Pest a bright, rich pink.

My next stop was Prague, where I met Václav Havel and his wife, Dagmar Havlová. I had long admired Havel, a gifted intellectual and play-wright who had spent years as a political prisoner under the Communists. Both Václav and Dagmar are funny and charming and wise. They showed me around the famous Prague Castle, the official presidential home, and later hosted me in their modest residence; they had no desire to live in the splendor of a castle. Being elected to the presidency of a nation that in a previous era had jailed him was, Václav said quite simply, "a gift of fate."

I joined Craig Stapleton, our ambassador to the Czech Republic— Debbie, his wife, is George's cousin and one of my close friends—for the ceremony marking the fifty-seventh anniversary of the liberation of the Terezin (or Theresienstadt) concentration camp. Just a year before, I had gazed upon the drawings made by children at the camp, images of flowers and of loaves of bread carried on hearses, displayed in simple frames on a wall of the United States Holocaust Memorial Museum. Nearly every child at Terezin died; only these pictures, hidden away, had survived.

As I laid flowers on the mass grave of ten thousand victims, I thought of my father and his fellow soldiers who had overseen the burial of some five thousand dead at Nordhausen in April of 1945. All those souls, now resting beneath grass and stones.

On Tuesday, May 21, I was slated to give a radio address directly to the people of Afghanistan from the studios of the U.S. government's Radio Free Europe/Radio Liberty, which now broadcast into Afghanistan, Iran, and many of the former Soviet republics from the old Czech parliament building. The name was a bit of a misnomer; there was nothing parlia-mentary about it. Instead, it was the place where Czechoslovakia's for-mer Communist leadership had met. Sandwiched amid Prague's bright Rococo architecture, the old parliament building is gray, angular, and unadorned, a perfect example of Stalinist construction. Now, in a touch of irony, it housed America's primary means of speaking to the people of Afghanistan. At Radio Free Europe/Radio Liberty's headquarters, my morning's events also included a media roundtable for the press.

But when my staff and I awoke, the Secret Service told us to cancel the address and the roundtable. They had received a specific threat.

The Secret Service is a remarkable institution. Its men and women are willing to risk their lives to guard the president's. They wait in broiling sun and subzero cold; their mission is to protect the first family from harm. My closest agents—Ron Sprinkle, Wayne Williams, Leon Newsome, Ignacio Zamora, and Karen Shugart, all of whom headed my detail—became like family. From the start, George and I made it a policy never to travel on Christmas, so that as many agents as possible could spend the holidays with their families. We knew they gave so very much.

We did not dismiss the risk, but I very much wanted to give the address. Finally, we arrived at a compromise. The agents sent out a dummy motorcade from my hotel. I departed later and was hustled into the parliament building via a rear loading dock, and from there, straight to the sound booth. My words were translated into the Afghan languages of Pashto and Dari. I spoke about the school kits being created, about the American children who had enthusiastically donated money to the children of Afghanistan, and about the educational, medical, food, and other humanitarian aid the United States was sending. The entire time, a helicopter hovered overhead.

I gave the address, and the threat never materialized.

But there was a constant stream of threats, and they seemed to increase in the following months.

After an overnight in Berlin, I met George and we traveled to Russia, first to Moscow, the sprawling city on the plain with the fortified Kremlin sitting high above, and then to St. Petersburg, with its western canals, ornate palaces, and czarist heritage. While George and Vladimir Putin signed a nuclear arms reduction treaty, I read *Make Way for Ducklings* to Russian children at the State Children's Library. They all laughed when they heard the names "Jack, Kack, Lack, Mack, Nack, Ouack, Pack, and Quack." In St. Petersburg, the Putins put grand Russian culture on display.

We saw the sprawling Winter Palace, the place where Czarina Catherine had once ordered a soldier to stand guard over the first snowdrop of spring. At the Hermitage, we glimpsed bits of the art that the czars had collected and other pieces later confiscated from the nobility by the revolutionaries. We saw only a small fraction of what is stored within those walls. There are over 3 million objects in the Hermitage Museum and Winter Palace; their corridors alone stretch for nearly fourteen miles. If we spent just one minute looking at each work of art, it would take eleven years.

By late May, St. Petersburg is light late into the night. Sundown is just before 11:00 P.M. At 9:15, the sky was still ablaze as we boarded a boat to cruise with the Putins along the Neva River. We dined on caviar as the sun slipped toward the western horizon on one side and the moon rose in the east. George looked at me and said, "Bushie, you are in Heaven." The translator immediately repeated it to the Putins, who gasped with pleasure.

We said good night after a barrage of fireworks.

The next morning, we toured the Kazan Cathedral, Russia's adaptation of the Basilica of St. Peter's in Rome and a monument to the Russian defeat of Napoleon in 1812, when captured French banners were placed in the cathedral. Inside the main basilica, there were no chairs. Worshipers stand as priests in long, flowing robes chant the liturgy. Under the Communists, the Kazan Cathedral had housed a museum of "History of Religion and Atheism." The museum remains, but the word "atheism" has been scrubbed away. From there, we made our way to the Grand Choral Synagogue, the second largest synagogue in all of Europe. It was built in the 1880s, with a special permit from the czar. Only select Jews, those with specific trades or advanced degrees, or those who had served in the military, were allowed to reside in St. Petersburg, and the synagogue's builders were told that they could not construct their place of worship near any churches or within view of any roads ever traveled by the czars.

The Putins hosted a farewell tea for us at the Russian Museum. George walked into the room where elegant tables were laden with trays of pastries and coffee samovars had been meticulously arranged. He turned to Vladimir and asked, "Are we going to eat this food or just look at it?" The Russian leader answered, with a twinkle in his eye, "This is a museum." Everyone in the room burst out laughing.

~⁀

I did not go with George to the G8 Summit in June. It was held atop a mountain outside of Calgary, Canada, enveloped in a security bubble so tight that spouses were not invited. In Washington, my Secret Service detail would no longer allow me to go for a walk outside the White House grounds, which I had done early on some mornings. Camouflaged in a baseball cap and sunglasses, I would traverse the gravel paths crossing the National Mall or the canal in Georgetown. But now I was to walk on White House grounds. It was ironic that as we hosted an official event in honor of the two hundredth anniversary of the great western explorers Lewis and Clark, my own physical space was shrinking.

Amid the uncertainty, we treasured the simplicity of our family life. For the girls' twentieth birthday the previous November, we had suggested that they invite twenty friends to Camp David for the weekend. George devised contests for the guests, including tennis, basketball, and bowling for the boys, and we put a karaoke machine in the main lodge so the kids would have fun activities all weekend. The girls stayed with us for holidays, breaks, and even some weekends, and I talked to my daughters on the phone almost every other day when I was home. On foreign trips, when they could accompany me, I found them to be wonderful companions. I looked forward to long flights and the hours of transatlantic mother-daughter time, chatting about friends and boyfriends, and whatever they found interesting. Echoing my path, Jenna was studying English and writing at Texas, while Barbara had chosen humanities at Yale.

In our own lives, George remained the biggest homebody known to man. When either one of us traveled around the country, we always tried to make it a day trip, flying out at the crack of dawn and returning home in time to eat dinner side by side. Except for solo visits overseas, we seldom spent a night apart. Many evenings we had quiet dinners, just the two of us, in the residence. We spoke about our daughters, about baseball in the summer, about family, and about friends.

But these respites could be measured in minutes; they never lasted long. There was, I realize now, a constant low-level anxiety that enveloped us each day in the White House after 9-11. We were always on watch for the next thing that might be coming. It was far more than simply scanning the skies; it was the threat reports, not merely from countries like Afghanistan or Iraq or Iran but from Yemen or North Korea or Somalia. It was earthquakes, tornadoes, or hurricanes. It was the constant knowledge that, in the span of thirty minutes or an hour, the world could change.

The pace inside the White House was brutal, not simply that year but for the entirety of George's two terms. George would arrive in the Oval Office by 6:30 or 7:00 every morning; his immediate staff came in by 6:00 A.M.; his chief of staff, Andy Card, was often in by 5:00 A.M., and everyone worked deep into the evening.

I remember vividly during 2002, when we would go to Camp David on the weekends, Condi Rice and Andy Card and his wife, Kathleene, would come along. Cabinet members frequently joined us as well. Condi and Andy would work the entire time, taking phone calls, reading papers, briefing George. Condi and I used to joke about her "inadvertent nap," the one she took when she was sitting on the couch to work and, from sheer exhaustion, fell asleep. Since the late 1990s, Condi had become like family. She traveled with us, joined us for dinner, and whenever she was in the room, her lively mind and sparkle were on full display. We are fortunate to have had not only her advice but her friendship.

At Camp, our Navy mess chefs became experts at comfort food, like fried chicken and chicken-fried steak, which we seldom had at the White House. Sometimes, early in the morning, Condi, Kathleene, and I would walk the two-mile perimeter trail with the steep hill at the end that we nicknamed Big Bertha. But even when we talked, in some corner, all of our minds were still working. There was no letting go.

In the late spring and early summer I attended the groundbreaking for the National Underground Railroad Freedom Center in Cincinnati, Ohio, and a preservation event for Louisa May Alcott's home in Concord, Massachusetts. I addressed an Early Learning Summit in Boise, Idaho, the third regional conference my office had helped to initiate after last summer's Early Childhood Summit, and I discussed the need to educate parents on creative ways for them to be their children's first teachers. I dedicated the Katherine Anne Porter home in Kyle, Texas, as a National Literary Landmark. At the White House, I had already hosted a conference on school libraries; now we were addressing character and community, gathering major leaders from character education programs across the nation to discuss what was working and what wasn't. Part of the conference focused on the increasing prevalence of service learning programs, in which students perform outside community service, often as a graduation requirement. Secretary of State Colin Powell gave the keynote address. But that entire summer it felt as if we were waiting, wondering where the next danger might lie, and whether the international community could persuade Saddam Hussein to disarm.

On July 17, Poland's president, Aleksander Kwaśniewski, and his wife, Jolanta, came to Washington for an official state visit. George and I had visited Poland the previous summer, and in one of my albums, I had a collection of photographs from the U.S. Embassy in Warsaw taken several days after 9-11. The entrance overflowed with flowers and notes that read, "We are with you." "We are all American."

In the wake of 9-11, President Kwaśniewski had helped mobilize central, eastern, and southeastern Europe to respond more aggressively to international terrorism and pursue terrorists. Although George had held more than fifty meetings with heads of state from around the world in the last eighteen months, this was just our second state dinner, and our first since September 11. State visits are precision displays, with everything organized down to the minute, and the protocol is almost as tradition-bound as the ceremonial opening of Parliament by the British monarch. That morning we hosted a formal arrival ceremony for the Kwaśniewskis with four thousand guests on the South Lawn.

As the final bars of the fanfare music, "Ruffles and Flourishes," sounded from trumpets on the Truman Balcony, George and I stepped into a small alcove outside the Diplomatic Reception Room. We stood there, completely still, barricaded behind two very tall, fully dressed Marine Guards until "Hail to the Chief" commenced. Then the guards parted and we began the walk down the red carpet to await our guests, who at that same moment were motoring up in their limousine. Military bands played the two national anthems; there was a twenty-one-gun salute, and the Revolutionary War–era Fife and Drum Corps marched past, playing "Yankee Doodle Dandy." Together George and Aleksander walked forward to review the U.S. troops representing all the military services, standing at attention in perfect formation. Afterward, both presidents spoke. At the conclusion we walked up the South Portico steps to the balcony and turned for a final wave before entering the Blue Room for an official receiving line. The two presidents departed to confer in the Oval Office; Jolanta and I retired to the Green Room for coffee. Between the arrival ceremony and the dinner preview for the press, and before the dinner itself, I slipped off to the National Cathedral for the memorial service for J. Carter Brown, the longtime director of the National Gallery of Art.

The evening was every bit as ceremonial as the arrival; there was another official greeting, and full-dress members of the Joint Service Color Guard, representing the military services, the Army, Navy, and the Marines—a fourth member is from either the Air Force or the Coast Guard, which alternate events—led us in a formal procession down the grand staircase and to the East Room to greet our guests. After the receiving line, we proceeded to the State Dining Room for the official toasts and dinner. The largest change in state dinner protocol in recent decades had come forty years before, when Jackie Kennedy traded in the traditional long, horseshoe-shaped table for round ones. For the Kwaśniewskis, the tables were decorated with red and white roses and daisies, in honor of the Polish flag. I had once heard the horrible tale of an official dinner where the flower arrangements had been in the colors of the guest nation's mortal enemy, and I was always deeply conscious of the flowers we chose. For the place settings, I had selected Nancy Reagan's red china and reproductions of Jackie Kennedy's West Virginia crystal; no one is able to use Jackie's original pieces, because too few remain. The glasses have been broken and chipped over the years; multiple glasses are lost at every party held, and the West Virginia glass blowers that once made them have long since shuttered their doors. Most crystal is now manufactured overseas. Fortunately, Lenox copied the Kennedy pattern, and it has continued to provide the White House with reproductions of Jackie Kennedy's glassware.

China dinner services are almost as much of a challenge. The earliest presidents brought their own porcelain sets, usually made in France or England, and dutifully crated up the pieces and carried them back home when they left office. There are a few scattered plates and teacups remaining in the White House collection, and we did host small dinners in the upstairs residence with plates from the Truman and Eisenhower administrations and Lady Bird Johnson's lovely wildflower pieces. But only the most recent china services, Nancy Reagan's famous red and Hillary Clinton's pale yellow, have enough pieces to be used for a state dinner. Every dinner takes a small toll on the china collections. Before Hillary Clinton ordered her pale yellow pattern, she asked Lenox to rerun pieces from some older china services to fill in the gaps from near constant breakage and chipping. Using privately raised funds from the nonprofit White House Historical Association, I added another china service near the end of George's second term. Manufactured by Lenox, its green lattice design is based on the few pieces of James and Dolley Madison's china in the White House collection. I ordered 320 place settings, but the pieces arrived in small batches, and we never had the chance to host a full dinner with them.

Three months of planning and preparation had gone into this dinner, but I had not planned on Jolanta wearing a long dress with a gauzy silk train. When we were walking into the State Dining Room, she stopped short. I stopped behind her, with an entire line of guests awkwardly pausing behind me. In a whisper I urged her forward, but she did not move. I spoke again, and at last she murmured, "I can't. You are standing on my dress."

After the high precision and gloss of the state dinner, Jolanta and I spent the next day in Philadelphia, where we toured the Thaddeus Kosciuszko house, home to the famous Polish soldier who was instrumental in our own Revolutionary War. Many Polish-Americans still lived in the neighborhood. I hosted a luncheon for Jolanta at the Philadelphia Museum of Art, and to commemorate the visit, the Pennsylvania Academy of the Fine Arts offered to loan us a painting for the White House. I chose a Karl Anderson piece, painted by the brother of the writer Sherwood Anderson, best known for his *Winesburg, Ohio*. We hung it in our bedroom.

The following week, I traded in my blush-colored tulle state dinner gown for jeans, a floppy hat, and hiking boots. My destination was Yellowstone National Park. I was meeting four of my childhood friends.

Our first summer hiking trip had been to the Grand Canyon National

Park, the year we turned forty. For three years in the 1990s, we had entered the lottery to stay at the tented campsites inside Yosemite National Park in California. But we were never picked. After George was elected president, I told my friends, "We finally won the lottery." In the summer of 2001, we at last hiked around Yosemite's gorgeous scenery. Then Ron Sprinkle, the head of my Secret Service detail and a former law enforcement ranger in Yellowstone, told me we had to visit his former national park. We stayed in rangers' cabins in the deserted backcountry and rode horses through a massive downpour one afternoon. We camped in a lone cabin on Peak Island, where an enormous old tree blew over and nearly landed on our roof, and in another spot where at dusk an awkward and skinny-legged teenage moose wandered past the five of us. We dipped our feet in hot, rushing creeks and watched as the mighty geyser Old Faithful spewed its water aloft. We hiked past the bubbling mud pots and gazed upon the forests where massive wildfires had blackened and scarred the trees, and where new, green saplings were now pushing their way up from the once-charred ground. With the cool tree canopy gone, the old forest floor was carpeted with wildflowers, blooming in the unexpected sunlight. We talked as we walked the trails and read poetry at night as the stars hung above us in the sky.

I came to cherish these annual trips, not simply for the uninterrupted pleasure of friendship but for the chance to be out in nature, to be unencumbered by schedules, appointments, and the constant forward rush of time. We could pick up our friendships as if one year had not passed, as if we had all been together the month or week before. It is hard sometimes, for women especially, to steal time for friends. The demands on us from families, from jobs, from every other commitment are so strong and unrelenting. But friendship is what nurtures us. My friends were often my sustenance during the White House years. We could talk, laugh, and simply be. Sharing those trails renewed me, body and soul.

I returned to Washington, and George and I began to contemplate the first anniversary of 9-11. On September 10, I spoke at the opening of the 9-11 exhibition at the Smithsonian National Museum of American History. It was in the same building that housed the first ladies' inaugural gowns, including my own. Gathered with me among the invited guests were Hillary Clinton,

Colin Powell, and Pentagon rescue workers. The exhibition, "September 11: Bearing Witness to History," was a collection of objects and artifacts from 9-11, including the briefcase that belonged to a woman who worked on the 103rd floor of the South Tower of the World Trade Center. She had miraculously escaped. There was a squeegee that had been used by maintenance workers to pry open an elevator in the Trade Center's North Tower and a metal crowbar used by a fireman to break through wallboard.

Fire Battalion Chief Joseph Pfeifer, who had helped direct the rescue operations that morning, stood beside the crowbar and spoke of sending another firefighter up into the burning towers. "I told him to go up, go up with his company, but not to go any higher than seventy. . . . After I told him, he stood there, and in the silence we looked at each other, and he turned around and he walked over to his men and took them upstairs. That was the last time I saw that lieutenant. That lieutenant was my brother, Kevin." The crowbar on display was the one that Kevin had been carrying. It was found next to his body in the rubble.

Near the crowbar, Joseph Pfeifer's helmet, boots, and coat were now also preserved. "My definition of a hero," Pfeifer said that morning, "is one of ordinary people doing the ordinary right thing at an extraordinary time." The exhibition also included a twisted piece of steel from the South Tower, a crushed fire truck door, and a partially melted television screen from the Pentagon. In its own glass display was the bullhorn that George had used, standing on the towers' rubble, to tell the rescue workers, "I can hear you. The rest of the world hears you. And the people who knocked these buildings down will hear all of us soon."

There was also a section from one of the many walls of prayers that had dotted Manhattan, this one by Bellevue Hospital, where people had posted notes and pictures, searching for loved ones. I spoke of the love we will always share with the heroes, "both here and beyond."

The following day, we began with a service at St. John's Church, across Lafayette Square from the White House. The Reverend Luis Leon, a refugee from Cuba sent to our shores by his parents to start a new life in freedom, delivered the sermon. He had fled on the frantic "Pedro Pan," or Peter Pan airlifts of children as Fidel Castro was seizing power. He would never see his father again. Leon spoke of that terrible morning of September 11. He likened it to a tattoo on our national soul. We who were alive on that morning were marked by it, indelibly and forever. "Mr. President," he said, "you never asked me why the terrorists did it. But I think they did it because this is a country where an immigrant can preach to the president."

At precisely 8:46 A.M., the moment the first plane had struck the North Tower of the World Trade Center one year ago, we stood on the South Lawn of the White House and bowed our heads for a moment of silence. Standing with us were Dick and Lynne Cheney, the cabinet, and the senior and White House staff, including the residence staff, the chefs from the kitchen, the doormen, the ushers and butlers, telephone operators, and maintenance workers, all of whom had come together to remember those we had lost. We observed that moment of silence each September 11 for the next six years, and the tradition continues still.

From there we went first to the Pentagon, where twelve thousand men and women in uniform had gathered, then to Shanksville, Pennsylvania, and then to New York. We laid wreaths and listened to prayers; in Pennsylvania the two ministers who spoke were relatives of the victims of Flight 93. At the Pentagon, in Pennsylvania, and in New York, we spent time visiting with the families of those who had died. They had survived their year of firsts—first Thanksgiving, first Christmas or Hanukkah, first New Year's, first Valentine's Day, first Easter or Passover, first birthday, first wedding anniversary, first Mother's or Father's Day. But I knew that as the years continued to pass, those absences would accumulate, and at some terrible tipping point, the days dead would outnumber the days alive. Nearly all the families had brought pictures, and they wanted me to know about the person they had lost. They talked about how funny he was, what a great mother she had been, or what a wonderful brother or sister. It was important for them to talk about those whom they had loved and lost. The talking soothed, and it helped to keep the one they loved alive in their hearts. So many had lost the person they loved the best.

We stayed in New York that night because on the heels of September 11 came the annual opening of the United Nations. It had been postponed the previous year, but this fall the General Assembly would be reconvening with its usual pomp and circumstance. The streets would be clogged with arriving heads of state and other world leaders making their way to grand receptions; roadblocks and traffic barricades would bring much of midtown Manhattan to a standstill. I had been working for weeks on a reception that George and I would host that night at the Winter Garden at the World Financial Center, just steps from where the Twin Towers had stood. But first, in the morning, George was slated to address the international delegates at the UN.

His announcement that the United States would rejoin UNESCO was warmly received. But the balance of his speech dealt with Iraq. He cited that fact that it had been four years since the last UN inspectors had set foot in Iraq. He reviewed Saddam Hussein's flagrant defiance of multiple UN resolutions. I listened as George said, "The first time we may be completely certain he has a nuclear weapon is when, God forbid, he uses one." He laid out a series of steps for Saddam, giving him a road map to peace, including disclose, remove, and destroy weapons of mass destruction and long-range missiles; end all support for terrorism; cease persecuting his civilian population; and stop exploiting the oil-for-food program for his personal gain. He then called on the world to hold Iraq's regime to account. "With every step the Iraqi regime takes toward gaining and deploying the most terrible weapons, our own options to confront that regime will narrow. . . . We must choose between a world of fear and a world of progress. We cannot stand by and do nothing while dangers gather."

What he did not say, but what everyone surmised, was that there were two paths now before us: peace or war. And what we would choose depended in large measure on whether, in Baghdad, Saddam Hussein was listening and would heed these words.

Days later, we had the chance to return Václav and Dagmar Havel's hospitality with a visit to Washington. Both Dagmar and I were wearing navy blue dresses for the black-tie dinner, and when we paused for White House photos on the red carpet, she was overcome with a fit of giggles; neither of us had thought to coordinate what we were wearing. It was a lighthearted evening, especially for the Havels. The previous August enormous floods along the Moldau River had engulfed the city of Prague. Marine guards and other U.S. Embassy employees, including our ambassador, Craig Stapleton, had gone to work cleaning out the knee-high mud and debris from flooded historic buildings throughout the city, saving priceless artifacts. The Havels wanted to express the deep gratitude of the Czech people. Ours, they told us, had been the only embassy and the only ambassador to help. It is easy to be proud of our country, because when there is a need, Americans' first instinct is to respond.

~~~~~

On the late afternoon of October 2, a single shot rang out across the D.C. city line in Montgomery County, Maryland. More than twenty-four hours later, after multiple sniper-style shootings in suburban Maryland and Northwest Washington, six people lay dead, among them a seventy-two-year-old retired carpenter, a thirty-nine-year-old landscaper who had been mowing a lawn, a fifty-four-year-old man who had been pumping gas, and a twenty-five-year-old mom who had been vacuuming her minivan. Each had been killed by a long-range rifle shot. Within a day the sniper had extended his deadly attacks into Virginia, shooting a forty-three-year-old woman as she loaded packages from a craft store, and then a few days later killing a forty-seven-year-old woman in the parking lot of a Home Depot. There were no suspects, no witnesses; the only clue was a tarot card left behind at one scene. Washington and the surrounding suburbs as far away as Richmond, Virginia, went into panic. Parks and playgrounds were suddenly deserted; parents were afraid to let their children wait at a bus stop or ride the bus to school. Parking lots sat empty. People crouched on their knees to fill their gas tanks, hoping to avoid giving the anonymous sniper a clear target.

After each new shooting, police set up roadblocks on major arteries and searched cars, vans, and trucks. Large black federal response vehicles idled along main roads, waiting to spring into action at the first report of another sniper attack. In the midst of these shootings, on October 6, we were invited to dinner at the Chevy Chase home of the columnist George Will and his wife, Mari, along with David McCullough and his wife, Rosalee, and the Civil War historian James McPherson and his wife, Patricia. It was less than a week after the first sniper attack, and there were still no leads. Hours in advance the local streets were blocked off, and when we arrived, with the usual police escort, a dark helicopter circled overhead, its rotors thumping against the evening sky. On the surrounding streets, neighbors bolted their doors and cringed in fear. They thought all the security gathered on the street meant that the sniper had struck again.

As the sniper's rampage continued, we were preparing for the second National Book Festival, to be held outside, underneath tents on the National Mall. Forty-five thousand people came to hear over seventy authors, and I brought a special guest, Lyudmila Putina. I had invited her during our spring visit. I liked Lyudmila, even though our conversations always had a slightly stilted quality because they were conducted via an interpreter. Lyudmila was engaging, and we both loved reading and books. I found myself thinking back to that long-ago Houston summer when I sat in the sweltering heat and read the classics of Russian literature, never knowing that my journey would lead me here.

Lyudmila accompanied me to the opening ceremonies for the festival in the East Room and then to the festival itself, where we walked through the tents and listened to authors. This was her first trip to the United States without her husband. She told me that she wanted to host her own book festival in Moscow, a remarkable step in a country where little more than a decade ago the bookstores were government-controlled. Many moments from that day stayed with me, but of particular note were the closing remarks by the historian David McCullough, in which he described John Adams's quest for knowledge: "The greatest gift of all, he was certain, was the gift of an inquiring mind." McCullough quoted Adams, saying, "I shall have the liberty to think for myself," and he added, "We face a foe today who believes in enforced ignorance. We don't." That plainspoken statement says so much about America, then and now.

On October 24, the Beltway sniper, John Allen Muhammad, and his accomplice, Lee Boyd Malvo, were finally captured, sleeping in their car at a rest stop off a Maryland highway. Malvo later testified that one of the aims of the killings had been eventually to extort money from the government so that they could "set up a camp to train children how to terrorize cities." On December 12, I made the annual Christmas visit to the

Children's National Medical Center, a tradition among first ladies dating back to Bess Truman and Jackie Kennedy. One of my escorts was Iran Brown, a thirteen-year-old boy who had miraculously survived being shot by the sniper in the chest outside his middle school in Bowie, Maryland, just after eight o'clock in the morning on October 7. He was one of only three victims who survived. Ten others died.

At the end of October, I was in the air again with George, off to Mexico for the APEC Leaders' Meeting. In November it was back to Europe with George for a NATO meeting and stops in Lithuania and St. Petersburg, where I saw Lyudmila. Our friendship was built not simply out of frequent meetings but the common threads of our lives. Like me, Lyudmila had two daughters, Maria and Yekaterina, both close in age to Barbara and Jenna. The Putins were proud that their daughters were fluent in English and several other languages. During a visit that previous summer to the Putins' dacha—a sprawling, steep-roofed house in the middle of a birch forest just west of Moscow—the girls played violin and piano for us. Another time, Vladimir proudly showed George the chapel he had built inside the compound and his stables, where a troop of Russian riders treated us to a command acrobatic performance. And as I walked through the dacha's brightly painted rooms with their massive fireplaces, I thought back to Lyudmila's surprise at seeing all the windows and open doors at our Texas ranch. Frigid Moscow winters and nights do not lend themselves to vast expanses of clear glass.

On this November visit to St. Petersburg, Lyudmila and I toured the beautifully restored Catherine Palace, and we were both drawn to Catherine's large, even indulgent, windows. Outside, the ground was covered with snow, and the lights from the palace reflected off the snow and then back off the windows until they resembled a kind of infinite light. I stood gazing out, imagining myself in some past century racing in a horse-drawn troika across the white, frozen ground. Off in other rooms, George and Vladimir discussed the complex issues of Iraq and Afghanistan.

The Republicans had won an unprecedented victory in the 2002 midterm congressional elections, the first time the party of a newly elected president had won seats in both houses of Congress since Franklin Roosevelt in

1934. According to a Gallup poll, George's approval rating stood at 68 percent. He was, the pollsters declared, "wildly popular." But we did not spend our days thinking about those numbers. Poll numbers are ephemeral; we did not live our lives by them. With the election now in the past, what stretched before us was the future, and every contour of it was unknown.

On December 4, I hosted thirteen women teachers from Afghanistan at the White House. Selected from across the country's provinces, they had already spent five weeks in a special professional training program run by the University of Nebraska at Omaha, where they lived with local families. I thought of them being welcomed into those solid, loving midwestern homes, eating Thanksgiving dinner, with heaping plates of turkey and dressing, biscuits and pie, and getting to know their American hosts. Each teacher who came had pledged to teach ten new teachers once she returned home. I hoped they would teach them everything they had learned, in the classroom and beyond. We had coffee, and as I walked them through the White House, I started to dream of making my own visit to Afghanistan.

We began our second holiday season, this time celebrating "All Creatures Great and Small," with animals incorporated into nearly every decoration, even cookies in the shape of Barney. We hosted night after night of events, including the annual Congressional Ball for nearly one thousand guests, all the members and their invitees. I had selected the image for our holiday card months before, a painting by Zheng-Huan Lu of the State Floor's beautiful piano, with its proud gold eagles, designed by Steinway for Franklin Roosevelt.

Christmas cards are a relatively new tradition at the White House. During the first half of the twentieth century, presidents primarily sent cards to family and close friends. But thousands of Americans mailed their own cards to the White House. Calvin Coolidge, who held the first National Christmas Tree lighting ceremony, received twelve thousand cards from the public in 1924, the same year that his beloved son died. In 1933, Franklin Roosevelt received forty thousand cards, so many that he needed to hire extra staff to open the mail. Christmas cards were rare during the time of Abraham Lincoln, but cartoonist Thomas Nast, the man credited with popularizing Santa Claus, had designed campaign posters for Lincoln's 1860 election. In 1863, at the height of the Civil War, Lincoln commissioned Nast to create a cover image for *Harper's Weekly* depicting Father Christmas welcoming Union troops. Among recent presidents, Dwight D. Eisenhower was the first to send out large numbers of White House Christmas cards. Six Eisenhower-era cards featured his own paintings, including portraits he did of Lincoln and Washington and several of his favorite landscapes. This December I inscribed our card with the words "May love and peace fill your heart and home during this holiday season and throughout the New Year."

On December 18, ABC broadcast Barbara Walters's annual special on the Ten Most Fascinating People of the year. Barbara had selected me as 2002's most fascinating person, calling me a "beacon of calm in the center of the storm." It was flattering, but even as it aired, I said to George with a smile, "Bushie, what goes up must come down."

On Christmas Eve at Camp David, George continued his annual ritual of placing calls to our troops. That day he was reaching out to men and women in the dusty, frigid landscape of Afghanistan and on other bases and ships around the world. At night we watched the Christmas pageant and Nativity play, retelling the centuries-old story of Christ's birth, performed by the children of the sailors and Marines stationed at Camp David. We smiled as a few pint-size angels, shepherds, and sheep scrunched up their faces in tears, overcome by sheer excitement and exhaustion. All of our family—George's parents, his brothers and sister and their children, Barbara and Jenna, and my mother—had gathered with us. On Christmas Day, George prayed that next holiday season he would not be calling men and women in yet another war zone.

On November 25, Barbara and Jenna had turned twenty-one. We celebrated just after Thanksgiving with a big party and a campout at the ranch with food from Tom Perini's Buffalo Gap chuckwagon. Our girls were now technically adults, looking out on a new world of their own. I treasured the few days and weeks that we had together through the year before they returned to their own lives. They were with us for that Christmas in the woods at Camp David, and a few days after they left, George sat down and typed out a thank-you note to them for his gifts. The note was full of fatherly love, but one line in particular has always stayed with me. He told Jenna and Barbara that he prayed that Saddam Hussein would disarm, that he would give up his weapons of death and destruction, and that there would be peace. He ended that paragraph with his usual effort to turn something so achingly serious into a lighter moment, assuring the girls that they need not worry that their dad somehow lacked for things to do.

George did not want war. No president ever does. He knew how precious any child is, and every person sent into war is someone's child, and often someone's mother or father too.

He turned to prayer in these times not with some newfound religion but because he had always turned to prayer. He found the first stirrings of his own faith after his sister Robin died. At age seven, at a Midland football game, he said to his dad that Robin, looking down from the stars in Heaven, had the better view. As a young Air National Guard pilot, when George came home, his mother would find an open Bible wherever he had been around the house. He was reading every word, as he would do, again and again, for years. His belief was always in something far larger than himself. He believed in the power of faith for compassion and comfort, as he must have felt it all those years ago, as a young boy watching his parents grieve the loss of their beloved daughter and who had grieved himself, as a small child would, with an ache beyond words.

I remember one late afternoon in the White House when Barbara was wrestling with a particularly difficult problem. George went to her room and sat down on her bed to console her as she told him what was wrong. He would not leave until he had begun to make it better. Afterward, I walked into my small upstairs office next to Barbara's room and found one of my young staff members in tears. She had heard bits and pieces of the conversation through the thin connecting door. She was sobbing, telling me how desperately she wished that she had had a father like George.

There would be no war for oil or for some kind of U.S. presence in the Middle East. There was war because only one man would not choose peace. That man was Saddam Hussein.

⁓

Before we would make any foreign visits, George and I would be briefed on the leaders and the conditions inside of the country. Often I was given printed biographies of national leaders. Occasionally, much to my surprise, those briefings would be wrong. It was usually just small details, such as what the first lady did—I remember once saying, "So, you are a teacher, like I was?" only to get a stare of disbelief after the translator had finished and the reply, "No, I am an engineer." Once we were told that the president of South Korea adored bowling. As a gift, because all leaders bring gifts for official visits, we had a beautiful custom-made bowling ball inscribed with the U.S. and South Korean flags. The South Korean president opened the gift and had no idea what it was; he had probably never been bowling in his life. The ball must have looked to him like some kind of lethal paperweight. More often than not, these embarrassing errors were based on gossip, on conversations overheard at cocktail parties or picked up by U.S. Embassy staff. Some mistakes were the results of simple language barriers or bad translation. But no one ever believed that our intelligence would make a mistake about whether or not Saddam Hussein had military weapons of mass destruction.

For that matter, our intelligence was confirmed by the Germans, the French, the Russians, the Israelis, the Jordanians, and the Egyptians. The major intelligence services in Europe and the Middle East, indeed in the rest of the world, stated that Saddam Hussein had weapons of mass destruction. In January of 2003, a key Middle Eastern leader warned U.S. general Tommy Franks that Saddam "will use WMD—biologicals, actually—on your troops." Here at home, Bill Clinton and Al Gore believed Saddam had weapons of mass destruction. So did leading members of Congress, including John Kerry, Hillary Clinton, Jay Rockefeller, Joe Biden, and John Edwards. The big open question was how close Saddam's scientists were to creating a nuclear bomb. The unfolding debate was over whether the United States and its allies should go to war to prevent Saddam from having the chance to use those weapons himself or to divert them to terrorists, or whether we should continue more years of sanctions, which had been in place since 1990.

After 9-11, George did not feel that he could subject the safety of other American cities or American civilians to the whims of one man. For George, the potential dangers we faced were numerous. What if he gambled on containing Saddam and was wrong? What if his gamble cost tens of thousands or hundreds of thousands of lives in a terror attack on U.S. soil?

Beyond the deep worry over weapons of mass destruction, in Saddam Hussein's Iraq, U.S. national security and common humanity intersected. Few tyrants on the world stage abused human rights like Saddam. The images were haunting and pervasive. Saddam had repeatedly ordered mass killings of Iraq's Kurdish minority. Best estimates are that tens of thousands of men, women, and children were gassed with chemical weapons or rounded up and executed in deserts far from their mountainous, northern homes. After the 1991 Gulf War, Saddam executed hundreds of his Kuwaiti captives and launched strikes on Shi'ites, Kurds, and other ethnic groups that he thought might be a threat to his regime. George and I heard stories of little children forced to witness their parents being gunned down with bullets to the back of the head. We heard of Saddam's opponents who were tossed from the open doors of flying planes, plunging to a grisly death; we heard about torture chambers where electrical wires were wrapped around young men's testicles and prisoners hung from molten hooks. Saddam read the works of Adolf Hitler and required his top Ba'ath Party officials to read *Mein Kampf*. He patterned much of his regime after that of the Soviet dictator Joseph Stalin, who had ruthlessly repressed his nation; as did the Nazis and the Soviets, Saddam and his Ba'ath Party elites recruited children to spy on parents and neighbors. No one can say for sure how many Iraqis were killed under Saddam's orders—the number is too high—but the estimates range from many hundreds of thousands to 1 million. Human Rights Watch has said that 290,000 Iraqis alone were "disappeared" by the Iraqi government over two decades.

Saddam had already been to war with Iran and had invaded Kuwait. Inside the national security community, in the age of al Qaeda and the post-9-11 world, there were fresh worries that he was a ticking time bomb.

Throughout the fall and winter, George attempted to persuade Saddam to disarm. He did not act alone. In October he sought a congressional resolution to authorize "the use of military force against Iraq." It passed the Senate 77–23, with Senators Kerry, Clinton, Biden, Edwards, and Reid all voting in favor. In November he sought and received a unanimous UN Security Council resolution calling on Saddam to disarm or disclose his weapons. He also sent private messages to Saddam through the French and the Russians. A few nations indicated that they could be persuaded to offer Saddam refuge if he chose exile. But when the offers were raised,

Saddam refused to go. We waited, hoping for a last-minute breakthrough, for some kind of reprieve.

On February 1, 2003, the space shuttle *Columbia* exploded as it began its reentry toward the earth, streaking like an enormous comet across the atmosphere. From thirty-nine miles above, debris and remains dropped from the skies over Texas. On board were seven astronauts, including two women and the first Israeli ever to fly in space. Ilan Ramon, the Israeli mission specialist, had said on January 29 that viewing the earth from the reaches of space made him realize how fragile the planet is, and also how important it is to strive for peace in the Middle East. Three days after that, I was hugging his wife at a memorial service in Houston.

Just as we returned to Washington, the FBI and other federal agencies raised the threat level for the District of Columbia. While residents continued to drive along the Beltway or hop the Metro, high-tech weaponry was quietly moved around the perimeter of the city. The military was placed on high alert. Unbeknownst to most people living in and around the capital, handheld missile launchers, capable of shooting down rogue airplanes or helicopters, were arrayed on mobile vehicles around Washington. The Pentagon also deployed other wide-ranging air defense and ground-to-air missile systems. Antiaircraft defense units were placed on alert in the vicinity of the capital, and heat-seeking antiaircraft missiles were visibly stationed on at least one Washington bridge. Blackhawk helicopters and F-16 fighter jets patrolled the skies. U.S. Capitol Police were issued submachine guns. Washington was the number one target for terrorists, and the White House was designated as the top terrorist target in D.C.

In the weeks that followed, residents were advised to buy supplies, like plastic sheeting and duct tape, to create windowless safe rooms that could withstand a chemical attack, and to lay in stockpiles of canned food. The anxiety was so great and the intelligence chatter so disturbing that some civilian assistant secretaries and others who worked at the Pentagon would, on some days, call their wives and children at 7:00 A.M. and tell them to stay out of the city for the next twenty-four hours. For those of us who lived in Washington, there was nothing to do but get up each morning and face the day.

In late February of 2003, I met with governors' wives and the Military Child Education Coalition to explore ways to make moves across state lines easier on military families. Many school districts wouldn't allow students to transfer their GPAs, so a straight A student and potential valedictorian's existing academic record vanished once he or she moved to a new school district. Together we worked to streamline the process. Commonsense initiatives like this aren't glamorous or headline-grabbing, but they solve problems. Many state first ladies helped to change rules and regulations to make transfers easier on the spouses and children of our armed forces. As March began, I called the mother of a ten-month-old girl who had received a heart transplant while her father was stationed with the Army in Kuwait. I could only imagine how hard it would be for a mother and father to face such a serious medical crisis under any condition, let alone when the dad was deployed half a world away.

In the winter of 2003, politics had begun to intrude more fully into the East Wing. From the beginning of George's term, I had worked to showcase American literature and the arts in the White House, first with music and then with writers. In late November of 2001, I hosted a symposium on Mark Twain, including Twain scholars and the filmmaker Ken Burns, who was preparing to unveil his documentary on the writer. Mark Twain is considered America's first real novelist, writing in the style and the vernacular of the young nation. George and I had always loved Twain's frankness and his razor-sharp mockery and wit. George's favorite Twain quotation is "Do the right thing. It will gratify some people and astonish the rest." After the symposium, we had the additional pleasure of going to Ford's Theatre to see the legendary Hal Holbrook's one-man show on Twain. In March of 2002, I hosted an event to highlight the Harlem Renaissance, where we discussed the syncopated, jazzy rhythm of Langston Hughes's poetry and the beautifully rendered novels of Zora Neale Hurston and other great writers of the age. The symposiums included scholarly addresses and lively panels debating the meaning behind the words. We talked about how these African-American writers began to create a twentieth-century and distinctly Black American identity with a rich culture of its own.

The following September my topic was women writers of the American West. We explored the lives and works of Willa Cather and Edna Ferber, author of the novel *Giant*, who wrote, "The sunbonnet as well as the sombrero has helped settle this glorious land of ours." The final author I selected for the event was Laura Ingalls Wilder, the writer I had loved since I was a little girl. Some of her descendants attended. Each of these writers had her own complex love affair with the wild, untamed land of the West that she called home and that I so loved.

But many of the scholars we invited did not, at first, want to come. David Levering Lewis, the Pulitzer Prize–winning biographer of W. E. B. DuBois, told *The New York Times* that he was shocked when my office invited him. A leading Twain scholar was so surprised he told my staff he'd have to call them back, and Ursula Smith, a scholar of the American frontier, also didn't initially want to come. I found that sad. Everyone can appreciate and enjoy literature; books do not come with a "do not read" sign for Democrats, independents, or Republicans. Some of the participants believed that I did not read widely. But they came away with their minds changed. The western scholar Patricia Limerick later said, "I did Mrs. Bush a terrible disservice thinking that maybe she didn't know, that she thought these [works] were all little houses on the prairie."

We ultimately had rich discussions, and all our literary events included Washington, D.C., high school students. But that was the end result. The first impulse, too often, was prejudice. Most of us over the course of our lives are guilty of some kind of stereotyping, but I have always found it a uniquely distressing attribute in people who study and teach. For these are the people who have chosen as their profession the life of the mind, and they are the ones whom we trust to teach our children. They, who have had every educational benefit, should welcome different thoughts and viewpoints. But so many responded to a White House invitation with their minds closed. And that was particularly true of a significant group of poets.

I have long been a reader of poetry, and I very much wanted to host a symposium featuring the works of Emily Dickinson, Langston Hughes, and Walt Whitman. I planned the gathering for February 12, 2003. But one of the invited poets sent a blast e-mail to fifty friends asking for antiwar poems and statements. He refused to attend but wanted another guest to present me with an antiwar anthology and have the event become an antiwar protest. What would have brought the works of three great American writers into American homes via C-SPAN was now set to become a forum for a purely political agenda. With real regret I postponed the event. It was never rescheduled. I had not selected the poets on the basis of politics, nor had the guest list been political. I wondered what victory the invitees thought they had won by keeping the East Room dark and silencing some of the nation's most eloquent writers.

In March of 2004 I held a symposium on Southern writers featuring Truman Capote, Eudora Welty, and Flannery O'Connor. It was to be my last literary symposium in the White House. Each of these writers was in his or her own way familiar with prejudice, which comes in many forms. I find particular beauty in the words of Eudora Welty, who over the years grew hunchbacked and misshapen but who created some of the most complex characters ever to appear on the printed page. She was a reader as well as a writer and once penned, "I learned from the age of two or three that any room in our house, at any time of day, was there to read in, or to be read to. It had been startling and disappointing to me to find out that storybooks had been written by *people*, that books were not natural wonders, coming up of themselves like grass."

⌒◡

The girls came home often that spring. Jenna flew up to spend a weekend with us at Camp David; Barbara spent her spring break at the White House. They wanted to be with us as the nation edged toward war. I tried to keep things as normal as possible inside the White House. Old friends, including Roland Betts, one of George's best friends from Yale, and his wife, Lois, and Mike and Barbara Proctor, came. Mike was George's childhood best friend, who had lived across the street and was a helicopter pilot in Vietnam. Mike and Nancy Weiss, our friends from Lubbock, also came. They all wanted to be there for George because they knew how their friend was agonizing.

The usual round of Washington events continued unabated. We hosted a reception for the annual Ford's Theatre gala to celebrate President

Lincoln and dressed in white tie for the dinner hosted by the Gridiron Club, Washington's oldest journalistic organization, founded in 1885. Jeannette Kagame, the first lady of Rwanda, visited Washington, and I had her to coffee at the White House. But with war increasingly looming, George's every thought was on our troops, Iraq, and Saddam.

For the better part of six months, I had been planning to host a group of my old Midland friends for four days at the White House, to tour Washington gardens, including Mount Vernon. I had been looking forward to seeing them, as had Susie Evans, my kindergarten friend and George's second-grade friend, who had moved from Midland to Washington, D.C., when her husband, Don, became the secretary of commerce. But when the days arrived, I regretted the invitation. I could tell that it irritated George to have a group of women sitting around, laughing, talking, opening a bottle of wine as he strode off to the Treaty Room after dinner for one of his frequent nighttime meetings with Condi Rice and her National Security Council deputy, Stephen Hadley. Many evenings, after most of official Washington had left its offices and gone home, they met in the residence to review, strategize, and question. The butlers put out chips and drinks, but they remained largely untouched.

Late one afternoon, Barbara called home. The teaching assistant in one of her classes at Yale had starkly told her, "I will only give you an A in this class if you tell your father not to go to war." Barbara handled the situation herself, making an appointment to speak to the dean of her residential college, who said that she should submit all her coursework directly to her professor.

We knew exactly how deep the passions ran before any American soldiers set foot on Iraqi sands.

In early March, antiwar protesters converged on Washington, waving signs and shouting epithets while George and Tony Blair worked to get the United Nations to vote on a final resolution taking Saddam to task for violating seventeen previous UN resolutions and authorizing military action if he refused to cooperate. In Washington, London, and New York, the days and nights turned into a marathon negotiating session, as our military began the final preparations for war.

On the night before the scheduled UN vote, George, Condi Rice, and I were eating dinner in the residence. All afternoon George had been placing last-minute calls to world leaders, including Vicente Fox of Mexico and Ricardo Lagos of Chile, soliciting their support for the resolution. George and Tony hoped the UN vote would convince Saddam of the international community's resolve and lead to a peaceful outcome, but other leaders were fearful that the two men were asking them to commit to war. The mood was somber as Condi and George reviewed the latest vote count and waited for word.

George never wavered under the pressure. It was the same as that moment after 9-11 at the height of the anthrax attacks, when he strode out to the mound, alone in the middle of Yankee Stadium, and threw out the first pitch. He has never been afraid to step up to the plate for whatever was required. When he first ran for president, he told his staff that he didn't want to make campaign promises that he could not deliver. He said, "If I run on something and say I'm going to do this, make sure it's something that really can be done." He is very disciplined and practical. He did not want to invade Iraq, but most of the global intelligence community was telling him that, the next time, a 9-11 could happen with chemical or biological weapons. We had been brutally attacked once; he would not allow it to happen again.

I remember too how during those weeks I would glance out from my sitting room window and see George walking Spot outside the Oval Office. On the lawn he could be alone with his thoughts. He was sending the best of America to fight and even die in Iraq because he thought it was the safest thing to do for our country. It was a decision that he had always hoped he would not have to make.

The UN resolution to authorize force was withdrawn in mid-March, after France, Russia, and Germany came together to announce their opposition. George and Tony Blair went ahead with their plans to depose Saddam Hussein. Troops from the United States, Great Britain, Poland, and Australia were readied; ultimately, more than forty nations would send troops or military support. On March 17, George gave Saddam and his sons one more chance, a forty-eight-hour deadline to leave the country and avoid war. Saddam and his sons did not leave. On March 19, at just past 9:30 P.M., U.S.-led coalition forces began high-precision bombing strikes on Baghdad. Less than twelve hours later, Americans and Iraqis had their first skirmish on the ground. We were at war.

I have often wondered if Jacques Chirac or Gerhard Schroeder could have done more, if one of them could have persuaded Saddam to go into exile, if they could have conveyed that the United States was not bluffing. After Saddam was finally pulled from his spider hole, looking like a madman, he said that he had not believed the United States would invade; he had not believed we were serious.

By June of 2003, American and British forces had located eighty of the countless mass graves in Iraq. Buried within were the remains of thousands of people whom Saddam Hussein had ordered to be killed. Long hair still hung from some of the skulls; they belonged to the women. United States forces found a police station with torture hooks hanging from the ceiling and a special "electrocution room," bare except for two tires and an electric cable. Saddam Hussein's regime was a regime of terror, in large ways and small ones. Uday Hussein, Saddam's son, who headed Iraq's Olympic committee, would torture athletes who failed to win, beating the soles of their feet until they could no longer walk. He raped women with impunity. In fits of rage, he would hit his victims with a metal bar or a cane.

When U.S. troops captured the Baghdad mansion of Uday and his brother, Qusay, I was in Austin, visiting Jenna. I was just walking into Regan's house when the head of my Secret Service detail, Wayne Williams, took me aside. He told me that pictures of Barbara and Jenna were found plastered on the walls of Uday's palace. American troops had torn them down, he said. He was stone-faced, but inside I felt as though we were both shaking. I spoke with George, and for months afterward, I was sick with worry. But we did not say a word to the girls.

George and I worried for our troops every day. I thought of them in the harshest conditions, sleeping, when they could, with the sand and the wind. I had told a group of soldiers at Fort Campbell, Kentucky, about how guilty I felt with my comforts while they went off to fight and had none. And each one immediately said, "Mrs. Bush, that's where we want to be." They loved their country, and they would do anything to protect it and to protect the men and women who served with them. But night after night I would picture our troops, I would worry, and I would pray.

Once, during an interview, Barbara Walters asked me if I could empathize with a mother who sent her child to be a suicide bomber. I said no, I could not imagine a mother who would want her child to blow himself up and kill other people at the same time. Mothers in our country have watched and prayed as their children left our shores to defend our freedom, and the freedom of people we will never meet in places we will likely never visit. Not only can't I empathize with the mother of a suicide bomber, I can't even imagine her.

On April 3, U.S. forces were racing toward Baghdad. Early that morning George and I flew to North Carolina, to the Marine training ground and base at Camp Lejeune. Already seventeen Marines from Lejeune's overseas division had been wounded and fourteen killed. Two were missing. They had lost the most of any base so far. George spoke to the troops still there and their families, as well as the loved ones of those who had been deployed. After lunch in the mess hall, we met with the families of the fallen Marines. One sergeant had left behind a six-year-old, a two-year-old, and two-month-old twins. We cried with their wives, parents, and children. The following week I joined George as he awarded Purple Hearts to wounded soldiers in the intensive care unit at Walter Reed Army Medical Center and to wounded Marines in the ICU at Bethesda Naval Hospital. We visited some seventy wounded troops and many of their families, and together we watched as two wounded Marines were sworn in as U.S. citizens. Twenty-year-old Lance Corporal O. J. Santamaria, from the Philippines, broke down as he took his oath. George walked over to hug him. Master Gunnery Sergeant Guadalupe Denogean from Mexico, the son of migrant farm workers, had spent twenty-five years in the Marine Corps and had fought in two wars before taking his citizenship oath. George told both men he was proud to call them "fellow Americans." We have, he said, an amazing country, where people are willing to risk their lives without even being full citizens.

On a trip to Arizona, I stopped to see the family of Army Private First Class Lori Piestewa, a twenty-three-year-old Hopi mother who had been killed during the first week of the war after an ambush by Iraqi forces near Nasiriyah. She had fought back bravely and had paid with her life. Lori was the first Native American woman to die in combat while serving in the U.S. Armed Forces. For two weeks she was listed as missing in action, until her body was found in a shallow grave. Her roommate and friend, Jessica Lynch, who was riding in the truck that Lori drove, had survived.

Lori Piestewa came from Tuba City, Arizona, home also to Moenkopi, a Hopi enclave in the heart of the Navajo Nation reservation. Some homes in the Hopi village still did not have running water; women and men carried buckets to a nearby river. For heat they burned tree branches, and the air hung with the scent of char and smoke, even in the spring. Most of the houses were the same adobe style that had been built for centuries in these dry desert lands. Lori, whose parents had both worked for the Tuba City schools, had grown up on the Navajo side of the reservation. Her father had fought in Vietnam; her grandfather had served in World War II. Lori had been the commanding officer of her high school Junior ROTC program. Her parents buried her on Hopi land. I met them, along with her three-year-old daughter and four-year-old son, one of her sisters, a brother, a sister-in-law, and her four nieces and nephews in a room at Page Municipal Airport, a tiny airstrip overlooking the Colorado River and Lake Powell. We had decided on this location so they would feel no obligation, on top of their grief, to host a first lady in their home. I invited them to come to the White House on Memorial Day.

George read the names of every man and woman who died in Iraq and wrote a personal letter to each family. The stories of those who received Medal of Honor citations deeply affected him. There was Sergeant First Class Paul Ray Smith, who after a surprise Iraqi attack leapt aboard a damaged armored vehicle and, completely unprotected, manned a fifty-caliber machine gun alone. He laid down his life for his friends and his men, and his selfless bravery saved the lives of more than one hundred American soldiers. There was Marine Corporal Jason Dunham, who played street soccer with Iraqi kids and who, when a grenade was thrown by an Iraqi insurgent, jumped on the explosive to save the lives of two other Americans. On a rooftop in the Iraqi city of Ramadi, Petty Officer Michael Monsoor of the U.S. Navy did the same, flinging himself upon a grenade to save two teammates.

Every day George read the casualty reports. He knew which military service, what city or province, and how. It was heartbreaking. One night at dinner he was particularly silent. Barbara and Jenna were there, teasing him, trying to get him to laugh. Eventually he just got up and excused himself. I told them then that a packed military helicopter had been shot down that morning over a field outside Baghdad.

But as George read the casualty reports, he read the threat reports too.

⌒

Just one week after I met with the Piestewa family, I was expected at an annual Washington tradition, the Congressional Club First Lady's Luncheon, for the wives, and occasionally the husbands, of senators and representatives. The luncheon is a fund-raiser for the club and is designed to honor the first lady. It is a demanding event for the organizers and the office of the honoree. Early in George's term, Hillary Clinton's former White House chief of staff confided to my chief of staff, Andi Ball, that "each year, the Congressional Club ladies made the Clinton staff cry."

Andi soon came to understand what she meant. In 2001 I had been told to walk on an elevated catwalk, like a fashion runway, so that the nearly two thousand women packed inside a giant hotel ballroom could catch a glimpse of me. As first lady I was accustomed to doing almost anything, but this was a bit too much. In 2002 I politely declined to do the runway. I also left the four-hour event a little early because Barbara had to move out of her dorm that afternoon, and I wanted to rush up to New Haven to help her. Indeed, it is rare for any first lady to stay for a four-hour-long luncheon. This year the organizers had started besieging my staff in February: they had specific requests for my remarks; they insisted that I stay for the entire lunch; and they wanted me to walk the runway again. The constant back-and-forth for these luncheons invariably, as with Hillary Clinton's staff, reduced one of the women in my office to tears.

But we admired and appreciated the enormous complexity of putting on such a large event, and at the lunch itself, the congressional spouses went out of their way to make me feel welcome. They invited singers they thought I would like, including Wynonna Judd. One year they even named a perfume for me and had tiny bottles of the scent waiting at each place setting as luncheon favors. There were other moments of genuine fun with the congressional spouses. I always looked forward to the smaller and more intimate annual Senate Spouses Lunch. Karyn Frist, wife of former Senate majority leader Bill Frist; Kathy Gregg, Senator Judd Gregg's wife; and Tricia Lott, wife of former Senate majority leader Trent Lott, were three of my closest friends in Washington. The Senate spouses, Republicans and Democrats, created special events for me each year. Once they surprised me with a re-creation of my first classroom, at Longfellow Elementary. Another year we ate at tables under the glass ceilings of the U.S. Botanic Garden, surrounded by exotic plants.

But while the Senate Spouses Lunch, at roughly one hundred, is a friendly, personal gathering, events held for the entire Congress instantly passed the one thousand mark: 535 elected officials, each with one invited guest. In sheer numbers, entertaining the Congress was one of the biggest challenges the White House Social Office faced, and we always looked for engaging ways to entertain the congressional multitudes. There are two events designed for the full Congress each year. The first is the Congressional Picnic, for all the members and their families, and the second is the Congressional Ball, held in December, for the members and their spouses. Every year the Social Office began working months in advance to develop a suitably exciting picnic theme that would honor different parts of the United States. One year it was cowboys, with pony rides for the small children. Another year, it was Mardi Gras, with a horse-drawn carriage on the White House drive and Paul Prudhomme as our celebrity chef, cooking up New Orleans fare. In 2006 the social secretary, Lea Berman, organized mini-Broadway musical numbers inside a large tent on the South Lawn, televised by PBS. In 2008 we borrowed a miniature train for the kids to ride. Beyond the numbers, though, there were other challenges that tested the patience of every social secretary and her staff.

Each year the social secretary's office would report that there were members who would not RSVP to the picnic, no matter how often White House staff called their offices to see if they were coming. Other members would call the Social Office and insist upon bringing more people, or they would arrive at the gate with eight interns in tow and expect to be cleared immediately, producing an outcry from the Secret Service, which required everyone's Social Security number days in advance in order to be admitted inside the White House grounds.

Occasionally the White House Social Office would find itself attempting to save members from themselves. At one picnic a member of the House leadership got drunk and threw up in the bushes. The social staff tried to maneuver him away from the nearby press pool. Alcohol is no stranger to some members of Congress. Social Office staffers were waiting to greet another member when he arrived at the White House. When his driver pulled to a stop, the man, who was already tipsy, took a swig of something and then proceeded to hop out of his car and teeter over to spit it into the bushes. It was mouthwash, presumably to mask whatever he had imbibed before.

The Congressional Ball, the largest event of the holiday season, was a substantial undertaking and often an adventure. It was held on a Monday night, always the night after the Kennedy Center Honors. The receiving line for photos lasted for three solid hours. Some senators and representatives wanted to bring additional guests, even their entire families, although the ball numbers already topped one thousand guests and the event was spread over every inch of two full floors of the White House.

Rather than just an outsize buffet, we worked to make the ball a real party. Downstairs was quieter and more reserved, but on the State Floor we had music and dancing. We searched the country for great, unusual bands, beginning with Rotel and the Hot Tomatoes in 2001. At every ball, by midnight, there would be sixty or more hardened partygoers still dancing, and more than once the staff had to intervene to prevent a conga line of senators and representatives from parading up the marble stairs to the private residence, where George and I were already in bed.

We invited members of Congress to the White House residence all the time, and these smaller events produced many memorable, laughter-filled evenings. We hosted cocktail parties for Republicans and Democrats in our private living room. When Nancy Pelosi became the House Speaker, George and I invited her and her husband, Paul, to dinner, just the four of us, in the residence dining room. Numerous times, when representatives or senators and their spouses arrived, my staff would hear them say as they rode the elevator, "I can't believe I'm going up here." One senator's wife wanted to take pictures of everything in the White House, even the basement kitchen, with racks of raw chicken waiting to be roasted in the oven.

On May 22, the Japanese prime minister, Junichiro Koizumi, came to visit us at the ranch. Koizumi had been one of the first world leaders to offer aid and assistance to the United States after 9-11, and he and George developed a close friendship. It was all the more remarkable because their two fathers had fought against each other in World War II. Indeed, in 1946, the year George and I were born, no one could have imagined that Japan would become one of our most steadfast international allies. During the war George's dad had been a naval aviator. In 1944 his plane had been forced down by enemy fire in a bombing raid on Japanese military installations; Gampy had survived by ejecting and parachuting into the Pacific. That same year Koizumi's father had worked to build an airfield for kamikaze pilots taking off to crash into American ships and carriers. Koizumi himself had been born in 1942, at the height of the war, when American forces were in retreat across Asia. And now, in a true historical irony, the sons of former enemies had become close friends. There is a comforting aspect to seeing history unfold in that manner and to knowing that the world can, in fact, change. After American and coalition forces entered Iraq, Koizumi later volunteered to deploy Japan's Self-Defense Forces in support of the mission, the first overseas deployment of Japanese troops since World War II.

When he arrived in Crawford, Koizumi and George walked out to our pool and sat side by side, talking for two hours. That kind of conversation, the personal give-and-take, was difficult to have inside the White House, with a legion of staff or formal seating arrangements. The following afternoon we had a cookout with hamburgers made from Texas beef. When I next saw the Japanese prime minister, he raised his arm and made a muscle, telling me, "That hamburger made me strong. I went home to do political battle, and I was strong because of that hamburger."

The 2003 G8 Summit was again held on a remote mountain. This time, the location was Évian, France. Before the summit opened, George traveled to Poland and then Russia to meet Vladimir Putin; for that leg of the trip, I joined him. In Poland we made a special visit to Auschwitz-Birkenau, the infamous Nazi death camp. George and I quietly walked along the train tracks that had carried carloads of human beings, piled on top of each other, without light or fresh air. I laid a single red rose at the terminus, where men, women, and children began to be herded left or right, to the gas chambers or to the labor camp, to work first and then die. We passed the barracks and the crematoriums, and I tried to imagine a blue sky that had once been covered over, black and gray, with human ash. "The inconvenient smell of smoke" was how one Nazi officer, who had gone free, later described it.

As I walked, I realized there are things that textbooks, photographs, or even graying documentary footage cannot teach. They cannot teach you how to feel when you see prayer shawls or baby shoes left by children torn from their mothers, or prison cells with the scratch marks of attempted escape. And I wept when I saw the thousands of eyeglasses, their lenses still smudged with tears and dirt. I, who would be nearly blind without glasses or contacts, could suddenly imagine people being driven into terror, with no way to see, groping about with their hands. And then there was the larger blindness, of the people who lived around the camps and around the world, of all of those who refused to see what was happening.

I thought too of Saddam Hussein, who had said how much he admired Adolf Hitler.

We waited for news out of Iraq. Some of it was positive and historic; we watched Iraqi citizens pull down statues of Saddam as people in the old Soviet Union and the Baltic nations had done to the images of Lenin and Stalin after the fall of communism. We heard reports of the Iraqis' joy at being able to speak freely for the first time in decades and to no longer live under the shadow of fear of Saddam and his henchmen. In some neighborhoods, Iraqi children trailed after American soldiers, staring in wonder at gifts of candy and crayons. But there were other disturbing signs. Museums and stores were looted. In sections of major urban areas, there was no rule of law. And there were attacks on our soldiers. At first, they were scattered incidents, a stray bomb or an errant shooter. But over the months the violence escalated. And no one was certain if the people behind it were disgruntled Ba'athists, the closest associates of Saddam, who had gone underground, or if they were Iranian-backed terrorists, or al Qaeda recruits. What we knew was American troops were under fire in a new kind of insurgent war.

In late September, after we had marked the second tearful anniversary of 9-11, I traveled to Paris as America's representative to the official ceremonies marking the United States' reentry after a nineteen-year absence into UNESCO, the United Nations' leading cultural and educational institution. The United States had withdrawn from UNESCO in 1984 to protest corruption and bias in the organization, but in the intervening years and with the end of the Cold War, UNESCO had made substantial efforts to reform, particularly under the leadership of its last director-general, the Japanese diplomat Koïchiro Matsuura. Among its new missions were global literacy and addressing the serious lack of education in the developing world.

I also made a "social call" to President Jacques Chirac, who had been fiercely opposed to the Iraq War. In full view of the assembled photographers, he greeted me by bending over to kiss my hand, and the photo was beamed around the world. When he raised his head, he told me, "Let bygones be bygones."

From Paris I jetted to Moscow to attend Lyudmila Putina's first book festival, which was devoted to children's literature. The Russian press called it the "Festival of School Libraries." When Lyudmila invited me, she asked that I bring along several American children's book authors. I selected two writers whose books were among the few American children's books that had been translated into Russian, R. L. Stine of *Goosebumps* fame, whose own ancestors had emigrated from Russia looking for freedom in America, and the teen thriller writer Peter Lerangis. Rounding out our delegation was Marc Brown, best known for his chapter books about Arthur the aardvark. At the festival R. L. Stine helped Russian children write a scary story about a boy named Mark and his father's ghostly car.

With Marc Brown drawing on a giant paper wall, the Russian children "created" a make-believe creature built from all different parts of the animal kingdom and invented a fairy tale. To the assembled school librarians and other invitees, I spoke about the need for families to turn off the television and read, and confessed my fondness for scary stories and mysteries and also Harry Potter. I added that to celebrate books is to celebrate freedom as much as it is to have fun.

Vladimir Putin joined us for lunch afterward, and he told me, "I heard your speech, and I saw that you had to mention freedom."

Lyudmila was particularly proud that her first book festival was what she called "legitimate." The attendees, nearly all women, were school librarians who had been selected to come to Moscow through an essay contest. They were not there because of family or party connections; none was, as Lyudmila put it, "a provincial governor's sister-in-law." Both Lyudmila and I very much agreed about the importance of education, and how difficult it is for books to compete with television, computers, and video games. The final night I was there, Lyudmila hosted a beautiful performance of the ballet *Don Quixote* at Moscow's enchanting Bolshoi Theatre.

In Washington, on Saturday, October 4, I hosted the third National Book Festival and then, two days later, a state dinner for the president and first lady of Kenya, Mwai and Lucy Kibaki. On October 10, at a speech in downtown Washington to the National Association of Women Judges, I was thrilled to tell them that Shirin Ebadi, the first female judge in Iran, had won the Nobel Peace Prize. "There can be no justice in the world," I told them, "unless every woman has equal rights." It saddens me that, in the twenty-first century, this point is one that still needs to be made. I think of our own lives and then of the lives of the women in Afghanistan and in Iraq. That day I spoke to the judges about how Iraqi women who came under political suspicion were "tortured, or raped, or beheaded. Some of Saddam's militiamen carried ID cards listing their official assignment as 'violation of women's honor.' Iraqi men were allowed to kill female relatives for supposed slights to the family name." By 2003, three out of four women in Iraq could not read. Over 60 percent of all Iraqi adults were illiterate. For the literate, Saddam had also succeeded in banning many of

Iraq's best writers and poets. Free speech was nonexistent; the Iraqi secret police were known to sit in classrooms to monitor what was studied and what was said. By contrast, American soldiers solicited donations of school supplies from their friends and families for Iraqi children.

We can and should debate all American wars, but can anyone truly say that the world was a better place and Iraq a better nation with Saddam Hussein in power? Or that it would not have become a full-fledged terrorist haven? And then there are the unanswerables. What, for instance, would the world have said if, in 1999, the United States had invaded Afghanistan? But had we done so, might the World Trade Center be standing today, its offices and observation deck crowded? We will never know. The world does not operate according to the principles of "what if?" All leaders make choices, and no one can say for certain what would have happened had a different path been taken. For myself, I prefer to stand against oppression, to stand, with George, for freedom.

In late October I was in Asia with George, stopping in Japan, the Philippines, and then Thailand, where we called on King Bhumibol Adulyadej and Queen Sirikit. During our brief stay, I visited an AIDS treatment clinic and met a young girl, shunned by her family, who came alone for her medicine. In Bali, Indonesia, the scene of a recent terror bombing, the security was so tight that our delegation staff was not allowed to walk in front of the buildings. Every entry, for us and for them, was through a back door. Ships and submarines hovered off the coast.

Meanwhile, Great Britain was reeling from another kind of security breach when we arrived in November for an official state visit. The tabloids went wild with revelations that a reporter for the *Daily Mirror* had spent the last two months working as a "phony footman" inside Buckingham Palace. Among his duties was serving breakfast to the queen and Prince Philip; his last act before he resigned was to arrange fruit and chocolates in the Belgian Suite, the rooms we would occupy on our four-day visit. George and I were amazed at the idea of a tabloid spy, while my staff members were a bit in awe of the palace, each having been assigned her very own lady-in-waiting.

We had a chance to explore Buckingham Palace, and the queen suggested that I go with my staff to watch the preparations for the white-tie state dinner being given in our honor. It was held in the palace's ballroom, which Queen Victoria unveiled in 1856 to honor the end of the Crimean War. At one end is a massive dais with golden columns and two royal thrones. We stood at the room's edge and watched as the royal staff walked on top of the perfectly set tables in their stocking feet, measuring tapes in hand, to check that each knife, fork, and spoon was perfectly placed at each setting.

After well over one thousand years of kings in England, there is a rare perfection to royal events that is truly breathtaking. Even the queen's china is revered. I remember the American ambassador to Liberia telling me the story of the British evacuation from Monrovia in the 1990s, when Liberian rebel forces began advancing on the capital city. As British diplomats prepared to abandon their cliff-side embassy, they opened the ambassador's supply of champagne and announced that they must destroy the china. The porcelain was too heavy to carry out, and it is against British law to allow the queen's china to fall into enemy hands. With champagne flutes in one hand and plates and teacups in the other, everyone stood on the balcony and hurled the pieces onto the cliffs below.

The royal family is not without its quirks. When Prince Charles and Camilla, Duchess of Cornwall, came to visit us, they requested glasses of ice before we began a long receiving line. The staff dutifully produced them, and the prince removed a flask from his pocket and added to each a small splash of what I presume was straight gin, so that they might be fortified before the hour or more of shaking hands.

The night of the royal state dinner for George and me at Buckingham Palace, I donned a Carolina Herrera burgundy dress, a fitted velvet top over a tulle skirt. Barbara Bush had loaned me the "Bush family jewels," diamonds and pearls. The next evening we reciprocated the hospitality of the queen and Prince Philip with a dinner at the American ambassador's residence, Winfield House, where the ambassador's dog roamed freely through the room. He began barking as George stood to give his toast, and Cathy Fenton, our social secretary, was left to scramble to scoop up the dog and remove him from the room so he wouldn't howl or yap when the queen rose and lifted her glass. After dinner Andrew Lloyd Webber and a small ensemble performed in honor of the queen. Our last stop was Sedgefield, England, Tony Blair's childhood home and his long-time parliamentary constituency, the British electors who placed him in Parliament. There we dined at the Dun Cow Inn with some of the Blairs' oldest friends.

The following week was Thanksgiving, which we were to spend at the ranch with Bar and Gampy and Barbara and Jenna, but for weeks I had known that George would likely miss our family feast. He was making a surprise visit to Baghdad to see the troops. I knew the exact moment he was supposed to land, and I immediately turned on the television to wait for the news. An hour passed. Then two hours. Still there was no film footage, no live feed. Late in the morning, I called the Secret Service agents' outpost on the ranch and asked, "Where's the president?" The agent in charge replied, "We show him in the ranch house, ma'am." I quickly said, "Oh, I'll go look again." The Baghdad trip was so secretive that even our own agents didn't know where George was. Condi Rice's Secret Service detail had spent the entire night in a car, with the motor running, outside our little clapboard house, where she usually stayed when she was in Crawford. They had no idea that she was on her way to Baghdad. A commercial plane in the sky that glimpsed Air Force One was told it was mistaken. When I did finally see the footage of George on television, I called Lisa Gottesman, the mother of George's personal aide, Blake. He was in Iraq, serving the troops from the chow line, alongside the president. I told her to turn on the television and see her son. She was in her kitchen making Thanksgiving dinner. When she looked at the screen, she burst into tears. Not because she was scared but because she was so proud of her son for having gone with George.

Our soldiers were thrilled to see George, who served a bunch of them supper in the chow line, visited, and ate a Thanksgiving meal. But it was he who was most grateful. His was a small gesture. Their service, every day, was the large one.

The December season was subdued that year. Every White House has had parties, even in wartime. The Lincolns hosted gatherings that lasted until the early hours of the morning. Eleanor Roosevelt installed an elaborate swing set on the White House grounds for her granddaughter's sixth birthday in 1933, during the height of the Great Depression. Lyndon Johnson ended the cycle of mourning for John F. Kennedy with a spur-of-the-moment decision to invite Congress over for a Christmas party. Layers of black crepe were removed and evergreens and poinsettias placed around the house. The kitchen rushed to prepare food and, at Johnson's request, mixed gallons of spiked punch.

This year we knew that, in many homes, families were missing a father or a mother, a son or a daughter, who was fighting in Iraq or Afghanistan. We held our annual children's party for military children who lived in or near Washington. Roland Mesnier, the pastry chef, displayed his cake-making skills, entertaining them with fabulous sweet creations. For our holiday theme, I chose "A Season of Stories," featuring favorite timeless storybook characters. The White House Christmas tree was decorated with storybook character ornaments that my mother-in-law had used over a decade before. There is great pleasure to be had in giving new life to old ornaments, just as many families over the generations do on their own trees. To adorn our annual card, I chose an image of the Diplomatic Reception Room, with a warming fire and George Washington above the mantel, painted by artist Barbara Prey. Our verse came from the book of Job: "You have granted me life and loving kindness; and your care has preserved my spirit."

On December 13, a grimy, unkempt Saddam Hussein was found hiding in a hole in his hometown of Tikrit. We had hope, but we were wary. Next year, 2004, would be another year of war abroad. At home, it was a presidential election year.

There would be no other political races after this one. Ten years after George had sought the Texas governorship, he would be running in his last election, this time for a second term as president. Come January of 2005, we would either be leaving or have four final years to serve. Some call serving in the White House a "burden" or a "sacrifice." The presidency can be, at moments, difficult, and in exchange for the enormous privilege of holding the office, you give up your privacy for a lifetime. But I believe it is a deep honor to be given the trust of the American people. For George and for me, it was a constant blessing to have the opportunity to witness, so often, the very best of America. I enjoyed this last campaign, with its enormous rallies and the chance to once again crisscross the country. I am grateful too to the tens of thousands of people who came out and cheered, to those who waited for hours to shake our hands on the rope lines and who said, "We are praying for you." I took strength and solace from their words.

Spot, our beloved springer spaniel, died that winter. I was away when she suffered a stroke. The only humane thing to do was put her to sleep, but George waited for me to return, so that I too would have a chance to say good-bye. The evening before Spot was going to be put down, George lovingly carried her out to the South Lawn, on whose lush grass she had rolled as a puppy and where, even as an old girl, she loved to chase after balls. George laid her down and then got down on the grass himself, encircling her in the chill dusk with the warmth of his body and gently stroking her head for a final farewell. Spot had been born in the White House to Bar's dog, Millie. She was the only dog to live and die in the White House, with two different presidents.

There was more private sadness to come.

On Valentine's Day, I hosted a dinner for some of our old friends from Midland in the Red Room. It was a dinner for Cathie Blackaller, my old next-door neighbor from Hughes Street, who was dying of metastatic breast cancer. On New Year's Day in Austin, Regan Gammon, Peggy and Ronnie Weiss, Cathie, and I had met for brunch. I told them that I wanted to do a mini-Midland reunion at the White House for a few friends, and Cathie, who used to sneak around outside with me in our pajamas on sleepover nights back when we were teenagers, said, "Why don't you do it sooner rather than later?" I heard her words, and I organized it for Valentine's Day. There were fourteen of us, including Mike Proctor, George's childhood friend. Cathie came in a wheelchair, with her scalp wrapped in a scarf, and Ronnie pushed her around. I seated her next to George, who kept her laughing all evening. That weekend we went to art galleries and enjoyed Washington. It was to be our last visit. Cathie died in April, at fifty-eight years old.

On April 28, CBS News' *60 Minutes II* broadcast the first images from a prison named Abu Ghraib outside Baghdad. They showed naked Iraqi prisoners being subjected to disgusting and degrading abuse by the American soldiers assigned to guard them. A *New Yorker* magazine article followed two days later with more gruesome images. I remember sitting with George over dinner as we did many nights upstairs in the White House, just the two of us, talking. George was nearly physically sick to think that any American troops could have behaved in this manner. He was angry too. "Laura," he said, "I have to know how this was ever allowed to happen and to make sure that it never happens again." There are times when the system of command fails, when soldiers fail their junior officers, when junior officers fail their senior officers, and when senior officers and their layers of civilian leadership at the Defense Department fail. Tens if not hundreds of people in authority across the system had not looked hard enough, had not done their duty. Suddenly the sacrifice, character, and hard work of more than 100,000 American troops in Iraq was being jeopardized by a few deranged men and women. It sickened and devastated both of us.

After two years of meeting on mountaintops, in 2004 the G8 came to the United States. George and I chose to host the leaders of the world's largest economies on Sea Island, Georgia. I invited the presidents' and prime ministers' wives—including Cherie Blair, Lyudmila Putina, Bernadette Chirac of France, and Sheila Martin of Canada—and created a special program for them. Later G8 meetings would do the same; in Germany, Angela Merkel's husband, Professor Joachim Sauer, put together a seminar on G8 population demographics for visiting spouses.

I took our group of wives bird-watching along a deserted beach, although they were most interested in seeing an alligator that made its home on the island's golf course. Lyudmila went swimming several times in the Atlantic's churning waves. The spouses' "work session" featured a roundtable and luncheon to which I invited Dr. Habiba Sarabi, the minister of women's affairs in Afghanistan; and two Iraqi women, the minister of displacement and migration and an Iraqi Fulbright scholar; as well as Paula

Nirschel, the wife of the president of Roger Williams University in Rhode Island. Paula had become galvanized by the plight of Afghan women, and in January of 2002, she woke in the middle of the night with an idea, to start scholarships for Afghan women at U.S. universities. Within two years, eleven women from Afghanistan were studying in the United States on full scholarships, and Paula had raised the money to cover their incidental expenses. At the summit's conclusion, Bernadette Chirac told us that France would build a maternity hospital for women in Afghanistan.

That spring Jenna and Barbara graduated from college, one day apart. We headed first to Austin for a celebratory dinner with Mother, Regan and Billy Gammon, and Jenna's friends at a local restaurant. The next night we were in New Haven, celebrating Barbara's graduation with a party at Dean Richard Brodhead's house—he was a friend and former classmate of George's. The only damper on the celebrations was George's nose, which he had scraped when his bike tire hit some loose soil and he toppled over. In all our photos, he is sporting a perfectly placed red mark. By the end of May, for the first time in four years, our girls came home to live.

A couple of months before school ended, Jenna had written a heartfelt letter to her dad, saying that she wanted to work for him in this, his final political race. She told George that she was tired of "hearing lies about you," and she wanted to help others to see "the Dad I love." Both Jenna and Barbara signed on with the Bush-Cheney campaign. It was, they said, their first campaign and also their last chance to volunteer for their dad. They answered phones in the headquarters and flew with us to campaign stops. By the fall the girls were going out and giving speeches on their own. We had the magic of watching the race unfold through their eyes. The constant rush of a full-throttle presidential campaign was new for them. They had been little girls when Gampy ran; they had been college freshmen, adjusting to their new, independent lives during George's first White House race. Now they would tear up when crowds of ten or twenty thousand roared in support of their dad.

Their friends came too. Many from Yale and the University of Texas moved to Washington to help on the campaign. Barbara would get e-mails from college friends with whom she had never discussed politics. They wrote, "I'm in New Hampshire" or "In New Jersey, campaigning for your dad."

I was so proud of the young women Barbara and Jenna had become, and to see how much they wanted to help their father. Both of them knew the world that was visited on presidential children. They had experienced its many privileges, the thrills of foreign travel, the glamour of meeting heads of state. But there are sacrifices as well, starting with the heightened scrutiny of their own lives. A few times they had strangers accost them on the street and scream profanity-laced epithets about their father and their family. They did not tell me about it when it happened, only much later. They knew the strains that George was under; they wanted to protect us. I would not wish what was said to them on any presidential child, or the child of any candidate for public office. But I fear that we have crossed a personal boundary in American political life, a boundary that we may not be able to recross. And the first crossing of that boundary began in the final month of the 2004 campaign.

⎯⎯⎯⎯⎯

The 2000 and 2004 national campaigns had a dividing line question. It was invariably a question on a social issue where the press made a concerted effort to find places where my views might diverge from my husband's. During the 2000 race, the media questions usually led, in various guises, back to the issue of abortion. Lisa Myers of NBC was the first to raise it, in the summer of 2000. The day before the 2001 inauguration, Katie Couric went further: Did I want *Roe v. Wade* to be "overturned"?

Hillary Clinton had been outspoken about White House policy and often commented on political decisions and politics. For eight years she had been a highly visible advocate in her husband's administration, so there was a belief on the part of the media that, even though I was not an elected official, they were entitled to ask me about policy, and also a curiosity about whether I would weigh in on policy with George. There was, from the start, a desire by some in the press and many of the pundits to discover any points of disagreement between us. It was an odd sort of Washington parlor game; I should have recognized it when I got the very first abortion query.

I knew the *Roe v. Wade* question was coming; Katie had already asked me two other questions about abortion in the minute before. I thought of

Barbara's and Jenna's shock when, as young girls, they first learned what abortion is. They knew how much George and I had longed for children, how much they were wanted. Talking with them around our small kitchen table, I, who had come of age during the bitter fights over *Roe v. Wade*, was also a bit shocked at their surprise and disbelief.

On the issue of abortion, I have always been struck by the deep divide between the sides. And how rarely the alternative of adoption is raised. We have so many friends and family members who found their children through adoption; George and I were fully expecting to be one of those couples as well. Today, for women in their twenties, thirties, and forties, infertility is the issue that is the most personal to them; it is the private struggle that breaks their hearts.

We are a nation of different generations and beliefs, seeing issues through different eras and different eyes. While cherishing life, I have always believed that abortion is a private decision, and there, no one can walk in anyone else's shoes.

When Katie Couric raised the issue of *Roe v. Wade*, I knew George's views, and I knew what the federal law is. I also knew the religious objections and the personal anguish of women on both sides. The simplest interpretation of her question was, Did I, as an incoming first lady, want to start off my husband's term by declaring that an existing Supreme Court ruling should be overturned? But the issue is so much more complex than that. Those were the split-second thoughts that filtered through my mind. Finally, to the question Did I think *Roe v. Wade* should be overturned? I answered no, and of course, that one word became the lead headline.

In 2004 the social question that animated the campaign was gay marriage. Before the election season had unfolded, I had talked to George about not making gay marriage a significant issue. We have, I reminded him, a number of close friends who are gay or whose children are gay. But at that moment I could never have imagined what path this issue would take and where it would lead.

Over twenty-four years, I had been at every Republican convention: Detroit, Dallas, New Orleans, Houston, San Diego, Philadelphia, and now New York. Once again the entire Bush family joined us, making it in part a mini-reunion of siblings, in-laws, cousins, and children and grandchildren. The Republican National Committee had chosen New York as its site in part to make a defiant stand against the terrorists. They wanted to show the world that the city had rebounded and that political leaders were not afraid to pack the hotels and eat in the restaurants. Being in the city reminded me how completely our country came together after 9-11, when for a time personal passions were put aside and we had a common care and a common purpose. Now I began to feel the country separating along new seams.

The campaign was highly personal for me in other ways too. In addition to my girls, I traveled with some of the families who had lost their loved ones on the morning of 9-11. Cheryl McGuinness, the widow of the copilot Tom McGuinness, whose hijacked plane had been flown into the World Trade Center, campaigned with me, as did David Beamer, father of Todd Beamer, one of the heroes of Flight 93. They did not, in the heat of a campaign, want the threat of terrorism to be forgotten.

Amid the rallies, speeches, and debates, George and I never forgot the sacrifice of our own troops at war. On almost every swing across the United States, George met with families who had lost sons or daughters, husbands or wives, or fathers or mothers in Iraq and Afghanistan. Many times I joined him; sometimes I visited with the families on my own. We met in stadium holding rooms and also on nearby military bases, any location that would give us a bit of privacy. We were there to thank and comfort them, to make sure that they were getting everything they needed from the Department of Defense or Veterans Affairs. But mostly we came to listen. Many of the families would show us photos, would tell us stories of the loved ones they had lost. They talked about a son's favorite sports teams, what position a daughter had played in high school. They talked about a brother's hobbies or pets, what a husband had said when he held his newborn son or daughter for the first time. They wanted us to know their loved ones as living people and to know the warmth and value of their lives. And I was struck by how similar their losses were to the losses of the families of 9-11. We came away humbled by these families' courage and sacrifice. There is no compensation for such a loss; we carried their stories in our hearts.

The same was true of our visits to the wounded at Walter Reed, Bethesda Naval, and Brooke Army Medical Center in San Antonio. We would see soldiers and Marines who had lost limbs and were asking to return to duty. We saw their spouses and small children clustered around their bedsides, and middle-aged mothers who had left their jobs and driven across half the country or flown from home with little more than the clothes on their backs to rush to the hospital and be there for their injured sons or daughters. We saw the hideous burns of IED bombs, and soldiers and Marines whose brains had been damaged beyond full repair. We saw their suffering. And I always knew when George had gone alone to visit the wounded or the families of the fallen. He was quiet, a deafening kind of quiet. And the grief shone in his eyes.

The last presidential debate of the 2004 election was held in Tempe, Arizona, on October 13 and was moderated by Bob Schieffer of CBS News. Bob is from Texas and has always been a straight shooter. His brother, Tom, a Democrat, had been one of our partners in the Texas Rangers, and George named him ambassador to Australia and later to Japan.

I was nervous before this debate, just as I was before every debate. Senator John McCain and his wife, Cindy, were with us in the holding area. The night before, for a brief respite, they had taken us to their favorite Mexican restaurant in Phoenix.

When George sat down to collect his thoughts, John, meaning well, went over and said, "Relax. Relax," which of course I knew would most likely distract George and make him anything but relaxed. George walked out onto the stage in a dark suit, white shirt, and red tie. John Kerry was wearing the same thing, except a slightly darker red tie. It was as if they had read the same handbook, what to wear to a debate. Jenna and Barbara were sitting on either side of me. We all heard Bob say, "Both of you are opposed to gay marriage. But to understand how you have come to that conclusion, I want to ask you a more basic question. Do you believe homosexuality is a choice?" John Kerry began his answer by saying, "I think if you were to ask Dick Cheney's daughter, who is a lesbian, she would tell you that she's being who she was, she's being who she was born as." Beside me, Jenna and Barbara gasped. They were utterly stunned that a candidate would use an opponent's child in a debate. John Kerry's statement did not seem like some off-the-cuff remark. His running mate, John Edwards, had also mentioned Mary during his vice presidential debate with Dick Cheney, the week before. Lynne Cheney was rightly furious to see her daughter be used by these men in a calculated attempt to score political points. Lynne called it "cheap and tawdry," and it was.

Seven days later I was the one in the campaign spotlight. In a brief interview, Teresa Heinz Kerry was asked by *USA Today* if she would be different from me as first lady. These are the trick questions of politics. They may seem benign coming off a reporter's lips, but they are minefields for whoever answers. Teresa began by saying, "Well, you know, I don't know Laura Bush. But she seems to be calm, and she has a sparkle in her, which is good." Had she ended at that sentence, there would have been no headline. But instead she continued, "But I don't know that she's ever had a real job—I mean since she's been a grown-up." Of course, Teresa had no idea that I had worked as a teacher and a librarian from 1968 until I married George, in November of 1977. Her husband's campaign issued an apology the same day. I was never offended. But from then on, at political rallies, I would see women holding signs: "I never did anything either, I'm a teacher" or "I don't do anything either, I'm a librarian."

Although the network news exit polls predicted that John Kerry would win, they were wrong once again. George and Dick Cheney won reelection by over 3 million votes.

In those months together out on the trail, we grew even closer as a family. And the 2004 race would ultimately add to our little foursome. During the campaign Jenna met another campaign aide, a young man from Virginia named Henry Hager. In May of 2008, they would marry under a sunset sky by the little lake at our ranch.

When Bill and Hillary Clinton entered the White House, *Saturday Night Live* debuted a few particularly cruel skits aimed at their then twelve-year-old daughter, Chelsea. The Clintons took a hard line, and the press was shamed into leaving Chelsea alone. The press did largely the same for Barbara and Jenna, although reporters from the tabloids and from more mainstream publications frequently called their friends, trying to entice them to talk about the girls. None ever did. But a postscript to the 2004 campaign was that it changed, perhaps irrevocably, how the families, especially the children, of national candidates are treated. The strategy of making Mary Cheney's private life an issue failed with the voters in November of 2004. But in the years since, it has become acceptable to mock candidates and their families, and other elected officeholders, in highly personal ways; David Letterman feels free to ridicule Sarah Palin's teenage daughters, and the audience laughs. That is the legacy of the 2004 campaign.

For the holidays that year, I chose the theme of seasonal music, and scattered across the White House we had scenes depicting our favorite songs, from "Frosty the Snowman" to "I Saw Mommy Kissing Santa Claus." In the front hallway, we created our own winter wonderland of snow-flecked trees with glittering icicle lights, a look that Nancy Reagan from sunny California had also loved. The Secret Service allowed us to resume tours, and some 44,000 people were able to come through the house to see the decorations. We hosted another 9,000 guests for the receptions, among them many military children and personnel.

We were at Camp David for Christmas Day when, deep under the Indian Ocean floor, the tectonic plates shuddered and the seabed cracked in the second largest earthquake in recorded history.

The entire planet vibrated from its force. Above, in the seawater, the energy from the quake unleashed a series of waves. The water began rushing toward shore, traveling as fast as an airplane, at speeds of some five hundred miles per hour. Off the coastline the pace of the water gradually slowed. Its power changed from speed to height, until it formed a wall of water that was in some places more than ten stories tall. In Thailand people on the beach saw the ocean race back, sucked into the tidal force of the wave. Then the water rushed forward. When it reached land, it crashed with the force of a small nuclear explosion. The tsunami was as high as one hundred feet, and it devastated not just southern Asia but the East African coast as well. Ultimately, more than 200,000 people in fourteen countries were killed. Thousands were drowned; many were sucked into the giant undertow and washed away. George and I watched the early television footage in horror, and he immediately asked his father and Bill Clinton to spearhead a fund-raising and relief effort in the United States. American citizens contributed more than $1.8 billion, and the U.S. government dispatched a total of $841 million in aid. Day after day we heard the stories of devastation: villages where only a few residents remained alive, survivors who clung to palm trees and waited with broken legs and arms, husbands and wives, parents and children of whom one remained and one was swept away.

There were no early warning systems for tsunamis in the Indian Ocean, just as there are none for earthquakes. But for other natural disasters, we could be confident that warnings could go out hours or even days before they arrived at our shores. In 2004 alone, four hurricanes had hit Florida in a period of six weeks. Two were Category 3 hurricanes, and one was a Category 4, the worst storm to arrive on the U.S. mainland since 1992. Forty-five people in six states died as a direct result of those four storms. Always, though, most of the people in their paths had fled to safety.

On January 6, George and I held a black-tie sixtieth-anniversary dinner for Ganny and Gampy. We had begun preparations for it before the election, not knowing if we would be packing to leave the White House or planning to stay. The singing Army Chorus performed, led by the moving bass singer, Alvy Powell, and we toasted Bar and Gampy's extraordinary marriage. One of their longtime friends, David Rubenstein, raised his glass and noted that Barbara and George Bush were the first presidential couple to reach the milestone of sixty years of shared life.

On her visit Bar also replaced her official White House portrait. She had never liked the image that had been painted of her; she and I both thought that it was flat and dull. When Bar mentioned this to the head White House usher, Gary Walters, he said with characteristic pragmatism, "Why don't you do something about it?" So Bar had a second portrait painted, and this one did capture her sparkle and wit. We proudly watched as her new and improved portrait was hung, proving that even first ladies can have a second act after they have supposedly been "immortalized."

Inauguration Day 2005 dawned cold and snowy. A light dusting fell over the Capitol, coating the dull winter grass in white. By the time George stepped onto the platform, a dazzling sun had broken through, but the air was still cold. Gampy spent the afternoon in a White House tub, trying to warm up. I later heard that the German ambassador, a big fan of Alpine skiing, described that morning, sitting in the shady section for diplomats, as "the coldest I have ever felt." I felt the cold too, but I was focused on George's words. His second inaugural address was a stirring discussion of freedom, not our unique American vision of freedom but the concept of freedom at its most fundamental. "America," he said, "will not pretend that jailed dissidents prefer their chains, or that women welcome humiliation and servitude, or that any human being aspires to live at the mercy of bullies."

He spoke of our own nation: "You have seen that life is fragile, and evil is real, and courage triumphs. Make the choice to serve in a cause larger than your wants, larger than yourself—and in your days you will add not just to the wealth of our country, but to its character."

George believes in the capacity of human beings to change their lives and the lives of others for the better. He believes in the generosity of the human spirit. And he believes that everyone, no matter what his or her circumstances, deserves a chance. I believe it as well. His inaugural words and ideals would inspire me in the four years to come.

My mother missed the family inaugural portrait. When I went to her room to get her, she was standing out in the hallway, not fully dressed, with rollers still in her hair. I knew at that moment that I should have had someone with her the whole time; the independent, confident woman who had been at the 2001 inauguration was gone. Travel was hard for her. She could no longer get on or off the plane unassisted. She visited less frequently during our second term, and when she came, my longtime Midland friend Elaine Magruder accompanied her.

In April of 2004, before the campaign had kicked into high gear, I'd cleared my schedule and gone home to Midland to help Mother move out of the last house that Daddy had built for her. Together, Mother and I packed up her belongings. As an only child, had I waited, I would have been doing it alone. We laughed over what we found in boxes or in closets. She moved her best things into her apartment in her new retirement home. The rest we gave away or I sent to Crawford. Mother was still thrifty too, cutting down "perfectly good" draperies to fit in her new, small living room. We hung her pictures on the walls and arranged her dwindling collection of furniture for what I knew would be the last time.

Two months later I was reminded again of the passage of time when President Ronald Reagan died and we sat with Nancy Reagan in her grief. I listened to the words of praise from many who had once mocked President Reagan. In the intervening years, they had reassessed his life and his legacy. Now he was seen as the man who had stood up to the Soviet Union and begun the end of the decades-long nuclear stalemate that was the Cold War. In those June days following his death, Reagan was hailed as a great statesman by many commentators, political opponents, and historians who had derided him during his lifetime.

We had our own transition as 2005 dawned. A second Scottish terrier, two-month-old Miss Beazley, a relative of Barney's, joined us in the White House. George had a new valet, Robert Favela, who grew up outside El Paso; the U.S. Navy had posted him to work for George in the White House. In an amazing coincidence, Robert had joined the Navy with his best friend, Carlos Medina. Carlos's parents owned the four-square orange-brick house in Canutillo that had been Grammee and Papa's home, where Grammee had laid each brick by hand.

Condi Rice was departing the West Wing for the State Department, as secretary of state. The new national security advisor, Stephen Hadley, is one of the nicest men I have ever met. His even temperament, dedication, and unmatched sense of fairness and balance made him a perfect advisor, and his compassion makes him a great person.

Inside the White House, Karl Rove was named deputy chief of staff.

Karl had been with us in the trenches of Republican politics for years. Not only did we respect his thoughtful and intuitive understanding of the political world, but his interests spanned well beyond vote counts and elections. As a person, Karl is funny and warm. He was invaluable to George as an advisor and would remain one of our closest friends.

My chief of staff, Andi Ball, who had been with me for a decade, since our first days in the Governor's Mansion and through the horrors of 9-11, and who had become a treasured friend, was going home to her husband in Texas. Replacing her would be the very talented Anita McBride, who had worked for Ronald Reagan and Gampy, and had most recently been at the State Department. We had a new social secretary, Lea Berman, a warm and gracious hostess; and I already had a second, sweet assistant, Lindsey Lineweaver. My first, the always cheerful Sarah Moss, had departed before the campaign and was now the married Sarah Garrison.

When I interviewed Anita, I told her there was one thing I wanted to do above all else: I wanted to travel to Afghanistan.

I had wanted to go to Afghanistan for years. My regular meetings in the United States with Afghan teachers and parliamentarians, lawyers and judges, as well as my work with the U.S.-Afghan Women's Council, had heightened my interest in seeing the country for myself.

I had tried to visit in previous years, but there were either security concerns or problems with planning. I did not want to divert vital military assets, such as helicopters or security, from the battlefield to accommodate one of my trips. I did not want people in our military to have to pay attention to me when they had other jobs and other duties. We needed to pick an optimum time for our military, but I was eager to go.

All the trip planning was done in secret, in the Presidential Emergency Operations Center, the same underground set of rooms where we had taken shelter on the evening of 9-11. A few representatives from the Secret Service and the White House Military Office worked with Anita on the arrangements; as did Paula Dobriansky, undersecretary of state for democracy and global affairs; and Deputy Chief of Staff Joe Hagin. Andy Card, George's chief of staff, had signed off on the trip, but on my staff, only Anita knew. The trip was so classified that she couldn't tell her own husband.

We had decided that I would travel to the Afghan capital of Kabul on the day of the U.S.-Afghan Women's Council meeting. The council, a unique public-private partnership that George and Afghan president Hamid Karzai had established in 2002, meets twice a year, once in Washington and once in Kabul. Through the council, American women partner with women in Afghanistan to share their expertise in education, business, politics, the law, and health care. Among its accomplishments the council has provided opportunities for Afghan women to open businesses, secure an education for themselves and their children, and begin to assume leadership roles inside Afghanistan. This is a sea change in a nation where, under the Taliban, women who had been widowed or left without fathers or brothers following years of war could not leave the house because they had no male relative to accompany them.

Many of the security assets that I would need would already be in place for the council's March meeting in Kabul. I could slip in under their cover. And that is exactly what we did. The members of the press who would accompany me on this trip did not know where we were going until thirty-six hours before our departure, and they were sworn to secrecy. American members of the U.S.-Afghan Women's Council were told that I was coming only after their plane had finished a refueling stop in England.

My plane left Andrews Air Force Base at 10:15 in the morning. Traveling with me were Anita; Margaret Spellings, the secretary of education; and Paula Dobriansky. To reach Kabul we would cross nine and a half time zones in fourteen hours. We would land at 11:35 A.M. local time at Bagram Airfield, our plane twisting like a corkscrew as we descended to evade any rounds of insurgent gunfire. Waiting to greet me upon arrival were a group of allied commanders from the United States, Germany, South Korea, New Zealand, Pakistan, Poland, Australia, Egypt, Estonia, and France. All had troops on the ground in Afghanistan.

I had a chance to personally thank the commanders before boarding a Nighthawk helicopter. Blades churning, it lifted off for the thirty-minute ride to Kabul. In the distance the Hindu Kush mountains rose, their pointed white snowcaps piercing the sky. Below us stretched brown dust and flat building compounds made of rough mud brick. Some looked like little more than stacked earth or ruins. I had the sense that I was flying over a scene out of the Bible, gazing down upon an ancient civilization and the distant footprint it had left behind.

Though we were far removed from shifting sands, the miles of ground looked like a desert. Afghanistan had once been renowned for its grapes and pomegranates; its fruits were favorite delicacies on the British ambassador's table in India. Remarkably, from my window, I could not glimpse even a blade of green. What trees had not been destroyed in the Russian invasion had been burned by the Afghans during the biting cold winters. Now, for heat, they burned things like trash or tires, whatever they could find, whatever would catch fire.

After years of war and Taliban rule, the country was decimated. Kabul was a shell of bombed-out buildings. Very few people had electricity. Water was carried by hand. Roads were collections of rubble. The country's physical infrastructure had been ruined, and the social infrastructure was worse. The most basic laws governing contracts, property rights, and business were absent in Afghanistan.

We had large scarves to cover our heads if needed, and while we flew, Anita and I pulled up our scarves as a fine, choking dust swirled through the open doors of the helicopter. The layers of dust that settled over us were far worse than the red sand that engulfed Midland. Here, there was nothing, not even scrubby mesquite, to hold the soil to the ground. The helicopter ride was like traveling in a wind tunnel, with the enormous thump-thump of the blades above us and bracing, cold air racing past. Soldiers leaned out of the doors and rear of the helicopter with their machine guns raised. These are the conditions our troops travel in every day, risking their lives. There is no special dispensation from either the elements or the insurgents; both are dangerous. The pilot who so gently set down my enormous helicopter was killed two months later in a crash in Iraq. Two of the crew chiefs were killed in a separate crash just a week later; their helicopter was brought down by bad weather in Afghanistan's Ghazni Province. I wrote to all three families. To Captain Derek Argel's widow, I penned, "Our nation has lost a hero, but you and your son have lost your precious husband and father. My heart aches for you."

Our destination was Kabul University, an austere, Soviet-style concrete building that had been partly bombed out during the years of conflict. The United States had renovated it to include dorm rooms and classrooms. In the yard outside, widows were planting trees as part of a nationwide reforestation project funded by Caroline Firestone, an American philanthropist and a member of the U.S.-Afghan Women's Council.

My first stop was the Women's Teacher Training Institute, which I had helped found in 2002. The program, overseen by the U.S. Agency for International Development, is designed to train teachers from the rural provinces. After completing the program, they return to their provinces to train other teachers. The idea was to create a cascading effect, so that as many teachers as possible could be trained as quickly as possible and more small villages could open their own schools. That spring the institute's first class would be graduating. The institute trained both men and women, but they were kept segregated, taught in separate classrooms.

When I entered the women's classroom, the women were sitting on the floor on cushions, their backs propped against the wall and their papers spread across their laps. The institute had few chairs or desks. Many of the women were completely covered in blue burkas, and I was immediately struck by the sheer weight of the material. These were small women, drowning in cloth, each forming a kind of triangle on the floor, as if they were pinned to the ground. And they seemed afraid even to lift their mesh-covered eyes and peer up at me. Perhaps they were wary of looking at me in my Western pantsuit, with my uncovered face and hair. But these women were brave enough to leave their homes and come to Kabul, to live in a dorm, go to school, study, and be trained. Two Kabul University students showed me the dorm rooms where the female teachers slept on bunk beds. Without these rooms, without this program, these women would have no chance for any kind of education, no chance at all to come to Kabul.

In the men's classroom, there were only cushions around the wall, not even a rug. The men had short beards, and most wore shirts that hung below their knees. Two had donned Western-style blazers over top. A lone man in the corner stood and struggled to say his name in English and to welcome me to Afghanistan.

I gave a speech in the university's cafeteria and announced the establishment of two new schools, the American University of Afghanistan and the International School of Kabul, a high school. "These are more than just development projects," I said, "they also signify the bond between the American and Afghan people. They are symbols of our shared hopes and dreams for the future. That dream is of a prosperous, peaceful, and above all, a free Afghanistan, where both men and women stand upright in equality. "

A nearby room had been set up like a grand Afghan bazaar, with piles of hand-woven rugs and rows of dresses on display. There were twenty booths, each showcasing goods made by women entrepreneurs, rug makers, weavers, embroiderers, and clothing makers, all microenterprise projects. The driving force behind many of these programs was a woman named Mina Sherzoy, who had escaped to California in 1979 after the Soviet invasion of Afghanistan. She had returned in 2002 following the fall of the Taliban to help her fellow countrywomen. But there were also women with no prior connection to Afghanistan. Connie Duckworth, the first female sales and trading partner at Goldman Sachs, had helped to found the Arzu rug company. "Arzu" means hope in the Dari language of Afghanistan. As an enterprise, Arzu works to preserve the traditional Afghan craft of rug weaving and pays women bonuses for high-quality workmanship. In return, Arzu weavers must agree to send their sons and daughters to school, to take literacy classes themselves, and to receive pre- and postnatal medical care for themselves and their babies. After I had returned home, I ordered two Arzu rugs for the White House collection to place in the hallways of the residence. I purchased a third rug for the small library at our ranch, so that we might always have something created by these Afghan women.

On the grounds of Kabul University, I helped plant a tree in a new grove on what had been barren land. That cluster of trees is still green and growing.

Behind the scenes, Anita had been in negotiations with the Secret Service to see if I could leave the grounds of the university and go into Kabul itself. The agent in charge, Joe Clancy, finally said yes, but the outing could not last more than twenty minutes. We had to be onboard our airplane and in the sky by nightfall. We drove into the city in a convoy, along one of Kabul's major streets, and stopped in front of three little stores, clustered together, sharing walls. One was a bakery, with a picture of a white frosted cake and a smattering of English words on its wooden sign. Through the window I could see shelves of fluffy breads and pastries. The sidewalk in front of the shops was concrete, but just beyond, the concrete gave way to packed dust. Trash, empty bottles, and papers, carried by the wind, came to rest where the fresh concrete lip rose. Three children in a nearby house peeked out from their windows, and Therese Burch, one of my advance staff, walked over and invited them to come outside. The older boy knew a few words of English, but his younger brother and sister looked at me in silence. They wore only thin jackets, and in the chill of March, the younger children had no shoes for their feet.

I said hello and offered them one of the small gifts that we had brought, a kaleidoscope. I held it up to my eye and turned the tube to show them how it worked. Their faces broke into smiles. Inside the bakery I looked at the display, and the employees insisted upon pressing a bag filled with sweet Afghan cookies into my hands. I paid for the bag and thanked them. The pastries looked delicious, but of course, the Secret Service agents wouldn't let us eat them.

In those few minutes, I had exhausted my unscheduled off-site visit time. We piled back into the convoy and returned to the helicopters that ferried us to the Presidential Palace, where Hamid Karzai was waiting.

The palace is old and, after years of neglect, was in terrible shape. Crumbling blocks had been repainted and fresh plaster patches hid aging bullet holes in the walls. It was a stark place, several years away from even a modest garden or grounds. The inside was furnished in heavy, carved wooden pieces and old, slightly worn tapestries. Only the official meeting area, where we sat on gold-trimmed claw-foot chairs, beneath a crystal chandelier, had any look of opulence. As we talked, President Karzai's staff served us bright glasses of pomegranate juice. The Secret Service blanched as I raised my glass. Lindsey, my assistant, rushed over to whisper that they didn't want me to drink it, so I left the beautiful glass of deep red liquid untouched; I was dying to drink that pomegranate juice.

After our meeting President Karzai walked me out of his offices and across a long, enclosed courtyard to a smaller, modern, rectangular building, made of concrete and blocks of stone. The woman who appeared in the doorway was his wife, who is so private that she is rarely seen in public.

Zeenat Karzai wore a long, gray coat, and her head was tightly swathed in a full white scarf. Unlike some Muslim women, who push their scarves back above their hairlines to reveal a tantalizing bit of their dark tresses, she concealed every strand of hair. In a nod to Western ways, she clutched a gray purse in her hand as we were introduced.

Sitting beneath a painting of her husband in her living room, Dr. Karzai offered me tea. She is a trained obstetrician-gynecologist in a nation with the world's second highest mortality rate for women in childbirth. In 2005 an Afghan mother would die every half hour trying to bring a child into the world. Dr. Karzai told me of the desperate need for a maternity hospital in Kabul. The French hospital that Bernadette Chirac had discussed at the previous year's G8 Summit had yet to materialize, and Dr. Karzai pleaded for help, hoping that the United States could do more. Clasping her purse in her hand, she walked me to the door and took a few brief steps into the sunshine before retreating inside. I turned around to wave as we hurried to the helos for the thirty-minute flight back to Bagram.

At the base, in a bare prefab room with Afghan throw rugs to warm the cold floor, I listened to a briefing by Lieutenant General David Barno and Major General Jason Kamiya on provisional reconstruction and military projects. As they pointed at provincial maps, my eyes were drawn to the vast, mountainous border between Pakistan and Afghanistan, the reputed hiding place for Osama bin Laden and the refuge for the Taliban. Even on paper, it looked formidable. By 4:55 that afternoon, I was standing in the chow line to eat dinner with the troops in the Dragon Chow Dining Hall. We ate chicken tenders, ketchup, and broccoli under a large American flag. Sitting on one side of me was a female soldier, wearing camouflage fatigues, her sandy hair pulled back into a ponytail. These were the two worlds, burka-clad women and women in combat fatigues, now inhabiting the same dusty Afghan ground.

At 5:45 P.M., we were on board the plane, chasing the setting sun. Touchdown was at 1:45 A.M. at Andrews Air Force Base.

I had told the Afghan students that it was "an extraordinary privilege" to be with them that day. It was. It was a privilege to see Kabul and to be able to thank our troops in Bagram. But it was powerful to see with my own eyes the complete devastation in Afghanistan. As years of Soviet war and then Taliban rule had shown, it is easy and quick to destroy, and slow and hard to rebuild. I can understand the impatience of many with the halting progress made by new democracies around the world. From our vantage point, our own democracy and government may appear to have come easily. But they did not. Thirteen years after America declared its independence, we had to completely revamp our government. And though in 1789 we started with a near perfect document, the Constitution, it took decades, even centuries, for us to build a more perfect country. It took over seventy-five more years to achieve the abolition of slavery. It was fifty-five years after the surrender at Appomattox before women earned the right to vote and another forty-five years beyond that before real civil rights came to our own nation. Only in hindsight do we feel the onward rush of progress and think of it as inevitable and unstoppable. In the moment, it looks like something else indeed.

Two days after I returned from Kabul, Pope John Paul II died in Vatican City. George and I, accompanied by Gampy, Bill Clinton, and Condi Rice, flew to Rome for the largest gathering of heads of state in history. In total, seventy presidents and prime ministers, four kings, and five queens gathered to mourn his passing. Four million other mourners packed the streets around the basilica, and millions had walked past his body as it lay in state. We too went to pay our respects, kneeling at the communion rail. Before us lay the once vibrant man who had helped rally millions in Eastern Europe to the cause of freedom and the end of communist oppression, and who had worked so tirelessly on behalf of the poor and the downtrodden. No effort had been made to cover his skin, which had grown mottled with age and illness. But his was a life of devotion, a life of blessings, a life well-lived.

Throughout the funeral service, the skies threatened rain. Then, at the precise moment when John Paul's plain pine casket with a simple inlaid cross was lifted high to be seen one final time by the mourners before it was carried into the Basilica of St. Peter's, a ray of sun broke through the clouds and shone bright upon the casket.

I thought of John Paul again the very next month as my motorcade raced along the flat desert highway leading from Jordan's main airport to the capital city of Amman, where stacked dwellings rose up the mountain-sides and the colors were muted desert browns and beige. I had arrived in the region where the world's three major faiths converge, moving from Jordan to Israel to Egypt.

In Amman I ate dinner at the private residence of King Abdullah and Queen Rania, whom we had hosted a number of times in the United States, including for a weekend at Camp David. We ate at a long, rect-angular wooden table, and during dinner Queen Rania excused herself to tend to her fourth child, a four-month-old baby, whose mews and cries drifted downstairs.

I was in Jordan to speak at the World Economic Forum, which was meeting at the edge of the Dead Sea. I would be addressing a large group of delegates before heading off to a smaller roundtable. As UNESCO's honorary ambassador for its Decade of Literacy, I spoke about education and literacy, and while I did, a desert fly buzzed around my face, attracted to the bright spotlight of the speaker's podium. My speech proved to be a different kind of irritant to some of the attendees. The message about edu-cation and opportunity for all citizens, including women, coming from the wife of a conservative American president, was too much for some of the men. "In my country," I said, "women didn't secure the right to vote until more than a century after our nation's founding. But now we know that a nation can only achieve its best future and its brightest potential when all of its citizens, men and women, participate in the government and in decision making." I continued, "I'm reminded of what Václav Havel, the former president of the Czech Republic, once told me, 'Laura, you know, democracy is hard because it requires the participation of all the people.'"

Below me, in the audience, there was a rustling, then a murmur, and then a delegation of white-robed men in red-checked head coverings walked out. They were from Saudi Arabia, where women cannot vote and cannot drive. They are not permitted to travel freely, and many have no chance for anything beyond the most rudimentary education, if that. I spoke of how, across the broader Middle East and North Africa, more than 75 million women and 45 million men are illiterate. Then I spoke about freedom. "As freedom becomes a fact of life for rising generations in the Middle East, young people need to grow up with a full understand-ing of freedom's rights and responsibilities: the right to discuss any issue in the public sphere, and the responsibility to respect other people and their opinions." I added, "Freedom, especially freedom for women, is more than the absence of oppression. It's the right to speak and vote and worship freely. Human rights require the rights of women. And human rights are empty promises without human liberty."

No one in the press reported the walkout—probably better for the delicate balancing acts of global diplomacy—but it was a clear reminder of how long the journey is for women to become men's equals in the wider world.

Afterward, I spent time with Jordan's king and queen at a roundtable with Arab youth, where we discussed education and economic improvement. Both King Abdullah and Queen Rania have charitable foundations devoted to improving lives in Jordan. I went on to nearby Mount Nebo, the last place where Moses stopped. Wearily, he ascended the mountain and glimpsed the Promised Land he would never reach. It was here that Moses died, leaving the Israelites to complete their journey alone. On clear days, from the rise, the scene is breathtaking; it is possible to see as far as Bethlehem and Jerusalem.

During the drive we passed encampments of nomadic Bedouins, their camels kneeling on the hot sands and their tents billowing in the desert winds. The heat was so searing and Mount Nebo so steep that my limousine broke down on the journey up the winding roads. My staff and I piled into the reserve vehicle to finish the climb. Waiting for me afterward in an old stone restaurant at the base of the mountain were a group of Jordanian women leaders. Before I left, I visited a girls' school and then the Jordan River Foundation, a special project of Queen Rania's to support women through microenterprise.

As we returned along the same flat desert highway to the airport, everything was routine. Then, a second later, it was not. The vehicles in my convoy swerved, evaded, and then accelerated. Something was very wrong. A rogue car had broken into my motorcade. In the seconds that followed, we did not know if it was a confused driver who had merely pulled out onto the road or if the people inside the vehicle knew that this was my convoy and that, in one of these vehicles, they would find me. Immediately an entire

Secret Service tactical team shouldered their guns and swarmed along the windows and back hatch of an accompanying Chevy Suburban, aiming their weapons and leaning out into the rushing air. Every cell phone signal was shut down. The fear was that a phone signal could be used to detonate a remotely controlled bomb or IED hidden inside the unknown car or pre-planted along the roads. The car was intercepted, and we continued on, racing to the airport at breakneck speed. I never knew from where or how, or why, that vehicle came. It was a stark reminder of the daily threats that hover over nearly everyone's lives in this part of the world.

A brief flight ferried me across the border and into Israel, to Tel Aviv. Hugging the coast of the Mediterranean, Tel Aviv is a city of glittering, modern buildings and some well-preserved old quarters, where it is still possible to imagine what life must have been like when this was a sleepy trading port centuries ago. From the air the lands of Jordan and Israel are a contrast of tightly massed towns and cities and vaster open spaces. We traveled the quick distance to Jerusalem, passing road signs for Bethlehem and Jericho. I was invited for tea with Gila Katsav, wife of the president of Israel. Israel is a beacon of democracy for the region and has had, since its founding out of the ashes of the Holocaust, a special relationship with the United States. It is one of America's staunchest allies, and the United States is in turn committed to Israel's survival.

Mrs. Katsav and Sheila Kurtzer, wife of the American ambassador, accompanied me to the Western Wall, one of the holiest places in Judaism, where the faithful come to pray. It is considered the sole remnant of the Holy Temple that was destroyed by the Romans, and religious and secular Jews make pilgrimages to this site. The original structures are attributed to King David; sections of the wall have stood on this spot since nineteen years before the birth of Christ, and their stones remain today. As is custom, I covered my head in a shawl and placed a tiny note in a narrow crevice in the limestone. On it was written a prayer for peace.

When I had arrived at the wall, there was a small group protesting for the release of Jonathan Pollard, the American civilian naval intelligence officer who pleaded guilty in 1986 to the charge of spying for Israel and was sentenced to life in prison. There were more confrontations to come.

On the hill above the Western Wall sit the Temple Mount and the Dome of the Rock, a shrine built by the Muslim conquerors of Jerusalem in 692. Its shiny gold-leaf dome reaches to the sky, and its ornate walkway of columns and mosaic art envelop the worn contours of an ancient, holy stone where the prophet Mohammed is believed to have ascended to Heaven and where the Jewish patriarch Abraham prepared to sacrifice his son Isaac. It is one of the most revered sites in the Islamic world. A visit to the Temple Mount by Ariel Sharon, when he was a candidate for Israeli prime minister in 2000, triggered a call for mass riots by the Palestinians' Hamas and Fatah organizations and formed the pretext for the Second Intifada or Palestinian uprising. Israeli police and officials, and even officials from the Palestinian Authority, are no longer permitted on the site; few non-Muslims routinely enter.

Both the dome and the Western Wall are holy places and always crowded with pilgrims. It had been decided that I would make the brief walk from the entrance to the Temple Mount to the dome itself, although in the crowds, people were pushing to get a glimpse of me. A few were worshipers who did not want me at the site, but the vast majority were paparazzi and members of the foreign press who wanted to call out questions and shoot photos. I had my Secret Service detail, but, seeing the mounting media frenzy, the Israeli security forces formed a ring around us. The security personnel brushed away anyone who came too close. Though the Israelis were not welcome beyond the gate leading to the dome, they would not allow me to enter without additional protection. I was not afraid, my Arab hosts were not afraid, but Suzanne Malveaux of CNN, who was accompanying me on the trip, was totally unnerved. In her televised report, a sixty-second walk looked like a major confrontation. The next morning she asked me if the president had been alarmed when he saw what happened. "Yes, Suzanne," I replied, "but only after he saw your report, on television."

I toured the beautiful holy site, which is managed by a special Muslim trust, and then drove to the ancient city of Jericho, upon whose walls Joshua's trumpets blew. Inside this Arab city, a sadly desolate place compared to the bustle of Jerusalem, I met with a group of Palestinian women. Afterward, I stopped to see one of the treasures of the Judean desert: Hisham's Palace, built in 724 by the Caliph Hisham, who ruled an empire that stretched from India to the Pyrenees. Although the palace had been damaged by an earthquake, the floor of the reception hall remained untouched. It is inlaid with the beautiful Tree of Life mosaic, depicting a pomegranate tree under which are gathered lions and gazelles. The gazelles are the visitors, coming to pay their respects and show their good wishes to the kingdom. But on the right is one gazelle that wishes the ruler harm, and so is savaged by a lion determined to protect his domain and take revenge. It was no accident that the mosaic graced a formal state receiving room. Perhaps diplomacy has changed little in thirteen centuries.

At day's end we traveled back to Jerusalem, to Yad Vashem, the Israeli memorial to the Holocaust. I had visited the memorial before, in 1998, when Barbara was spending a semester abroad in Rome. George, Jenna, and I had spent Thanksgiving with her, and then George and I had gone on to visit Israel with a group of American Jews and Christians. One was a man named David Flaum, the child of Holocaust survivors who had come to the United States. His older brother and sister, born in Europe, had perished at the hands of the Nazis. Worn by years of suffering, David's mother had died when he was still young. As we entered the area that commemorates the children killed in the Holocaust, David broke down. Together George, David, and I gazed upon the lights of thousands of tiny candles, each one reflecting its image into a mirror until the reflections stretch out toward infinity. Every light represents a child lost, a living, breathing child who is no more, like the brother and the sister whom David had never known.

For a first lady, there are moments of maximum political controversy, and they often strike without warning. Mine was to come the next morning, just after we visited the Church of the Resurrection in Abu Ghosh, an Arab-Israeli town. The nuns and monks sang Psalm 150 in Hebrew, a beautiful display of voice and faith. Indeed, here in this peaceful spot, it seemed that all faiths might exist together in peace. A couple of hours later, I arrived at the Ittihadiyya Palace on the outskirts of Cairo to call on Suzanne Mubarak, first lady of Egypt. Suzanne is close to my mother-in-law. In one of my albums, I have the official vice presidential photo of Bar showing Suzanne Jenna and Barbara's first real baby pictures, taken just a few weeks after they were born.

I had arrived two days before a nationwide referendum on future presidential elections. I had known that elections were scheduled, but in weeks of staff meetings and in my National Security Council briefing for the trip, no one had mentioned that my visit would be so close to the referendum vote. Egypt is an important U.S. ally, but it also jails political opponents. I had walked, unprepared, into a potential minefield. In retrospect, it was probably one of the worst possible times for me to be in Egypt. Right away the Egyptian and American press asked me about the upcoming vote. And while I had reams of official talking points on educational programs and compliments about cultural sites, such as the pyramids and the library at Alexandria, no one had thought to include a detailed briefing paper on current political issues in the country. I answered that holding elections was a "bold step" toward democracy, but both the referendum and the actual presidential elections that followed were later criticized as insufficiently democratic for not allowing a full slate of opposition candidates to participate. Days after I left, protesters against the May referendum were beaten in the streets. And when one of Egypt's leading opposition figures, Ayman Nour, who was jailed early in 2005, strongly petitioned for a "rerun" of the presidential vote, the election commission denied his request.

I imagine that people at the NSC thought the first lady was going abroad to do cultural events and ladies' things and assumed that I would never be asked about politics. After all, I was taping an episode of Egypt's version of *Sesame Street, Alam Simsim,* and visiting the Egyptian Muppet version of the grocery shop, the house and carpentry workshop, the invention corner, and the garden and library. But we had selected that event in part because 85 percent of Egypt's preschoolers and 54 percent of their mothers watch *Alam Simsim.* An appearance there had the potential to reach more ordinary citizens than high-level summitry. Yet while I might have been better prepared, the fact is that, for all first ladies, improvisation comes with the terrain.

After the television taping, Suzanne Mubarak hosted a lunch in my honor and then we toured Abu Sir, one of Egypt's thousand "girl-friendly schools," dedicated to girls and built in 2003 in the shadow of the pyramids. From there we saw the pyramids themselves. With the press in tow,

I was in the middle of a tour with Dr. Zahi Hawass, who directs the Giza pyramids excavation. He was preparing to unveil a new discovery when Jim VandeHei, then a political reporter for *The Washington Post*, elbowed his way to the front of the press pool, climbed onto the pyramid plateau, and began shouting out questions about the Egyptian referendum and Hosni Mubarak's political and election plans. Dr. Hawass appeared dismayed and completely taken aback to have this outburst happen in the middle of Egypt's premier historical site. It was a violation of protocol, and as far as the Egyptian antiquity experts were concerned, Jim VandeHei was part of the U.S. delegation. Sometimes members of the press forget that they are not seen as independent entities abroad. I quietly apologized, knowing that this incident would not be attributed to an individual reporter or *The Washington Post*; it would be blamed on me and, by extension, on George.

My first solo trip to the Middle East had been a series of land mines. The Saudi walkout during my World Economic Forum speech seemed positively mild by the time I boarded the plane to return home. But these moments were fleeting, while the region's problems were far more intractable. My meetings with Israeli and Palestinian women were vivid confirmations of the often deep distrust that exists among some on both sides. When I sat down with the Israeli women, they spoke of the horrid things said about Jews in Arab textbooks. When I sat down with Palestinian women, they lamented the security barrier that Israel was constructing along the West Bank, and how it made their lives more difficult. Each time, in their words, there was a quality of "if only." If only they would change their textbooks, if only they would take down the barrier, then we would get along. There were so many if onlys.

From my first encounter with the British tabloids, when I was dubbed a "cowgirl," I was fascinated to discover what parts of American culture struck a chord overseas and how other countries saw us. But I never imagined that one innocent speech I gave on a Saturday night in a hotel in Washington, D.C., would have such a lasting impact abroad. It was April 30, 2005, the night of the annual White House Correspondents' Association dinner. The correspondents' dinner is the culmination of a

Washington ritual of roasting the president. It begins with the Alfalfa Club in January and continues through the late winter and early spring with the Gridiron Club, the White House News Photographers Association, and the Radio and Television Correspondents' Association, all building up to the crescendo: the correspondents' dinner, some three thousand people gathered in black tie in the basement ballroom at the Washington Hilton hotel. There, beneath a white cutout ceiling that looks as if it spent its previous life on the set of *Star Trek*, the president sits and listens while comedians and members of the press crack barbed jokes about him. Then the president is expected to give his own humorous speech. As George put it, "People make fun of the president and then it is the president's turn to get up and make fun of himself." The evening's purpose is to honor members of the White House Press Corps, but news organizations also try to fill their tables with celebrities, the famous and the infamous, from all walks of life, and the evening may be the closest thing Washington, D.C., has to a glitzy Hollywood party.

That night, as George began his speech, I quickly interrupted him. "Not that old joke, not again," I said. "I've been attending these dinners for years and just quietly sitting here. I've got a few things I want to say for a change.

"George always says he's delighted to come to these press dinners. Baloney. He's usually in bed by now. I'm not kidding. I said to him the other day, 'George, if you really want to end tyranny in the world, you're going to have to stay up later.'" I had been close to petrified when I started, but by now the room was convulsed with laughter. I moved on to my *Desperate Housewives* bit. "Here's our typical evening: Nine o'clock, Mr. Excitement here is sound asleep, and I'm watching *Desperate Housewives*—with Lynne Cheney. Ladies and gentlemen, I am a desperate housewife. I mean, if those women on that show think they're desperate, they ought to be with George." I ended my comedic stand-up career by comparing George's penchant for brush clearing to *The Texas Chainsaw Massacre* and my mother-in-law to *The Godfather*'s Don Corleone. The speech got a standing ovation, but my last lines were serious. "So in the future, when you see me just quietly sitting up here, I want you to know that I'm happy to be here for a reason—I love and enjoy being with the man who usually speaks to you on these occasions."

Around the world that last sentence was left out, and for years people from Europe, Africa, Asia, South America, and the Middle East couldn't imagine why I would publicly go onstage and rib my husband. The whole concept of "roasting" a president or other prominent figure is particularly American and can be hard for other cultures to grasp. In hushed voices, foreign leaders or their spouses would ask me, "Are you really a desperate housewife?"

On July 7, just after the G8 leaders arrived in Gleneagles, Scotland, for their summit, four coordinated bomb blasts were detonated in London's subway and bus system during rush hour, killing fifty-two and injuring seven hundred. The bombings were carried out by Islamic extremists. Only twenty-four hours before, Tony and Cherie Blair had arrived in Scotland to the triumphant news that London had won the 2012 Olympics. Their elation was swiftly replaced by grief. George and I could so well understand the horror of seeing ordinary citizens attacked and murdered as they went about their daily working lives. The summit continued, but Tony immediately raced to London. The blasts overshadowed one of his central goals for the G8 meeting, persuading the world's industrialized nations to forgive the often crippling developing world debt. The problems of debt were particularly acute in sub-Saharan Africa.

George and I had traveled to the African continent twice, once when his father was president and again in 2003, to the west coast nation of Senegal and the continent's southern tip, South Africa and Botswana, then to Uganda in the east and Nigeria along the western coast. In Senegal, under a blistering sun and amid blinding white sands, we walked with Condi Rice and Colin Powell to the infamous slave fortress on the island of Gorée and imagined the routes that had carried their families to our shores.

The fortress is a dark and isolated place, sitting on a cliff with the waves breaking below, and its very darkness and dampness are testament to the mournful horror of what occurred inside and outside its walls. Together George and I stepped through the Door of No Return, from which captured Africans were herded on board slave ships bound for the Atlantic's deep waters. We stood in silence, as we had at other memorial sites and battlefields both in the United States and abroad. I had no desire to talk;

I remained in solemn contemplation, knowing what had happened to the people who walked through this door and the doors of other coastal fortresses. I wanted to honor the lives of the men, women, and children who had been held here and those who had survived the horrific journey aboard a slave ship only to arrive on docks in the New World and be sold at auction.

This summer, I was returning to the continent with a cautious bit of hope. In 2003, at his State of the Union address, two years before sub-Saharan Africa became a central G8 cause, George had proposed a $15 billion U.S. initiative to combat the overwhelming devastation of AIDS around the world, particularly in Africa. Called PEPFAR, the President's Emergency Plan for AIDS Relief, it focused on cutting transmission rates between mothers and children, lowering the rate of new infection among youth and adults, and putting those who were infected on antiretrovirals, with which they could often lead nearly full lives. PEPFAR also devoted resources to caring for the vast numbers of AIDS orphans. The fifteen focus countries targeted by the plan had 50 percent of all AIDS infections around the world.

Many African nations, like South Africa, have lost vast portions of their populations, including much of their middle class and their workforce, to AIDS. They were economically devastated and coping with massive human suffering. The tragedy was compounded by the fact that for well over a decade, people across the African continent were not being tested for AIDS. A positive test was a death sentence because there were almost no medicines available in these nations to treat or manage AIDS. Infected men and women continued to spread the disease. But now having treatment available meant that getting an AIDS test was no longer the equivalent of learning you were going to die. Helping to halt the spread of HIV/AIDS and to care for the sick would have a transformative effect on the continent as a whole. In July of 2005 I was going to see PEPFAR's early results.

I was thrilled to have Jenna traveling with me. Barbara had accompanied George and me on that first trip in 2003, and afterward, so moved by what she had seen and so proud of her dad's role in helping to combat HIV, she enrolled in Yale's comprehensive survey course on AIDS.

Meeting with Afghan president Hamid Karzai at the Presidential Palace. (Susan Sterner/ White House photo)

Holding up a kaleidoscope for an Afghan child on the streets of Kabul in March of 2005. (Susan Sterner/ White House photo)

On board a U.S. military helicopter in the skies over Kabul, Afghanistan. (Susan Sterner/White House photo)

Dinner with U.S. troops and commanders at the Dragon Chow Dining Hall at Bagram Air Base. (Susan Sterner/White House photo)

A visit to Homeboy
Industries, which works
with twelve thousand
young people from
L.A. gangs each year.
(Krisanne Johnson/
White House photo)

At a Rwanda church,
Jenna and I hold
feverish HIV-infected
children on our laps.
(Krisanne Johnson/
White House photo)

With Jenna, Cherie
Blair, and Jeannette
Kagame at a memorial
for the victims of
Rwanda's genocide.
(Krisanne Johnson/
White House photo)

Serving meals to victims of Hurricane Katrina in Lafayette, Louisiana.
(Krisanne Johnson/White House photo)

Listening to the stories of families who had escaped the storm.
(Krisanne Johnson/White House photo)

Hugging a child in Mississippi. In many towns, there were only piles of debris.
(Krisanne Johnson/White House photo)

Building a new home in Louisiana. By August 2008, the New Orleans metro area had reached 87 percent of its original population.
(Eric Draper/White House photo)

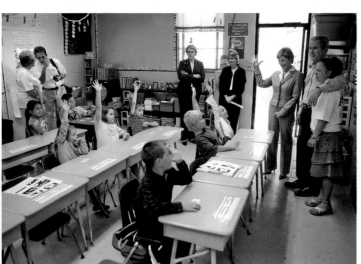

The reopening of Delisle Elementary School in Pass Christian, Mississippi, October 2005.
(Eric Draper/White House photo)

Thanking our troops at Bagram Air Base in Kabul in March of 2006.
(Eric Draper/White House photo)

HIV-positive mothers from South Africa's Mothers2Mothers program visit me in the White House.
(Kimberlee Hewitt/ White House photo)

The wonderful pomp and circumstance of a state dinner for Queen Elizabeth II and Prince Philip, April 2007. (Joyce Boghosian/White House photo)

Our annual National Park hike in New England, with Jane Ann, Marge, Peggy, me, and Regan. Those unhurried days of friendship renewed me, body and soul. (Peggy Weiss)

With the Dalai Lama in the White House residence.
(Eric Draper/White House photo)

Meeting with breast cancer survivors in the Pink Majlis, the Pink Tent, in Abu Dhabi, October 2007. (Shealah Craighead/White House photo)

Riding a camel through the ancient Jordanian city of Petra.
(Shealah Craighead/White House photo)

Pope Benedict XVI came to visit us at the White House on his birthday, and we surprised him with a cake, April 2008. (David Bohrer/White House photo)

A bird's-eye view of the annual Congressional Picnic. (Grant Miller/White House photo)

Jenna married Henry Hager, whom she met during George's 2004 campaign, at dusk by the little lake on our ranch. (Paul Morse)

En route to the Mae La Burmese refugee camp with Barbara in an Air Force cargo transport plane in August of 2008. (Shealah Craighead/ White House photo)

Showing a Burmese family their first digital photo. (Shealah Craighead/ White House photo)

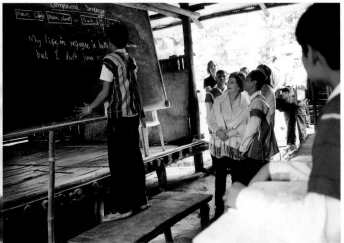

A Burmese boy writes a message to me on a blackboard in his classroom: "My life in refugee is better than Burma, but I don't have opportunity to out outside." (Shealah Craighead/ White House photo)

Cheering on our athletes at the 2008 Summer Olympics.
(Eric Draper/White House photo)

A private moment with George.
We are anchored to each other.
(Paul Morse/White House photo)

Home to Texas, January 2009.
(Eric Draper/White House photo)

She was now living in Cape Town, South Africa, and working at the Red Cross War Memorial Children's Hospital, which treated AIDS patients and other sufferers. South Africa was to be our first stop.

The press pool included Ann Curry from NBC's *Today* show, who was making her first visit to the continent and would later tell me that this trip changed her life.

Africa as a continent is life-changing. In so many places, the scenery is beautiful beyond description and the wildlife a marvel of creation. Barbara, who loved her little cat, India, with all her heart, once told me, "The existence of cats proves that there must be a Heavenly Creator," and indeed to look at lions and tigers in their full majesty is to glimpse some of that splendor. Barbara and Jenna and I were mesmerized as we drove through the Madikwe Game Reserve in South Africa, amid the lions, elephants, and warthogs, accompanied by a cacophony of hundreds of birds. But too often, mere steps from this striking beauty are poverty beyond imagination and tremendous human suffering. In that Cape Town hospital, Barbara held tiny babies as they struggled with the ravages of AIDS. About 70 percent of the globe's AIDS patients live in Africa.

I saw the reality of those numbers for myself when Jenna and I drove to the Khayelitsha township, where the streets were little more than packed dust and the houses woven together from strips of tar paper and tin. The bathrooms are a line of Porta-Potties strung along the edge of the township, and the walk to them is fraught with peril. Almost daily, women are raped and abused. I had come to meet mothers with AIDS, part of a special Mothers2Mothers program founded in 2001 by a California doctor, Mitchell Besser, along with Robin Smalley. Pregnant women are encouraged to come to the health center to be tested for HIV. If they test positive, they start treatments with antiretrovirals, to help prevent the AIDS virus from being transmitted to their babies. Each month 28 percent of the four hundred mothers who delivered children in the clinic were HIV-positive, but less than 5 percent of the babies born had the virus. Most of these women not only are sick with HIV/AIDS but live in cold, tiny shacks, without plumbing or electricity. They cannot see at night, and what little water they have must be stored in buckets or bowls.

Mothers2Mothers also counsels pregnant women and trains HIV-positive mothers to mentor and work with new groups of expectant mothers. In addition to paying these trained counselors, the program provides an opportunity for the women in the township to make and sell beadwork. After this visit, my staff wore their White House credentials on brightly colored Mothers2Mothers beaded lanyards.

In the clinic a small group of women, many with babies balanced on their laps, called me Grand Mama Laura and told me their stories. I held their hands as these mothers told me of how they had been disowned by their own mothers when they revealed that they had AIDS. Some women's entire families had barred them from returning home. A woman named Babalwa told me that she had tested positive for HIV when she was thirty-four weeks pregnant. She called her husband. "He thought I was lying," she recalled, "so he went to get tested himself and was positive." Her voice caught as she explained, "My life before was so violent and he was beating me and not sleeping at home and this was the result. Because he was ashamed of what had happened, he pulled himself up and we started to build up a new life for us."

Babalwa told me of accompanying another pregnant mother to her home to tell her family that she had tested HIV-positive. "When I went to her family house, there were five brothers and sisters and a mother." The young woman announced that she had tested positive. Everyone sat, shocked and quiet. Then the woman's brother stood and said, "You are not alone. I am also HIV-positive." One by one, every sibling in that room, all six children, stood up and told their mother and their brothers and sisters that they too had tested positive for HIV/AIDS. Babalwa ended with a plea "that we don't have more orphans who are losing their parents. We need more mothers staying alive to take care of their babies. We don't want any more HIV-positive babies." I thought of Barbara, holding those little babies as they fought for life.

I hugged the mothers, and I left with tears in my eyes. "Please," I said, "come and visit me in the White House." When I returned to the United States, we began making the arrangements, and they arrived in the winter of 2006. There Babalwa told me, "Dr. Mitch is our father, Robs is our mother, and we want Mrs. Bush to be our grandmother."

The stigma of AIDS cuts wide and deep across South Africa, which in 2005 had more people infected with the disease than any other nation in the world. Talking frankly about AIDS in South Africa requires talking about sexual abuse of women and infidelity, which is rampant. Men who leave their families to find work in other cities may take up with new girlfriends. Historically, women who were the victims of sexual violence and abuse have had few legal protections; Babalwa could do nothing when her husband struck her. I told the women I met, "Ending domestic violence, rape, and sexual abuse is also essential to fighting the spread of HIV/AIDS." I hoped that if I, as an American first lady, discussed those issues openly, many of them would feel less afraid to do so as well.

From South Africa, I flew to Tanzania, where, with Mrs. Anna Mkapa, the first lady of Tanzania, I visited two Catholic-run organizations working to provide AIDS prevention and care. I then traveled to a concrete-block-and-tin-roof school on the Muslim-majority island of Zanzibar, where I was joined by Zanzibar's first lady, Mrs. Shadya Karume. The school was built with seed money from the United States, replacing the mud-and-thatched-roof hut that had been the students' prior classroom. Public and private American aid had financed the construction of sixteen schools, and public and private American funds had purchased twenty thousand books for children to read. Before I departed, President and Mrs. Karume presented me with a beautiful chest filled with exotic spices, recalling Zanzibar's storied past as a fabled destination for early Western spice traders.

The final stop on my trip was Rwanda, scene of the horrific 1994 genocide, in which some 800,000 Tutsis and moderate Hutus were shot and hacked to death by rampaging Hutu militias. Many women who survived the massacres were raped; many contracted AIDS. It is hard to envision the rivers of blood that must have run across the red, dusty hills that rise up like walls around Kigali, the capital.

Waiting for me on the tarmac was Cherie Blair. For months we had planned to travel together to Africa after Gleneagles. Her work as a human rights lawyer had made her uniquely passionate about the efforts of Rwanda to come to terms with its genocide and to try the perpetrators, both in international tribunals and in local Gacaca courts, based partly on tribal customs and also on the Truth and Reconciliation Commission that South Africa had adopted after apartheid. (There was no way to try the vast numbers of perpetrators in international courts.) The Gacaca courts gave the victims the chance to confront those who had slaughtered their families and offered an opportunity for all to begin the extraordinarily difficult process of making amends.

Great Britain had invested millions of pounds per year in helping to redevelop Rwanda. The British government initially balked at covering the costs of Cherie's trip because she had no official title. She flew on a commercial jet, with one staffer and a lone protection officer—the British government had rejected my offer to take her on my plane. At the airport, she rode in the back of the British ambassador's Range Rover as it fell in behind my motorcade.

Our first stop was the Kigali Memorial Center, where we laid a wreath at one of the mass tombs; 250,000 Rwandans are buried in the soft, rain-drenched earth on the memorial's grounds. Inside were rooms containing unvarnished stories of human brutality. Babies and toddlers had been held upside down by their legs as their heads were cracked against walls, ridding the nation of the Tutsi "cockroaches," as the propagandists called them. Cherie and I stood, looking at the photos of children who died and reading the heartbreaking inscriptions underneath each image: "He loved ice cream." "She loved Daddy."

At the FAWE Girls' School the next day, Jenna and I listened as young Rwandan girls told us about their lives. After their presentations, one teacher asked his students, "Now, do you have any questions for Mrs. Bush?" A lone girl shyly raised her hand. "What did you do in the United States after the Civil War?" She was hoping to find an answer to her future in our own blood-soaked past. I told her about our president, Abraham Lincoln, who had wanted a healing rather than a punitive peace at the war's end. I told her of his dream that the two sides would reunite as one whole nation.

Some of the most pioneering humanitarian work in Africa is being done by American religious institutions. A special project of the organization World Relief encourages local ministers to be tested for AIDS and to share the results with their congregations. Inside a circular church with rough wooden benches, a concrete floor, and simple cream walls, Jenna and I held feverish small children with HIV on our laps as a Rwandan minister preached to the congregation. Just that year he had announced to his worshipers that he'd tested positive for HIV/AIDS. By speaking openly about his disease, he was hoping to help break the stigma and to convince them to be tested as well.

The toll from AIDS is enormous, but the numbers cannot capture the consequences. One in particular is orphan children running their own households. In Rwanda I met a girl named Tatu, who had lost her father to genocide when she was only two; her mother had died of AIDS when she was eleven. Now twelve, she was caring for three small half brothers, ages eight, six, and three. She had been abandoned a third time by an older brother, who after their mother's death had returned to the family house, sold it, and disappeared with the money. Tatu had dropped out of school to work and was hawking fruit at a market stand to provide for her younger siblings. She sobbed as she spoke, and I took her into my arms. American church groups were building a home for her and her young brothers.

Rwanda is, of necessity, a society of women. In the genocide, hundreds of thousands of men were killed. By 2005, women held nearly 50 percent of all the seats in the National Assembly. Before we left, Cherie and I, accompanied by Kay Warren, wife of Reverend Rick Warren, whose Saddleback Church has been active in Rwanda, attended a dinner hosted by Jeannette Kagame, Rwanda's first lady, who had been born in a Rwandan refugee camp in the Republic of Burundi and who had herself fought as a Tutsi soldier. Seated with us, amid candlelight, overflowing flower vases, and white linen tablecloths, were some of Rwanda's most prominent women. The ministers of justice, the environment, education, labor, and economic planning, as well as the head of the National AIDS Control Commission and female senators and parliamentarians, were all in attendance. At my table were leading government ministers. We talked about the many challenges facing Rwanda. At one point, I asked a simple question: How many of you have had malaria? Malaria is a debilitating and even fatal disease carried by the bites of mosquitoes: the United States eradicated it from its swamps and marshlands decades ago. Each of the Rwandan women seated at the table answered, "Yes, of course I've had malaria." All of them had been bitten, had fallen ill, and could have died.

I have been changed by Africa on each visit, in large measure because of the tremendous hope I have seen among its people in the midst of overwhelming despair. When George and I returned in 2008, we traveled again to Rwanda, where we stopped at a school for teenagers. Some were orphans who had lost a parent to AIDS or to genocide. As we left the school, we saw a group of teenagers waiting outside to greet us. One had a sign, "God is Good." George nodded and said, "God *is* good." And these teenage children replied, in unison, "All the time." To suffer as they have suffered, with genocide, disease, and poverty, and to still believe "God is good. All the time"!

"I Told You
I Would Come"

Greeting Governor Habiba Sarabi, Bamiyan Province,
Afghanistan. (Shealah Craighead/White House photo)

On Tuesday, August 23, 2005, a cluster of rain and thunderstorm clouds coalesced over the Bahamas into what the National Weather Service named Tropical Depression Twelve. The next day the depression became a storm, with winds above forty miles per hour. It was the eleventh tropical storm of the 2005 season, and the weather service christened it Katrina. Within twenty-four hours, Katrina was upgraded to a Category 1 hurricane, and forecasters predicted that it would make landfall in Florida, then turn toward the Alabama-Florida panhandle. At 6:30 that night, August 25, Katrina arrived at the Dade and Broward county lines. Its winds were eighty miles per hour, its rainfall up to sixteen inches. Three people drowned as the storm hit; three others were killed by falling trees. More than 1.4 million homes and businesses lost power. Unsure of where Katrina would head next, the Federal Emergency Management Agency began positioning ice, water, and food at logistics centers in Alabama, Louisiana, Georgia, Texas, and South Carolina. Within three days the federal government would have finished the largest prepositioning of emergency assets in its history. But still, forecasters could not say with certainty where the hurricane would turn.

Katrina passed over Florida and then reached the Gulf of Mexico, but instead of heading north, it drifted west, its winds and rains growing stronger over the warm, late summer waters of the gulf. At the end of the afternoon on August 26, weather forecasters began predicting a new path, saying that the storm would now make landfall in the Mississippi-Louisiana region. They also predicted that it would be a Category 4 or 5 storm. A Category 5 is considered a catastrophic storm, with winds in excess of 155 miles per hour. It can produce, as weather scientists clinically put it, "complete building failure" in its immediate path. There are only three Category 5 storms ever recorded in the United States; one of the worst was Hurricane Camille in 1969. When it came ashore in Mississippi, it caused a twenty-four-foot storm tide, about one-quarter the height of the 2004 Indian Ocean tsunami.

At five in the afternoon on Saturday, August 27, New Orleans mayor Ray Nagin called for a voluntary evacuation of the city. Early on August 28, Katrina officially became a Category 5 storm.

George and I were at the ranch for a late-summer break. Inside the secure federal trailers on the property, White House staff members, including Joe Hagin, deputy chief of staff for operations, were monitoring the storm around the clock. The National Hurricane Center began issuing advisories warning that the levees in New Orleans could be "overtopped" by Lake Pontchartrain and "significant destruction" would likely be experienced far from the hurricane's center. In the morning of August 28, George began calling the governor of Louisiana, Kathleen Blanco; the governor of Mississippi, Haley Barbour; and Michael Brown, the head of FEMA. When he reached Kathleen Blanco, at 9:14, he told her that she needed to issue a mandatory evacuation order for New Orleans. She responded that she did not think everyone could get out in time.

But by 9:30, Governor Blanco had heeded George's advice; along with Mayor Nagin she did issue a mandatory evacuation call, the first ever in New Orleans's history. Residents now had only hours to leave. By nightfall, heavy rains and high winds began to lash the Gulf Coast. At 6:10 A.M. on Monday, August 29, Katrina made landfall in Plaquemines Parish, Louisiana, a peninsula that juts out into the Gulf of Mexico. It arrived as a Category 3 storm with sustained winds of 115 miles per hour and gusts of 130 miles per hour. Katrina sliced through Plaquemines with a twenty-foot storm surge, killing nine people. It continued northeast, clipping the eastern edge of the giant Lake Pontchartrain and St. Bernard and Orleans parishes, along the Mississippi border. Its main track was now over Mississippi, and after it made landfall, its force began to weaken. By 1:00 P.M. Monday, Katrina had dropped to a Category 1 storm; by 7:00 P.M., it was downgraded to a tropical storm. And it had passed east of New Orleans. But the damage was done.

The Gulf Coast storm surge had been as high as twenty-seven feet. Flooding extended six miles inland and up to twenty-three miles along rivers and bays. But all day Monday, the first reports George and the

White House received from the Department of Homeland Security and the Department of Defense and Army Corps of Engineers were that New Orleans's levees had held. When Deputy Chief of Staff Joe Hagin asked Governor Blanco for an update on the status of the levees during an 11:00 A.M. conference call, she told him her information was that New Orleans's levees had not been breached. Instead, she reported, the main floodwaters were engulfing another, smaller parish to the east. Not until after midnight, early on Tuesday morning, nearly eighteen hours after the hurricane had swept through, did the Department of Homeland Security report widespread breaches and flooding to the White House. New Orleans's levees and floodwalls gave way; pumping stations that had lost electricity stopped working. Up to 80 percent of the city was filled with water that in low-lying sections was as much as twenty feet deep. First responders could not reach the city, but prepositioned Coast Guard units immediately swung into action. Over several days the Coast Guard rescued and evacuated more than 33,000 people. The first of their teams began searching for survivors just hours after Katrina came ashore.

On Wednesday morning, the day after we received word that the levees had broken, George returned to Washington. He decided against landing in Louisiana or Mississippi but flew over the devastated region instead. His decision was, on a much larger scale, the same one I had made not to go to Afghanistan in 2002, 2003, or 2004. Whenever a president, or even the first lady, travels, a huge infrastructure of personnel accompanies him or her. And there is another huge infrastructure waiting on the ground. In Afghanistan I had not wanted to use military assets, like helicopters, when they might be needed on the battlefield. With people still trapped in their flooded homes and thousands not yet evacuated from the Superdome, George did not want a single police officer or National Guard unit or any other type of first response team to be diverted from the rescue efforts to assist with a presidential visit. He had visited Ground Zero in New York on September 14, only when he knew that it was highly unlikely anyone else could or would be found alive. He did not want one single life to be lost because someone was catering to the logistical requirements of a president. He did not want his convoy of vehicles to block trucks delivering water or food or medical supplies, or to impede National Guardsmen from around the nation who were arriving to help.

By Friday, September 2, nearly twenty-two thousand National Guard soldiers and airmen had reached the region. Sixty-five hundred troops were in New Orleans alone. Over fifty thousand guardsmen and -women from all fifty states, as well as U.S. territories and the District of Columbia, would ultimately assist along the Gulf Coast. That morning George traveled first to Mobile, Alabama, and then to two of the most devastated cities, Biloxi, Mississippi, and New Orleans. I flew to Lafayette, Louisiana, to see some of the six thousand people who had fled New Orleans and surrounding towns and were now huddled in the Cajundome.

Already, people from across the country had arrived to help. As soon as the storm hit on Sunday night and Monday morning, Red Cross volunteers, many of them retirees, had begun driving from Iowa and other states to Louisiana and Mississippi, prepared to live out of their cars if necessary. By the end of the week, thousands of men and women from the Southern Baptist Convention began to arrive. The Southern Baptist Convention has the third largest disaster relief organization in the United States, after the Red Cross and the Salvation Army. Like many Red Cross volunteers, with whom they often partner, the Baptists rolled out sleeping bags and unfurled hard cots inside local churches. When one team of sixty first arrived, the only dry and empty place they could find to stay was a local jail. For weeks these volunteers cooked thousands of meals each day, sometimes on generators that they had hauled themselves in the backs of trucks. When they could, they used donated food from Walmart and Subway, but knowing supplies would be tight, they also brought their own. A single team of Baptist men and women from Oklahoma cooked sixteen thousand meals a day in Louisiana. Other sites routinely made ten thousand hot lunches and dinners. Red Cross volunteers helped distribute this food and also began gathering clothes for families who had lost everything.

Inside Lafayette's Cajundome, 137 miles west of New Orleans, many Katrina victims had been separated from friends and family; in some cases, mothers could not find their toddler children. And in these early days, they did not know if they would ever see their loved ones again. I served up plates of jambalaya and sat with elderly men and women who were struggling with the thought of a lifetime of memories having vanished and who were stunned by the prospect of having to start over again.

Sixty miles away, in Baton Rouge, I visited Acadian Ambulance, an ambulance service that covers a wide swath of Louisiana and Mississippi. Because it was in Baton Rouge, Acadian's communications facilities had not been knocked out by the storm or the flooding. When patients were left stranded, and state and city officials had either disappeared from New Orleans or were completely unreachable by e-mail or phone, Acadian and its volunteers almost single-handedly evacuated hospitals and spent days treating the sick and injured at the packed Superdome. The company, helped by spouses and siblings of its employees, located more than forty military and out-of-state helicopters, as well as 150 ambulances from other parts of the country, to transport critically ill patients, some of whom exhausted doctors were keeping alive by manually squeezing oxygen into their lungs. They packed newborn babies into cardboard boxes to fit more of them inside the helicopters. With their satellite telephones, a mobile antenna, a portable generator, and incredible determination, Acadian employees and volunteers saved hundreds, if not thousands, of lives. I wanted to thank Richard Zuschlag, the chief of Acadian Ambulance, and his team, who had done what some professional city, state, and federal disaster management officials had failed to do: help people and save lives in some of the most horrific conditions imaginable.

On Sunday, George and I traveled to the American Red Cross National Headquarters in Washington, D.C., to ask for donations of blood and for volunteers. On Monday, I returned with George to Baton Rouge, Louisiana, for a briefing on the emergency operations and then visited with more evacuees at the Bethany World Prayer Center. In total, after Katrina, I made twenty-three visits to Louisiana and the Gulf Coast; the first year, I traveled there nearly every month.

At the Bethany Prayer Center, I sat on the ground with children, and I saw in their eyes the same devastation that I had seen in New York after 9-11. For the kids in New York, the fears were loud noises, traveling on planes, or riding in the subway. Here, the fear was of water. Some children were terrified of getting in a bath, or even of the sound of the tap running. I heard stories about people who had driven out just as the storm hit, people in pickup trucks who had been caught in the flood surge and spent a day or a night trapped inside, with water up to their doors. And in the chaos, thousands were still missing.

In tragedies there are heroes, and Hurricane Katrina produced a tremendous share, from the volunteers who came not just in the first weeks but also in the first years. They helped build new homes and fed and clothed the displaced. There were the heroic Coast Guard rescuers who had maneuvered boats and helicopters to pick people off of rooftops as the floodwaters engulfed their homes, and the National Guard troops and airmen who saved lives and brought order and relief, as well as the volunteer medics and ambulance crews. But there was also a group of retired law enforcement officers, including former sheriffs and former Secret Service agents, who volunteered to find the missing. They were activated as part of a special project run by the National Center for Missing and Exploited Children in Alexandria, Virginia. On September 5, the center opened a Katrina missing persons hotline. It processed over eleven thousand calls in its first nine days of operation. Five thousand eighty-eight children were reported missing; by September 15, the retired lawmen had resolved 701 cases.

One reason there were so many missing kids was that when evacuation boats and helicopters arrived, there were often only a few seats left. Without hesitation, parents and grandparents said, "Take the children." But frequently families were evacuated to different centers, even different states. One child who was plucked from the top of a New Orleans apartment building amid the floodwaters was two-year-old Gabrielle Alexander. But no one knew her name. She was evacuated to a children's center in Baton Rouge, where she would not speak a word. Volunteers from the National Center for Missing and Exploited Children traveled to Baton Rouge and photographed the children. Their pictures were repeatedly broadcast on television, particularly by CNN and CBS News. When a center volunteer knelt down to photograph Gabrielle, he turned the camera over to show her the digital image, hoping to get her to speak. She pointed at her picture and said, "Gabby." Now the volunteers had a name to put with a face. They began combing the lists of missing children and found an entry for a two-year-old Gabrielle Alexander. Her mother had been evacuated to San Antonio, Texas. After confirming with law enforcement that these were mother and child, the center arranged for a special Angel Flight to fly Gabby to her mom. They raced into each other's arms on the tarmac in San Antonio.

Within six months center volunteers located and reunited every missing child on the list with his or her family. The center volunteers came from around the country and worked, many of them, eighteen to twenty hours a day, because they had the skills to help. And they did it solely from the goodness of their hearts. The following spring, I had the center volunteers and some families that they had helped to reunite, including Gabby's, come to the White House to meet in person and to share their stories.

Other heroes were the teachers and the principals in schools throughout Louisiana, Mississippi, and Alabama. Many of them had lost everything. They were living in their cars or with relatives, yet from the first days after Katrina struck, they were back at their schools, using buckets to clear the mud from the floors and walls. I spoke with one teacher who had to throw out every book from her second-floor library; they were entirely mildewed by the time she reached the school. In Pass Christian and Southaven, Mississippi, and Chalmette, Louisiana, and New Orleans, I saw so many teachers who were stressed and weakened and, if not crying, on the verge of tears. They could cry with me when they could not at other moments or in other settings. The rest of the time, they were trying so very hard to be strong for their students, their schools, and their communities. And they knew that if parents had schools for their children to attend, they would be more likely to return home.

There were countless lessons to be learned. Katrina was in many ways the perfect storm; everything that could go wrong, did. There was virtually no communication on the ground. The New Orleans mayor had retreated to the Hyatt Regency hotel, where phone service was lost even before the storm hit. For three days his command center could not receive e-mails or incoming calls. The White House gave him a mobile phone on Friday, September 2, but he had to lean out a window to get a signal. Police officers in New Orleans didn't have cars; they broke into the local Cadillac dealership and drove off with whatever they could find. During the first few days, George and the White House repeatedly offered to send thousands of additional federal troops to stop the looting and violence in New Orleans, but Governor Blanco declined the offer because she wanted her office to be in charge, rather than the federal government. No one in a position of authority for emergency planning at the state or city level had envisioned anything like Katrina, and when it came, almost no one was prepared for the devastation.

Perhaps there was never any way to be fully prepared. The destruction was so huge, a near tsunami-size surge and violent storm covering an area larger than all of Great Britain. Over the next few years, when I landed in New Orleans and drove into the city, I would pass street after street where the houses were boarded up and marked with orange X's to show that they had been searched. Sometimes they had another code, a black circle, spray-painted alongside, to show that the body of a person or an animal had been found within the walls. The National Hurricane Center's official estimate is that, in Louisiana and Mississippi, fifteen hundred people died as a direct result of the Katrina storm.

When I landed in New Orleans on October 10, I saw packs of abandoned dogs running through the streets, barking and scavenging. Some eight hundred abandoned dogs and cats were rescued in a special airlift organized by Madeleine Pickens, wife of the oilman T. Boone Pickens. Volunteers located watermelon trucks to ferry the weak and dehydrated animals to the airport, where they were flown to shelters as far away as California. About 50 percent of the animals were reunited with their owners; the others, some whose owners could no longer care for them, were fostered and adopted. One New Orleans man spent seven days with his dog on the roof of his house, until he ran out of heart medication and had to be airlifted out of the city. The dog, Brutus, was transported to San Diego for care. A female volunteer at the San Diego animal control office located the hospital where the owner had been taken, but the man had been released. She began combing phone books and calling every number with the same last name, eventually finding the man's cousin. The owner was flown to San Diego for a tearful reunion with his dog—the reason he had spent seven days on his roof was that he had not wanted to abandon his pet. To this day, every two months a New Orleans animal shelter worker drives to San Diego with forty animals in need of adoption, in a custom van donated by Madeleine.

But as bad as New Orleans was, the devastation was often worse in other places along the Mississippi Gulf. In parts of Louisiana, houses had been flooded, perhaps moved slightly off their foundations, but inside something might be salvaged. In Mississippi, for miles on end, there was nothing but bare foundations. I drove through coastal towns where hundreds of gorgeous antebellum homes, houses that had withstood over 150 years of other storms, had been completely washed away. Blocks were empty except for the debris. Week after week I met young mayors in these towns; many of them had been in office only since January. Now their homes and stores were wiped out; there were no businesses, no economy. They were presiding over ghost towns. All knew that, no matter what, some residents would never return.

I visited with those who had lost their homes, and I came back as communities were rebuilt, as they opened schools or cut the ribbons on playgrounds. But I wanted to do more. In 2001 I had started, with the help of some very good friends, the Laura Bush Foundation for America's Libraries. Money was raised to provide small grants for school libraries around our country so that they could purchase books and research materials; many times these grants would double or triple a library's annual book budget. By May 2005, the Laura Bush Foundation had given grants to 428 school libraries nationwide.

I had already invited the foundation's fund-raisers for breakfast at the White House on September 24, 2005, the day of the National Book Festival, to thank them. That morning I asked them to continue to raise money, to be given only to schools along the Gulf Coast; a basic elementary school library book collection costs $50,000, a high school collection at least $100,000. My friends Bill Marriott, Marshall Payne, Ruth Altshuler, and Pam Willeford agreed. They raised and we have given nearly $6 million to rebuild the library collections of these devastated schools.

And the schools were devastated. In January of 2006, I visited Chalmette High in St. Bernard Parish, which had been used as an evacuation center because it was two stories tall. When the levees broke, it took less than ten minutes for rushing waters to reach the ceilings of local homes. Terrified residents climbed onto rooftops or went up to their attics as the waters kept rising. Some drowned. Those who could took to boats. One seventh grader at Chalmette, Erika Guidroz, told of being knocked out of her family's boat and into the rancid floodwaters. She also watched her father and another man peel back the metal roof on a home to save a woman and her grandson. The woman's husband and her own son, the boy's father, had already drowned. Some twelve hundred residents in St. Bernard had sought refuge in Chalmette High School. The school's entire first floor had flooded. Stranded residents and families had gathered on the second floor, eating boxes of Froot Loops cereal from the cafeteria and rationing small sips of water. There were disabled teenagers with ventilators. One elderly man died; a blanket was placed over his body.

As the waters rose, evacuees began arriving by boat. The school's principal, Wayne Warner, and the school superintendent, Doris Voitier, lifted scores of refugees into the building by hoisting them through a second-story window using a yellow plastic chair. For three days the storm refugees huddled in the school, without working toilets or a sewer system, until rescue boats reached them. Some first responders were Canadian police officers, who had sailed down the length of the Mississippi River. In parts of St. Bernard Parish, other residents waited six days for rescue. They walked through waist-high floodwaters and were forced to break into local stores to find food. Ironically, in 1927, during the Great Mississippi Flood, St. Bernard and its neighboring parish of Plaquemines had been decimated by floodwaters on purpose. To save the city of New Orleans from the raging river, engineers stacked thirty tons of dynamite and blew a hole in the levee at Caernarvon, Louisiana, to divert the water. In 1927 St. Bernard and Plaquemines were submerged while the city was saved. This time, none had been spared.

When the waters receded, Doris Voitier and Wayne Warner began cleaning up Chalmette High School's second floor first. Even with families living in tents and out of the backs of trucks, they were determined to reopen their school. By the time I visited, they were still working to remove the mud on the first floor. Lost in the flooding were all 29,000 books in the school's library as well as a complete set of original *Life* magazines. This little high school had saved every issue since 1936, and they used them as primary sources to study history. I contacted Ann Moore, the chairman and CEO of Time Inc., and in May of 2006 she came with me when I returned to Chalmette. She brought an entire replacement set of original *Life* magazines, as well as a hundred large, framed classic *Life* photographs, including twenty-five from New Orleans, such as the iconic portrait of the jazz great Louis Armstrong. The Laura Bush Foundation also gave the school two grants to replace its collection of books and materials.

Getting kids back to school, even if it was just a temporary school, was one of the most important things that could be done to return some normalcy to their lives. I met so many children who had lost everything but held on to a library book and, weeks or months later, brought the book back to their school librarian and nervously asked, What is the late fine? Books matter. Schools matter. And at times like this, I am again struck by how strong teachers, principals, and superintendents are. They matter in ways we often take for granted.

It takes years, even decades, to recover from a disaster like Katrina, and the destruction spared no one in its path. In Mississippi, Democratic congressman Gene Taylor, who represents Gulfport and Biloxi, lost almost everything he owned. Republican senator Trent Lott and his wife Tricia's family home was destroyed. At the Congressional Ball that December, a few in attendance complained to the White House social staff that we were not serving shrimp—the gulf shrimp industry had been decimated by the hurricane and there were few shrimp to be had that year. But Congressman Taylor was reluctant to come with his wife because the ball is black tie, and most of their clothes, including their dress clothes, had been ruined along with their home. The Taylors arrived late and stayed off to one side, hesitating to go through the receiving line. My chief of staff, Anita McBride, spotted them and urged them to walk through, saying, "President and Mrs. Bush will want to see you." And we very much did.

For eight years, every day that I was in the White House, I walked past the black lacquer screen that Nancy Reagan had added to the cavernous, yellow upstairs hallway to make it appear a bit smaller and more intimate in scale. Day after day Bar Bush and Hillary Clinton had passed it too, and there was great comfort in that continuity. To live in the White House is to live with your predecessors, with their decorating, their renovations, their furniture; Bill Clinton's Oval Office couches, re-covered, were now in our residence upstairs. George and I both pored over biographies and histories of the men and women who had inhabited these walls; our bedside tables were crowded with books about their lives. And there was a real solace to these constant reminders of what had gone before, to know that from within these walls Franklin Roosevelt had faced the

Pearl Harbor attack, Abraham Lincoln had agonized over the Civil War, and tens of other presidents had struggled with their Congresses and their consciences as well. Our presidents have overwhelmingly been good and decent men, men who did the best they could under the circumstances they faced, with the knowledge they had. They loved their country and wanted the best for it and for the office they held.

I loved the White House. I took great pleasure in the chance to keep and to conserve it, restoring the elegant silk wall covering in the Green Room that Jackie Kennedy had selected more than four decades before, or embarking on a project to renew the library and many of the ground-floor rooms, as well as to restore the Lincoln Bedroom, working on each space with White House curators and preservationists. I was delighted too whenever former presidents and their families returned. We had Nancy Reagan to the White House on several occasions, sometimes to stay overnight in the Queens' Bedroom. We hosted a ninetieth birthday party for Gerald Ford. And in the fall of 2005, Lynda Johnson Robb called to tell me that her mother, Lady Bird Johnson, would be making what was probably her last trip to Washington, D.C. I gladly invited her to the White House. I had always admired Lady Bird, the first Texas first lady, and had been so proud that she had recognized the great natural beauty of our home state and nation. When we drive our vast highways, past waving grasses and blooming flowers, acres of bluebonnets or black-eyed Susans or Queen Anne's lace, that is the legacy of her touch, of how she worked to beautify America with native plants and wildflowers.

A series of strokes had left Lady Bird unable to speak or walk. I met her in her wheelchair with Lynda at the South Portico. Joining me was the retired White House maître d', Wilson Jerman, who had worked under President Johnson, and when the two of them saw each other, they fell into each other's arms. We wheeled Lady Bird inside to the Vermeil Room, so she could see her portrait hanging above the carved mantel. Her face broke into the most beautiful smile. When I began redoing the Vermeil Room on the ground floor, I had asked the painters to adjust the color of the walls to more closely match the pale gold-yellow of the dress Lady Bird is wearing in her portrait, which also blends with Jackie Kennedy's pale and elegant column dress in her portrait on the adjoining wall, so the room is all of a piece.

When we took Lady Bird up to the State Floor to see the portrait of her husband, she reached her arms out as if to touch him. And as we passed through the rooms, she would put her hands together and clap lightly or utter a bit of gasp when she saw a piece of furniture or a painting that she remembered.

By 2007, when the U.S. Department of Education building was renamed in honor of Lyndon Johnson, who had signed some sixty education acts as president, Lady Bird was too frail to travel to Washington. George invited her daughters, sons-in-law, and grandchildren to the bill signing. Inside the Oval Office, he placed a call to Texas so Lady Bird could listen to the ceremony. George said, "I'm signing this bill right now, Lady Bird." Then we had the whole Johnson family up to the residence so that Lynda and Luci, now long grown, could see their old rooms and show their children and grandchildren the home where they had once lived.

The months of travel during the 2004 reelection campaign had given me time to reflect, and as I moved about the country, I began to consider what I would like to work on if George won a second term.

For years I had known that, as a nation, we are not focusing on boys the way we should. The statistics tell a particularly bleak story: Boys are more likely to drop out of high school than girls; boys are more likely to have a learning disability; fewer boys than girls attend college—girls are soon expected to make up 60 percent of all college undergraduates; fewer young men than young women attend graduate school. Boys are much more likely to be incarcerated and to get into trouble for drug and alcohol use. In the last forty years, the nation has entirely rethought how we raise girls, fostering their belief that they have every opportunity. But we have not given that same thought to boys; they are still locked in traditions as much as our daughters were two generations ago. And as they grow into men, the importance of their role as fathers is often demeaned. We expect men to provide financial support, but many of their other skills have been marginalized. They are too often viewed as the television caricatures of bumbling, hapless people, not as vital nurturers.

Yet that is very far from the truth. Since I was a young child, I had seen the difference that fathers made, in my life and others. I remember my second-grade friend Georgia, whose own father had died, and how my father would take her and me to the father-daughter events at school or with the Girl Scouts. And I remembered the many boys I met on school visits or during other events, such as the twelve-year-old in Austin who talked to me about not having a dad to play catch with and do the things that dads do. As he spoke, he struggled with the words; he felt the loss of a father so deeply. And of course, I had seen the consequences of absent fathers when I taught and worked in Dallas, Houston, and Austin. When you are missing a parent, you live with a special sadness for your entire life.

I knew the statistics, I knew the stories, and in August of 2004, I decided that if George won, I would start a special White House initiative to focus on boys. By January of 2005, I had expanded that idea to include troubled and at-risk girls as well, but the major focus remained on boys. George announced the Helping America's Youth initiative in his 2005 State of the Union speech. The initiative was my responsibility to lead. My goals were several: to raise awareness about the problems young people face and to motivate caring adults to connect with our nation's young people in their families, schools, and communities. I also wanted to examine the myriad of federal programs for at-risk youth, scattered across twelve departments as diverse as defense, justice, education, and health and human services. Each agency gives millions of dollars in grants every year to programs that serve youth. But sometimes programs duplicated each other, or the effect was unfocused or uncoordinated, and the different agencies did not always communicate with one another. As part of Helping America's Youth, my staff and I created one interagency working group, bringing together all these agencies and government entities so this disconnect would change.

Almost immediately that winter, I began traveling the country to visit some of the most innovative and daring private programs focused on at-risk youth, such as a Chicago program that cut shootings by 68 percent in one police district and the largest gang intervention program in the nation, in Los Angeles. Over the next four years, I would do fifty separate events around the nation, focused solely on Helping America's Youth.

Starting in the winter of 2005, my staff and I also began planning a major conference, to be held in October at Howard University, a historically African-American university chartered in 1867 and located in Washington, D.C. We gathered over five hundred civic leaders, educators, faith-based and community service providers, teen experts, and parents to highlight the most serious problems facing American boys and youth—and to showcase successful solutions. In this way, individual communities would not have to keep reinventing the wheel. The thought was, where success stories exist, let's find them and share them, so that more children and teens have a chance. We invited people from all political persuasions; this is an issue beyond politics.

On the day before the Howard University conference, I sat for an interview with the *New York Times* reporter Jason DeParle. Jason's beat was poverty and welfare, and on the campaign trail the previous year, I had read an article he had written for *The New York Times Magazine* about a young man named Kenyatta Thigpen, who was trying to turn his life around. Ken had been a drug dealer and pimp who had done time in jail, but now he had a three-year-old son, and he was determined to be a good parent. He was trying to become the father that he had never had, even driving a pizza delivery car at night so that he could be with his boy during the day. I had met Ken, his girlfriend, and his son in March during a visit to the Rosalie Manor Community and Family Services Center in Milwaukee. When we met, I told him that this article about his life and struggles had helped crystallize my thinking about ways to reach out to the young people who are most in need. Now, as we prepared to open the Howard University conference, where I had invited Ken to speak, I was also eager to meet the reporter who had first written about him.

I had long ago resigned myself to what was written about me in the press. First ladies generally have an easier time than presidents, but that doesn't exempt them from criticism. In the beginning, much of the commentary focused on how I looked. Whereas Hillary Clinton was mocked for her hairstyles and headbands, I was told, "Laura Bush is begging for a makeover" and "She's no Jackie O." On January 15, 2001, before George had even taken office, *The New York Times* wrote, "Some historians predict that the first lady she may come to resemble most is Mamie Eisenhower . . . whose division of labor was simple: 'Ike runs the country and I turn the lamb chops.' And," the *Times* continued, "Mamie wasn't such a great cook either, but understood the symbolic need to look as if she were a great cook," thus managing to zing me and Mamie Eisenhower in the same line.

In March of 2001, *The Washington Post* asked: "Everybody wants to know: Is she publicly genteel and privately tart? Is she smarter than he is? Does she work to make herself somehow smaller next to him?" By George's second term, it was lines like *The Boston Globe*'s "Maybe Laura Bush will finally break out of the plastic." I was used to all of this. It comes with the job.

I was also used to questions that began with negative poll numbers about George, and then went on to ask "How does that make you feel?" such as when Ed Henry of CNN said, "But you know what people are saying, which is that your favorability rating in the latest CNN poll is 68 percent, about twenty-two points higher than your husband. . . . Does that annoy you?" Or the reporter who began our interview by asking me if I had ever Googled myself, then proceeded to discuss nasty entries about me that popped up on a Google search. I was used to having my words reinterpreted, as when, on my July 2005 Africa trip, I was asked if I wanted George to name a woman to Sandra Day O'Connor's soon-to-be-vacant spot on the Supreme Court. "Sure," I said, "I would really like for him to name another woman. I know that my husband will pick somebody who has a lot of integrity and strength. And whether it's a man or a woman, of course, I have no idea." But the headline was "First Lady Wants New Female Justice," as if I were pointedly instructing George and drawing a line in the sand.

But I never expected what would happen on the afternoon of October 26, when I sat down with Jason DeParle in my office in the East Wing. In a tone that was adversarial and more than a touch offensive, he began by asking, "So what's a nice woman like you doing with a guy like him?" Meaning Ken Thigpen. It was demeaning to me, and it even seemed demeaning to Ken. I thought it radiated cynicism, as if Jason did not believe in the sincerity of Ken's efforts to choose a different path for himself and his son.

In these exact words, Jason later said, "One of the people wrote, this is a *Saturday Night Live* skit, that people—you're vulnerable to people—being a wealthy woman in the White House, vulnerable to people rolling their eyes and making fun of your ability to talk to gang members. What do you think about that? Did that—does that go through your mind?" And then I recounted yet again that I began my adult career as a twenty-one-year-old teacher working with predominantly African-American kids in inner-city schools. It was not a new interest. It had been my interest for nearly forty years, while I taught and while George was governor. But Jason kept on trying to bait me, saying, "Well, that's what so interesting about your association with Ken. You're not put off that he was a drug dealer or a pimp in his earlier life?" At that point I was incredulous. The assumption by this reporter was that he knew all there was to know about me, and that of course, I couldn't be, wouldn't be, interested in anyone who was different from me. I had already spent hours talking with ex–gang members. I was happy to meet Ken.

Jason DeParle's tenor suggested that he saw my efforts as some kind of a joke. His article after the conference was no better. It opened by smugly saying that I was "wealthy and white," while Ken was "poor and black." As it happens, Jason DeParle himself is wealthy and white, but does that disqualify him from writing about poverty and African-American welfare mothers?

There are hardworking, stellar members of the press who cover the White House. They are highly dedicated to their work under demanding and difficult conditions. Two journalists, NBC News' David Bloom and *The Atlantic* magazine's Michael Kelly, had died covering the early days of the Iraq War, David of a blood clot, and Michael in a vehicle accident.

Many regional reporters from outside Washington also did their homework and were quite fair. On the national stage, I was always happy to do interviews with the highly professional Jonathan Karl, Robin Roberts, and Diane Sawyer of ABC News; as well as Deb Riechmann of the Associated Press; Ann Curry, Matt Lauer, and David Gregory of NBC News; and Greta Van Susteren and Chris Wallace of Fox News. And in the early months and years after 9-11, the snide remarks about my looks largely evaporated. There were far bigger things to discuss. It was the press who had graciously called me the "comforter in chief."

But as in every White House, from the beginning some in the media came with preconceived notions and an adversarial point of view. Some of it was sloppiness, reporters who didn't know an issue and got basic facts wrong. But some of it was bias, where journalists, rather than being objective, could not put their own emotions and assumptions aside. Jason DeParle was a classic example of a reporter coming with his story already written.

And how some journalists saw me often had very little to do with me and very much to do with how they perceived George. What was written and said about him was far worse.

The misperceptions about George were manifested in many ways, large and small. I remember interviewing in February of 2004 with Elisabeth Bumiller, then the *New York Times'* White House correspondent. She had just written a piece about George and John Kerry both being members of the same secret society at Yale. At the end of the article, Elisabeth repeated a previously circulated story about George's dad appearing at his son's dorm room door and telling George to join his old society and "become a good man." But the story wasn't true. Gampy was a congressman at the time. He wasn't concerned about whether George joined a Yale secret society or not; he certainly didn't make a special trip to New Haven to speak to George. At the end of our interview, I asked Elisabeth about the article, and it was clear from her reply that she had never checked the story herself. But apparently the anecdote was just too good not to use. That was the problem. While the truth may not be as interesting, it is the truth.

For me, the greatest casualty of this media cynicism was what the press frequently would not cover: stories of amazing people doing extraordinary things across America. The people I met and places I visited as part of my Helping America's Youth initiative inspired me as first lady.

In April of 2005, I traveled to Homeboy Industries in Los Angeles. Founded in 1988 by Father Gregory Boyle, a Jesuit priest, Homeboy is the largest gang intervention program in the nation. Los Angeles County is home to eleven hundred gangs, with an estimated eighty-six thousand gang members. Each year Homeboy opens its doors to twelve thousand gang members from eight hundred separate gangs. If a gang intervention program has a 30 percent success rate, it is considered effective. The University of California–Los Angeles puts Homeboy's success rate at 80 percent. The program has given tens of thousands of gang members new lives.

"Father Boyle would ride his bicycle into the middle of our gang fights," one of the young women working at Homeboy told me in 2005, shaking her head in disbelief. But Father Boyle couldn't ride into the middle of every gang fight. He designed Homeboy to give ex–gang members, many of whom have criminal records and very little formal education, a fresh start. His motto, he told me, is "Jobs, jobs, jobs," and his belief is that if gang members could be taught work skills and could get good jobs, they would choose a different path. Although drug dealing may look lucrative, Father Boyle contends that many of the young men and women standing on street corners or working out of neglected buildings live with enormous anxiety. They fear being shot, being arrested, being robbed. They fear the people they buy from and the people they sell to. But they don't know anything else. Getting out is, in fact, a relief.

Homeboy Industries operates five businesses and a solar-panel installation training program, all staffed with ex–gang members. Homeboy also helps to provide job training and placement, even things as basic as how to behave on the job and how to dress. Young people in the program who are not ready for the private work world are given jobs in the Homeboy businesses, where they can learn everything from landscaping and T-shirt silk screening to baking and working in restaurants and food service. They learn how to take direction from a supervisor, how to get along with co-workers, and how to develop a work ethic. Father Boyle's program provides mental health counseling, alcohol and drug abuse treatment, anger management programs and domestic violence classes, ways to get a GED high school degree, and help for people who have recently been released from jail and need to make the transition from detention to a free life. One other major component of Homeboy is gang-tattoo removal. Sitting in his spare office with a simple desk, Father Boyle told me of one young man who came to him when Homeboy was relatively new and said, "I've got a huge tattoo on my chest that I want removed." Father Boyle thought for a moment and then replied, "Don't worry. You can wear a shirt. Tattoo removal hurts. No one will see it." The young man answered, "My son will."

Thousands of the young men in the program are covered in gang tattoos. Father Boyle has convinced twelve Los Angeles doctors to remove those tattoos for free; these twelve doctors conduct four thousand tattoo removal treatments each year.

Father Boyle was one of the people I invited to the conference at Howard University. He came and brought some of his ex–gang members. It was their first plane trip and the first time they had ever worn suits. After the conference I invited them to a reception at the White House. Over the years Father Boyle would travel to Washington with other ex–gang members, and we always made sure that they could get a White House tour. Young men who had been in gang fights and had even spent time in jail could learn that, having started down the path to change their lives, they were welcome in the most prominent home in the nation.

There were so many other remarkable programs across the nation. Dr. Gary Slutkin, a physician and epidemiologist at the University of Chicago, had spent most of his career combating tuberculosis in San Francisco, cholera in Somalia, and AIDS in Uganda with the World Health Organization before he returned home to Chicago. He thought he was done with public health crises until he realized that in some Chicago neighborhoods 20 to 30 percent of children have directly witnessed violence. In other areas the numbers are even higher. In the South Side of Chicago during the 1990s, as many as one in four children at three elementary schools had witnessed a shooting; one-third had seen a stabbing. By 2002 Chicago's homicide rate was nearly three times that of New York. Slutkin's model was to treat violence as an epidemic, like AIDS in Africa. His program, CeaseFire, works to reduce violence in communities by treating the entire community.

Whereas in Uganda he had used former prostitutes to spread the message about AIDS, in Chicago he recruited reformed ex-convicts and ex–gang members. Called "violence interrupters," they return to the same neighborhoods where they once got into trouble. If they see a fight or hear of one brewing, they literally interrupt it and say, "Don't ruin your life over this petty slight," or "Don't shoot someone or pull a knife because he looked at your girlfriend or because he cut in front of you in line." Slutkin matches at-risk kids with older trained mentors in their communities, and he brings together the whole community, law enforcement, clergy, teachers, school administrators, and parents, so each of them can deliver the message that violence is not accepted here. They march in the streets to protest after shootings and put up billboards with the pictures of beautiful young children, saying, "I want to grow up." In its first year, CeaseFire cut shootings in one police beat by 68 percent. In six communities, it reduced shootings by 42 percent. By 2004 CeaseFire had been implemented in fifteen Chicago neighborhoods. Within a few years, it would be used in cities throughout Illinois.

After the Howard University conference, my staff and I held six regional conferences, to highlight more programs and reach more people; in short, to help the helpers. We searched published reports and interviewed hundreds of experts to find organizations that were turning around what might otherwise have been tragedies. Each organization had to have independent statistics measuring its success and a track record to pass our vetting process. What we found amazed us.

The human needs in parts of our society are so great that fatherhood initiatives must teach young men the most basic lessons of being a dad. One program I visited in Kansas taught fathers and their children how to hug. They started with a thirty-second embrace. For most of these children and their dads, it was the first time they had ever been wrapped in each other's arms.

I traveled again to Los Angeles to visit Will Power to Youth, a program founded by Ben Donenberg and sponsored in part by Tom Hanks and Rita Wilson, which uses Shakespeare to reach at-risk kids. Instead of hanging out with gangs, teens in L.A. are paid to spend a summer producing a Shakespeare play, building scenery, acting, and learning Shakespeare. One of the young men I met was hired by Home Depot for its kitchen design department because of what he had learned designing sets for Shakespeare plays. I saw a program in Atlanta where Emory University students coach debate teams in housing projects, to teach kids to use their minds and their words to settle disputes. In upstate New York, I watched as teenagers were taken through a mock arrest and jury trial to see how evidence is presented and what their sentences would be for a potential crime. I played the Good Behavior Game with kids in Baltimore. Dr. Sheppard Kellam helped pioneer the game; his idea was that many children do not know how to be students; they have never seen a parent read, have never sat still in a chair to listen. The Good Behavior Game teaches them how to behave in school.

I also told these success stories to other audiences, speaking to the National League of Cities, the Big Brothers Big Sisters conference, and other organizations around the nation. After three years my office had helped to develop a more organized way for these innovators and pioneers to share their findings and their wisdom. We created a special website to help new organizations get started and existing ones to expand. And George signed an executive order to make the special interagency working group permanent.

There are still gangs, still teenagers going to jail, still children without fathers, but there are also more people giving their time and their lives to offer kids another path. In December of 2008, Gary Slutkin of CeaseFire wrote to me, "I believe that someday we may be able to contain violence, as we have so many other epidemic problems of history." However difficult that may be, there is no reason not to try.

⁓

On November 2, 2005, Prince Charles and his wife, Camilla, came for an official visit. For their arrival lunch, we served ginger biscuits from Charles's Duchy Originals food products, which the prince founded to raise money for his personal charities. During their stay, Charles, Camilla, and I visited the SEED School, a charter boarding school in Washington, because the prince has a particular interest in education.

In the evening we hosted an official black-tie dinner. State dinners can be held only for heads of state, thus the only state dinner that can be held for the United Kingdom is a dinner for the queen, not for the prince or the prime minister. Japanese prime ministers can have only official dinners; according to protocol, the emperor remains Japan's head of state. The same is true for many other nations, including those with prime ministers and presidents. Israel and India, for example, can have official dinners only for their prime ministers because the presidents outrank them. At our official dinner, the Marine Band played themes from famous British shows, such as *Reilly: Ace of Spies*, and Nancy Clarke, the White House florist, and I chose white orchids for the tables because Charles and Camilla were newlyweds.

From Washington the royal couple was going on to New Orleans, so I invited Joe Canizaro, a friend of ours from there, who shares the prince's interest in architecture and planned communities. Also on our guest list was Lieutenant General Russel Honoré, the commander of the Joint Task Force Katrina, who led the Department of Defense's response to Hurricane Katrina and Hurricane Rita, which followed. The prince, who has frequently been in the crosshairs of the British tabloids, was particularly amused by General Honore's story of admonishing the American press, "Don't get stuck on stupid" during a news conference three days before Rita struck.

Charles's eclectic interests made for a fun guest list; I invited architects, including Robert Stern, the dean of Yale's architecture school, and writers Red Steagall, the cowboy poet from Fort Worth, and Azar Nafisi, the author of *Reading Lolita in Tehran*. Afterward, I gave Charles and Camilla signed books from all the authors who had attended. For our official gift, George gave them each a handcrafted Texas saddle because of their love of horses. They acted thrilled, but I imagine they must have entire tack rooms in their stables devoted to the saddles that have been given to them on various world tours, not to mention the fact that ours were designed for Western-style riding, not English.

On November 9, the Dalai Lama visited George and me for the second time at the White House. The Dalai Lama is a dear and gentle man whose example is an inspiration; he eloquently embodies the hopes for freedom in Tibet. Once, at the White House, he tickled a ramrod-straight, stoic Marine guard under his chin, saying, "Smile." The Marine did. But underneath his soft nature is a man who has been denied his rights and his homeland since he was a boy. He told us that he genuinely feared for Tibet, feared that its culture would be erased from memory as China resettled vast numbers of its citizens inside Tibet's mountainous, landlocked region. George believes that acknowledging the Dalai Lama is a special American responsibility. The world looks to the United States for leadership, and if we do not stand up for freedom, who will? During his eight years in the White House, George met with dozens of dissidents from Cuba, Venezuela, China, Russia, North Korea, Burma, Belarus, and other countries.

For the holiday season, I had chosen the theme "All Things Bright and Beautiful," and we decorated the White House with flowers and fruit, plants, and things that people can find in their yards and gardens. We put pears in our evergreen garlands and on our centerpieces. After a year of so much natural devastation—a tsunami, Katrina—it was a way of remembering the special beauty of nature. The White House was filled with retired staff who came back to work at the Christmas parties, when the sheer number of guests and events made everything hectic. They had been through so many holiday seasons that they knew the rhythms, knew when the food tables were running low or how to ladle punch without dripping. They knew just what needed to be done, and they would introduce themselves saying, "Mrs. Bush, I am Alfredo. I was here in the Kennedy administration." That is the type of love and devotion the White House inspires.

At the parties, some guests produced unexpected moments of levity. One woman, waiting to be screened by the magnetometers as she arrived for a White House function, asked the Social Office aides if the machine could see that she wasn't wearing any underwear. Another asked if the machine could tell that she was wearing two pairs of Spanx, modern-day girdles. And at the Congressional Ball, one of the members coming through the receiving line told me, "My wife and her friends think you wear a wig." I looked at him dumbfounded, then smiled and said, "No, it's my own hair," and pulled on it, just so that he would know for sure.

I had asked the third-generation artist Jamie Wyeth to paint a scene for the official White House holiday card, and he featured the Andrew Jackson magnolia covered in snow, with Barney, Miss Beazley, and India the cat in front. When we sent out our holiday greetings we wished everyone "hope and happiness" for the season and the year to come.

In any given year, it is possible to count the nationally elected female leaders around the world using little more than the fingers of two hands. Some of the most famous female leaders are women who served decades ago, such as Indira Gandhi, Golda Meir, and Margaret Thatcher. In January of 2006, on Martin Luther King Day, I represented the United States at the swearing in of Liberian president Ellen Johnson Sirleaf, the first woman ever elected to lead an African nation. Liberia was founded by former American slaves, who colonized the west coast of Africa as early as 1820. President James Monroe asked for U.S. government funds to purchase the original tracts of land. The Liberian settlements became a haven for slaves freed by the U.S. Navy from the last of the transatlantic slave ships, and today about 5 percent of all Liberians are descended from these early settlers, who escaped slavery for freedom and who, in 1847, created their sovereign state.

But the country's recent history has been brutal and tumultuous. In 1980 a military coup ushered in a decade of authoritarian rule, followed by rebellion and bloody civil war. Finally, starting in 1997 the country had two years of calm, until war erupted again in 1999. It took over three years to achieve another cease-fire and the beginnings of peace, and the price of conflict has been enormous. Two hundred thousand people died in the violence; about 1.5 million fled as refugees. Many of the nation's children were forced to fight as tiny soldiers and had grown up with guns and ammunition rather than parents.

In 2005, when Ellen Johnson Sirleaf was elected, she was one of only four previous Liberian cabinet members who had escaped execution. That January morning she was taking office in a capital city, Monrovia, which had no electricity or running water, and where it was not safe to stay overnight. Instead, Condi Rice, Barbara, and I stayed in neighboring Ghana. To reach downtown Monrovia we passed thatched huts made of woven reeds and roofs that were little more than plastic sheets or corrugated metal strips, held in place from wind and rain by rocks scattered about the edges. Liberians lined the road to watch our convoy pass, transistor radios pressed to their ears for a bit of news. I smiled and waved, and they shyly did so in return.

It was a remarkable moment of promise to see a strong woman inaugurated as the president of an African nation, a woman so determined to lead her country out of the ruin of decades of war and conflict. As I read the program for the inauguration, I saw the irony that Liberia's early leaders, like ours, were born in Virginia or Kentucky or other Southern states. But while our presidents and statesmen had often been born as sons on landed estates, Liberia's leaders had been born as slaves. When they came to Africa to found a new nation, they created its name as well. The word "Liberia" is meant to denote liberty.

In her inaugural address, Ellen Johnson Sirleaf spoke of how women in Liberia had long been "second-class citizens," forced to endure rape during the civil wars, forced to endure the loss of their families and their dignity. She said that she prays for the reconciliation of the country.

Liberia's last leader, Charles Taylor, had allegedly flown arms traded for diamonds into the airport while his own citizens fought and killed each other. In July of 2003, George had repeatedly called for Taylor to resign and leave the country. He then dispatched three American warships with two thousand Marines to Liberia's coast. After weeks of back-channel diplomacy between the United States and Liberia's neighbor Nigeria, Taylor was persuaded to leave, and departed Monrovia on August 11. That summer Charles Taylor did what Saddam Hussein would not the previous spring.

A small group of Marines went ashore to assist West African peacekeepers and to clear the way for humanitarian aid. The United States was the only Western nation to provide such direct political and humanitarian help, and many Liberians were grateful to George; the vice president's wife later told me: "President Bush said 'leave,' and Charles Taylor did."

In Ghana, I launched the Africa Education Initiative, which linked U.S. universities with African nations including Ghana, Senegal, Zambia, Tanzania, South Africa, and Ethiopia. The first partnership was with six minority-serving universities, most African-American, plus the University of Texas at San Antonio, which is predominantly Hispanic. Each university shares its expertise and its education department to develop kindergarten through eighth-grade textbooks written in native African languages, illustrated by African illustrators, and if possible, printed in each African country. The presidents and representatives of the American universities—Chicago State, Elizabeth City State, Tougaloo College, South Carolina State, University of Texas at San Antonio, and Alabama A & M—joined me at the launch.

As part of the United States' work in international development, we had made a special commitment to improving education in Africa, where a staggering one-third of young children do not attend school. American resources help provide textbooks and teacher training and scholarships so that orphans and other vulnerable children, especially girls, have a chance at an education. With education we can reduce disease, poverty, suffering, and violence, and with better education, we can work to stop future genocides. In sub-Saharan Africa, girls especially are denied the opportunity to learn. In 2005, of the 42 million African children who had never set foot inside a classroom, who did not know how to read or to do simple math, 60 percent were girls. In fact, Ellen Johnson Sirleaf has made it a priority to teach the sidewalk market women in Liberia the basics of addition and subtraction so they might earn a better living.

By 2006, the United States had helped provide more than 2.1 million books to schools and libraries and had implemented programs to train

300,000 teachers. I met with some of those teachers that January morning in Ghana. Then I visited, as I did in every African nation, an HIV/AIDS treatment center. Between 3 and 4 percent of all Ghanians have HIV or AIDS, and as in other African nations, the stigma is particularly great for women.

It is tragic that while the United States and Western nations have made tremendous strides on behalf of women and women's rights, many other parts of the world lag far behind. During a South American summit meeting, when I was attending a lunch with the first lady of Brazil, she told me that she wanted to work on "birth records." The translation was spotty, and I thought she said "bird records." I immediately started thinking of the Amazon, ecotourism, and the fabulous ways that they could protect their bird species, because I am an avid bird-watcher. And I replied, "Oh, that's great." She never realized that I thought she was talking about birds when she started. But what she was discussing was so much more basic yet vitally important. In Brazil and many other parts of the world, countries do not have adequate data on their populations because they do not record births or produce birth certificates. Tens of thousands of children, especially girls, are never counted. Boys may make it into the system eventually because they join the military, but girls remain invisible. They literally do not count, in nation after nation around the globe.

Before I left Ghana, I had lunch with President John Kufuor at what was then the official presidential palace, inside the Osu Castle, or Slave Castle. It was the place where slaves were shipped to Europe and the Americas, and for years it was where Ghana's president made his official home. Underground, I saw the small "storerooms" where Africans were kept chained in the dark, waiting for months for ships to arrive. Many went blind because, after so much time in the darkness, their eyes were irreparably damaged when at last they stepped into the brilliant tropical light.

On January 26, 2006, I returned to New Orleans and the Gulf Coast, along with Secretary of Education Margaret Spellings, to visit local schools and a playground. I began at the Alice M. Harte Elementary School in Orleans Parish. It had been one of the lucky schools, suffering only minimal damage. But it had also experienced "the Katrina effect" in education. Before the storm, the state of Louisiana had launched a state takeover of some of New Orleans's most troubled schools. When tens of thousands of families evacuated the city and temporarily enrolled their children in other school systems, many parents realized how substandard the city's schools were. Parents and teachers began to demand better for New Orleans. By November 2005, the Louisiana legislature gave the state full control of 107 of the city's 128 schools. Within eighteen months, half of New Orleans's schools would reopen as charter schools, available to all students but independently operated, with more comprehensive curriculums, and required to meet strict performance standards. One of the first of these public schools to become a charter school was Alice M. Harte, where I helped celebrate the return of its students.

My second stop was the St. Bernard Unified School, which had opened its doors on November 14, 2005, to serve 354 students. That number had risen to 1,500 students, from kindergarten through high school. This was now the only school in the entire parish. Some students were traveling from Baton Rouge, ninety miles away, where they had been evacuated, so they could attend classes in what had been their home. With portions of the school still being cleaned out from the flooding, teachers and administrators were using trailers and tents as classrooms. Doris Voitier, the determined school superintendent, had been unable to get temporary buildings or emergency funds from either FEMA or the Army Corps of Engineers. But instead of waiting, she took action so her students could resume their education. In St. Bernard Parish, nearly every school, home, church, and business had been destroyed by the flooding in Katrina's wake.

In Mississippi, even before the floodwaters had receded, Governor Haley Barbour had begun putting together a rebuilding commission. Despite the immense devastation, every Mississippi school had reopened by November of 2005. This January afternoon in the tiny town of Kiln, the pro football quarterback Brett Favre and his wife, Deanna, were waiting for me. Favre had grown up in Kiln and had played his first "big-time" football in its modest high school stadium. Together we dedicated a new KaBOOM! playground, built by local volunteers that very same day. Through its Operation Playground, KaBOOM!, a nonprofit that builds play spaces for children in low-income areas, had pledged to build or restore one hundred playgrounds across the Gulf Coast over two years. Each project was completed by volunteers. People from around the country came to the Gulf Coast to help with all aspects of the rebuilding. Jenna and Barbara did as well. They spent a New Year's in Louisiana, constructing a house with Habitat for Humanity.

On nights and weekends, I had a second career inside the White House: movie critic. After years of barely being able to squeeze in time for a movie or waiting until it came to the video rental stores, George and I were now the happy beneficiaries of the White House movie theater and a supply of feature films from the Motion Picture Association (movies have been shown in the White House since Woodrow Wilson was in office). We showed movies to heads of state visiting at Camp David, and Jenna, Barbara, George, and I entertained the girls' friends with new releases and hot popcorn. We loved to have the children of the White House staff in to see the latest Disney offering or movies about Nancy Drew and Kit Kittredge. Each fall, after the National Book Festival, I would spend Sunday afternoon watching a chick flick or a foreign film with my friends. My inner movie critic decided that many films were too long and could stand a good bit more editing; for his part, George did not like films that depended on the F-word for much of their dialogue.

The White House theater is on the ground floor. For state occasions it doubles as a coat check, but the rest of the time, it looks like an old-time movie theater, with oversize red plush seats and a big screen. Our first showing in 2001 was *Thirteen Days*, the story of the Cuban Missile Crisis and the Kennedy presidency. We invited Senator Ted Kennedy and many members of his family to attend.

In February of 2006, we debuted *Glory Road*, the story of the Texas Western Miners, one of the first integrated basketball teams and the first to be desegregated in the South. To win the NCAA championship in 1966, Coach Don Haskins started his five best players, all African-American, making sports history. We invited the producer and the central star, but most of our spots were reserved for the former team players and the family of Coach Haskins. I remembered well the story of El Paso's Texas Western Miners. For two years my mother had gone to Texas Western, when it was called the Texas College of Mines and Metallurgy, and I had attended summer school there in 1965. Afterward, we had the entire team, most of whom were our age, nearly sixty, to dinner in the State Dining Room, where players reminisced and swapped stories.

February was also the month the Winter Olympics opened in Turin, Italy, and I led the American delegation, which included a great group of former Olympians: the skaters Dorothy Hamill and Debi Thomas, the gymnast Kerri Strug, the football star Herschel Walker, who had competed in the bobsled, and the speed skater Eric Heiden, who was now the skating team's orthopedic doctor. In Rome, Barbara and I went to meet the new Pope, Benedict XVI, and all of us visited with our troops stationed at the air base in Aviano. The troops were thrilled to meet the former Olympians.

As with every international event, there were scattered groups of protesters in Turin, arrayed against a variety of causes. Most were antiglobalization; some were protesting Coca-Cola, smog, fast food, and plans for an Italian high-speed train; and some were protesting the Iraq War. Media reports before the Olympics had predicted large-scale demonstrations, but they did not materialize. What protest groups did form stayed far away from most Olympic sites. But when Brian Williams interviewed me a few hours before the Opening Ceremony, his second question was: "How much do the protest signs get to you along the motorcade route?" I told him I had seen only a few protest signs. And I wondered whether he, tucked away in his broadcast booth, had seen any at all.

Inside, at the ceremony, only the Italian athletes received louder and more resounding cheers than the American team. Spectators stood and clapped.

I sat with Cherie Blair for the opening, and behind us was the very charming Giorgio Armani. I spoke no Italian, he spoke almost no English, and the noise from the celebration was deafening, but we communicated with hand signals and got along fine.

As we were preparing to fly home from Italy, I received word from my Secret Service detail that there had been an accident on a ranch in Texas; Dick Cheney had accidentally shot a friend while they were hunting quail. I was sick with worry, for Harry Whittington, who had been hit, for Dick, and also for George. I asked my chief of staff, Anita McBride, to call Andy Card, George's chief of staff, though it was the middle of the night at home. I wanted to urge the vice president's office to state the facts, to be open, and to answer questions. There was no need to say anything but the truth. Silence, which was all that was coming from the West Wing, was worse. Dick Cheney did speak to the press, and Harry Whittington recovered. And it gave George a great joke for his next black-tie roast: that the vice president had shot the only trial lawyer who'd supported him.

Back home and around the world, there was mounting dissent over the Iraq War, and George was deeply troubled by how badly the situation inside Iraq had deteriorated. Iraq had already held two sets of national elections, including one in December of 2005 for a 275-member Council of Representatives. But there were near daily terror attacks and bombings, and in parts of the country neither our troops nor the Iraqis were safe. Suicide bombers were killing day laborers and market shoppers, police and National Guard recruits, and even religious pilgrims at mosques. As many as one hundred Iraqis would be killed in a single incident. One of the most devastating events occurred in late February, when bombers struck a holy Shi'ite shrine, the Askariya shrine in Samarra, some sixty-five miles north of Baghdad. In the weeks and months after the bombing, Iraq would be crippled by fresh waves of sectarian violence between Shi'ite and Sunni Muslims. It seemed that each time Iraq began to stabilize, after it held elections, after it began to form a broad-based government, a new incident or threat would appear and undermine that precarious stability. How to drive the insurgents out was occupying most of George's waking hours. This would be a decisive year.

On March 1, Air Force One, with George and me on board, had just finished refueling in Ireland for a scheduled trip to India and Pakistan. I called my assistant, Lindsey Lineweaver, into the president's cabin and asked if she could keep a secret. "We are not going to be landing in New Delhi," I told her. "Air Force One is headed for Afghanistan."

George and I arrived at Bagram Air Base outside of Kabul and then headed to the city on board Marine One. Hamid Karzai was waiting for us at the presidential palace compound. George and President Karzai conferred while I joined his wife, Dr. Zeenat Karzai, for lunch, a traditional meal of chicken, green vegetables, flatbread, and several kinds of rice. Just as on my previous trip, we spoke intently about the needs of women, especially their medical needs. Even something as simple as cooking can be deadly in Afghanistan. Because so many women cook with primitive fires using highly flammable kerosene, they often suffer severe burns. Their children are frequently burned too, by falling into the flames or as a result of kitchen explosions. We discussed mothers' health and infant mortality. There was still no maternity hospital in Kabul, but I had spoken to Secretary of Defense Donald Rumsfeld after my last trip, and by late 2005, the U.S. military had set up a program to train midwives in Afghanistan.

In downtown Kabul, George cut the ribbon on the new U.S. Embassy building. Our day finished back at Bagram with a visit to U.S. troops. At dusk we were in the air flying to India, where Prime Minister Manmohan Singh appeared at the airport to welcome us. I was in awe of the enormous presidential residence, the Rashtrapati Bhavan, which was completed in 1929 by the British as a monument to the permanence of their rule; eighteen years later, India was independent. The palace's walls contained 700 million bricks and 3 million cubic feet of stone. With 340 rooms and 200,000 square feet of space, it dwarfs the White House.

Over a whirlwind three days, I made a number of stops. I visited one of Mother Teresa's homes for disabled children in New Delhi; Mother Teresa's ministry cares for some ten thousand children, many of them abandoned. The homes are a true testament to her love for those so many others consider "the least." I chatted with Indian Muppets as they taped part of *Galli Galli Sim Sim*, their version of *Sesame Street*. George and I laid a wreath at the memorial to Mahatma Gandhi, then bowed for a moment of silence and threw rose petals in honor of his memory. Before we departed, Prime Minister Singh and Mrs. Gursharan Kaur hosted a lovely lunch for us at Taj Palace Hotel. The prime minister is one of the kindest and gentlest world leaders, a quiet and elegant man, and George and I were happy that the United States had developed such a warm and rich relationship with India. At the lunch George stood up and walked with Prime Minister Singh to each table, to greet everyone in the room. Our final night, the president of India, A. P. J. Abdul Kalam, held a giant outdoor dinner for us on the perfectly manicured lawns of the Presidential Palace. Waiters in white gloves served us from overflowing platters of food, and the grounds were decorated with hundreds of glimmering white lights, echoing the bright stars above.

From India we flew to Pakistan, where the previous day a bomb in Karachi had killed a U.S. diplomat. There had also been angry street protests, and the security surrounding us was so tight we barely glimpsed Islamabad. Our ambassador, Ryan Crocker, invited George to take a few swings with a cricket bat, but most of the time was spent on high-level talks with President Pervez Musharraf. At a dinner in our honor, we watched a beautiful display of folk dancing. But at my table, Sehba Musharraf, the prime minister's wife, lamented that so many young Pakistanis knew very little about their nation's arts and culture. When I returned home I reached out to Michael Kaiser, the president of the Kennedy Center and an arts ambassador for the state department. Michael flew to Pakistan to offer advice, and later that year Mrs. Musharraf made her own trip to the United States to attend a Pakistani cultural event at the Kennedy Center. It was the beginning of a number of fruitful arts partnerships between the Kennedy Center and other nations around the globe.

In mid-March I returned to New Orleans for a tour of the levees with the Army Corps of Engineers, who explained where they had been breached and what was being done to repair them. It was six months after Katrina, and there was still devastation. I also visited several schools to follow the rebuilding efforts. On May 3, the Laura Bush Foundation would make its first grants to restock school libraries across the Gulf Coast.

Yet each time I returned to New Orleans, I could see progress. At first it was just the collection and disposal of debris, but little by little the empty buildings were being removed or reclaimed. We saw strip malls and groups of stores slowly return to life. Parking lots that had been empty now had a few cars. Where windows had been dark, there were bits of light. But there was still so far to go.

That spring Andy Card retired from the White House after over five years as George's chief of staff. He had served in the post longer than any other chief of staff in recent White House history. Under incredibly intense pressures, Andy had kept his even-tempered and fair style, which earned him bipartisan praise across Washington. We valued him not just for his skill but for his friendship. We had become especially close with Andy and his wife, Kathleene. They had spent many weekends with us at Camp David, invariably leaving late Saturday night or at dawn on Sunday so Kathi could return to her church in McLean, Virginia, where she was an assistant minister. After 9-11, Kathi and Alma Powell, Colin Powell's wife, had reached out to the spouses of George's cabinet secretaries and White House staff. That September many were new to Washington; some had young children, and now their husbands or wives were gone from their houses and their lives, working at a breakneck pace seven days a week. Kathi, together with Alma, who had spent years managing the separation and sometimes isolation that came when her husband was deployed overseas with the military, gave these spouses refuge, a place to talk, and a way of supporting each other.

Andy and Kathi's caring, calm, and compassion were and are invaluable to us.

The annual White House Easter Egg Roll dates back to Andrew Johnson's administration. Then it was just a family affair. Eggs were dyed on Easter Sunday and rolled along the lawns on Monday morning. The larger gathering of local children, eggs, and spoons was held on the Capitol grounds. But in 1876, Congress grew tired of divots in its grass and rotting abandoned eggs. It passed a law forbidding the Capitol grounds to be used as a children's playground. The roll was rained out in 1877, but in 1878 President Rutherford B. Hayes opened the gates of the White House to the displaced egg rollers. Only two world wars and horrible weather have canceled the event since. When they were six, I had taken Barbara and Jenna to the roll while Gampy was vice president.

By the time George and I arrived at the White House, the roll had become an elaborate production. We hosted entertainers, including the singers Miley Cyrus and the Jonas Brothers, as well as magicians and celebrity storybook readers, featuring sports stars like Troy Aikman of the Dallas Cowboys and cabinet officials. Thousands of small children rolled their eggs with wooden spoons. As a reward, each would be sent home with an inscribed wooden White House egg.

For me 2006 will always be known as the year of the great egg caper. That Easter Monday morning, a member of the Social Office noticed a seventy-year-old lady who was a longtime volunteer at the roll. Instead of working she was repeatedly visiting the Porta-Potty on the South Lawn. Concerned, the staffer told a member of the White House Visitors Office, who walked over and opened the bathroom door. Inside the volunteer was stuffing masses of wooden Easter eggs into her girdle. The White House staff then began a search of other senior citizen volunteers and uncovered a widespread ring. The women were surreptitiously taking the eggs and coloring books into large Porta-Potties and slipping them under the stalls to a "ringleader," who was hiding the contraband in a bright yellow trash bag that she had removed from a bathroom trash can. From there they planned to smuggle them off the grounds. Instead of creating a scene, White House staff redirected the women to work at the food tent, serving egg salad. The staff then took down their names, and they were permanently removed from the volunteer list.

Sadly, pilfering was a common problem at the White House. Guests would walk out of the washrooms with hand towels stuffed in their jackets or purses. One prominent television personality was known for having a collection of White House paper hand towels, monogrammed with the presidential seal, in her powder room. She had "accumulated" them when she came for interviews. Over the years, guests had removed pieces of flatware to the point where one set of silver engraved with the words "The President's House" was so popular as a "souvenir" that we used it only in the private dining room upstairs. Guests also helped themselves to the vermeil eagle place card holders. After these repeatedly vanished from the dinner tables, we asked the butlers to remove the card holders before dessert was served. Some visitors even took the dangling cut glass pieces from the sconces that hung in the ladies' room on the ground floor. There were times when the social secretary's staff joked that we should have guests walk through the magnetometers on the way in, and again on the way out.

Occasionally a guest was apprehended before making it onto White House grounds. One very well dressed woman, who had been placed on a guest list at the request of a Senate office, was detained by the Secret Service at the entry gate. She had three federal bench warrants out for her arrest. The warrants popped up when the officers ran her Social Security number through the database. As the officers led her away in handcuffs, she insisted upon draping her fur coat over her wrists and hands. Another time an aide accompanying a preschool tour group was detained because she was in the country illegally, and one guest's driver was nabbed for having thousands of dollars in outstanding parking tickets.

There were also moments of entrepreneurial daring, such as the time a group of singers opened huge black cases inside the Vermeil Room, placed them on the antique furniture, and began selling jewelry to the other performers right underneath Eleanor Roosevelt's portrait. They had concealed the jewelry inside their voluminous clothing bags, and the Secret Service had assumed it was for them to wear.

Some other performers who came to entertain would send over pages of requirements, down to what type of water they wanted to drink and what snacks they would eat. One celebrity singer wanted us to create a White House dressing room for him, complete with a star on the door.

On April 20, we hosted the president of the People's Republic of China, Hu Jintao, and his wife, Madame Liu, for a state visit. The United States' relationship with China is one of our most important, and George had his own special Chinese relationship. His father had served as the U.S. envoy to the People's Republic in 1974–75, after relations between America and China were reestablished following the Cultural Revolution and the Vietnam War. As a young man, George had bicycled through the streets of Beijing. But this morning disaster lurked at every turn. At the arrival ceremony, President Hu was introduced as being from the Republic of China, which is the official designation for Taiwan. During the ceremony itself, Wenyi Wang, a forty-seven-year-old woman who had been admitted as part of the press pool—she had credentials from *The Epoch Times*, a newspaper that had covered other White House events—stood up and began to scream at the Chinese leader, denouncing him for his treatment of Falun Gong, a Chinese religious sect. She yelled, "President Bush, stop him from killing." It took several minutes for uniformed security officers to remove her—the plainclothes Secret Service are charged to act only if there is an immediate threat to the physical security of the president—and until the officers arrived, her curdling, high-pitched cries echoed across the South Lawn. President Hu and his wife were gracious, but George and I were embarrassed. There are no do-overs for events like state visits. Controversy can follow any state leader, not only Americans, abroad.

Two months later we were back on the South Lawn to welcome Prime Minister Junichiro Koizumi of Japan. Koizumi, who had become our good friend, would be staying for two days, and that night we planned an official dinner in his honor, with flower arrangements reminiscent of a Japanese garden, green orchid topiaries rising over the tops of tall glass cylinders. More than the black-tie evening, we knew Koizumi was looking forward to the following morning, when we took off from Andrews Air Force Base for Memphis, Tennessee. He is a huge fan of Elvis, so we had planned a trip to the King's home, Graceland. Waiting on the front steps to take us through the house were Priscilla and Lisa Marie Presley, and when Koizumi saw them, he began singing the Elvis classic "Love Me Tender" to Priscilla. After the tour, we stopped for lunch at the famed Memphis barbecue restaurant the Rendezvous, where Koizumi donned big gold sunglasses, hopped up on the stage, and asked a three-piece band to play the Elvis hit "I Want You, I Need You, I Love You," while his face beamed and he sang along. He was overjoyed. As a gift, we gave him a 1950s jukebox filled with songs by Elvis and other rock 'n' roll classics.

My late spring was filled with return trips to New Orleans, projects for Helping America's Youth, and a UN General Assembly High Level Meeting on HIV/AIDS, as well as another trip with George to Austria and Hungary. In June, U.S. troops in Iraq had reached their lowest levels in two years, 125,000, but the violence around the nation was not abating. On June 13, George made another surprise visit to Baghdad to meet with Iraqi prime minister Nouri al-Maliki. He increased U.S. troop levels and knew that the 2006 midterm election would likely be a referendum on the Iraq War.

We now had two late-summer anniversaries to mark, the one-year anniversary of Katrina and the five-year anniversary of 9-11.

For the Katrina anniversary, George and I returned to New Orleans on a day that was bright and sunny with thick, swampy heat. We stopped for hotcakes at Betsy's Pancake House and visited a school. We also visited the devastated Ninth Ward and Lower Ninth Ward, which before it was settled had been a low-lying cypress swamp and early plantation land. Sitting below sea level, and positioned between the Mississippi and Lake Pontchartrain, the Lower Ninth Ward had been the site of some of Katrina's worst flooding. More than four thousand homes had filled with water; many had washed away or been destroyed.

We called on the music legend Fats Domino, who had been born in that ward and whose rhythm and blues had poured out of my radio when I was a teenager in Midland. When the floodwaters came, Fats's tan-brick house was engulfed. The waters rose past the priceless collection of gold and platinum records adorning his walls. Decades of mementos washed away or were ruined in the flood. One item that had been lost was the National Medal of Arts given to him by Bill Clinton. Before we left George had asked Bill whether he would mind if we had the medal recast. Bill was thrilled. So we presented Fats Domino with a second gold medal, cast from the same mold, and draped it over his neck.

Our final event was held on the tarmac at the airport, where we met the New Orleans Saints football team, who were about to play their first game of the season in the Superdome. A year before, the Superdome had held thirty thousand evacuees from the floodwaters. Now New Orleans was happily celebrating the Saints' return to the city for NFL competition.

For the five-year anniversary of 9-11, in addition to the traditional wreath laying and visit to Ground Zero, we made a special visit to the "Fort Pitt" firehouse to observe the day with rescuers who were mourning their buddies, some who had been lost and some who were still scarred by that day. The UN General Assembly opened immediately after the remembrances for 9-11. I was there to hear George's address to the UN, and I had a special event of my own.

In 2003 I had been asked to serve as UNESCO's honorary ambassador for its Decade of Literacy, and my staff was working feverishly to convene a White House global literacy conference at the New York Public Library to coincide with the United Nations meeting.

Almost three-quarters of a billion adults in the world cannot read or write; two-thirds of the illiterate are women. UNESCO's focus was on the thirty-five countries with the highest illiteracy rates, where less than half the population can read and write. But although the problem was easy to enumerate, the solutions are far more challenging. In 2003 UNESCO had announced its goal of increasing global literacy by 50 percent by the year 2015. By 2005 UNESCO realized that it could not meet its goal. That fact alone gave this September 18, 2006, meeting particular urgency.

At the New York Public Library, amid great books by some of the finest writers, the White House Conference on Global Literacy brought together forty-one education ministers, thirty-two first ladies and spouses, and literacy experts from seventy-five countries to share information and learn about which programs work best. Among our presenters was Dr. Perri Klass, a renowned pediatrician who is also the director of the Reach Out and Read National Center. I had started the organization's first programs in Texas when George was governor. Reach Out and Read was founded in 1989 by Doctors Barry Zuckerman and Robert Needlman, along with three early childhood educators. Pediatricians like Zuckerman, Needlman, and Klass saw the absence of reading and literacy skills among their young patients and began giving parents "prescriptions" to read aloud to their children just as they prescribed medicines to combat disease. Each child is given a free book at every checkup from age six months through five years, about ten books in all. More than 4,500 Reach Out and Read programs nationwide serve 3.8 million children.

We heard from Dr. Klass about encouraging family literacy and from Florence Molefe of South Africa about how parents who learn to read and write become role models for their children. Two other panels discussed literacy for health and literacy for economic self-sufficiency. Those who cannot read are limited to the most menial jobs, and they cannot follow simple directions to take lifesaving medication or to administer it to their children.

⁓

Late that afternoon I took some of the presenters down to Wall Street, where we toured the floor of the New York Stock Exchange and I rang the exchange's closing bell. It was a far cry from my first visit with Regan, nearly forty years before. Traders on the floor applauded, and I leaned over to shake their hands. But not quite everything had changed. I smiled when I saw that *The Wall Street Journal* began its coverage by reporting that I was wearing "a pink skirt-suit."

⁓

The United States is the world's largest supporter of public health improvements overseas. We generously provide medicines, materials, training, and lifesaving aid. Our hospital ships set sail for the Indonesian coast to treat tsunami victims or Haiti after a devastating earthquake. American doctors spend their vacation weeks in Africa or Asia or South or Central America, treating those who otherwise would not have care and performing operations, like eye surgery that returns a patient's sight. Two American doctors, twins named Vance and Vince Moss, have traveled twice at their own expense to Afghanistan. Working sometimes in caves and in bombed-out buildings, with only flashlights and cell phones to see by, they have operated on sick and injured Afghan men, women, and children. When villages heard they were coming, hundreds would line up to be seen by the men they called the "same-face healers." Through the passionate work of private citizens like the Mosses, private foundations, and government programs, the United States shares its ingenuity and know-how to save lives. Fortunately, we are not alone. French doctors helped to found Médecins Sans Frontières, or Doctors Without Borders, in 1971; it now operates in nearly sixty nations. Israeli doctors created Save a Child's Heart, the world's largest global pediatric heart surgery program, which operates in Africa, China, Jordan, Iraq, Vietnam, and the former Soviet republics, and also treats hundreds of Palestinian children.

Yet in 2006, every day around the world, 3,000 children under the age of five were dying from malaria; 1.5 million lives were lost each year. Hundreds of thousands of children and adults were succumbing to malaria comas and never waking up. Malaria, which is transmitted by a single mosquito bite, is a preventable disease. The United States eradicated malaria from our swamps and lowlands in the early part of the twentieth century; before then Washington had regular malaria outbreaks. George's great-grandparents the Walkers, who lived in St. Louis, started going to Maine in the summer to avoid malaria outbreaks along the Mississippi River.

In the twenty-first century, we know that systematic programs can wipe out the mosquitoes and arrest transmission of the disease. Something as simple as sleeping under a bed net or treating infested areas with insecticide can greatly reduce malaria outbreaks. But in some of the poorest countries in the world, very little was being done to combat malaria, which is every bit as deadly as AIDS. George wanted to change that. In June of 2005, he announced the President's Malaria Initiative, which focused on combating malaria in fifteen of the world's hardest hit nations, where more than 80 percent of all malaria deaths occur. To receive aid and funds, these nations' governments had to become active partners in malaria eradication.

Eighteen months later, the President's Malaria Initiative was entering its next phase. As we had done with Helping America's Youth, I wanted to get all of the organizations that were addressing malaria to meet in the same room on the same day. On December 14, for the first time, experts from the World Health Organization, the World Bank, and UNICEF met with Admiral Tim Ziemer, director of the president's initiative, as well as with representatives from private foundations, such as Malaria No More and the Gates Foundation, which was announcing $84 million in new grants; it had already spent $682 million to combat the disease. They came together as part of the White House Summit on Malaria, which I led at the National Geographic Society. Our goal was simple: cut malaria deaths by one-half across these fifteen nations and share the resources and knowledge to do it.

Already there were signs of progress. After the initiative began, communities on the island of Zanzibar reportedly cut their infection rates from 45,000 cases to near zero in a mere four years. When George left office, the overall number of malaria deaths among children under five had dropped by one-third in both Zambia and Rwanda. And on the island of Zanzibar, where just three years before, 22 percent of all children seen in local health clinics had tested positive for malaria, now that number was less than 1 percent. I thought of the female leaders I'd met in Rwanda, all of whom had contracted malaria. Now their children might be spared. Thanks to the compassion of the American people and the President's Malaria Initiative and its partners, there are now tens of thousands of mothers who no longer have to weep over the death of a child from an entirely preventable disease.

The week before the malaria summit, I was reminded of the less than life-or-death issues that dominate the news from the White House. My ultimate in clothing faux pas received about as much attention as the summit. The dress debacle occurred on December 3, 2006, at a White House reception before the Kennedy Center Honors, and the guilty party was a red Oscar de la Renta gown. George and I were standing for the long receiving line greeting guests when I saw a good friend of mine from Houston. She was wearing the identical red lace dress. We posed for the camera with slightly awkward smiles. A few minutes later a friend from Washington walked through in the exact same gown. Then came a good friend of mine from California. Now there were four of us in the identical dress. We tried to turn it into a lighthearted moment, and the four of us gathered for a group photo, but I could tell that no one was amused. I had chosen the de la Renta gown because it blended so nicely with the brilliant red of the Kennedy Center's interior. But after the last camera click, I raced upstairs to change into a navy blue dress from the back of my closet to wear to the awards ceremony.

Thus continued my fashion education. It had started when the press made fun of the purple suit I wore to that first White House visit with Hillary Clinton. After that I had begun visiting New York fashion houses; my favorites were Oscar de la Renta and Carolina Herrera. I paid for all my own clothes and took to attaching an index card to each outfit, writing down what event it had been worn to, so that I could avoid duplications. Each season my assistant would remind me of the different occasions for which I would need a new dress or outfit: state dinners, annual galas, and the like. I would glance through the designers' "look books" and make selections, usually asking that the color or style be slightly altered. But in the book, that red dress had looked perfect. It had vaguely crossed my mind that someone else might see the dress and think exactly the same thing, but what were the odds of that woman wearing it to a White House party? I let the thought pass from my mind until December 3. Unfortunately, no one else had thought to check on how many of the red lace dresses had been sold around the country, and one of the women who wore hers to the White House that night was so infuriated that she returned it to the store and demanded they give her a refund.

My dress, however, had a long life. Not only did I wear it for the official White House holiday photo but I sent it to travel the country as part of the Heart Truth Red Dress campaign to raise awareness about heart disease.

When I arrived in the White House, if I had been asked what was the leading cause of death among American women, I would have replied cancer. But the correct answer is heart disease. In 2003 heart attacks and related diseases were responsible for one out of every three female deaths in the United States. Very few American women knew this devastating statistic, and thousands of doctors were insufficiently aware of the risk for women's heart health. Most modern heart procedures, like stents and angioplasty, had been developed for men. Even the instruments used by heart surgeons were designed to fit men's far larger arteries and veins. At the start of 2003, Dr. Elizabeth Nabel of the National Heart, Lung, and Blood Institute asked me to be the ambassador for Heart Truth, a campaign to educate women about the risk of heart disease, and what they could do to prevent it. The keys to prevention are exercising, maintaining a healthy weight, quitting smoking, and monitoring blood pressure and cholesterol. I immediately said yes.

My first message was that women's heart attack symptoms may be different from men's. For women, common symptoms are often extreme fatigue and pain in the neck or the jaw, not just pain in the arm or the chest, the most frequent symptoms for men. In September 2003, I visited St. Luke's Hospital in Kansas City, Missouri, where I discussed the warning signs of a heart attack. A local woman named Joyce Cullen watched me on television. That night, as she was getting into bed, Joyce began to feel ill. She remembered what I had said and told her husband to pray and rush her to the hospital. Doctors performed heart surgery and saved her life. Joyce joined the Heart Truth campaign and began speaking to local churches and women's groups to try to save other lives. In February 2004, I invited her to the White House to help me launch American Heart Month. I heard from other women as well. A daughter told me how her mother's life was saved after they watched me discuss heart attack warning signs on the *Rachael Ray* show. Another woman dialed 9-1-1 because of an article I wrote in the *AARP Bulletin*. This is the remarkable platform that a first lady has. By 2005 women's deaths from heart disease had fallen to one in four. The heightened attention in the media, especially in women's magazines, to heart health and the national effort to educate women and their doctors saved countless lives.

The Heart Truth campaign put me on the cutting edge of fashion when I unveiled its Red Dress Project during New York City's famed Fashion Week. More than one hundred top models and celebrities have walked the runway in red dresses to highlight the importance of heart health. Today the red dress emphasizing heart health has become almost as iconic as the pink ribbon for breast cancer. And my now famous 2006 Kennedy Center red dress has traveled the country to remind women to care for their hearts.

That December, George and I hosted a retirement dinner at the White House for Kofi Annan, the outgoing secretary-general of the United Nations. America has a long history with the UN; during the darkest days of World War II, President Franklin Roosevelt was the one to coin the name United Nations, and the organization's charter was signed in San Francisco in 1945. Kofi Annan had been a fierce opponent of the Iraq War but a good ally in working to combat violence, disease, and illiteracy around the globe.

During dinner in the upstairs Yellow Oval Room, Kofi Annan asked me about the protesters who gather in Lafayette Park, across from the White House. He was most likely thinking of antiwar protesters, but in fact, many of the people who come in sun, rain, sleet, and snow are not protesting against something but are imploring the American president to do something. Many are pro-democracy protesters, demonstrating on behalf of freedom. We heard the chants of protesters asking George to do more to support human rights in Vietnam. "Mr. President," they called, "please say, 'Vietnam must be free.'" We heard voices calling for an end to political imprisonment in China or freedom for Tibet. Ethiopians came to hold candlelight vigils to call for greater freedoms and an end to civil war. We would look out and see hundreds of their flames waving in the darkness. Week after week people came asking for the United States to use its power and influence to make lives better in other corners of the world. They did not come out of anger or hate, I explained, but out of hope. Kofi Annan looked vaguely surprised, then nodded his head.

The theme of Christmas 2006 at the White House was "Deck the Halls and Welcome All," and the decor was primarily red. The tree in the visitors' reception room and another outside the Oval Office were decorated with ornaments made by artisans in the North Carolina community of Spruce Pine, which had been hard hit by the loss of manufacturing jobs when local textile factories shut their doors. Helped by a generous donation in 2003 from Gloria Houston, who wrote *The Year of the Perfect Christmas Tree*, Spruce Pine had established nearly one hundred small businesses dedicated to producing handmade Christmas decorations. They called their economic development program the Home of the Perfect Christmas Trees. I chose their hand-blown red glass balls and Carolina snowflakes, woven from colored reeds. Roland Mesnier returned from retirement to make the gingerbread White House, using over three hundred pounds of dark chocolate and gingerbread and adding eight hundred hand-piped snowflakes. At the Hanukkah party, the Marine Band played the traditional Jewish tune "Hava Nagila," and guests began dancing the hora in a large circle around the central hall. To inscribe our holiday card, a scene of a glowing Oval Office exterior bathed in a fresh coating of snow, painted by the landscape artist James Blake, I chose Psalm 119, "Thy word is a lamp unto my feet, and a light unto my path."

For George and me, the holidays were once again the season of receiving lines, where we spent long hours shaking hands. To manage the receptions, sometimes two in a single night, Blake Gottesman, George's personal aide, started the practice of counting how many photos were taken in an hour. During the early parties of the season, we averaged about fifteen seconds per photo, but as the weeks progressed, we, and the ever-longer lines, would whittle that down to about seven seconds. Each morning our staff would e-mail around the numbers from the previous night, but even at seven seconds, we could be standing, shaking hands, and smiling for hours in a single evening, so that every guest had a chance to be greeted by the president and the first lady.

For several years during the month of December, I had noticed pain in my left forearm. I brushed it off as coming from too many hours spent standing and holding my arm at my side. But this year, the pain continued into the spring, and it escalated after my hiking trip in Zion National Park. I scheduled an MRI, and the White House doctor, Richard Tubb, told me that I had a pinched nerve in a cervical vertebra. In August of 2007 the chief of neurosurgery at the George Washington University Hospital scraped away bone spurs and calcification that were pressing on the nerve in my neck. For the first time in months, I woke without any pain. Pinched nerves are harbingers of creeping age, and even though this required surgery, the press interest was not nearly as intense as when I had a small squamous cell skin cancer lesion, likely the result of too many hours spent around the Ranchland Hills Country Club pool in Midland, removed from my shin. One of the White House correspondents caught sight of my postsurgical Band-Aid and asked me if I had been bitten by Barney.

In 2006, as always, we spent Christmas at Camp David with the girls and much of our extended family, and George made phone calls to our troops overseas. In November, following the midterm elections, George had replaced Secretary of Defense Donald Rumsfeld with former CIA chief Robert Gates. In Iraq, Saddam Hussein's yearlong trials had concluded; he was scheduled to be hanged on December 30. But that was not enough to turn the tide of bombings and violence; three thousand American troops had died since the war began. At this stage, George was convinced that the United States needed a new strategy. Many Americans now blamed him for the war; the attacks were shrill and personal. For popularity's sake, it might have been easier to withdraw U.S. forces, but the easy course is not always the right one. Instead, George chose to implement a policy known as "the surge."

On January 10, 2007, he announced to the American people that he had decided to commit some twenty thousand more U.S. troops to Iraq, to protect the Iraqi population, to isolate the extremists, to push the Iraqis to lead, and to create space for political progress. More than 70 percent of eligible Iraqi citizens had voted in the last election, but the nation still had a long road ahead.

Many in and out of government, including prominent Republicans and nearly every Democrat, opposed the surge. Many inside George's administration also disagreed with the plan. It was a hard and lonely decision, and it was one of his bravest moments in office.

Day in and day out, the criticism of George from all sides was withering. He was denounced and caricatured in ways far worse than his father had been. I survived it because George did. He is not a self-pitying man. He is not a man of outsize ego or arrogance, despite what his critics said. He simply did what he believed to be right and expected to be judged based on outcomes and history, not by daily headlines or pundits on talk shows. But it was still painful to see the man I loved, the man I knew, so misrepresented by his opponents to the American people. And the hardest part was knowing that our daughters saw it too. The dad who had held them as babies, who had loved them unconditionally, was now the target of mocking late-night comics and near hysterical cable television hosts. It hurt me to think of our daughters picking up the newspaper or reading the Internet or walking into a room where the television was on. Their resilience in the face of this onslaught was remarkable. As a family we have listened to some of the worst things that can be said about us or someone we love, and never has our own love dimmed. But what we endured is a meanness of spirit, a viciousness, and a cruelty that I hope no political family will ever be subjected to again.

We could do nothing but wait and hope for the tide to turn. Our friends and our family waited with us. George had the unwavering love and support of his parents. He also had the special companionship of his youngest brother, Marvin, who lived in nearby northern Virginia. On the weekends, Marvin would call and say, "There's a great game on, why don't we watch it together?" The two of them could lose themselves in sports for an hour or two, and in that easy way that brothers have, the unspoken language of friendship would pass between them. I had my sisters-in-law.

Margaret Bush, Marvin's wife, came several times during the week when I was in Washington to exercise with me in the White House gym. George's sister, Doro Bush Koch, and her husband, Bobby, and their children frequently came for dinner and joined us at Camp David. The richness of their friendship and their love for me and for George was of great solace as we waited for improvement in Iraq. The Bush children had seen their father lead the nation during the Gulf War; now it was their brother, in a longer, more difficult fight. They understood, as few people could, the burdens of leading a nation in wartime. And this was a war unlike any our country had ever faced.

In World War II, we knew that if we crippled the enemy in one place, other fronts would weaken and eventually collapse. During the Cold War, the United States could cede some countries, such as Cuba or Eastern Europe or Vietnam, or even Afghanistan up until 1979, to the Soviets' sphere, and still the fundamental balance of power would remain unchanged. Yet in this new type of war, against not an army in uniform but a radical ideology bent on destroying the very framework of our shared civilization, we could not write off one country to the enemy. Never before in history had such small numbers possessed the potential to inflict such horrific damage. So wherever the terrorists were plotting destruction, we had to engage them. And wherever terrorist cells might be trying to gain a foothold, we had to turn them back. It was a war of terrorist acts and a contest of ideology, and we could not win unless we met them firmly on every front. We could not let Iraq fail, or let the United States fail in Iraq. We could never again allow a full-fledged haven for terror to flourish if we wanted to protect Americans inside the borders of our own nation. Nor could we give up on the millions of Iraqis who were hoping that the extremists would be turned back and a free society would have a chance to take hold. George chose the best way he thought to win, and we waited. And we prayed for the men and women who had pledged to fight for our country and for our freedoms.

⌒

The nasty personal criticisms of George had begun in earnest in 2004. In a May 2004 interview with her hometown paper, the *San Francisco Chronicle*, Nancy Pelosi, the leader of the Democratic Party in the House of Representatives, said, "Bush is an incompetent leader. In fact, he's not a leader. He's a person who has no judgment, no experience and no knowledge of the subjects that he has decided upon." She went on, "Not to get personal about it, but the president's capacity to lead has never been there. In order to lead, you have to have judgment. In order to have judgment, you have to have knowledge and experience. He has none." In 2005, after being invited to a meeting at the White House, she called George "dangerous." Meanwhile, the Democratic leader in the Senate, Harry Reid of Nevada, called George a "loser" and a "liar." Subsequently, in a private, one-on-one meeting in the White House Cabinet Room, Reid said to George that he would stop calling him names. But he didn't stop. And he later told both *Rolling Stone* and then *The New York Times Magazine*, with apparent pride, that he had "never" apologized for the liar comment.

These two congressional leaders also made those statements about the sitting United States president when the country was at war, though as George and I knew, similar invectives had been hurled at presidents during wartime from the earliest days of our republic. Franklin Roosevelt had complained that "every senator is a law unto himself and everyone seeks the spotlight." Interestingly enough, when Pelosi and Reid were asked to suggest their own policy proposals, their answer invariably was withdraw from Iraq immediately, whatever the consequences.

Nevertheless, George and I repeatedly invited Harry and Landra Reid and Nancy and Paul Pelosi to the White House. They came for small gatherings and for black-tie dinners, and received invitations to major state events. When the Queen of England visited in the spring of 2007, Nancy Pelosi danced in the White House in her long ball gown.

Of course, I hated hearing all those terrible things said about my husband. The comments were uncalled for and graceless. While a president's political opponents, as well as his supporters, are entitled to make what they see as legitimate criticisms, and while our national debates should be spirited, these particular words revealed the very petty and parochial nature of some who serve in Congress. George, as president, would never have used such language about them. It demeans honest debate; it debases the office of the presidency; and just as importantly, it does little to produce good decisions or good policy. George did not use interviews to call political opponents "losers" or "liars," and if he had, the outcry would have been enormous. The president doesn't have the luxury of behaving like a smart-aleck kid on a school playground; he has to work not just with Congress but with leaders around the world. The cockiest thing George did was say that he wanted to get Osama bin Laden "dead or alive."

Pelosi and Reid and others got to say whatever they wanted, and George and I were still polite. We still shook their hands in receiving lines and posed for photographs, and George did not exclude them from important meetings or White House events. He respected the offices that they held. Indeed, past congressional leaders, including Senator Lyndon Johnson and then Senate Majority Leader Mike Mansfield, who was a vocal critic of Johnson's during Vietnam, took great care not to utter uncivil words about their presidents in public.

In the Texas statehouse, the governor's office sits in the middle. George could walk down the hall to speak to legislators all the time, and he did. He worked in a thoroughly bipartisan manner. As president, George had great appreciation for the separation of powers, which lies at the heart of how our government works. But in Washington, Capitol Hill was like its own fiefdom, a cacophonous place where no one House member or U.S. senator has the ultimate responsibility for anything. No one has ultimate responsibility for our national security or for our economic security. It is easy to throw mud and pass the buck when there are 534 other people to hide behind. George didn't have that luxury. Every problem in the world comes to the desk of the President of the United States.

⌒

On the night of February 11, 2007, as Washington lay huddled under a deep chill, we lit the lights on the East Entrance and welcomed guests to celebrate Abraham Lincoln, on behalf of Ford's Theatre and the Abraham Lincoln Bicentennial celebration. Senator and Mrs. Harry Reid were two of our guests.

The White House in winter looks like something out of Abraham Lincoln's time, with the soft glow of light bathing it in creamy whites. Marine guards moved with precision as each vehicle approached. In long dresses and tuxedos, the guests walked across the shiny tiled floors of what is called the booksellers' corridor on the ground floor. They then climbed the marble stairs up to the formal State Floor. Time and again, at this event and at many others, people's eyes would overflow as they reached the State Floor. To walk through the corridors, to enter the Green, Red, and Blue rooms, to stand where our own leaders have stood for generations is a deeply patriotic and moving experience. But tonight we had also invited them upstairs to see the Lincoln Bedroom and Sitting Room, whose renovations were now complete. In Lincoln's day, the room had not been a bedroom but the president's official office.

Working with the Committee for the Preservation of the White House, I had re-created the rug based on photographs of an 1861 English carpet that was in Lincoln's office. We commissioned it from the same company that had woven his original rug. Hand-blocked wallpaper that approximated Lincoln's office design was used for the walls, and we reproduced the room's period marble fireplace mantel, which had been discarded in 1902. The bedroom furniture suite that we used had been purchased by Mary Todd Lincoln, and every other piece in the two rooms had been part of the White House collection when the Lincolns resided here. In the sitting room, I installed the only marble Victorian-era fireplace mantel that had survived the numerous White House expansions and renovations. On a simple Victorian desk in a corner of the bedroom, we displayed the fifth and last known copy of the Gettysburg Address written in Lincoln's hand. He had made this copy so that his words might be sold at auction to raise money to buy bandages for wounded Union troops.

In this room, on January 1, 1863, Lincoln had signed the Emancipation Proclamation, and night after night he had waited for word on his war. For this night, I had asked the Marine Strings to play a selection of Lincoln's favorite songs, including "Dixie." As the melodies drifted upstairs, echoing about these pieces of our history, some of the guests wiped tears from their eyes.

⌒

Three weeks later, on March 1, 2007, I was landing in the pitch darkness in a small Air Force plane on Midway Island, scene of one of the most bloody and decisive naval battles of World War II in the Pacific. Today the guns are silent and the island is the centerpiece of one of the largest environmental conservation efforts on earth. Midway is home to eighty people and about 400,000 pairs of Laysan albatross, as well as tropic birds, black noddies, white terns, and other nesting and migratory birds. In Hawaiian, the island has long been called Pihemanu, or "the loud din of birds." From November through July, planes are not allowed to land or depart during daylight because of fears that birds in flight will be sucked into the engines.

In the blackness, my staff and I rode on golf carts to aging military barracks; I spent the night in a tiny house belonging to Barry Christenson, the manager of Midway Atoll National Wildlife Refuge, and his wife, Elise. When I awoke, it was to a deserted island paradise of gleaming sands and rustling palms, with waters so clear that it was possible to see the fish beneath. We had to watch each step we took, for fear of stepping on an albatross nest or a young chick. On Midway Island the albatross have no natural predators; the danger to them comes instead from the seas. Parents fly low over the water, skimming the ocean top for fish and squid. They eat what they catch, then regurgitate the half-digested food to feed their babies. The tragedy is that an albatross cannot distinguish between a squid and a piece of floating plastic. Scattered across the sands and grasses were abandoned albatross nests and chick carcasses, the remains of bird babies who had died after being fed. John Klavitter, a wildlife biologist, opened the partially decomposed bodies. Inside were plastic bottle caps and other refuse, including toothbrushes, cigarette lighters, and plastic tires from a child's toy.

Ocean currents in the Pacific have created a plastic garbage dump estimated to be twice the size of Texas. Most of its contents float just under the swells of the waves, where bits and pieces are ingested by bird and marine life. The Department of the Interior and the National Oceanic and Atmospheric Administration, as well as other U.S. agencies, are working to mitigate this plastic debris and prevent new trash from accumulating. Twenty-one tons of debris had been collected around the Hawaiian Islands in 2006. But so much more needs to be done; there are 6.4 *million* tons of trash polluting and destroying our global marine habitats.

In 2006 George had designated nearly 140,000 square miles of these vulnerable Pacific waters as a marine national monument. It is the single largest U.S. conservation area, bigger than all our national parklands combined. Among the string of tiny islands and atolls in these waters, Midway Island is the only spot inhabited by humans. But the entire region is home to some 14 million seabirds and seven thousand marine mammals, nearly two thousand of which cannot be found anywhere else on earth. The next morning, in Honolulu, I would christen the monument with its Hawaiian name, Papahānaumokuākea.

On the Midway atoll, after stepping carefully around the albatross nests, Interior Secretary Dirk Kempthorne and I knelt in the dirt to replant native plants that were being crowded out by invasive species attacking the shores, another environmental danger. I stood in the water in my bare feet and fed endangered Hawaiian monk seals, of which only about thirteen hundred remain. And I saw the rusting antiaircraft guns and shell craters, the pitted runways and weapons depots where American soldiers and sailors had won their first major victory against the Japanese. We paused in silence to remember as the wind and birdcalls reverberated in our ears.

At the start of 2007, we received word that Queen Elizabeth of England wanted to make another visit to the United States, and the White House immediately sprang into action to host a state dinner in her honor. The preparations involved two social secretaries, Lea Berman, who was departing after over two years of service, and Amy Zantzinger, who would be with us through the remainder of George's term. We invited the violin virtuoso Itzhak Perlman to play for the queen. We decorated the State Dining Room with white roses in vermeil vases and used the gold-edged Clinton china. Our menu tastings, with our talented White House chef Cris Comerford, were done weeks in advance, and everything was designed to showcase the best of America with a nod to British favorites, from spring pea soup with caviar to a first course of Dover sole, followed by lamb with seasonal, local vegetables and salad. And the dinner was to be white tie. George of course didn't want to wear white tie, but at Buckingham Palace, Prince Philip and the queen's guests had donned them for us. So Condi Rice and I made an executive decision that this evening would be white tie as well, much to George's chagrin.

The arrival ceremony was perfect, under blue skies, with a twenty-one-gun salute and a parade by the Old Guard Fife and Drum Corps. That afternoon, Queen Elizabeth, followed by George, greeted dozens of British expatriate and American schoolchildren, who came bearing flowers and shyly asking for autographs. We had invited Bar and Gampy to join us, and when the queen asked to visit the newly opened World War II Memorial, we suggested Gampy as her escort. The eighty-two-year-old World War II fighter pilot lent his arm to the woman who had been a beautiful teenage princess when the war raged. Then Princess Elizabeth had volunteered to drive and repair heavy transport vehicles only after her father, King George VI, refused her request to become a nurse. Now Gampy and the queen walked slowly through this monument to their shared past.

The guest list for this dinner was fun to compile, particularly the invitation I was waiting until the very end to extend. The queen is a fan of horse racing, and she had attended the Kentucky Derby the weekend before coming to the White House. I watched the derby on television, and the moment it ended, I called Amy Zantzinger with a request: invite the winning jockey, Calvin Borel. When she finally reached him, he thought it was a joke. Amy convinced him that indeed the White House was calling, and he said yes, he would attend, but he and his fiancée, Lisa Funk, had nothing to wear. After they heard about the invitation, the stores in Louisville, Kentucky, where the derby is run, stayed open on Sunday so that Lisa could find a dress. For Calvin, Amy arranged to rent a set of white tails from the same man who was outfitting George for the evening.

Both Calvin and Lisa were beaming when they walked through the receiving line, and then Calvin did the sweetest thing. It is strict protocol not to touch the queen, not even to shake her hand, until she extends hers to you first. But as Calvin stood between the queen and me, he wrapped his arms around both of us for the official photograph. All during the dinner, I could see Calvin and Lisa at a nearby table, and they looked so happy. He had his arm draped over her and an expression of bliss, winning the Kentucky Derby on Saturday, and on Monday night dining with the Queen of England at the White House.

On the evening of June 5, George and I landed in Heiligendamm, Germany, site of the country's oldest seaside spa, nestled on the coast of the Baltic Sea, for the G8 Summit. I arrived and began my events, but by the afternoon of the seventh, I could barely stand up. My head inexplicably throbbed; I was horribly dizzy and nauseated. I went to bed, pulled up the covers, and for several hours felt so awful that I thought I might die right there in that hotel room.

I was not the only one to fall ill. Over the next day nearly a dozen members of our delegation were stricken, even George, who started to feel sick during an early morning staff briefing. For most of us, the primary symptoms were nausea or dizziness, but one of our military aides had difficulty walking and a White House staffer lost all hearing in one ear. Exceedingly alarmed, the Secret Service went on full alert, combing the resort for potential poisons. In the past year, there had been several high-profile poisonings, including one with suspected nuclear material, in and around Europe. The overriding fear was that terrorists had gotten control of a dangerous substance and planted it at the resort.

After my stay in bed, I managed to get up and return to the summit. George, who almost never gets sick, refused to postpone a meeting with French president Nicolas Sarkozy, but he canceled a press conference and remained in his room to rest during the G8's final morning meeting. Indeed, George felt so ill that he met with Sarkozy in his hotel room and did not even stand up to greet him. Sarkozy walked over to the sofa to shake his hand and then sat nearby. The White House press office announced to the media that the president had contracted some kind of virus or stomach flu. European papers began scrutinizing every meal that George had eaten and even examined the Baltic fish that had been served.

We all recovered, although a few of the staff had lingering aftereffects; our military aide's gait has never returned to normal, nor has our senior staffer regained full hearing in that ear. The most concrete conclusion any doctors could reach was that we contracted a virus that attacks a nerve near the inner ear and is prevalent in Heiligendamm. But we never learned if any other delegations became ill, or if ours, mysteriously, was the only one.

❦

Later in June, I returned to Africa, to follow the progress of the President's Malaria Initiative and our work to combat AIDS through PEPFAR. Jenna came with me. She had just spent the better part of a year working with UNICEF in Central America, where she had met an AIDS orphan who she called Ana, a young woman who had suffered the trauma of contracting HIV/AIDS from her mother at birth and then lost both parents to the disease. As a teenager, Ana was sexually abused in her grandmother's home. Jenna had been so moved by Ana's determination to build a new life for herself that she asked to write a book about her, *Ana's Story*.

In Zambia, Jenna and I glimpsed the widespread consequences of AIDS. Together we toured the Mututa Memorial Center, founded by Martha Chilufya, whose husband had died from AIDS. Mututa, whose name means "drumming" in the Bemba language, provides home-based care for some 150 Zambians living with AIDS. We sat in brilliant sunshine on the hot red earth, surrounded by baby dolls and bicycles. World Bicycle Relief had donated 23,000 bicycles to nonprofits in Zambia so that care-givers can ride through villages and out to the countryside to deliver medi-cines and check on neighbors. Some of these men and women on bicycles had gone to their neighbors' houses and found them in bed, half dead from the ravages of AIDS. They would get them up, get them to a clinic, and get them started on antiretrovirals for another chance at life. As we sat in a circle listening to their stories, two girls told us about how they had each been victims of sexual abuse and were now HIV-positive. Tears streamed down their cheeks as they spoke. Afterward, Jenna went over, took their hands, and said, "You are not alone. This story happens all over the world," and she told them about Ana. I added that Jenna had just written a book about this young woman. They raised their faces to ours and then they said, "I wish you would tell our stories. Write about us."

⟳

Since 2002 I had been following the repressive Burmese junta and its harsh treatment of the Nobel Peace Prize winner Aung San Suu Kyi. Elsie Walker, George's cousin and my good friend, who had once worked for the Dalai Lama, was a longtime advocate for Burmese human rights.

The Burmese are a tragic example of a people striving for democ-racy and being cruelly denied. The brutality of Burma's current military regime is even more ironic because the inhabitants of one of the earliest kingdoms there, the Pyu, eschewed war and jails and even, as legend has it, would not wear silk because they did not want to harm the silkworms. Like the ancient kingdoms of central Asia, Burma was invaded and con-quered by the Mongols, and it too felt the reach of imperial Britain. The first Anglo-Burmese War was the longest and most expensive in the history of the British Indian Empire. By 1885 Britain had annexed the entire kingdom and the Burmese king had been forced into exile in India. The Japanese invaded Burma during World War II, and late in the war, the Burmese joined with the British to oust Japan from their soil. Burma gained its official independence in 1948, but it was marked by internal strife. A coup in 1962 placed it under control of the military. The military maintained power, despite repeated protests, until a 1990 election, which Aung San Suu Kyi's National League for Democracy won in a landslide.

The junta placed her under house arrest, nullified the election, and would not allow the National Assembly to be convened. Although she was eventually allowed to move about Rangoon, Suu Kyi was returned to house arrest in 2000 and again in 2003.

While I was in the White House, some of what I did to aid the Burmese had to be done in secret. But by the fall of 2006, I could no longer remain publicly silent. To coincide with the annual opening of the UN General Assembly in September of 2006, I convened a roundtable at the UN to address the deteriorating situation in Burma. While the United Nations uses "Myanmar," the word that the junta has selected to rename the country, for the meeting I sat under a map inscribed with the traditional name, "Burma." As in Iraq and other nations, in Burma rape is routinely used as a weapon of war. The day of the roundtable, we heard stories of the victims. Among the oldest to be raped by government forces was a woman of eighty; the youngest was a girl of eight.

I followed that conference with op-eds in major newspapers and several meetings with the UN's special envoy to Burma, Ibrahim Gambari, and my office participated in the weekly White House meeting on Burma. In May I joined the Senate Women's Caucus, comprising all the female senators, and we publicly appealed for Aung San Suu Kyi's release. In June I met with Burmese exiles and refugees at the White House. By August, Burma was dominating international headlines because of the government's brutal crackdown on Buddhist monks who had peacefully taken to the streets to protest soaring prices for fuel and other basic goods. The government responded with beatings and arrests. Here and abroad, the usual round of diplomatic protests were launched, but it was not enough. I decided to speak out.

I telephoned the new UN secretary-general, Ban Ki-moon, and asked him to denounce the junta's crackdown. I called for a new UN Security Council resolution against the regime, even though China and Russia had vetoed similar U.S. efforts just eight months before. Determined to help mobilize public opinion, I sent testimony to the Senate Foreign Relations Committee, wrote another op-ed for *The Wall Street Journal*, and gave interviews. The U.S. government imposed new sanctions, including sanctions aimed at the junta generals' personal wealth. I wanted the people inside Burma to know that we heard them, and the junta to know it too. Things might not change, but that is no excuse for not speaking out when the need and the opportunity arise.

On September 20, I hosted a tea at the White House. It was a special tea for what was called the First Lady's Prayer Group. The group had begun in 1993, as Hillary Clinton was entering the White House. The idea had come from Susan Baker, Jim Baker's wife, who was very close to Barbara and George Bush and was dismayed when they lost their bid for reelection. Susan already belonged to a Christian prayer group that met each week and included women of all political backgrounds, including Janet Hall, wife of former Democratic congressman Tony Hall, and Holly Leachman, wife of a Washington Redskins chaplain who herself was a lay minister at the McLean Bible Church. Among the other members were Carolyn Wolf, wife of Republican congressman Frank Wolf, and Joanne Kemp, wife of former congressman Jack Kemp, whose husband would run for vice president against Bill Clinton and Al Gore in 1996. Grace Nelson, wife of Democratic Florida senator Bill Nelson, also joined. To assuage her disappointment over the 1992 race, Susan suggested that her prayer group begin to pray for the new first lady, and they soon became known as the First Lady's Prayer Group. Hillary Clinton met with them occasionally. When George and I moved to Washington, they began to pray for me and each week would send their prayers and Bible passages to my office for encouragement. Many of these women became my good friends.

They were far from the only ones who prayed for the first lady and the president. George has long said that the United States is a remarkable nation, maybe the only nation on earth where so many people pray for their president. We knew that people were praying for us, and we were raised up by their compassion. We are grateful for those millions of anonymous prayers.

In the early 1960s, my grandmother found a lump in her breast. She never told Mother or Daddy or me. She simply found a surgeon, checked herself into the hospital, and had her breast removed. On our next visit to El Paso, after she was well and healed, Grammee matter-of-factly mentioned that she had had a breast tumor. The cancer never spread, and two decades later, when she was eighty-two, Grammee died in her backyard, watering her flowers, from what must have been a stroke or a heart attack. Papa found her body amid the flower beds.

My mother is also a breast cancer survivor. Her lump was discovered during a routine mammogram a few years after Daddy died. She had a mastectomy in Midland with her own doctor. I was with Mother when she was wheeled into surgery, and we said a tearful good-bye in case she did not wake up. Afterward, I spent several days at her house caring for her, but she refused to allow a home health aide to come help her once I left. She told me, "I don't need any more help."

But I knew all too well the ravages of breast cancer, which had killed my former Midland next-door neighbor and close friend, Cathie Blackaller. In Dallas I had volunteered with the Komen Foundation when it was in its infancy. In the United States we have benefited from years of advocacy for breast cancer treatment and prevention. There are still, though, many places where cancer remains a highly taboo topic and where it is difficult to mention the word "breast." One such region of the world was the Middle East, where many women live their lives shrouded behind abayas.

Health diplomacy is an important way for American women to reach out to other women around the world, and a key component of that health diplomacy was the U.S.–Middle East Partnership for Breast Cancer Awareness and Research, launched in 2006 by the U.S. government, the Susan G. Komen Breast Cancer Foundation, and the M. D. Anderson Cancer Center at the University of Texas. As this partnership took off, I became an advocate for women's health not just at home but overseas. In October 2007, I visited some of the countries hardest hit by breast cancer.

In many Middle Eastern nations, breast cancer is the most commonly diagnosed cancer in women, and in some nations, such as the United Arab Emirates, it is the second leading cause of death.

I arrived after dusk in Abu Dhabi, one of the seven United Arab Emirates, and was hit by a wall of searing, humid heat when I stepped off the plane. Sheikha Lubna Khalid Al Qasimi, the UAE's minister for foreign trade, was waiting to greet me. Sheikha Lubna was educated in California and is a member of the ruling royal family; she is the first woman to hold a ministerial post. We walked into the enormous and thoroughly modern gilt and marble dignitaries' airport terminal for the ancient Arab custom of offering tea to an honored guest. Then my motorcade left, illuminated by the brilliant reflected light from the skyscrapers that soar above Abu Dhabi.

The next morning I awoke to the hum of giant cranes and the skeletons of massive buildings rising from what had less than a century ago been a desert home to nomadic fishermen and herders. In 2007 *Fortune* magazine had declared it the richest city in the world. Yet its vast riches had done little to protect women from disease. In Abu Dhabi, breast cancer is the leading cause of death for women; only 36 percent of all women find their cancers when they are most treatable, in stage one or two. Many women do not want to be examined by a physician because they fear social ostracism if they are found to have breast cancer. Their husbands may leave them; their sons may turn their backs. Their daughters may be considered unmarriageable.

Away from the glint of the city's modern towers, I gathered with breast cancer survivors inside a large circular tent whose walls were draped in billowy pink fabric. The emirates were a largely Bedouin society before the discovery of oil, and this tent, which had been erected within the walls of a hospital, spoke to those ancient traditions. The women who came to this Pink Majlis, literally, in Arabic, "the pink place of sitting," were veiled and covered. A few had sewn pink ribbons on the black cloth of their abayas. In a voice barely above a whisper, one survivor told me of having been abandoned by her husband. Another spoke proudly of how, when her hair fell out from chemotherapy, her husband and her two sons shaved their heads in solidarity. I listened to these women and heard in their voices the common fear of all women, the fear of a disease that causes sickness, disfigurement, and death.

Before I left Abu Dhabi, I visited the seaside palace of Sheikha Fatima, the widow of the late ruler of the emirates. Her home was decorated in marble and gold, and every table fairly groaned with enormous platters of food, overflowing bowls of fruits, and trays of dates and nuts. Abundance is the sign of hospitality. Sheikha Lubna joined us, along with many of Sheikha Fatima's female relatives, and it was a striking confluence of the changes in women's lives, behind the veil, in just a few generations. While the young, veiled women talked about participating in Abu Dhabi's business and political life, Sheikha Fatima remained firmly rooted in traditional ways. She not only covered herself but she wore a leather face mask. Her husband, she told me, thought it was very provocative to see only the tiniest bit of her eyes.

The neighboring emirate city of Dubai is even hotter; it is the largest of the emirate states. Dubai had already begun a major initiative through the Chamber of Commerce and local businesses, including American-owned firms like FedEx, to create an education program about breast cancer. I marveled at the massive buildings, the man-made islands, and the second largest man-made marina in the world. The entire city, a modern wonder where towers twist and point to the sky, has been fashioned on top of a sandy outcropping.

The third Middle Eastern partnership was located in Saudi Arabia. In the newly opened King Fahd Medical Center, I spoke to reporters as a female doctor watched me from behind a dividing wall, her entire body covered except for a thin opening for her eyeglasses.

In the Saudi Kingdom, women contract breast cancer at far younger ages than in the United States, often a decade earlier. Over coffee in the city of Jeddah with breast cancer patients to "break the silence," I looked around and realized that every woman in the room was young, many two decades younger than I. Many were mothers with small children. One of the country's most outspoken cancer patients, and one of the first Saudi women to speak openly about her disease, is an obstetrician and gynecologist, Dr. Samia al-Amoudi. In 2007 she was forty-nine years old.

As we talked, a cancer survivor asked me what I thought of Saudi women. I told her the truth, that at first I had found it disconcerting to sit with women who were covered, that the covers seemed like barriers between us, closing them off from me, and that I had expected it would be difficult to talk to them, but I was wrong. It was surprisingly easy to talk about such an intimate subject as breast cancer. A woman held up a bit of her black abaya and said, "These covers may be black, but they're transparent," meaning that underneath we are all very much the same.

As our visit ended, two women gave me a black head scarf decorated with pink ribbons. Most of the women in the room were wearing them. As a sign of respect to them and to their disease, for a minute I placed the scarf over my head. The hastily snapped photo capturing the moment spawned a small uproar: by wearing the symbol of Saudi cancer survivors, I was thought to be endorsing veiling across the globe, as opposed to sitting with mothers and their daughters who were looking for hope when facing a disease that is, far too often, a death sentence.

From Saudi Arabia, I went on to Kuwait, where I met with a group of about twenty women leaders, including a lawyer, the first female government minister, and an assistant government undersecretary for tourism. I asked to meet with female leaders in nearly all of the countries I visited, but this meeting was special. Just a year before, in 2006, Kuwaiti women had won the right to vote. In pleading their case, the women's activist Roula al-Dashti had said, "Half a democracy is not a democracy." Twenty-seven women ran for office in the 2006 national elections, and while up to 58 percent of Kuwait's women voted for the first time, every female candidate lost.

Three of the women I met with had been among the candidates. We gathered in the home of a female Kuwaiti politician and member of the ruling family, Rasha Al-Sabah. We sat on thick, cushioned sofas around the edges of the room, and it was clear when they spoke that the women were deeply disappointed and hurt that other women had not turned out to elect them. Gently, I asked the women, What did you run on? What was your platform? And they looked surprised. It apparently had not occurred to them to run on issues, something we take for granted in our political campaigns. They had run simply on the fact that they were women. We forget when we look at other nations trying to democratize how much there is to be learned. I am reminded of the story of China when it began expanding its relations with the West at the close of the nineteenth century. Vast numbers of traders, emissaries, missionaries, and other visitors saw Chinese women hobbling on bound feet. Shamed, China began to abandon the practice; it was formally banned in 1912. Yet even now, there are old women whose feet are wrapped in rags.

I mentioned to the Kuwaiti women that George in his campaigns, starting with the one to become governor of Texas, had run on specific issues that were important to him. His goal was to explain what he would do if he were elected and how his plans differed from those of his opponent. In May of 2009, sixteen women ran for public office in Kuwait, and this time four of them were elected to the country's assembly.

After meeting with the Kuwaiti women, I had a chance to meet and thank some of our troops who were stationed in Kuwait, helping to support U.S. forces in Iraq.

I paid a call as well on the emir of Kuwait, and we sat in two very fancy chairs surrounded by members of his government and my staff, attempting to make small talk. When our supply of topics dwindled, I began to look for a way to gracefully excuse myself. Just then he stood up, and a door opened onto a beautiful and elegant tea party. Drinking from a dainty china cup and nibbling on delicacies, I walked about and spoke with the Kuwaitis in one of the most gracious parties I ever attended.

On this trip I returned to Amman, Jordan, where I announced a U.S.-Jordanian partnership at the King Hussein Cancer Center, named for King Abdullah's father, the late King Hussein, who had battled cancer for years. Indeed, with cancer, we do not know from where a breakthrough treatment will come or when. Perhaps it will be a doctor in Amman, or a study of Bedouin women in Abu Dhabi that helps us unlock some of the mystery of this disease.

On my previous visit, everyone in Jordan had told me to go to the ancient city of Petra. Before my plane took off for home, this time I did, walking through its intricate buildings carved deep in the sandstone, rather like the ancient Buddhas in Bamiyan, Afghanistan. Along one street I spotted a group of camels and their handlers, and I turned to our ambassador, David Hale; my chief of staff, Anita McBride; and my press secretary, Sally McDonough, and said, "Let's ride." On our camels, we meandered through the twisting, narrow gorge that surrounds the ancient city and its rose-colored walls. Much of the city has lain largely silent since the 300s, when an earthquake struck, but it is still possible to imagine the people who once made their homes amid this cavernous stone. As we rounded one final bend, almost like a hallway cut through the earth, we came upon a group of Americans. When they caught sight of me, they spontaneously raised their fingers to make the sign of "hook 'em horns" and began singing "The Eyes of Texas." It was a tour group from home.

⌒

The November 6 visit of Nicolas Sarkozy, the new president of France, to Washington was surrounded by high-level intrigue: would he or would he not be bringing his wife? In August the Sarkozy family had chosen to vacation on a New Hampshire lake. Cecilia Sarkozy, France's first lady, had mentioned this to me during the G8 Summit. I knew George and I would be in Maine visiting his parents, and I suggested that the Sarkozys and their son come to Kennebunkport. We planned a kid-friendly meal of hamburgers, hot dogs, and blueberry pie, but Cecilia stayed behind and Sarkozy came alone. Now, before we printed the invitations for the state dinner, the National Security Council was working with the French government to determine whether this visit would also be a solo one.

George and I like Nicolas Sarkozy very much. He is young and dynamic and blunt, and he has a great sense of humor and understanding of the frequent absurdity of political life. Sarkozy's father was a Hungarian immigrant, a refugee from World War II and the Communists. Over lunch Sarkozy told us that when he was young, his father said to him, "You must move to the United States." When Nicolas looked at him quizzically, his father had added, "I know that you want to be president, but a man named Sarkozy will never be president of France."

Sarkozy did come by himself. Shortly afterward, he and Cecilia divorced, and a few months later, he married the model and singer Carla Bruni. Single or married, the French president arrived in Washington with a very interesting entourage. Rather than the typical group of political people, his delegation included a chef, Guy Savoy, from one of Paris's top restaurants and the director of the Louvre Museum, Henri Loyrette, as well as a retinue of cabinet ministers.

In contrast to the sometimes testy relationship that George had with Jacques Chirac, Sarkozy was pro-American and interested in building a strong partnership with the United States. It was no accident that he timed his visit to coincide with the 250th anniversary of the birth of the Marquis de Lafayette, the young Frenchman who had become one of George Washington's closest aides during the Revolutionary War and who is buried in France beneath soil that he himself carried home from the ground around Bunker Hill. In January, at the request of Jim Billington, the Librarian of Congress, I had paid a visit to the Marquis de Lafayette's La Grange, a fifteenth-century château outside of Paris, where he lived after his brutal imprisonment during the French Revolution. The chateau's attic contained a treasure trove of artifacts and personal Lafayette papers, and the Library of Congress had overseen a special effort to digitize the collection. So entwined was Lafayette's life with the young United States that on the grounds of La Grange are trees from every U.S. state he visited; he brought their saplings home and planted them. He kept a rare letter written by Martha Washington, American newspapers from 1776, a signed copy of the Declaration of Independence, and an American flag that he took with him to prison. Across the ocean President George Washington labored for Lafayette's release, sent his dear friend books, and gave Lafayette's son refuge in the young America.

I thought that to commemorate this extraordinary French aristocrat who had such love for the United States, we should host Nicolas Sarkozy at Washington's Mount Vernon home. My initial hope was to do a formal state dinner on the grounds, but the visit could not be scheduled until November, and by then the weather was likely to be changeable and cold. Instead, on Sarkozy's second day in Washington, D.C., the two heads of state traveled to Mount Vernon and sat at the table where Lafayette and Washington had once dined to discuss the security of the globe. But unlike that George and the marquis, George and Nicolas were banished to Mount Vernon's greenhouse for lunch. The Mount Vernon Ladies' Association, which oversees the historic treasure, does not permit food or drink of any kind inside Washington's home, not even for two presidents.

Before he left, Sarkozy also addressed a joint session of Congress—the Marquis de Lafayette had been the first foreign dignitary to do that, in 1824—and told the House and Senate that he was committed to sending more French forces to help secure Afghanistan.

By late fall the Iraq surge had reached its maximum point, with 170,000 U.S. troops on the ground, and there were positive signs of change. In the summer Iraq had met eight of eighteen political and security benchmarks, but on another eight, its progress was still, according to a White House review, "unsatisfactory." There had, however, been no catastrophic bomb attacks. Violence was markedly declining, as were attacks on U.S. troops and U.S. combat deaths. In mid-December, British troops would return control of the once violent port city of Basra to the Iraqis and the Iraqi army. It appeared that the surge, which earlier that year had been so derided by its critics, was beginning to bear fruit.

December brought another round of Christmas parties. Our pastry team commandeered the ground-floor China and Vermeil rooms to frost the thousands of Barney and Miss Beazley cookies they baked each season. The theme I had chosen was "Holiday in the National Parks." I had come to love the national parks from all my summer hiking trips. With my childhood friends, I had hiked not just in Yosemite and Yellowstone but also in Olympic, Glacier, Denali, Mesa Verde, Acadia, the Everglades, Zion, and Death Valley, all truly some of the most beautiful and striking spots on earth.

In 2005 my hiking group and I had returned to the Grand Canyon, where we began our hiking ritual in 1986, the year we turned forty. This time we took our daughters on the route that started with a river trip through the canyon and then a ten-mile hike out along the South Rim. There were five women in their late fifties and six in their twenties. The twenty-somethings walked out in about four hours; their mothers finally made it in seven. The dry heat and the hike had so exhausted me that at one point I thought about lying down to rest alongside the trail. Then I imagined the headlines: "First Lady Carried from Canyon on a Gurney," and I doggedly kept going. When the girls asked us if they could come again next year, we looked at each other for an instant, sweat beading on our faces, and answered with a resounding "No."

During our summer hikes, we always invited the park superintendent and rangers to join us, usually on our last night. After our 2002 visit to Yellowstone, Suzanne Lewis, the superintendent, surprised us by nominating my childhood friend Regan Gammon to the National Park Foundation board. Started in 1967 with support from Lady Bird Johnson and funds from Laurance Rockefeller, the foundation serves as a charitable partner for the park system, helping to increase parkland, protect fragile ecosystems and species, conduct school outreach, and protect park history. Although we had hiked in the parks for years, none of us had been aware of the foundation and its work. After Regan, I joined as well, as the foundation's honorary chair.

To decorate the White House for "Holiday in the National Parks," the official title of the holiday celebration, we sent a plain gold ball to each of the 391 parks and historic sites and asked park service officials to select a local artisan to create an ornament that would represent the site. When we think of national parks, we tend to think of the Grand Canyon, Yellowstone, and Yosemite, but the list is long and includes the White House grounds, Independence Hall, the Statue of Liberty, Gettysburg, and Valley Forge. Every state in the nation has a national park or monument except Delaware, which is creating a national historic trail.

For the fir tree in the Blue Room, we received ornaments painted or etched with scenes from the Shiloh battlefield and from the Pennsylvania site where Flight 93 had crashed, which was now our newest national monument. In the niches at the entry to the State Floor, we hung oil paintings by Adrian Martinez of Hopi Point at the Grand Canyon and a waterfall in Zion National Park to bring scenes of the parklands into the White House. He created the paintings especially for the curved spaces, working on scaffolds as well as down on his knees. White House carpenters built replicas of the missions in San Antonio, the Cape Hatteras Lighthouse, and the Statue of Liberty to decorate the rooms and halls. The chefs reproduced Mount Rushmore in chocolate. In the Palm Room, the decorative tree was made entirely from seashells to represent our national seashores. It was a wonderful chance to showcase our diverse parklands, and our holiday card depicted a scene from the first lady's garden—itself national parkland—painted by David Drummond. We added our wishes that "the joy of all creation fill your heart this blessed season."

At our Hanukkah party, Judea and Ruth Pearl, the parents of Danny Pearl, *The Wall Street Journal* reporter kidnapped and murdered by terrorists in Pakistan, lit the menorah. For the six previous years, we had borrowed magnificent menorahs from Jewish museums and synagogues around the nation. Many had been saved from Europe before the Holocaust. But this year the Pearls brought their family menorah.

The Pearl family menorah had belonged to Danny's great-grandfather Chaim, who had carried it with him when he moved from Poland to Israel to help found the town of Bnei-Brak, where today there is a street named in Chaim Pearl's honor. From there the menorah had come to the United States. Year after year it was lovingly lit in the Pearls' home. Judea, who is also a cantor, movingly sang to us during the ceremony and his melodic voice left many guests wiping their eyes. When George spoke, he said that Daniel Pearl's "only crime was being a Jewish American—something Daniel would never deny. In his final moments, Daniel told his captors about a street in Israel named for his great-grandfather. He looked into their cameras and said, 'My father is Jewish, my mother is Jewish, and I am Jewish.' These words have become a source of inspiration for Americans of all faiths. They show the courage of a man who refused to bow before terror—and the strength of a spirit that could not be broken."

On December 10, International Human Rights Day, I spoke via teleconference to Burmese refugees living in Thailand and then issued a call for greater international pressure on the junta, which was still persecuting those who had peacefully protested in the late summer. In Iraq the violence was continuing to ebb. The surge was showing further signs of working.

For us, the year 2008 was to be a year of lasts, the last NATO Summit, last Summit of the Americas, last international trips and visits, the last state dinner, the last chance for me to work on the White House initiatives I had begun. The final year in office, especially after seven years, is in many ways its own long good-bye. But there were firsts as well, and though the year was sometimes difficult, it was also remarkable.

I could now walk the halls of the White House and have my own memories come flooding back, such as the 2006 Veterans Day, when we invited all the living members of my father's World War II unit, the Timberwolves. Those who could came to the White House with their wives and children. Some apologized that they didn't have a jacket or a tie to wear, and we said, Come just as you are. One veteran didn't believe that he was actually being invited to the White House—he thought it was a scam and called the Better Business Bureau. After a chain of phone calls up to his congressman, he was assured that the invitation was in fact real. I watched those men, who had once been so young and brave, come with their canes, walkers, and wheelchairs to the house of presidents and wished my father could have been among them.

In June 2008, we invited the Classes of 1964 from all three Midland high schools—Midland, Lee, and George Washington Carver—for a reunion at the White House. In the fall we held a dinner for the justices on the Supreme Court and their spouses.

And now, in addition to our American guests, I could recall the many times when I had walked women from Africa and Afghanistan through these famous rooms and halls, so they might glimpse our history as well. In the East Room, George had paid tribute to Medal of Honor recipients, his voice breaking as he recited their acts of heroism until he himself could barely speak. I could pass each doorway and remember a conversation I had had, a person I had met, a memory that was my own.

We had hosted dinners in the State Dining Room in honor of Benjamin Franklin and William Shakespeare as well as two black-tie dinners to recognize Eunice Kennedy Shriver and the Special Olympics, which she helped to found. We had celebrated the Dance Theatre of Harlem, the Thelonious Monk Institute of Jazz, Thomas Jefferson's 265th birthday, and also baseball. For my entire eight years, I had wonderful partnerships with our leading national cultural arts agencies. The poet Dana Gioia, who headed the National Endowment for the Arts, helped Americans rediscover the pleasure of reading through his Big Read program, highlighting such classics as *To Kill a Mockingbird, Fahrenheit 451*, and *The Joy Luck Club*. I was there when Dana and the NEA launched the largest tour of Shakespeare in American history, bringing the Bard's words to some 2,300 small and midsize communities in all fifty states, as well as to 3,600 schools and major military bases. Dana pioneered a special NEA effort called Operation Homecoming, which paired returning war veterans with writers to help them tell their stories. A special anthology of soldiers' writings was published in 2006.

I was happy to support Chairman Bruce Cole's efforts at the National Endowment for the Humanities to reinvigorate the teaching of history through programs such as We the People, which put some of our most important national documents within reach of school classrooms. I helped launch Picturing America, which gave public and private schools, libraries, and communities access to top-quality reproductions of iconic images of America's past, so they might experience our history through art, from *Washington Crossing the Delaware* to the works of Winslow Homer, Depression-era photographs by Dorothea Lange, and the scene of Martin Luther King marching from Selma to Montgomery.

At the Institute of Museums and Library Services, Dr. Robert Martin, and later Anne-Imelda Radice, worked with the nation's 122,000 libraries and 17,500 museums to recruit and educate new professionals. I was proud to be part of IMLS's presentations of the annual National Medals for Museum and Library Service. Among its many contributions, IMLS helped to provide opportunities to train Native Americans to preserve their past in Arizona, and support interpreters for African-American history in Brooklyn. It worked with the Cleveland Metroparks Zoo to assist with the conservation of endangered animals, and also to assist with the 190 million objects around the nation that are in serious need of conservation.

At the White House we hosted each year's winners of the Cooper Hewitt National Design Awards, given to the best architects, landscape architects, fashion designers, and others whose design work make our country more beautiful. I enjoyed meeting many of these talented creators, whose work I had admired for years. At the President's Committee on the Arts and Humanities, my good friend Adair Margo expanded the Coming Up Taller Awards for excellence in children's arts programs to add an international focus, by recognizing programs in Mexico, Egypt, and China. The idea is that when a child takes a bow, afterward he or she comes up taller. I am proud to have helped make the White House a strong partner for the nation's artistic and cultural life.

Many of our happiest moments came from welcoming Americans from across the nation into the home of presidents. We had military families, from Jewish veterans of the Korean War to the cousins and friends of soldiers in Iraq. Fifteen hundred military spouses came for breakfast. We invited people we'd met out along rope lines or who had written us letters. We hosted Girl Scout troops and school groups. I invited high school students from Washington's Ballou High, which was grieving several murders, to come to the East Room for a special screening of a documentary on their high school band. We invited a dance troupe from Atlanta, comprised of girls from at-risk neighborhoods, to perform for the Coming Up Taller Awards. When travel funds were an issue for this troupe and others, we found the money to pay their way to the White House. We had over a thousand college athletes come for NCAA receptions. Almost every week, Diane Bodman, wife of Energy Secretary Samuel Bodman, brought through small groups of wounded soldiers, veterans, and their families. I wanted everyone who walked through the doors or onto the grounds to feel comfortable. During the late-spring and summer months, George and I watched children play T-ball, as a thousand visitors strolled around the South Lawn during each game. We were happy that the White House grounds had become a place where families could gather on a Sunday afternoon. Opening this house, opening our days to others, also opened our own hearts.

In February, George and I made our last trip to Africa. We began in the West African nation of Benin and then flew to Tanzania, where at the airport crowds of dancers awaited us dressed in fabric imprinted with George's picture, surrounded by the country's traditional colors of blue, green, black, and yellow. Tanzania's first lady wore a dress made from fabric with George's picture stamped on it and the American and Tanzanian flags intertwined. On one of her scarves was written the words "We cherish democracy."

Everywhere we stopped, in Benin and Tanzania and Rwanda and Ghana and Liberia, thousands of people lined the sides of the roads, waving American flags and the flags of their nations, singing and cheering, to thank George for what he had done for them, for the lives that his efforts had saved. The Ghanaian president, John Kufuor, invited a thousand people to celebrate at a dinner in an overflowing ballroom, where the band played Ghanaian highlife music, a combination of Glenn Miller–style swing and jazz. President Kufuor asked me to dance, and within minutes everyone was on his or her feet, even George, dancing with Theresa Kufuor.

There had been an incredible change from our first trip, in 2003. I remember one mother in Botswana who had heard that the American president was coming to visit a local medical clinic, so she dressed her daughter in a lovely white, fluffy dress with bits of lavender, already looking like an angel. The little girl lay on an examining table, so frail and sick but with her mother's last hopes to make her beautiful. Today, with anti-retrovirals, that child would have a chance. Millions do have a chance. Whereas once a visit to Africa was about holding the hands of the sick and dying, now it is about hope. People who were waiting quietly for death are taking antiretrovirals and, in what they call the "Lazarus effect," are now celebrating a second chance at life.

Our history has made us a free nation, but history has not been so kind to much of Africa, where colonialism, the slave trade, poverty, war, and pandemic disease have ravaged nations not just for decades but for centuries. Yet after just three years, nearly 25 million people in sub-Saharan Africa, living in the fifteen countries of the President's Malaria Initiative, were protected by insecticide-treated nets. In 2003, only fifty thousand people in sub-Saharan Africa received antiretroviral treatment for AIDS. By 2008, after George's PEPFAR program, that number had grown to more than 2 million. Another 4 million orphans and vulnerable children had been cared for, and more than 200,000 babies whose mothers had AIDS were born HIV-free. People thanked us with such enthusiasm and warmth that we left each stop with tears in our eyes.

In March I traveled to Haiti, one of the first nations to receive PEPFAR funding. It is the poorest nation in the Western Hemisphere, with the greatest HIV burden. In the early 1980s, Haiti was the epicenter for HIV. It was the first country on earth to have a clinic devoted solely to HIV/AIDS care, the GHESKIO Center in Port-au-Prince, founded in 1982 by Dr. Jean Pape, a native Haitian who trained as a doctor at New York's Weill Cornell Medical College, one of the center's longest sponsors. Each year the clinic sees over 100,000 people, many of them the poorest of the poor. Even in March, the island heat was stifling, and the brightly colored buildings belied years of suffering. For most of the decade, Haiti's political situation had been so volatile that the Secret Service had refused to allow me to visit earlier in George's term. But in the Haitians I met, I saw a deep warmth, rich spirit, and hope for the future. And there were reasons to hope. By 2008, Haiti's infection rate from HIV had fallen, and PEPFAR programs were helping to provide antiretrovirals to nearly eighteen thousand men, women, and children. We left hoping that more things would change, never imagining the devastating earthquake to come.

In April, Benedict XVI made the first visit by a Pope to the White House in almost thirty years. He came on April 16, his birthday, and more than thirteen thousand guests welcomed him on the South Lawn, spontaneously serenading the Pontiff with "Happy Birthday" during the arrival ceremony. It was the largest gathering on record at the White House.

The papal nuncio told the White House that the Pope had decided to arrive on his birthday because "you spend your birthday with your friends." He wanted the visit to be a reflection of his respect for the United States, for its generosity and charity. We were deeply touched.

We decorated with yellow and white tulips, in honor of the papal colors, and under a sky of brilliant blue, the soloist Kathleen Battle performed "The Lord's Prayer," rather than a traditional anthem or marching song. We had asked if there was any song the Pope would like to hear, and the papal nuncio said the song with the words "Glory! Glory! Hallelujah." So Sergeant Alvy Powell led the Army Chorus in singing the Civil War anthem "The Battle Hymn of the Republic." Then George spoke. "Here in America, you'll find a nation of compassion. . . . Each day citizens across America answer the universal call to feed the hungry and comfort the sick and care for the infirm. Each day across the world the United States is working to eradicate disease, alleviate poverty, promote peace and bring the light of hope to places still mired in the darkness of tyranny and despair. . . . In a world where some invoke the name of God to justify acts of terror and murder and hate, we need your message that 'God is love.'"

Pope Benedict talked of America's pluralistic society and how "all believers have found here the freedom to worship God in accordance to the dictates of their conscience." He continued, "Freedom is not only a gift, but also a summons to personal responsibility. Americans know this from experience—almost every town in this country had its monuments honoring those who sacrificed their lives in defense of freedom, both at home and abroad."

He ended with the words "God bless America."

When the arrival ceremony was complete, we walked inside the White House and up to the State Floor. I'd asked the pastry chef to prepare a birthday cake for the Pope. When we wheeled out the four-tier cream and white cake, adorned with white icing ribbons and a single white candle, his eyes lit up with surprise.

The visit was deeply meaningful for George and for me, and also for the many members of our family who are Catholic, including Jeb and his wife, Columba, and Doro's husband, Bobby Koch, and their children.

That night Pope Benedict had a private dinner with his American cardinals while we held a special dinner in honor of his visit, inviting Catholic bishops and other Catholic leaders, especially from charities, who had done so much to help at home and abroad. We had Catholic members of the cabinet and the Congress, including Nancy Pelosi, and Catholic members of the Supreme Court, as well as many of our good friends who shared the Pope's faith, including Joey and Jan O'Neill, who had introduced George and me, now more than thirty years ago. That April 16 was one of the loveliest days we spent at the White House.

Just over two weeks later, on May 2, Cyclone Nargis devastated the Burmese coast, causing the worst natural disaster in Burma's recorded history. More than 100,000 were reported dead, and many, many more were missing. And that was just the official count; unofficial totals suggested that the number of deaths might be far higher, approaching the toll of the deadly 2004 tsunami. To add to the suffering, the Burmese government would not allow outside aid. The United States had naval vessels that could have docked and provided clean water and medical care for those in need, as we had done after the tsunami, but the ruling junta would rather inflict more loss of life than give up an inch of power. So at three in the afternoon on May 5, I walked into the White House briefing room to speak to the press, and via them to the world, about Burma, including the fact that the only warnings about the cyclone the Burmese people had received had come from the United States, from our Radio Free Asia and Voice of America. I hoped that Burma would accept aid from India at least. In my remarks, I called on the junta to postpone a scheduled May 10 vote on a new sham constitution, written largely to bar Aung San Suu Kyi from running for office. The constitution banned anyone who had ever been married to a foreigner from holding office—as it happens, her late husband was British.

The vote was postponed, and as the days passed, the junta did relent and allow one hundred American C-130s flights fully loaded with emergency medical supplies to land in Rangoon. But the devastation outside the capital was far worse, and the junta would not permit our ships to dock and offer immediate, lifesaving aid. To maintain their brutal control, Burma's rulers preferred death and disease to life.

On May 10, Jenna married Henry Hager at our ranch, overlooking our tiny lake, the old cattle watering hole, where we now stocked fish and grew prairie grasses. Henry was waiting for her as the sun set. Barbara was her maid of honor, and Jenna's tearful dad walked her down the aisle as mariachis played "Here Comes the Bride." Our longtime friend the Houston pastor Kirbyjon Caldwell performed the service. Jenna and Henry were wed before an altar and cross carved from the same limestone that forms the walls of our house. It was the sturdiest of foundations for their new life together.

Mother was there, and Bar and Gampy read to Jenna and Henry from First Corinthians. Jenna's cousin Wendy and her husband, Diego Reyes, read a Pablo Neruda poem in English and in Spanish. And Henry's parents, John and Maggie Hager, spoke of what they had learned about how to keep a marriage strong, of how they had faced and triumphed over adversity when John Hager contracted polio shortly after Henry's older brother was born.

That evening, as Jenna and Henry slipped on their shiny new rings, George and I basked in their love. Come fall, we would mark our thirty-first year of marriage. Our daughter was a newlywed, and we had now been together for exactly half our lifetimes.

We held their celebratory dinner in a large tent decorated with giant festival staffs, trailing flowers, and streams of brightly colored ribbons. After tearful toasts the guests danced to the music of Super T and then, late in the evening, gathered around the warm glow of a firepit. A few weeks later, we hosted a reception for Jenna and Henry in the White House.

Jenna had dreamed of marrying at the ranch since we first bought the land, and she and Henry very much wanted to marry at a place they could return to. Each spring, when the bluebonnets open and the pink evening primrose blooms, carpeting the ground as they did on that perfect early evening, I am reminded of how Henry and Jenna took their first steps together as husband and wife, beaming smiles on their faces, walking beneath a shower of fragrant rose petals.

As Jenna and Henry left on their honeymoon, George and I made our final presidential visit to the Middle East. We arrived to celebrate the sixtieth anniversary of the founding of the State of Israel. After joining in the official commemorations, George and I walked the heights of the ancient desert fortress of Masada, atop a massive, weathered outcropping of rock where 960 defenders held out for three years against the Roman Tenth Legion's attempt to conquer them all. Today Israeli soldiers make the promise that "Masada shall never fall again." On May 15, the anniversary of Israel's birth, George addressed its parliament, the Knesset. "The alliance between our governments," he said, "is unbreakable, yet the source of our friendship runs deeper than any treaty. It is grounded in the shared spirit of our people, the bonds of the Book, the ties of the soul. When William Bradford stepped off the *Mayflower* in 1620, he quoted the words of Jeremiah: 'Come let us declare Zion in the word of God.' The founders of my country saw a new promised land and bestowed upon their towns names like Bethlehem and New Canaan. And in time, many Americans became passionate advocates for a Jewish state." George recalled how he too, on previous visits, had prayed at Yad Vashem and touched the Western Wall.

We paid a call on some of our Arab friends as well, first King Abdullah of Saudi Arabia. There I returned to visit with breast cancer patients at King Fahd Medical Center. The same female doctor, covered entirely except for the slit for her eyes, approached me and then was surprised when I did not immediately recognize her through her veils. I was delighted to learn that, though its partnership with the United States was less than two years old, the King Fahd Center had already scheduled a breast cancer conference for October, to include oncologists and cancer specialists from around the Middle East.

In Egypt I visited the coral reefs around the Red Sea port of Sharm al-Sheikh and from a glass-bottomed boat watched as sea life moved in silence among the brilliant-colored coral. On land I launched an international Big Read program between American and Egyptian high school students. The Egyptians read *To Kill a Mockingbird, The Grapes of Wrath,* and *Fahrenheit 451*, while the American students read *The Thief and the Dogs*, a novel by the Nobel Prize–winning writer Naguib Mahfouz.

Come June, I made my third and final visit to Afghanistan.

I began in Bamiyan Province, where those ancient Buddhas had been destroyed seven years earlier. From almost any spot in the valley I could gaze up and see the empty niches, hollowed deep into the stone. Today Bamiyan has a female governor and is one of the safest provinces in the nation. In my 2005 visit, when I met her in Kabul, I had promised Dr. Habiba Sarabi that I would come to her home. When my helicopter landed, Governor Sarabi was waiting on the dusty ground. We embraced, and I said, "I told you I would come."

On full display was a group of Kiwi troops, who were there as part of the New Zealand army and New Zealand's provincial reconstruction team. In tan desert camouflage, they did a full native Powhiri dance; a few men had donned body paint and waved long, pointed spears as the Secret Service watched warily.

A short way from the landing strip, where the helicopters remained parked and ready and surrounded by armed guards, Governor Sarabi and I entered a police training facility. In spare prefab buildings, Afghans were learning the basics of law enforcement, and in one room, with dark curtains on its high, tiny rectangular windows, the trainees were women. Eleven Afghan women had come here to study basic police work. Seated at their rows of desks, their slightly bent heads veiled and bodies fully covered, they asked that no photographs be taken of their faces. At that moment, I felt the depths of their bravery; they were concealing their identities not merely from local insurgents or opium poppy merchants. Many of these women's own families did not know that they were training to be police officers.

From the academy, Governor Sarabi and I traveled farther into the valley, past scrubby fields. There, in the shadow of the ancient Buddha's remains, mud-brick walls were rising. It was the first floor of what would become a new, two-story school for Afghan boys and girls. The school was being constructed by the Ayenda Foundation, an offshoot of the U.S.-Afghan Women's Council. Ayenda was founded in 2006 by two council members, Shamim Jawad, the wife of the Afghan ambassador to the United States, and Timothy McBride, who had worked for Gampy as an assistant to the president in the White House. The money to build the school had been donated entirely by American and Afghan citizens.

Before I left Bamiyan, I cut the ribbon for a new highway built by the U.S. Agency for International Development. The new road followed one of the ancient Silk Road pathways, but today it led not over the mountains but to the airport, so local entrepreneurs might sell and ship their goods to Kabul and beyond. Then the helicopters lifted off for Kabul and the Presidential Palace, where President Karzai was waiting. We met and spoke to the press. In other rooms of the palace I visited with students, young men and women from Kabul University, as well as from the new American University of Afghanistan and the International School of Kabul, whose formation I had announced only three years before. For these students it was their first time on the Presidential Palace grounds. But I had to remain inside the palace compound; I could not walk the streets of Kabul, past store windows and open front shops, and my plane had to be in the air by dusk.

Vast swaths of Afghanistan still had no electricity or running water. But the lack of knowledge was the worst of all. Bamiyan, for example, has for years been a rich potato-growing region. But local farmers now had no storage facilities for their crops. They could not preserve their harvest to eat during the harsh winters, nor could they keep their surplus to sell when prices were high. Instead, they hawked their freshly dug crops in local markets, and whatever they did not sell rotted. Then an Idaho potato farmer recalled how his own grandparents had stored their potatoes, in a simple dugout cellar. He taught Afghan farmers to do the same. There are hundreds of stories like this, of soldiers who came back after they left the army, of retired police officers who came over as police trainers. Colonel Gary Davis, who served as surgeon general for the U.S. Army in Afghanistan, returned to Kabul after he retired from the military to teach Afghan doctors and nurses how to care for some of the country's most serious pregnancy-related complications. Despite the obstacles and the dangers, these Americans have given so much of themselves to make other lives better and have asked nothing in return.

And the obstacles are many. In January of 2008, a group of female Afghan parliamentarians came to see me at the White House. They spoke of the severe threats that women continue to live under in all parts of

Afghanistan and of how much they feared the Taliban's return. One of them told me, "This is our only chance."

But I remember too one of my friends who said, "We talk so much about helping Afghan women. What about the men? It seems to me they are the ones who need to change most of all."

Slowly, some are changing. There are illiterate men who are happy to have their daughters enrolled in school and learning to read. Days after my Afghan visit ended, I spoke at an international donor conference in Paris hosted by President Nicolas Sarkozy. He had convened eighty nations and organizations to secure more global aid for Afghanistan. Already over 6 million Afghan children were attending school; 1.5 million of them were girls, who had been banned from the classroom before 2002.

I made my case and hoped that this "only chance" would be enough.

After Paris, George and I traveled together to Slovenia, to attend our last U.S.–European Union Summit. As I left Europe, I thought of the many friendships we had made with foreign leaders. I would miss German chancellor Angela Merkel and her husband, Joachim Sauer, whose quick minds and lively conversation warmed our visits. We had stayed with them in the German version of Camp David, an old manor house located in the former East Germany that had been fully restored. In return, we had invited them to visit our ranch, where we hiked and talked. I had built a friendship with Aliza Olmert, wife of the Israeli prime minister, Ehud Olmert, who was herself an accomplished artist. And I had taken great joy in my visits with the king and queen of Jordan. But it was also time for us to move on. Tony and Cherie Blair had already left 10 Downing Street. Soon we would be leaving the White House.

But first I wanted to see the Burmese border lands.

From the air, on August 7, everything below me was green, that rich, over-grown green of Southeast Asian jungles and the wide plumes of stunted mangrove and towering native oak trees. As the small American military cargo plane descended, I could see the roadways cutting through and catch a quick glimpse of the narrow city streets of Mae Sot, punctuated by the brilliant gold-leaf dome of the temple pagoda. I was in northern Thailand, and just beyond lay the country of Burma.

George and I and Barbara were on our way to the Beijing Olympics, and George had wanted to make one last visit to South Korea and then to Thailand before we arrived in China. If we were going to Thailand, the two places I wanted to go were the Mae La Refugee Camp and the Mae Tao Clinic. Barbara was eager to join me.

The summer air was wet and humid, and people were waiting impatiently for the onslaught of the rainy season. My clothes stuck to my skin almost from the moment I stepped off the plane. A large welcoming party was waiting for us on the tarmac, the governor of Thailand's Tak Province, the deputy governor, the chief judge, the Mae Sot district officer, the commander of the provincial police, the mayor, the chairman of the municipal council, the U.S. consul general, and sixty schoolchildren waving flags. From there we departed for the Burmese border.

The Mae Tao Clinic is the place Dr. Cynthia Maung calls home. She is a Burmese doctor who fled into Thailand in 1988, when she was twenty-nine years old. She was running from chaos; in the cities, Burmese troops knelt and fired repeatedly on unarmed demonstrators protesting the repressive junta. To silence some of the protesters, the regime's forces rounded them up and drowned them. Dr. Cynthia escaped by walking through the jungles at night. When the sun rose, she slept in fields. She crossed the border at Mae Sot and began life in a refugee camp. Soon she was setting up a primitive medical clinic to treat refugees who arrived with war wounds or who had contracted malaria. She sterilized her instruments by boiling them in an aluminum rice cooker and thought she would return home in two, possibly three months. Twenty years later, she has made only brief forays across the jungle-laced border to care for the sick in Burma. She remains in Thailand, at her clinic, where she is known as the Mother Teresa of the Burmese.

I had already "met" Dr. Cynthia via a White House teleconference on Burma, but now I had the chance to talk to her face-to-face and to shake her hand. I walked into her open-air clinic, and the first thing I saw was a volunteer American doctor performing cataract surgery in a building with open windows. Outside the rains of a tropical thunderstorm poured down, turning the paths to mud. In another section was a row of picnic tables covered with plastic shields. That was where they placed the newborns. They weighed the babies on a vegetable scale, laying each on a paper napkin. The clinic also fits prosthetics—legs, arms, feet—for all the people who lost limbs to the many land mines planted by the military junta. Refugees are being trained to make the prosthetic molds and casts, for which there is near-constant demand. Fifty thousand Burmese also cross the border each year to visit Mae Tao to seek medical care. Many walk hundreds of miles from deep inside Burma to the clinic. I left behind crates of donated supplies, including thousands of bed nets to help prevent malaria, which is rampant in the region.

Thirty miles away, pushed up against the sides of steep, forested mountains, their tops obscured by drifting clouds and rain, is the Mae La Refugee Camp. The sprawling camp winds its way around six hills at the Thai-Burma border. Today children who were born in Mae La two decades ago are having children of their own. None of them has ever set foot outside Mae La's compound of muddy paths and hutlike homes. Thai law requires them to remain confined to their camps in a stateless limbo. More than 140,000 Burmese refugees live in camps like this strung along the Thai-Burma border, nearly 40,000 in Mae La alone, at least according to official estimates. The actual totals may be much higher. Beyond the camps, as many as 1.5 million other Burmese live inside Thailand.

At Mae La there are now twenty-six schools, built from weathered bamboo, with open sides and topped by thatched roofs. What few desks and chairs they had rested on damp, earthen floors. At the school I visited, two young American women were helping to teach English. One of the boys stood and wrote a slightly halting message to me on the blackboard, "My life in refugee is better than Burma, but I don't have opportunity to out outside the camp. I would like to speak English, so I am now trying hard." They lived in a camp without jobs, where there is no electricity and no running water, yet they came to learn and dreamed of a better life. A few would get that chance.

In 2005 the U.S. Congress changed the immigration requirements for

Burmese refugees. By the time of my visit, over twenty thousand Burmese had been cleared to resettle in the United States. Three families were preparing to board a bus for the first stage of their trip when I arrived at Mae La. One family was going to Florida; another was headed to South Carolina; and a third was leaving for Texas. Their belongings were packed into brightly colored rice sacks.

At Mae La, I was greeted by teenagers performing a traditional Burmese dance. It was a dance from a land over the mountains, a land they had never seen from outside their bamboo walls. The next day, August 8, 2008, would mark twenty years since the brutal government crackdown that drove so many Burmese to run for their lives into Thailand.

That is part of what is ultimately so tragic about these repressive regimes, in Burma, in Afghanistan, in Liberia. They go on for years, in some cases, like Burma, for generations. Whole generations pass, and the culture erodes. Under the junta, half the people in Burma suffer from malnutrition and hunger. And when these regimes finally do collapse, everything has to be rebuilt. There is no infrastructure for people to even begin to start over, no economic infrastructure, no civil infrastructure, no physical infrastructure, no power lines or good roads. It takes years to rebuild.

It was almost surreal to leave the refugee camp and arrive that night in Beijing, China, which had spent years preparing for a grand Summer Olympics. In a speech in Bangkok, George had called on the Chinese to cease detaining political dissidents, human rights activists, and religious activists. He spoke out in support of a free press, freedom of assembly, and labor rights, saying, "The United States believes the people of China deserve the fundamental liberty that is the natural right of all human beings. . . . Trusting its people with greater freedom is the only way for China to develop its full potential."

China was consumed with its global spectacle. And we relished every minute of watching our amazing athletes compete on the world stage. We waved flags and cheered, moving from the Olympic swimming pool to the basketball stadium to the imported sand court for beach volleyball. It was a stunning sight to see the Chinese cheering for the American basketball players, chanting "Kobe, Kobe" for Kobe Bryant. And we were equally proud when our basketball team lined the seats of the Olympic pool to shout as Michael Phelps won his string of gold medals. The men's team came and cheered at the women's games. It was a genuine display of camaraderie and sportsmanship.

I was particularly touched by one event, the men's 400-meter freestyle in the Olympic pool. Michael Phelps won the gold, while fellow American swimmer Larsen Jensen won the bronze. After the ceremony, all three medalists made a celebratory walk around the pool, and George and I waited at the rail to greet them. As he took his first steps, Michael Phelps tossed his bouquet of red roses into the crowd, and the silver medalist soon did the same. But Larsen Jensen held on to his. When he reached me, he lifted his arm to hand me his flowers, saying, "I want you to have these."

Gampy joined us, remembering the days thirty years before when he had been the United States' official diplomat to China after President Nixon reestablished relations. President Hu Jintao had us to lunch in the Forbidden City, the centuries-old compound of the emperors, tucked behind massive red walls. There were small meandering streams and gardens, but the ancient rooms are now largely bare, leaving their past to our imaginations.

⁓

As September opened, we expected a harsh presidential campaign but an otherwise calm fall. Within two weeks our assumptions had been thoroughly dashed. George's presidency would be bookended by two Septembers, the September of 9-11, when the nation was devastated by forces without, and the September of 2008, when it was threatened with collapse from within.

My own experience with economic collapse came from the fierce boom and bust oil cycles in Midland. Each time, people were lulled into believing that the boom would last, and each time, the oil markets collapsed with the slimmest of warnings. Economics was not part of my portfolio in the White House, but along the dusty streets of Midland I had known highly educated geologists who lost their jobs and families who left town because when the well drilling ceased and the derricks were shut down, there was nothing left for them. But the crisis we now faced was engulfing not one Texas town but vast swaths of the nation. Week after week the White House was working around the clock to manage the financial crisis. Some staffers barely left their desks. George's term began just after the dot-com bubble had burst, plunging the nation into recession. In his final months, he was working to contain another bursting bubble as it direly threatened the entire U.S. economy.

In the news and on the presidential campaign trail, George was attacked ruthlessly. We had both long ago given up stewing over the things said about either one of us. When you are president, there simply isn't time. George did not have time to be mad at a press person who wrote or said something nasty about him. He did not have time to be upset at a candidate who lashed out at him in an effort to secure higher office. Then too, as we had long ago learned, there is a certain luxury that comes from being a candidate. It is easy to criticize a sitting president when you are not the one in the Oval Office, when you are not responsible for the decisions that must be made and for the whole of the nation. I thought of that when I heard the daily rants from the campaign trail. It got so that even the weather seemed to be George's fault. And I wondered if Barack Obama, who spent far more time attacking George than he did his opponent, John McCain, would want to amend his words once he discovered the reality of the White House and was himself confronted by the challenges and crises that hit a president every day, all day.

There is also a larger picture to consider. No one, not even a president, is going to make the right decision every time. Presidents may have more information on which to base their decisions, but they do not have the benefit of hindsight. They must be prepared to take risks for what they believe is right. And they must try to anticipate the future, not just two years or four years out but what the consequences will be decades ahead.

George believes, and I believe as well, that the presidency is larger than the men who are in it. The Founding Fathers, who in the spring of 1787 wrestled with this issue, designed it that way. Each president's responsibility is to the office, the sole national institution that speaks for all Americans, regardless of their party or class or home or age. George always believed that it was his responsibility to treat the office with great care.

Presidents are not always right, but history tells us that our core values are right and that our country is good. Those are the values that guided

George, the touchstone by which he measured what he did. George knew that in the heat of the moment, presidents tend to get much of the blame and little of the credit. Not all of his decisions would be popular, but as a nation, we would not want our presidents to make decisions solely on the basis of their personal popularity, or poll numbers, or daily headlines. The challenges we face are too great for that.

I am proud that, as president, George acted on principle, that he put our country first and himself last.

Just as the financial crisis was roiling America, the surge in Iraq was cementing some of its largest gains. Iraq, which had once been cited as a failure, was becoming a far less violent, far more peaceful and stable place. It was not perfect, but it had an opportunity to build a better, healthier society, and perhaps in time, ten or twenty-five years from now, it would help transform the Middle East into a more peaceful region. The loneliest of George's decisions, the surge had been the right choice. But ironically, drowned out by the din of a political campaign, Iraq's success was pushed out of the headlines, if it was mentioned at all.

I never visited Iraq, one of my genuine regrets from my time in the White House. I did spend several years working on a project to open a children's hospital in Basra; Iraqi children have one of the highest incidences of pediatric leukemia in the world, likely caused in part by Saddam Hussein's use of chemical weapons, and their need for care was great. But the location chosen for the hospital was for years a high security risk. There were lengthy delays, and when I left the White House, the state-of-the-art facility had still not opened. There are, however, many moments at which I could look back with pleasure and a bit of pride. I had worked to support better education and women's rights and human rights around the globe, and I had worked to better people's lives here at home. I had reached out to victims of oppression in Burma and to tattooed American teens struggling to break free from the cycle of gang violence. I had sat on mud floors in African health clinics and inside Bedouin-style tents for breast cancer survivors. I had visited seventy-five countries, including five trips across Africa and three to Afghanistan. I had been to many of the countries hardest hit by AIDS and malaria. I had held the hands of the dying and looked into the eyes of children who had been orphaned in the most hideous ways, as well as children who were raising other children younger than themselves. Yet amid heartbreak and horror, I had seen individual miracles. I saw how medicines or simple bed nets were giving millions of people a new lease on life. I had met Burmese who were still able to dream of freedom, and Afghan women who were proud to earn an education. I had seen the worst of man in the 9-11 attacks and the worst of nature in Katrina. But I had also seen the very best of America in the hundreds of thousands of people who had put their lives on hold to help the victims and to help our country rebuild. I witnessed the compassion of strangers comforting, clothing, and feeding those in need. I had seen young men and women abandoned by their parents choose to raise their own children in love. I had been blessed to meet and to know many of the bravest men and women the world has ever seen, our soldiers, Marines, airmen, sailors, and Coast Guard men and women.

At home and abroad, I was inspired by stories of resilience. I could think of Doris Voitier in St. Bernard Parish, who was determined to keep her promise of an open school for her students after the ravishes of Katrina, or of Habiba Sarabi in Bamiyan, Afghanistan. I could think of military families whose grandfathers, fathers, and now daughters and sons wore our nation's uniform. My greatest keepsakes and treasures from the White House are the people, the ordinary yet so very extraordinary people I met, day after day, week after week.

Inside the White House, I had helped restore five historic rooms and refurbish over twenty-five rooms in the residence for future families. At Camp David I had worked on redecorating the cabins with privately raised funds; many of the buildings were now more than half a century old. Foreign leaders had been staying in a cabin where the front hall looked directly into the bathroom. It was a pleasure to make them comfortable. We gathered a historical archive of photos capturing famous visits to Camp David so that every president from FDR forward and numerous foreign leaders are remembered and recognized. I helped to renovate the James S. Brady Press Briefing Room, which had last been modernized in 1981. Every seat now has Internet access and energy-efficient lighting. I worked on updating the Cabinet and Roosevelt rooms in the West Wing. In the

White House, George and I had hosted over fifteen hundred social events; many were to award medals or honor accomplishments or great moments in American arts and literature. With Jim Billington I had started the National Book Festival, which now draws some 120,000 visitors each fall, and I had worked to combat illiteracy worldwide. I had done what I had hoped to do: I had worked to be a good steward of the White House for our nation. Every day, even the difficult ones, had been a privilege.

In October of 2008, I was finally able to travel to the Laura Ingalls Wilder house in Mansfield, Missouri, where she and her husband had settled on Rocky Ridge Farm.

I had long wanted to visit the last home of the woman whose Little House on the Prairie stories I had grown up with and had spent hours reading to my own daughters. From the Laura of those books and her family, I relearned the lessons that no matter how impoverished the lives of those on our frontiers, they were rich in character and strength and love. I proudly presented the home and museum with a certificate from the National Trust for Historic Preservation designating it an official project of Save America's Treasures. One of the great treats I had as first lady was the chance to visit the homes of some of my favorite authors—Mark Twain's residence in Hartford, Connecticut; Carl Sandburg's home, Connemara, in Flat Rock, North Carolina; and Edith Wharton's Lenox, Massachusetts, home, the Mount. In the case of the Mount, preservation work has been vital to save it from closure and decay. Today it is a thriving place, honoring one of America's best female writers.

In November, as the banking system began to stabilize after its near collapse, George hosted a world economic summit, where there were so many foreign leaders that the White House had to place the translators in a tent on the roof of the East Wing, with wires running through the bottom of the residence and up into the State Dining Room, so everyone could hear what was being said simultaneously. Thirteen languages were spoken at the dinner, and the arrivals alone took close to an hour, because each head of state had to arrive and receive the same recognition of protocol.

December brought the renewed joys of Christmas. I chose a red, white, and blue theme to honor our country during this election year. We recycled many of the decorations from previous seasons, turning old towering Nutcracker statues into flag-waving Uncle Sams; even Santa wore red, white, and blue. We sent ornaments to every member of Congress and asked each representative to select a local artist to decorate them. Three hundred and sixty-nine returned, decorated with paint, fabric, beading, and images of our varied regions.

Mother came for that last Christmas, and as she had done in previous years, she pulled a chair to the very top of the residence stairs and listened to the beautiful sounds of the carolers and bell ringers as their voices and music rose and echoed off the marble below. Each year, aside from the formal parties, we opened the White House on December afternoons and weekends to members of Congress and their guests and every person on the White House staff; we did the same for hundreds more across the government. They were invited to tour the house with family and friends, and we asked choirs and orchestras and carolers from around the nation to perform as the guests walked among the decorations, the garlands, and the trees. Those were the sounds that Mother so loved.

But it was too much for her to spend Christmas Day with us at Camp David. The prospect of getting her from the cabin to the lodge in the cold and ice was too daunting. With a knot of regret, I let her return home to Midland. But we did have our girls and the entire Bush family—George's parents, his siblings, their spouses and children. It would be our last gathering at Camp David, "Camp" as we called it, the place where George's sister, Doro, had married Bobby Koch at the end of Gampy's term. When he left office, she had assumed she would never see Camp again. Instead, when George was inaugurated, Doro was issued a standing invitation to come with us, not just for the holidays but for any weekend.

It was the season for good-byes. George was busy with departure photos for the staff. But he insisted upon adding something else. He invited everyone who worked at the White House—the butlers, the painters, the ushers, the telephone operators, the secretaries, every White House employee—to come to the Oval Office for a photo. And they came, these wonderful people who had been such an important part of our lives for the past eight years. Some had worked at the White House for four decades but had never before been invited into the Oval Office. They entered with tears in their eyes.

We would also be leaving not just close staff but true friends. George's second chief of staff, Josh Bolten, had been a steadfast guiding presence during the difficult months of the Iraq surge and through the economic crisis. He had been with George since 1999, the earliest days of his presidential run. Josh is a fine person, with a wonderful sense of humor and a great and versatile mind. We had treasured his company, and that of his longtime girlfriend, Dede McClure, on our Camp David weekends.

My own staff had a special place in my heart. I remained very close with Andi Ball, my first chief of staff. My second, Anita McBride, had become a confidante and a cherished friend. She and my other staff members had been instrumental in so many accomplishments. Our lives were interwoven far beyond the walls of the office, and it was with real sadness that we watched as this period of shared days came to an end.

Long before the November election, George was determined to make the transition to the new president the most seamless in history. He created a Transition Coordinating Council, to ensure that "each office was left in better shape than when our administration had arrived." It was part of George's interest in the continuity of government, and it was also because we knew how vital a smooth transition is, particularly given the ever-present threat of terrorism and the challenges to the economy. He believed that one of the paramount responsibilities of the president is to do all that he or she can for the next occupant of the Oval Office. Every White House department was instructed to prepare detailed briefing binders for its successors. In my office, the projects team left behind detailed lists of all their contacts at federal agencies, as well as timelines for events and even for producing the White House Christmas card. The correspondence shop left binders filled with sample letters, and we left scheduling information as well. And that practice was repeated across all parts of the administration. The Social Office gathered hundreds of pages of instructions, timelines, and sample invitations to leave behind detailed information for their successors. The same was done for Homeland Security, national security, economic policy, commerce and trade, everywhere that there would be a new team. Because this was also the first presidential transition during a period when the nation was under terrorist threat, the White House held a full Homeland Security exercise, a mock attack on major city subways, bringing together the outgoing and incoming administrations, including National Security Advisor Steve Hadley and his successor, General James Jones, and Homeland Security Secretary Michael Chertoff and his successor, Arizona governor Janet Napolitano, as well as Fran Townsend, the long-serving assistant to the president for Homeland Security and counterterrorism, so that there would be full continuity for the government and for the American people.

Barack and Michelle Obama came to visit the White House, and while George and the president-elect met in the Oval Office, I gave the next first lady a tour. Upstairs I showed her the dressing room window, with its view across the Rose Garden and into the West Wing, and told her the story of my mother-in-law first pointing it out to Hillary Clinton sixteen years before. I also invited her to come back with her daughters and her mother. She did, in December, and Jenna and Barbara came to show the girls the parts of the house that they had always found the most fun.

As in so many years past, Inauguration Day 2009 was cold. It was also historic, as the nation swore in its first African-American president.

After the inaugural ceremony, we made our last walk down the steps of the Capitol with the Obamas; inside Marine One, Bar and Gampy were waiting, so that they could join us for the final helicopter ride to Andrews Air Force Base, where nearly one thousand of our staff and friends were waiting to bid us a fond farewell.

The love of the Bush family had come full circle; the pride George had felt for his parents, they felt in return for their son. They too had made this journey we were about to begin and had found unexpected joys in the years beyond.

As the helicopter rose over the Capitol, George took my hand. We looked at the city below and out into the vibrant blue January sky, toward home.

Prairie Chapel
Mornings

George and me, Crawford, Texas, 2009.
(Photo © David Woo)

Late that January afternoon in 2009, we stopped in Midland, where George spoke to a cheering crowd. We had left from Midland to travel to the White House; it was fitting that it be our destination on the journey home. Thirty thousand people were waiting for us on the downtown square. George thanked them for welcoming us. "I am grateful that you all came out," he said, "and I am thankful that I had the honor of being president of the U.S. for eight years," noting that we all offer Barack Obama "our prayers for his success." As the afternoon faded, he said, "The days have been long, but the years are short," adding, "This guy who went to Sam Houston Elementary spent the night in Buckingham Palace.

"The presidency," George said, "was a joyous experience, but nothing compares with Texas at sunset." He paused briefly, then spoke. "It is good to be home." From there our plane carried us to Waco, where four thousand more of our cheering friends lined the edges of the runway.

On that plane ride home to Texas were many of the staffers who had served with us—Josh Bolten, Andy Card, Karl Rove, Karen Hughes, Andi Ball, and Anita McBride—and also our lifelong friends. From Waco we headed to our ranch with a few of our closest friends. We reached our land, Prairie Chapel Ranch, in the dark. Barbara was with us; Jenna had to return to Baltimore, Maryland, to teach the next morning. George parked his mountain bikes in the garage, and we unloaded the luggage. I was struck by the stillness. There were no staff members, no briefers, no military aides. The grounds were quiet, except for the rustle of the Texas winter wind, the murmur of our own voices, and the soft shuffle of our feet on the crushed stone.

The next morning we were up, as we always are, before dawn, and for the first time in eight years, George made the coffee himself before he brought it into our bedroom.

Outside, as the day broke, our land was the color of dull wheat, and the prairie grasses were dry and brown, waving in the wind. The sky, when the sun rose behind the clouds, was a leaden gray, wrapping snug above us and beautiful in its repose. We could drive out and see cattle grazing in our pastures, hear the water rushing down in the canyons. We saw where we wanted to plant blackberry vines and where the bluebonnets would begin blooming in the spring. We gazed upon the spot where Jenna and Henry were married; each morning from our kitchen table I can see the warm glow of the limestone cross where they exchanged their vows.

There are still physical reminders at Prairie Chapel Ranch of our eight years in the White House: Secret Service watch huts remain scattered around the edges of our house, and a giant treetop enclosure, a place where sharpshooters once paced, scanning the perimeter for trouble, stands draped in vines. Someday it might make a wonderful fort for a grandson or granddaughter.

And there are other reminders. We live behind gates now; our Dallas house has one at the end of its curving block. Until the gate was installed, carloads of the curious would wind down our dead-end street, running their tires over our neighbors' lawns, to get a glimpse of our new home. Bar and Gampy faced the same problem when they returned to Houston, and the Texas legislature passed a special law allowing gates to be installed on the residential streets of former presidents. George and I are the second-generation beneficiaries.

At home our pace of life has hardly slowed; after the White House, requests and invitations continue unabated. There are many days when, just as during the presidency, nearly every minute is accounted for. We live by the block schedule, a 6:00 A.M. flight to Florida or Pennsylvania, and then on to Minnesota or Indiana. I am asked to give speeches and to serve on charitable advisory boards, like that of the Salvation Army or of the Smithsonian's new National Museum of African American History and Culture; George speaks, works on building his presidential library and institute, and has joined with Bill Clinton to coordinate a national relief effort for earthquake-ravaged Haiti. There is much meaning and purpose to be found in a postpresidential life.

I am aware, though, that a completely normal life remains just out of reach. At the airport with my mother, well-wishers ask for pictures, and I stop to smile underneath the dangling Hertz Car Rental sign. In restaurants, in passenger terminals, amid the shelves of a bookstore, strangers approach me like long-lost friends, or rotate their heads to offer up smiles, second glances, or polite stares. At times I wonder when this curiosity will fade, when the novelty of our lives will diminish, and George and I will occupy more of the background.

I wonder too about the passions that seem to be so permanently entrenched in all sides of American politics, where elected officials become near instantaneous celebrities, and crowds are expected to swoon as teenagers once did for the Beatles almost half a century ago. Celebrity is a particularly poor model for politics. At the White House, there is no off-season hiatus or a director to yell, "Cut, that's a wrap." The demands of not just the nation but of the world are fierce and unrelenting. I am certain that all presidents have moments when they simply ask God, "Please do not let anything happen today."

We have lived through four seasons now on our ranchland, a spring bloom of wildflower carpets and flowering prickly pear; the baking heat of summer, when the air shimmers and even the cicada whine slows to accommodate the stifling air; a fall of crisp mornings and brilliant colors; and a winter when at night we can hear the howls of the coyotes and the rush of biting prairie winds. Four seasons. Hardly enough time to reflect on eight years, let alone a lifetime. When I was born, there was a blacksmith shop on one of Midland's main streets; today, our news is disseminated via blogs.

But each morning, when I watch the sun lift itself over our eastern hill, cutting through the tree line and illuminating the gentle prairie grasses and the two young shade trees that our White House staff gave to us, I am reminded of the joy to be found in the day that is coming. George will soon open his presidential library at Southern Methodist University in Dallas. The George W. Bush Institute is already functioning, and as part of that, I am pursuing many of the causes that were especially dear to me in the White House. I am eager to continue to advocate for women's rights and women's health. Through a special women's initiative, I have begun working on new ways to help the women of Afghanistan and the Middle East and to promote education and literacy for the millions to whom alphabets are a mystery and basic addition a complex puzzle. And through the institute, we will help to promote basic human freedoms for these women and their families.

But as much as I treasure my public life, I also treasure the quiet of my private one.

Sometime during that first spring and summer back in Texas, I began to feel the buoyancy of my own newfound freedom. After nearly eight years of hypervigilance, of watching for the next danger or tragedy that might be coming, I could at last exhale; I could simply be. When I raise my eyes to the sky, it is to see the drift of the clouds, the brightness of the blue, or the moon and the ever-shifting arrangement of the stars.

"Look up, Laura," I can still hear my mother say, with a hint of awe and wonder, and I do.

ACKNOWLEDGMENTS

Before the first sentence of this book was written, my family was there. I am deeply blessed to have the love of my husband, George, and my daughters, Barbara and Jenna, and Jenna's husband, Henry Hager. They enrich my life beyond words. And I am grateful for their thoughts, suggestions, and encouragement throughout this process. Most of all, I am grateful for their presence and comfort, for the affection that we share, and for the gift of being able to share my life with them.

My mother lovingly reached into the depths of her memory for stories of the past, and on the Bush side, I have a wonderful, sprawling family to call my own. To my friends, thank you for your steadfast role in my life, for all that we have shared, and for the journey we have taken together.

I was a bit wary about embarking on a book, a memoir in particular, but I am immensely fortunate in having the very best guides. I am especially grateful to Lyric Winik, who helped me put my story into words. Lyric is a talented and beautiful writer who worked tirelessly, logging thousands of airline miles and many hours away from her patient husband, Jay, and their two boys, Nathaniel and B.C. I cherished our conversations about everything from growing up in Midland to life at the White House, and I will miss working with her. She is a dear friend.

My thanks to Bob Barnett of Williams & Connolly, whose judgment and advice are without peer. He is a terrific advocate. At Scribner, I could not have asked for a better team than Publisher Susan Moldow and Editor in Chief Nan Graham. Both of these talented women share my deep love of language, literature, and storytelling. From beginning to end, they have masterfully nurtured this book, and it has been a pleasure to work with them and the rest of the Scribner team, including Paul Whitlatch, Rex Bonomelli, Brian Belfiglio, and Rosalind Lippel.

Emily Kropp Michel has been outstanding and invaluable as a researcher, locating documents and other materials that were essential to writing this book and fact-checking. She did it all with consummate professionalism and good cheer.

Peter Rough was helpful with checking and coordinating specific materials from the White House years. My thanks to the archivists at the George W. Bush Presidential Library, led by Alan Lowe, particularly Tally Fugate, who located well over one thousand documents, and Jodie Steck, who searched through vast databases of photos. I especially wish to thank William G. Allman, the White House curator, who shared his rich knowledge of White House history and artifacts with me during my tenure as first lady.

A significant portion of this book centers on the White House, and there I was deeply appreciative of Lynne and Dick Cheney, who have served our nation with devotion and are valued friends. I was fortunate to have two terrific chiefs of staff. Andi Ball came with me from the Texas governor's office to the White House, where she remained for the first four years. She was with me for the events of 9-11 and the challenging days that followed, and her warmth and good humor were a welcome presence in the East Wing. I treasure her friendship. Anita McBride, who served for my last four years, was instrumental in so many accomplishments. She embraced the toughest challenges and destinations—Afghanistan, Africa, and the Burmese border—and I am grateful for her service, counsel, and special friendship. I am indebted to my wonderful personal assistants in the White House, Lindsey Knutson and Sarah Garrison, for being at my side every minute on the road and at home.

Andy Card and Josh Bolten, chiefs of staff to George, are two of the finest individuals we have known. I have benefited greatly from the wise counsel of Karen Hughes, Karl Rove, and Harriet Miers.

I want to thank the members of my staff who worked long hours in the East Wing, particularly Anne Heiligenstein and Sonya Medina, who were instrumental in developing the policy behind my initiatives and worked closely with the West Wing on many of our efforts. Ably assisting them over the years were Maria Miller Lohmeyer, Kristin Mende, Page Austin, and many others to whom I am grateful. Good writers and my longtime friends, Joan Doty and Sarah McIntosh, served as the staff elders guiding many of the young aides and wrote charming documents and letters, including penning hundreds of hilarious replies from Barney and Miss Beazley. Year after year, my skilled press secretaries smilingly braved the media whirlwind. I'd like to thank Sally McDonough, Susan Whitson, Gordon Johndroe, and Noelia Rodriguez. My hardworking speechwriters helped ensure that I always said the right thing: Nikki McArthur, Meghan Clyne, Ed Walsh, Elizabeth Straub, and Charlene Fern. On my staff, I'd also like to thank the dedicated Melanie Jackson, January Zell, Quincy Crawford, Deanna Ballard, and the other young people who worked in the East Wing, who served both the White House and their country. I had many great people, including many volunteers, who worked for me as advance people, traveling the country and the world to scout sites and prepare for visits, and I appreciate their days of hard work. I'm appreciative too of the White House photographers—especially Susan Sterner, Moreen Ishikawa Watson, Joyce Boghosian, and Shealah Craighead— who expertly captured our eight years through their lenses.

At the White House, we had three elegant and outstanding social secretaries, Cathy Fenton, Lea Berman, and Amy Zantzinger, who, with their very able staffs, planned fabulous events and paid attention to every detail, from working with the West Wing, Secret Service, and the Military Office to standing near us for every hour of receiving lines. They were responsible for many treasured and memorable events and evenings throughout George's presidency.

I'd also like to thank the directors of the White House Visitors Office, Clare Pritchett, Sara Armstrong, and Amy Allman, who along with their staffs coordinated the Easter Egg Roll, managed every tour and the Christmas open houses, and worked with all 535 congressional staffs to arrange constituent tours. And I spent many great hours with five terrific young men, Israel Hernandez, Logan Walters, Blake Gottesman, Jared Weinstein, and David Sherzer, George's personal aides, who traveled with us and have become like family.

In the White House residence, I wish to thank the many wonderful people who took care of George and me every single day, the ushers, led by Gary Walters, who served four presidents and devoted a large part of his life to the White House, lovingly caring for the home and the families who reside there. We also thank current chief usher Rear Admiral Stephen Rochon, Dennis Freemyer, Daniel Shanks, Claire Faulkner, Worthington White, and Nancy Mitchell. We recall fondly Dale Haney, who cared for the beautiful gardens and expertly looked after Spot, Barney, and Miss Beazley. Thanks to the great White House butlers and our dear friends William Carter, James Ramsey, Von Everett, Ronald Guy, George Hannie, Cesar Rodas, and the late Smile Saint-Aubin. We were also appreciative of the great valets, Sam Sutton, Fidel Medina, and Robert Favela, for their kind and constant service to the president and our family. We had an excellent White House physician, Dr. Richard Tubb, and caring doctors and nurses. My thanks also to Tom Driggers of the White House Communications Agency, particularly for his generous assistance during our yearly hiking forays. I appreciate the hard work of the calligraphers, especially Debra Brown. Thanks to the doormen, who we saw first in the morning and last in the evening, Vincent Contee, Wilson Jerman, Jay Warren, and the late Harold Hancock, and the housekeeping staff, including Mary Arnold, Silvia da Silva, Ivanez da Silva, Annie Brown, and Steven Gates. The floral shop, led by the remarkable Nancy Clarke, and also Robert Scanlan and Keith Fulgham, made a beautiful home more beautiful. We had a talented kitchen staff, led by the lovely chef Cristeta Comerford, and assisted by Tommy Kurpradit, and in pastry, the creative skills of Roland Mesnier, then William Yosses and Susan Morrison. And we were fortunate to have a myriad of operations personnel, painters, carpenters, plumbers, engineers, and electricians who saw to the care of the White House.

Finally, my lasting thanks to the wonderful Maria Galvan, who has for years been a faithful companion and friend.

At Camp David, we received great care from camp commanders Captain Charles Reuning; Captain John Heckmann; Captain Robert McLean, III; Captain Michael O'Connor; and RDML Michael Giorgione; as well as the Navy chaplains CDR Stanley Fornea, CDR Patrick McLaughlin, and CDR Robert Williams. George and I are grateful to all the men and women at Camp David for their service to our country.

During my tenure as first lady, I had terrific partnerships with many individuals, starting with Dr. James Billington, the Librarian of Congress.

Together, with the help of his assistant JoAnn Jenkins and my staff, we established the National Book Festival, highlighting many of our nation's best authors and the great institution of the Library of Congress. The festival remains today as a favorite of book lovers. I enjoyed working with many talented administration officials and good friends on key issues, including secretaries of state Condoleezza Rice and Colin Powell, secretaries of education Margaret Spellings and Rod Paige, secretaries of the interior Dirk Kempthorne and Gale Norton, Homeland Security secretaries Tom Ridge and Michael Chertoff, and secretaries of defense Donald Rumsfeld and Robert Gates. Their staffs worked with mine on initiatives for women abroad, the environment, education, and Helping America's Youth, among others. A special thanks to the directors of the National Park Service, Mary Bomar and Fran Mainella, and the National Park Foundation's past president, Vin Cipolla, as well as the many park rangers and staff who were so helpful.

I particularly enjoyed my partnership with our nation's cultural agencies, led by Dana Gioia of the National Endowment for the Arts, Bruce Cole of the National Endowment for the Humanities, and Robert Martin and Anne-Imelda Radice, who directed the Institute of Museums and Library Services. I also want to thank John Nau, chairman of the Advisory Council on Historic Preservation; Dick Moe of the National Trust for Historic Preservation and Save America's Treasures; Henry Moran, the executive director of the President's Committee on the Arts and Humanities; and the committee's terrific past president and my good friend, Adair Margo. Thanks to Dr. Elizabeth Nabel of the National Institute of Health's National Heart Lung and Blood Institute and the Heart Truth Campaign. On Afghanistan issues, my thanks to Paula Dobriansky; the members of the U.S.-Afghan Women's Council; Dr. Phyllis Magrab, the council's vice chair; and Georgetown University, where the council now resides. Many thanks also to Sarah Moten for her work with me in Africa.

Since 2003, the Laura Bush Foundation for America's Libraries has provided grants to school libraries across the nation to purchase books. In 2005 leading board members began a separate initiative to help rebuild devastated school library collections following the hurricanes. My heartfelt thanks to Pamela Willeford, the chair, and to the Leadership Council of the Laura Bush Foundation, J. W. Marriott Jr., chair; Ruth Sharp

Acknowledgments

Altshuler; Chris Boskin; John H. Bryan; Delphine Daft; Annette Kirk; Frederic Malek; Lowry Mays; Marshall B. Payne; Lee Scott; John F. Smith Jr.; and Judi Hadfield. I also thank the foundation's advisory committee—who read the thousands of grant applications, make school visits, and conduct workshops for librarians—Jose Aponte, Dr. Eliza Dresang, Dr. Gary Hartzell, Marilyn Joyce, Dr. Larry Leverett, Dr. James Maxwell, Dr. Barbara Stein Martin, Dr. Timothy Rex Wadham, Julie Walker, Dr. Junko Yokota, Barbara Correll, and Dr. Yunfei Du, the technical adviser.

A number of individuals and institutions provided key assistance in preparing this book for publication, including Chris Michel in the Office of George W. Bush; the Honorable Stephen Hadley; Ambassador Zalmay Khalilzad; Senator Judd Gregg; Jo Shuffler; Mary Jones, chief of staff of the Senate Rules Committee; Harry Ogg and the library research staff of the Midland County Public Library; Judy Bezjak, historian of the 555th Antiaircraft Artillery Battalion; Leslie Meyer of the Petroleum Museum in Midland, Texas; Brent Glass, director of the National Museum of American History, and his curators; Ernie Allen of the National Center for Missing and Exploited Children; Jim Wallwork; the Office of the President's Malaria Initiative; Ambassador Mark Dybul; Tonia Wood and Jessica Tucker of the Texas State Library and Archives; Colonel Gregory Woods of the White House Military Office; and John Meyers.

Finally, I am grateful to my dedicated current staff; to my chief of staff, Charity Wallace, who spent eight years working in the administration, many of them as the director of my advance team, where her hard work and commitment were invaluable; as well as to my personal aide, Molly Soper. Their excellent work and dedication to this project have been invaluable. My special thanks to them and to everyone else who contributed to bringing this book to fruition.

BIBLIOGRAPHY

Numerous books, articles, and papers were consulted during the course of preparing this book. The most significant books are listed below. In addition, I relied heavily on my private papers and the block and daily schedules from my office as First Lady of the United States and First Lady of Texas, as well as schedules and papers from the presidency of George W. Bush. I am particularly appreciative that Andi Ball and Anita McBride, my two chiefs of staff, shared their private notes and papers with me during the preparation of the manuscript, as did others on my White House staff, including press secretaries Susan Whitson and Sally McDonough and my then-director of advance, Charity Wallace. Also Lea Berman, Amy Zantzinger, Lindsey Knutson, and Amy Allman shared their own private notes and materials. In addition, United Nations and UNICEF studies on Afghanistan provided useful background information. And the powerful and detailed reporting of the New Orleans *Times-Picayune* was particularly helpful in refreshing my memory on Katrina and its aftermath.

A note as well for future researchers: significant parts of the overall presidential timeline from 9-11 and a few parts of the timeline from Katrina are incomplete. The 9-11 Commission cited in its final report its concerns with record keeping for the location of the president and other key government officials on that day, and in fact some time logs kept that day have up to a one-hour discrepancy. In addition, human memory is faulty. Senator Ted Kennedy, Senator Judd Gregg, and I all independently recalled spending hours together at the U.S. Senate that morning. In fact, the entire time was about one hour or slightly less, according to the best estimates of the reconstructed official logs.

George's presidency was also the first electronic presidency, meaning that its documents were all electronically archived, but in some cases, during my travels, I added unscheduled stops that were not always noted on the original logs. Where there are differences with the official trip logs, this book should be considered as the definitive source.

"Ancestry of Laura Welch Bush, First Lady of the United States of America." Family History Library. The Church of Jesus Christ of Latter-day Saints. Salt Lake City, Utah, 2002 (unpublished).

Angelo, Bonnie. *First Families: The Impact of the White House on Their Lives.* New York: Morrow, 2005.

Anthony, Carl Sferrazza. *America's First Families: An Inside View of 200 Years of Private Life in the White House.* New York: Touchstone, 2000.

Blair, Cherie. *Speaking for Myself: My Life from Liverpool to Downing Street.* New York: Little, Brown and Company, 2008.

Bonnifield, Matthew Paul. *The Dust Bowl: Men, Dirt, and Depression.* Albuquerque: University of New Mexico Press, 1979.

Bush, Barbara. *Barbara Bush: A Memoir.* New York: Scribner, 1994.

Clemens, Gus. *Legacy: The Story of the Permian River Basin Region of West Texas and Southeast New Mexico.* San Antonio: Mulberry Avenue Books, 1983.

Cochran, Mike, and John Lumpkin. *West Texas: A Portrait of Its People and Their Raw and Wondrous Land.* Lubbock, Texas: Texas Tech University Press, 1999.

Fehrenbach, T. R. *Lone Star: A History of Texas and the Texans.* New York: Da Capo Press, 2000.

Filkins, Dexter. *The Forever War.* New York: Alfred A. Knopf, 2008.

Firestone, Caroline Hudson. *Afghanistan in Transition.* New York: New Hudson Foundation, 2009.

Fleming, Candace. *The Lincolns: A Scrapbook Look at Abraham and Mary.* New York: Schwartz & Wade Books, 2008.

Franks, Tommy. *American Soldier.* New York: HarperCollins, 2004.

Griffin, John Howard. *Land of High Sky.* Midland, Texas: First National Bank of Midland, 1959.

Hoegh, Leo A., and Howard J. Doyle. *Timberwolf Tracks: The History of the 104th Infantry Division, 1942–1945.* Washington, D.C.: Infantry Journal Press, 1946.

Metz, Leon Claire. *City at the Pass: An Illustrated History of El Paso.* Woodland, California: Windsor Publications, 1980.

Nader, Ralph. *Unsafe at Any Speed: The Designed-in Dangers of the American Automobile.* New York: Grossman, 1972.

The New Handbook of Texas. Austin: Texas State Historical Association, 1996.

Payne, Darwin. *Big D: Triumphs and Troubles of an American Supercity in the 20th Century.* Dallas: Three Forks Press, 2000.

Pickens, Jennifer. *Christmas at the White House.* Dallas: Fife and Drum Press, 2009.

Bibliography

Rashid, Ahmed. *Taliban: Militant Islam, Oil, and Fundamentalism in Central Asia.* New Haven: Yale University Press, 2000.

Seale, William. *The President's House.* Vols. 1–2. 2nd ed. Washington, D.C.: In association with the White House Historical Association, 2008.

Sirleaf, Ellen Johnson. *This Child Will Be Great: Memoir of a Remarkable Life by Africa's First Woman President.* New York: HarperCollins, 2009.

Sonnichsen, C. L. *Pass of the North: Four Centuries on the Rio Grande.* El Paso: Texas Western Press, 1968.

Storey, John W., and Mary L. Kelley, eds. *Twentieth-Century Texas: A Social and Cultural History.* Denton, Texas: University of North Texas Press, 2008.

Timmons, W. H. *El Paso: A Borderlands History.* El Paso: University of Texas at El Paso, 1990.

Truman, Margaret. *The President's House: 1800 to the Present; The Secrets and History of the World's Most Famous Home.* New York: Ballantine Books, 2005.

U.S. Congress. House. Select Bipartisan Committee. *A Failure of Initiative.* 109th Cong., 2nd sess., 2006. H. Res. 437.

U.S. Congress. Senate. Committee on Homeland Security and Governmental Affairs. *Hurricane Katrina: A Nation Still Unprepared.* 109th Cong., 2nd sess., 2006. S. Rept. 109–322.

Wead, Doug. *All the Presidents' Children: Triumph and Tragedy in the Lives of America's First Families.* New York: Atria Books, 2003.

Welty, Eudora. *One Writer's Beginnings.* Cambridge, Mass.: Harvard University Press, 1995.

West, J. B. *Upstairs at the White House: My Life with the First Ladies.* New York: Coward, McCann & Geoghegan, 1973.

The White House. *The Federal Response to Hurricane Katrina: Lessons Learned.* http:// georgewbush-whitehousearchives.gov/reports/katrina-lessons-learned. Washington, D.C., 2006.

Woodward, Bob. *Bush at War.* New York: Simon & Schuster, 2002.

———. *Plan of Attack: The Definitive Account of the Decision to Invade Iraq.* New York: Simon & Schuster, 2004.

Worster, Donald. *Dust Bowl: The Southern Plains in the 1930s.* New York: Oxford University Press, 1979.

INDEX

Index